THE POLITICS OF ECOSUICIDE

THE POLITICS
OF ECOSUICIDE

edited by LESLIE L. ROOS, Jr.
NORTHWESTERN UNIVERSITY

HOLT, RINEHART AND WINSTON, INC.
New York   Chicago   San Francisco   Atlanta   Dallas
Montreal   Toronto   London   Sydney

Preface

This book was designed with the hope that it would prove valuable to teachers and students concerned about national and world environmental problems. Informed ideas about the ways in which society might deal with these problems have been scattered throughout a number of journals. Environmental issues cut across disciplines, but many of the relevant decisions are inherently political. Thus, although this book strives for an interdisciplinary perspective, its focus is on politics.

Although some of the selections employ mathematics, it is my belief that the book can be read profitably by students at various stages in their university careers. A broad range of approaches is presented here, organized around a set of analytical concerns. These essays should be useful for both political science courses and interdepartmental offerings concerning the environment.

A number of these essays have previously appeared elsewhere; I would like to thank the journals and publishers concerned for their permissions. Several papers were written especially for this volume. The authors were uniformly cooperative.

Finally I would like to express my appreciation to Sharon Symcak, Alice Perlin, and Carol Anderson for their work in typing and proofreading this manuscript. Johnna Barto at Holt, Rinehart and Winston has been most helpful in the various phases of preparing this manuscript.

Leslie L. Roos, Jr.

Evanston, Illinois
January 1971

Contents

THE POLITICS
OF ECOSUICIDE

INTRODUCTION

Problems connected with environmental management (or lack thereof) are among the most significant facing the United States —and the world—today. Given the interest in and importance of environmental problems, what questions might the student of politics address himself to? Three sorts of questions are emphasized in this reader:

1. How are decisions about environmental problems made at the national and at the state level?
2. What is the role of analysis in selection of the "proper" environmental policies? Might different types of analysis lead to different conclusions?
3. What are some methods for bringing about change in the ways Americans treat environmental problems? What institutional and behavioral patterns might be altered to facilitate such change?

The selections in this reader reflect both the concerns of the editor and a desire not to duplicate that which is readily found elsewhere. For this reason, particular substantive areas are not emphasized; specialized studies of population issues and pollution problems have not been stressed. Moreover, because of the availability of a topical volume linking environmental issues with a radical analysis of American society, such a critique has not been included here.

The readings differ among themselves in the answers forwarded. Considering the uncertainty that surrounds our approach to environmental problems, perhaps offering a diversity of answers is appropriate. The structure of the readings reflects the questions listed above. The selections on public opinion, on new institutions, and on the bureaucracy deal primarily with influences on government decision making about the environment. Subsequent section headings reflect the readings' concerns with the role of analysis and with problems of change.

This division of questions and readings limits neither the topics discussed nor the issues raised by the selections. Thus, several readings imply different sorts of orientations on the part of American business. The survey data reported by Miss Trop and the editor suggest that business leadership may be quite responsive to pressures for environmental improvement and that governmental regulation will be favorably received. However, the behavioral data presented by Caldwell tells a different story. Despite media campaigns and voluntary compliance agreements, pollution of Lake Michigan by oil and steel companies has shown few signs of abating.

Another issue discussed by several authors concerns "externalities," costs and benefits that occur outside the market system. Here there is not disagreement among the contributors, but rather a question as to what can be done to take these externalities into consideration. Analysis and regulation are mentioned by several authors as possible partial aids, but the problem is a larger one: changing our approach to the processes of production and consumption.

How to bring about meaningful change is a theme that emerges throughout the readings included in this volume. Although the last section concentrates upon change, both the introductory essays and those dealing with political factors discuss related problems. The essays do not resound with optimism. There is considerable agreement that things are not going very well now, but such statements are generally tempered by the authors' suggestions for the future. The suggestions are important; but what if they are not followed or not successful? The alternatives are continued environmental deterioration, overpopulation, and a declining quality of life.

The possibilities for achieving meaningful change via incrementalism—by means of a succession of relatively small changes—are discussed by a number of contributors. Advocates of systems analysis call for a comprehensive, planned approach to change, while activists suggest legal action, protests, and so forth. Bargaining may also enter into any change situation.

While Schick seems to link bargaining with incremental approaches to change, there are other possibilities. Analysis can aid each side in understanding what is at stake, even when political considerations are significant. In his essay, Hagevik discusses how, even when only partial knowledge is available, such knowledge can be put to use to help decision making.

Interest group demands and concerns are one reason why change may tend to be incremental. Many groups seek veto power over legislation and regulations that affect the environment; pressures are put upon local and national representative bodies—as well as upon regulatory agencies—to slow down the change processes. Interest group activities are mentioned at various points in this book. In particular, analysis is an alternative to "normal" politicking by pressure groups.

One approach to handling change might emphasize the use of experimentation of various types. In the face of substantial disagreement about the good faith of those being regulated (business interests, for the most part) and real questions about the proper mode of regulation, relatively small-scale experimental projects trying different sorts of regulations would certainly seem in order. The Caldwell article is particularly timely in applying an important technique—that of interrupted time-series analysis—to the evaluation of experimental programs. If planned change is to be meaningful, such techniques must achieve a wider recognition.

Several different approaches to the regulatory process have been suggested. In comparing these approaches with those used to regulate the oil and steel companies in the Chicago area, it is noteworthy that voluntary compliance is not treated by Hagevik, perhaps because he has little faith in its efficacy. Effluent fees and payments systems are rejected on the basis of both practical and theoretical considerations. Hagevik ends up with a number of suggestions for improving the regulatory process and setting enforceable abatement schedules.

The relationship between the environmental issue and other problems is also noted by several authors. The press of other societal needs may direct decision makers' attentions away from the environment toward what seem to be more pressing problems. This is partly because of the normal tendency to deal with crisis situations first. Despite talk of an environmental "crisis," such a situation may seem temporally remote to a politician having to deal with day-to-day crises of other types. In similar fashion, the decision makers are likely to neglect the environment because of an inability to keep track of more than a certain number of pressing concerns. Because of such tendencies, dramatic events like the Santa Barbara oil spill aid the conservationist's cause by keeping both the public and its political leadership aware of environmental concerns.

The questions regarding the environment as a political issue are relevant to another problem. What is the relationship between social reform and environmental reform? What do the poor think of the newfound concern for the environment? The contribution by Miss Trop and the editor considers this latter question by utilizing public opinion data. From another perspective, the reaction of leaders of the poor seems to have varied according to the facet of the environmental issue under discussion.

Efforts to protect the environment are threatening to the poor in several ways:

1. Concern is directed away from social reform and psychic energy is drawn off to be applied to this new issue.
2. Funds which might go into poverty programs may be diverted into various kinds of environmental programs.
3. Development of backward regions—with the jobs and higher living standards implied by such development—may be postponed or prevented in the name of conservation and environmental protection.
4. Incorporation of stricter standards to lower pollution tends to raise the costs of essential goods and services. These costs may be disproportionately borne by those who can least afford it.

All these questions have been raised by spokesmen for the poor, but with differing amounts of forcefulness. The regressive aspects of raising the prices of various goods have received comparatively little attention. In an inflationary environment, such added costs seem surprisingly accepted.

On the other hand, vigorous statements have been made and lively politicking taken place regarding some of the other "threats" mentioned here. Roadblocks to developments that might provide jobs for the poor have been particularly attacked. Attempts to preserve an undeveloped resort area in South Carolina for upper-class whites and a comparatively few black fishermen have aroused a black population needing the work which a projected chemical plant would bring. More broadly, the system of National Parks and Wilderness areas seems to appeal primarily to middle- and upper-class tourists. By and large, the poor have not had the resources and inclination for the use of wilderness recreational opportunities.

But when the environmental cause becomes tied to urban problems, some interesting coalitions seem possible. Social and environmental improvement might be linked together. It is the urban poor who cannot escape to clean air and private beaches; thus, in metropolitan areas public health and environmental health overlap. Threatened closings of accessible public beaches due to water pollution certainly decrease recreational opportunities and may increase the possibilities of riots. Most urban mayors are attuned to these kinds of problems, but there must be a solution better than keeping the beaches open under highly dubious health conditions. In such cases, spokesmen for the environment and representatives of the ghetto might profitably join forces to seek antipollution legislation.

Such coalitions are possible on a national scale, but the signs are not overly encouraging. What Crowe has labeled "tribalism" is clearly on the increase in the United States, thus making it more difficult to find the means to deal with problems of the "commons"—problems of the polity as a whole. Societal developments may be making the polity less able—rather than more able—to deal with environmental problems. There does not yet seem to be a national commitment to spending the kinds of funds necessary to preserve the environment. More dynamic leadership, leadership committed to environmental reform, may emerge, but informed optimism is difficult to sustain.

PART ONE

STATEMENTS OF THE ENVIRONMENTAL PROBLEM

Observers who have seriously considered the many facets of our present environmental plight must realize that solutions are neither clearly evident nor certain of implementation. Yet few are probably aware of the actual enormity and complexity of the task facing the nation. Across the country commuters and hippies, housewives and sportsmen, church groups and politicians, and students and professors have gathered to spread the message and formulate plans of action. Government has wrestled with the tangle of overlapping environmental agencies and bureaus in an effort to cope with pollution of the American environment. But behind the flurry of meetings, public outcry, and political pressure looms a question with awesome implications: Given our present political social structure, is a significant, comprehensive solution possible? Though the articles in this part adopt quite different perspectives, this question is central throughout.

As a polemic to incite action, "The Politics of Ecosuicide" maintains traditional political theory to be irrelevant in a world faced with the problem of survival. Can crisis be averted only through fundamental restructuring of our present political system? After summarizing current human trends and conditions that, if unchecked, will gravely endanger human and other life forms, Anthony D'Amato suggests some of the likely reactions of individuals and groups as population and pollution increase and life-supporting natural resources are further depleted. His projection implies that the majority of individuals will neither

7

truly comprehend the impending threat nor be capable of any
rational, cooperative action to avert irreversible environmental.
destruction. And a projected pattern of group reactions predicts
scenarios of several possible grim outcomes. An analysis of basic
societal perceptions—the context in which an environmental action program must be considered—also points to the low probability of effective action. D'Amato identifies a number of "mass"
values held by the global populace and by the science establishment. Without exception, these mass attitudes reinforce the status quo and work directly counter to the achievement of a significant solution. D'Amato concludes that, left to its own resources, political society will become increasingly totalitarian
as environmental destruction becomes more evident. The only
viable, liberal approach is a crash program of research into creative cooperation that may lead people to change their values
and life styles.

In a more systemic political and social analysis that disa-
grees with some of the ideas of D'Amato, "The Tragedy of the
Commons Revisited" offers a no more hopeful outlook. Responding to the statement of a natural scientist that the critical problems of population, atomic war, and environmental corruption
are more amenable to political than technical solutions, Beryl
Crowe analyzes three social myths on which this statement is
based. Crowe exposes the fallacies of the natural scientist's proposed solution, concluding that the myths probably cannot be
revitalized or reformed in time to avert a full-blown tragedy of
the commons—the destruction of our water, soil, air, and living
space. This prophecy of environmental apocalypse assumes,
however, that comprehensive solutions are dependent upon a set
of conditions in which the myths are valid—and perhaps this
assumption may be open to question. Crowe maintains that the
structure of our present political and social institutions makes
comprehensive solutions impossible, and thereby implies that if
we are to achieve solutions, it will require basic and fundamental change. Having concluded that the most crucial problems
that threaten existence are politically as well as technically insoluble, suggestions for interim contributions of science are offered.

The D'Amato and Crowe articles present a bleak outlook
when considered singly. When they are taken together, the picture is darker still. The suggestions for action proposed by
Crowe are dismissed by statements of D'Amato. The analysis by

Sprout is somewhat more optimistic in presenting the possibility that those proposing social reform might enter into coalition with the advocates of environmental reform. Crowe, of course, sees cooperation between such distinct "tribes" as highly unlikely.

Finally, we should note that the magnitude of the problem is even greater than the articles suggest. The discussion emphasizes events and conditions within the United States, and clearly the problems demand transnational solutions; with the unity of the world's ecological system, all mankind is dependent upon the same shrinking resources.

1

ANTHONY D'AMATO *

The Politics of Ecosuicide

I Perceived and Actual Threats to the Environment

Political thought down through the ages has never had to confront the hypothesis that man in organized society was so rapidly destroying his environment that the human species would not have very long to live. It is clear that if such an apocalyptic vision had come to the great political philosophers, they would have drastically revised their theories of the state and the community to organize them along the lines of a common fight for human survival. Instead, political theory operates upon the luxurious level that the environment is mere background, and that people can *afford* to engage in wars with other people or engage in internal struggles for power, goods, and values.

Today we have to abandon all our heritage of political theory and most of our heritage of political science, for it is irrelevant to the problem of survival now confronting us. Instead, we have to engage in speculation into the future, into models of alternative futures, into events that have never happened before. If it has been foreordained that the demonic genius of the human intelligence would lead men inexorably to extinction, then we have a nonrecurring historiography to contend with. All cyclical theories have to be abandoned; experience is no longer a teacher but a great misleader; and we have to be prepared to throw away all or nearly all the "intellectual skills" that we have been taught in school which were based upon the assumption that what was rational and productive for one generation would be equally useful for the next.

A brief inventory of current human trends should be enough to convince the most cynical eco-skeptic that the human species is gravely

* Professor D'Amato is teaching at Northwestern University. His article was prepared for this volume.

endangered and that the near future will have to be unlike anything that has ever been experienced in recorded human history.

1. Let us first consider the population explosion. The human species is now threatening to overrun the planet, leaving no room for food. At current rates, which include all extrapolations for birth-control programs, it will take just 600 years (or less than a third of the time span of Christianity) for people to be packed one hundred persons per square yard of all the land space on earth. Well before that time we may expect cataclysmic events which will guarantee that people will not be packed all over the face of the earth in such density.

2. This leads to the second tendency, which is not wholly a function of the population explosion—the depletion of natural resources. The food productivity of the soil, the cleanliness of the air, and the wholesomeness of the world's supply of water, are all endangered by increased human usage. More and more land space is rendered unfit for farming yearly, due to overfarming, erosion, soil-depletion through the use of single-crop farming and intensive fertilization, and the spread of the population, resulting in a paving-over of farmland for housing, factories, streets, and highways. Water is used for industrial cooling and cleaning, and it is now impossible to find water anywhere in the world that is not partially contaminated with man-made wastes. Atmospheric oxygen is being depleted, and replaced with carbon dioxide, due to human population growth (consumption of oxygen through respiration), killing off of plant life (thus reducing photosynthetic restoration of oxygen), industrial combustion (consumption of oxygen in the burning of fossil fuels, and such), and iron oxidation (the iron and steel products of technology left out in the air to rust). At some point, no one knows when, there will simply not be enough oxygen in the earth's atmosphere to support human life. And apart from the population explosion, the rapidly accelerating pace of technology—the industrial revolution—endangers the soil, air, and water. The rising rate of technological capacity for exploitation of these resources guarantees through the simple logic of economics, whether in capitalistic or in socialistic systems, that they will be exploited at an increasing rate.

3. A third tendency concerns the depletion of living organisms—the vanishing species. As people accelerate in numbers, there is less room for nonhuman animals to roam around and less room for plant life when man cuts down forests and paves over wilderness areas so that he may construct his home, his schools, his factories, and his highways. More men take to "sport hunting" in addition to increased (and ecologically reckless) hunting and fishing to satisfy growing human hunger. When an animal or plant species vanishes, it cannot be replaced no

matter how much "technological genius" is devoted to the task. In recent years animal and plant species, and especially insects and small
plants, have been disappearing from the face of the earth in accelerating
numbers, resulting in a simplification of the global ecosystem. Ecologists
tell us that living organisms interact in complex ecosystems; with fewer
species, the interconnectedness of plant and animal life becomes more
precarious, breaks down, and hastens the simplification process. Ultimately the simplest system is one in which there is no life at all. The
moon and the other planets are simple systems of this type. (They have
high positive entropy, whereas living organisms are negentropic, introducing order into a randomizing world. But, to be possible at all, "life"
requires a delicately balanced environment, and as species die off, simplicity and randomness—positive entropy—come into the system, jeop-
ardizing the remaining living organisms.)

4. The greatest threat is pollution. With population growth and
the push of the developing nations to industrialize, world pollution increases at an accelerating rate. Individual components of pollution inter-
react to form, in many cases, more deadly types. "Smog," for instance, is
a more deadly gas than the sum of its individual components, for they
react chemically in sunlight and in air to produce smog. The vast
amount of oil now spilled into the oceans may also give rise to new
kinds of chemical pollution of the oceans, as well as hasten eutrophication due to the deadly effect of oil upon some microorganisms. More in-
sidiously, as we introduce increasing amounts of pollution into our air
and water, we may be breaking down the ability of these natural resources to resist marginal increments in pollution. Air pollution, for instance, is now worldwide; lichens in Lapland, it is reported, are suffering from the air pollution of West European industrial centers. Twenty
years ago, "smog" was associated with Los Angeles; now it is found in
Phoenix, San Francisco, Honolulu, Rome, Sydney, Moscow, and indeed,
in all major cities. Perhaps this is happening because a saturation point
has been reached in the Earth's atmosphere so that just a little more
pollution anywhere results in smog.

Some people have argued that we had almost as much pollution
twenty years ago, only now that ecology has become a "craze," the
newspapers naturally are filled with reports of it. People who argue this
way tend to discount the alarming effects of pollution because they
think that the issue has been overly publicized and that the reality is far
less significant. To an extent, it must be conceded that the public's interest in phenomena, whether it be wars or moon shots or ecology, comes
in waves, and at the peak of a wave may be just as overexaggerated as
it is ignorant at the trough of the wave. Nevertheless, it would appear to

be impossible to get worldwide public interest in a nonevent. Mass perception must be based upon some real changes in the physical world. So we must ask ourselves, what is it that has changed? Let us consider both population and pollution in this regard.

Although the slope of the world population curve is moving sharply toward the vertical, there have been no abrupt advances or declines in the population graph itself. Popular perceptions of the danger of population growth have been more or less gradual (until very recently), with peaks of awareness coinciding with some historical events. In the nineteenth century, when Malthus was writing gloomily about wars, famines, or plagues as the solution to the world population crisis, Europeans felt some sense of incipient crowding. But emigration to America was the safety valve, both in terms of the numbers of people who came here and in psychological terms of a feeling of open spaces westward. World population of one billion in 1850 then doubled in eighty years to two billion by about 1930. Ortega y Gasset, writing at that time, perceived with considerable discomfiture the emergence of mass man, invading and utilizing culture havens previously open only to sensitive intellectuals, and lowering the quality of the political atmosphere so that demagogery could rear its head. The late 1930s witnessed Japanese expansionism and German demands for *lebensraum;* the case of crowded Japan was obviously more persuasive than the German situation, but crowding—as Professor E. T. Hall and others have shown—is a matter of how we perceive it. Japanese citizens had, and still have, a much higher tolerance for crowding than West Europeans; so it is psychologically possible that in the late 1930s, Japan and Germany equally felt the need for more real estate.

The next doubling of population, to four billion persons, will occur by about 1975. Under the shadow of thermonuclear destruction, national lebensraum movements have been pretty well contained. Japan, for one, succeeded in lowering its birth rate since 1945, and although the population kept growing (due to concomitant lowering of the death rate), it did not grow as rapidly as in the 1930s. High immigration barriers in most nations are fencing off population movements, and countries such as India (which itself adds to its population every ten years the equivalent of the present population of Japan!) seem to have so much trouble feeding themselves that the level of industrialization needed to support an aggressive army cannot be reached; as a result, a few border skirmishes are all the threat to external real estate that India can muster.

Thus, although the geometric rate, as well as the even more pronounced arithmetical growth, of the population "bomb" continue on their suicidal course, these facts could have been, and in some cases (for example, Malthus) were, projected long ago. The Stalinist purges and the second World War did not put a noticeable dent into world population growth, nor have there been any noticeable spurts—just an inexorable, hyperbolic rise.

The worldwide attention to the overpopulation menace, therefore, must be due to an exogenous variable, a factor that *did* change in the 1960s. This variable is pollution. The degradation, and in an increasing number of cases the destruction, of the environment upon which our bodies depend for nourishment and breath visibly underwent a qualitative turn for the worse in the 1960s, and has been noticed as a universal phenomenon in the early 1970s. Since many people discount the reality of pollution because of its newsworthiness, in actuality pollution is much worse than anyone's perception of it. DDT, for instance, is a persistent pesticide; already it is thinning the eggshells of bird life throughout the world and endangering many species. Like radioactive isotopes, chlorinated hydrocarbons such as DDT may have carcinogenic and mutagenic effects upon humans over a longer term. An effect that is acute in lower forms of life may, in us, simply be chronic. Nor can we get rid of radioactivity in the environment once it is introduced as the by-product from the nuclear electric power stations that are proliferating all over the United States and being copied in all other countries as well. Governmental scientists, paid to be mollifiers of the public, will simply continue to raise their estimates of the "safe" levels of radioactive pollution. The so-called peaceful uses of nuclear power (which may indeed eventually bring eternal peace and stillness to this planet) have only been with us in the past decade or so, and radioactivity from them (plus fallout from the many nuclear weapons tests) may have contaminated our bodies to the extent that we are more susceptible to other kinds of pollutants. Thus, cancer, which is on a sharp increase throughout the world, may result from smog or smoking *because* the lethal effects have been enhanced by radioactivity in the environment. Results such as these are naturally very hard to measure statistically, and the vested utility and uranium interests can be expected to use their political power to keep a lid on any attempt to get funding for such an enormous statistical study.

It is possible, therefore, that the many news stories about pollution that we are now seeing daily will *increase* in number in the next few years and be pushed somewhat into the background only because they have become a permanent fixture of our lives. On the other hand, more "dramatic" pollution effects will occupy headlines because, as the earth becomes increasingly saturated with types of pollutants, their synergistic effects will cause increasingly dangerous and visible results.

At this point we close the circle back to population. If the current high level of global pollution is caused by 3.5 billion persons now alive, can mankind survive an increase of at least 30 percent in pollution as world population increases 30 percent in the next decade? Can we survive an increase of over *100* percent in pollution as the population doubles by the year 2000? (Pollution increases should outpace population increases by the result of rapid industrialization of the vast majority of countries that now call themselves developing nations.) It is this now extremely noticeable threat of pollution of the environment (plus considerable world starvation resulting from the inability of depleted and polluted soil to produce more and more food) that has caused a great reassessment of the population problem. Each new baby that now comes into the world, though innocent and harmless-looking, represents an actual threat to the survival of everyone else. It is no wonder that birth control and abortion have, with incredible rapidity considering the traditional slowness of human attitudes on basic issues to change, become respectable.

II A Projection of Political Reactions

a. *Individual Reactions*

Let us consider here what might be the political reactions of mankind to a growing awareness of the threat to the environment outlined in the preceding section. At the outset we must start with the obvious proposition that men are quite different from one another in their ability to act rationally in the fact of impending disaster; and we must add the not-quite-so-obvious proposition that man has not been programmed by natural selection to react emotionally or instinctively to gradual threats that span more than a generation's reproductive cycle.

The first proposition tells us that although there are some people today who understand the impending disaster to our life-supporting environment with sufficient rationality that they are devoting the bulk of their personal efforts to help mankind attempt to avoid catastrophe, the majority of people do not, and perhaps cannot, conceptualize the threat so concretely. The threat, after all, is scientific-intellectual; it requires a person to look about him, to make extrapolations, to listen to others, and to project into the future the probable effect upon nature of what a proliferating human species is now doing to nature. Not many people can intellectualize this. As the threat becomes more obvious (for example, as people have to wear air-filter masks in cities), more people might become aware of the threat. Yet, we can be quite sure that some people will not be aware of the threat of imminent destruction until the last minute—when they are themselves gasping for breath. Moreover, we cannot simply assume that as the environment becomes less livable, more and more people will become aware of the problem and that, at the eleventh hour, the people of the world will rise in rational concurrent action and somehow save themselves. For it is quite possible that air pollution or hunger will make people less rational and less intelligent. The lead from automobile exhausts, for instance, is known to be a form of poison dulling the intelligence. It has been suggested in some studies that carbon monoxide, another component of automobile exhausts, has a dulling effect upon the nervous system. Hunger and malnutrition, too, not only render a person less energetic and less able to cope with stress, but also tend to wipe out in a person's mind all thoughts other than the desire to get food by any means. Thus we cannot assume that the environmental threat that we face will contain the seeds of its own amelioration by virtue of the eventual triumph of mass human rationality. The opposite may result from the very poisons that constitute the environmental threat.

The second proposition is a generalization from all forms of higher animal life: that evolution has created this form of species well equipped to mature to the point of sexual reproduction, but not particularly equipped to do anything after that point except grow old and die. For, from an evolutionary point of view, what an animal does after he engages in the sexual reproductive act is almost totally irrelevant. Animals have evolved with great ability to react to short-term dangers that might interfere with the generation cycle that leads to reproduction of the species. For the human animal, ten or fifteen years marks the limit of the "long run," for a conscious child of, say, five years will reproduce in ten or fifteen years, and thus he only has to be biologically equipped to survive in that time period. The human animal, in consequence, is very well equipped to respond to immediate and visible threats. If attacked by an animal or another person, a man is quick to respond in self-defense. He has fashioned tools and used his wits to become "master" of the animal kingdom. In modern times, man has turned his defenses against other men. People readily perceive the threat of a war so long as national leaders make sure to personify the enemy. Domestically, people readily perceive a threat in "street gangs" or "hippies" (as in the movie *Easy Rider*); great sums can be expended to fight crime as well as to fight wars. In addition to personal threats, people will respond readily to the threat of deadly poisons; our food and drug safety laws are fairly good in reacting immediately to deadly poisons or deforming drugs (for example, thalidomide). In short, dangers that are immediately or at least quickly apparent are well suited to human avoidance. The human race would not have survived in natural selection if it had not had the ability to avoid dangers to life and limb that would manifest themselves at least within ten or fifteen years.

The opposite is true of dangers that might kill a person over a longer term. Once the period of fifteen or twenty years for reproduction is over, it is irrelevant, evolutionarily speaking, when or how a person dies. Thus we have no emotional programming to enable us to react to slow-acting dangers such as air, water, or radioactive pollution. The only way we can react to such dangers is to use our intelligence, an intelligence which, from an evolutionary point of view, exceeds the minimum necessary to survive for a reproductive period. In other words, it is possible for some people to perceive and intellectually articulate a threat to the entire species that may become manifest in longer than a twenty-year time span. We know from the fact that many species have died out (for example, dinosaurs) that either these species did *not* have the intelligence to perceive and react to a species threat, as opposed to an individual threat, or that events simply overpowered them. In humans, at least, we can articulate the problem. But whether many others will perceive the problem intellectually when they are not programmed to perceive it emotionally is, at present, unknowable.

b. Dialectics of Group Reactions

Moving from individual perceptions to group behavior, a Hegelian pattern of mass initiatives and reactions might in the future run somewhat as follows.

THESIS. Incipient awareness of the environmental crisis generates activities such as teach-ins on college campuses, hour-long and hour-boring TV "specials" on the environment, vast amounts of printed words, political promises, agencies, commissions, and—especially important for our purposes—action programs in the form of lawsuits and "eco-tactics." The lawsuits promise initially to "punish" the polluters, to make them cease and desist, and further serve to encourage people to work "within the system" in combating environmental degradation. Ecotactics will also consume a considerable amount of activist energy. Typical ecotactics include writing letters to your congressmen, using and reusing your own shopping bag (instead of the store-furnished disposable bag), recycling your own garbage in your own yard, bicycling instead of motorbiking or driving an automobile, refusing to buy chopped-down

Christmas trees, refraining from litterbugging, and so forth. These and many more are promoted with missionary zeal by save-the-environment organizations. Teach-ins, lawsuits, and ecotactics all provide a heady initial dose of optimism that the environmental problem can be solved.

ANTITHESIS. Environmental activism invites an immediate form of backlash. Other "liberals" and activists complain bitterly that societal problems of poverty, war, and injustice are being subverted by the "establishment," which is taking a politically safe form of environmental activism as opposed to correcting the ills of society. Energies are thus channeled into the wrong directions, say the backlashers. A visible manifestation of this tendency was seen in early 1970 at various college campuses holding environmental teach-ins; these were actively and passively boycotted by the black student movement on the theory that pollution is a middle-class white man's issue. An underprivileged member of society might argue that we must have equality before we can have survival; his opponent might say that by the time we get equality, the species will have perished. Some writers—notably Paul Ehrlich, who for the most part has been an invaluable contributor to studies of the environment—would like to have it both ways. Ehrlich sees no reason why we can't work on all fronts at once, and argues that once blacks get to the level of affluence of whites in the United States, they will then reduce the size of their families, as do economically comparable whites. In the meantime, presumably, population control is for whites only.

This initial kind of backlash thus itself contributes to the prevailing optimism as activist groups join common cause and attempt to restructure the entire world. However, it becomes apparent with the passage of some time that this kind of activism will not work, at least as far as the environmental crisis is concerned. Some people may recycle their garbage, but most people will not. Moreover, the people who recycle their garbage probably will restrict the size of their families for ecological reasons, while the majority will not. The result is that the ecotactics people will not gain in numbers relative to the majority of the public. Even as more people join the ecotactics movement, their membership will probably be outnumbered by the population growth of the majority of the public that is unsympathetic to ecology. Thus a certain amount of despair will seep into the ecology movement. This will be reinforced by the relative nonsuccess of lawsuits. While judges may be expected to become more sympathetic to environmental concerns, the fact is that lawsuits against polluters will engender a new interest group: the workers who are employed by the polluters and the consumers who want the products of the polluters. If a paper mill, for example, says that it will be forced out of business competitively if it loses a given lawsuit and is ordered to add expensive antipollution devices, its workers may be expected to take up the company's cause and make it politically, as well as legally, difficult for such an adverse verdict to issue from a court. Or if a utilities company is blocked from putting in a nuclear power plant, at some point or other there will be an electric "brown-out" or "black-out" in the area. Then the public will clamor for more electricity (we have become so dependent upon it for heat, light, "work-saving devices," and so on), with the result that courts and legislators will be reluctant to put any further obstacles in the way of new power plant development.

SYNTHESIS. Thus despair, resignation, and depression may result from the antithetical societal forces just outlined. However, this synthesis in turn becomes a thesis; it contains the seeds of its own contradiction, in Hegelian terms. As environmental despair sets in, many people will adopt a highly hedonistic philosophy. "Eat, drink, and be merry, for tomorrow we die," will in various verbal disguises be the slogan of the era. This is nothing other than a form of human value adaptation to crisis. When there is too much cognitive dissonance in living at a time when the species is doomed, the mental overload results in a new value orientation that allows the human animal psychologically to adapt to his new perceptions. The form of adaptation will undoubtedly be that of "dropping out" of the pursuit of artificial inner experiences (drugs, for instance), and of reckless behavior in a spirit of abandonment. In a sense, the extreme of the present hippie movement is exactly this. It is the ultimate form of realism: adaptation to a doomed planet.

ANTITHESIS. The previous synthesis-turned-thesis deals predominantly with perceptual adaptation. But physical events predictably will intrude. Overcrowding, overpollution, simplification of the ecosystem, and exhaustion of resources will take their physical toll upon the hedonists. Perhaps vast plagues (started from the germ warfare research laboratories, as Paul Ehrlich suggests, where ultimate toxins are developed that have no effective antidote) will sweep the earth, killing off vast numbers of people and maiming the rest. Or there could be thermonuclear war (resulting, perhaps, from population pressures for more land) which might kill outright one or two billion people but leave the rest under a radioactive cloud that might either be lethal or permit only severely mutated descendants of the persons still alive. Or atmospheric pollution itself may slowly suffocate the race, weeding out all but the most healthy (who will themselves be stunted by the pollution).

SYNTHESIS. Under some of these scenarios, no human race will be left. This would, of course, be the final synthesis, a concept that is left unexplained in Hegel and unconvincing (the "classless society") in Marx. The earth's ecosystem would be greatly simplified; it would resemble the ultrastable moon. Under other scenarios, future dialectics might take place. For instance, atmospheric pollution might result in killing off 90 percent of the human race and leave the rest in a debilitated condition. This group, the cheerless society, will obviously not continue to pollute the atmosphere at anything like former levels. Eventually it is possible that the atmospheric pollution will settle back to earth. Or, a new ice age might result from the particulate matter in the atmosphere blocking the rays of the sun; in this case, the human survivors will be reduced to a primitive form of existence and probably not contribute any more pollution for thousands of years. Thus, from a cosmic perspective, planet Earth's current environmental crisis may be only a convulsion that effectuates an ecologically sound reduction in human population but still leaves the species living so that, in thousands of years, it may again repopulate the planet. However, present readers who find optimism in this possibility should not forget the alternative possibility that the convulsion might be 100 percent effective, wiping out all higher mammals. If we were dealing in Malthusian terms alone, we might expect the human race to be self-regulating by the processes of wars, famines, and plagues. The difference today is that certain possible types of environmental destruction or depletion (using up the oxygen, covering the earth with lethal radioactivity, polluting the air until it is completely poisonous, and so forth) might leave no survivors.

III   The Socio-Perceptual Context

a.   Global Values

Turning from speculation of futures to the present, we must compile an inventory of basic societal perceptions in order to understand the context in which any environmental action program must be based. Key mass perceptions include the following four values.

1. DEMOCRATIZATION AS A VALUE. As electronic communications increase, people increasingly expect to run their own governments. Quite the contrary of Orwell's *1984*, the inevitable mixed and conflicting messages in the mass media result in a heightening of individual claims to individual sovereignty. Governmental officials in countries having a

high degree of communication transactions must increasingly pander to the popular will. Soviet leaders are not much different from American leaders in this respect: The Russian people want housing, automobiles, the "good life" of gadgets and styles; and the Russian leadership caves in to these demands. The percentage of Soviet expenditures for military defense is not much different from that in the United States. Both governments, as well as the leaders of other countries, can fool their publics part of the time, but over the long haul they are responsive to popular demands. While the governments become quite adept at channeling these demands along certain lines that are more profitable or lead to more leadership power, at the same time the governments are becoming less adept at educating the public. Short-run maneuvers (for example, a Czechoslovakian invasion or a Vietnam war) can be brought off despite basic popular resistance, but hardly any government now wastes its time in the long-run education of the public. The net result is that the lowest common denominator—that is, the mass of people—is in charge. So long as this mass wants better housing, more TV sets, automobiles, mass digestible entertainment, and so forth, it will be very hard to bring about a drastic reorientation of values toward preserving the environment. In the eighteenth century one might have had to convince one man—the enlightened despot—to have a good chance of bringing about social change. Today, one must convince the uneducated, unenlightened masses, and such a "grass roots" campaign might be immeasurably difficult in light of the fact that governments themselves have despaired of doing anything so ambitious.

2. EGALITARIANISM AS A VALUE. The most trivial form of democracy is one in which there is perfect egalitarianism. Its conceptual simplicity, as opposed to the more subtle notion of Rousseau's general will or the complexities of Edmund Burke's conception of representative government, probably assures that it will be the reigning political system in years to come. Everyone can understand "one man, one vote," whereas hardly anyone can be persuaded (if he is asked!) that since he is less informed and stupider than others, his opinion should not count as much as theirs.

The combination of democratization and egalitarianism should serve to project on a worldwide basis the worst fears of De Tocqueville and Ortega y Gasset: That the mass mind will rule in what should be an intellectual aristocracy. Instead of the best ideas holding sway, political power will turn on the ideas that attract the most votes. Intricate ideas for preventing ecological disasters may take a back seat to simple ideas. Mass man sees nothing wrong, for instance, in unlimited hunting for "sport"; he might never be persuaded to relinquish forever his shot-gun or fishing reel because of the imminent threat to the survival of var-ious animals or fish.

3. A RADICAL CHEAPENING OF LIFE. Any commodity in plentiful supply becomes cheap; the same is true for human life, particularly when it is *too* abundant. The proliferating human species has already seen a cheapening of each man's political power. Each representative to every government on earth today "represents" far more people—sometimes ten to a hundred times more people—than his counterpart a century ago. Of course the quality of the representation, as well as the power of any single constituent, declines sharply. A similar cheapening of the value of an individual life is already manifest in crowded places such as Calcutta or Hong Kong; this pattern will rapidly spread with in-creases in population density. As life becomes cheaper, it may become increasingly hard to save in the face of environmental deterioration. Studies of overcrowded rats reveal a pattern of disregard for, and then cannibalism of, newborn rats, and a deterioration and finally extinction of the reproductive process. It may be very hard to convince the mass man to undertake a great effort to preserve human life if a general atti-tude of disregard for life takes hold in the majority mind.

4. PROGRESS AND MATERIALISM AS A BURGEONING VALUE. As al-luded to earlier in this essay, it is not so much the population growth of the underdeveloped countries per se that threatens the global environ-ment, but rather the increasing pressures for industrialization and devel-opment in these countries. By attempting to follow in the pattern of the United States, the underdeveloped nations could well overpollute our small planet.

Industrial development is not a value in itself; it has to be per-ceived to be such. The poor farmer in India or China today has his own set of values. His values will be relative to his own position; they will be ecologically determined, so to speak, so as to avoid too great a cognitive dissonance between the ideal and the real. If the farmer is on the verge of starvation, and if there is no prospect for an improvement in his or his family's condition, it is quite possible that he does not place a high value on living. He may, for example, feel that a long or a short life is irrelevant, since either way the important thing is that he will be rein-carnated into another form which might have a much shorter or longer life than his present existence. He may also place little or no value upon material possessions. On the other hand, he might place a great value upon having as many children as possible so that he will be doing his share to reincarnate previous life. By contrast, the average American places a great value upon living as long as possible, upon gadgetry and possessions and material comforts, and probably much less value upon having children (a child can be a "nuisance" and a "bother" to an American, whereas the Indian or Chinese farmer might not think at all in those terms but rather simply feel that he is fulfilling some divine plan).

It is the American, not the Indian, who is polluting the global environment with his jet planes, automobiles, nuclear power plants, guns, poison sprays, and so forth. But it is the American, too, who is doing his best to convince the Indian to adopt the American values. In the United States we simply assume that the world's masses want to live the way we do, and value the prolongation of life, and we act upon these assumptions by showing them how we live, by helping them industrialize, by exporting medical and nutritional technology to prolong their life spans, by promoting birth control in their countries, by inviting their best students here on scholarships to view the American scene for a while and then go back and spread the message, and by supporting political leaders in those countries (with heavy military foreign aid) who favor industrialization and a healthy business climate. Behind much of the American impetus for exporting birth control methods to foreign countries is a big-business lobby that has felt for many years that India, Latin America, and Africa would be better markets for our products and better workers for American-owned factories on their home territories if they didn't have so much population growth. Too many mouths to feed creates a bad labor pool and desperate governments which resort to confiscation of foreign companies. If we could only thin out their populations a bit and then give every family a TV set so that the American way of life could be dramatically portrayed, the underdeveloped countries would become ideal consumers for our products and ideal sources of cheap labor for our foreign investment programs.

Unfortunately, the Madison Avenue techniques that have been used to sell to underdeveloped countries the materialistic values of the industrialized nations have proved to be remarkably efficacious. Every political leader of every underdeveloped country has gotten the message. Everyone wants to modernize and industrialize as rapidly as possible—which means ignoring the pollution consequences. It may be impossible to reverse the image of the American "good life" that we have successfully exported, and even if it were possible from a communications standpoint, it is unlikely that the American mass media and business interests would ever allow it. Those who control the media are far too sincere! Being successful businessmen, they daily preach the value of business success. It is probably beyond their psychological ability to teach over the airwaves and in the newspapers that the American business ethic is ecologically unethical.

b. Values of the Science Establishment

A charge frequently heard in the pollution area is that a person will attempt to clean up the world before he has cleaned up his own back yard. In the matter of societal perceptions, it might similarly be said that natural and social scientists should look first to their own attitudes before attempting to change the minds of others. Three pervasive notions among others engendered by our cult of scientism are as follows:

1. A DEEP CONVICTION THAT PROGRESS IS DESIRABLE AND RE-LENTLESS. This notion found its most forceful propagandists among the French *philosophes* in the eighteenth century. Condorcet, for example, tried to prove that progress was historically inevitable. He admitted that the medieval period was a step backward toward darkness rather than light, but nevertheless this admission was not to him at all inconsistent with his thesis that mankind has progressed in a straight-line development and that the future would inevitably be greater than the past. Voltaire, in his attacks on established religion, happened to use the same kind of theistic language to launch a religion of scientism, a faith in mechanistic progress. In the past two centuries the *philosophe* attitude has uncritically spread throughout the world, reinforced time and again by widely publicized scientific breakthroughs that gave man new abilities (such as flying through the air or rocketing to the moon), new powers (creating and enslaving machines to do man's work, the atomic and hydrogen bombs), new invulnerabilities (vaccinations, transplants), and new amusements (radio, movies, television). Moreover, these triumphs of applied science reinforce each other (we have movies in our airplanes, we see space travel as it happens on television). The gadgetry of scientific progress is our own "cargo cult." The pursuit of money to be able to buy more and more of these "good things of life" is the overriding force in our lives, supplanting by far the impetus of the old religions.

2. A NEED TO USE SCIENCE TO CONQUER NATURE. With the dethronement of religion in industrialized society, the natural world begins to look hostile and alien to us. All religions teach that nature is either part of God's plan or part of God, and some religions deify and animate natural phenomena (fire, lightening, the winds). But when scientism re-

places religiosity, a kind of individual detachment from nature takes place. The human being is a unit, a discrete thing with a mind of its own, operating in a vast, dead universe. Nature becomes antagonistic to man, and man, to survive, must conquer nature. Our hospitals are symbols of antinature: whitewashed walls, square unrelieved rooms, unnaturally gleaming instruments, impersonalized doctors and nurses dressed in alien white and wearing masks. Where the technicians of science have their unfettered way, as doctors do in hospitals, no sign of nature is allowed to break in. Nothing is random, nothing is green, nothing is dirty. Sterilization has become a cult extending beyond the hospital: housewives compete with each other (encouraged by the delighted detergent companies) to have their kids wearing unnaturally white shirts, shoppers select fruits that have no blemishes and are artificially colored, and people scrub and polish their homes and apartments and yell at their children for tracking in mud or touching the walls. Dirt is our enemy, Mr. Clean our hero.

Early toilet training is the modern analog to the religious ritual of baptism. Corporations, as well, "hide" their waste products and sewage; no attention is paid to these unglamorous aspects of business, and there is a tacit agreement that the less said and done about them the better.

If the universe is alien and dead, then of course science can be expected to attempt to "conquer" it. Unfortunately, to bastions of applied science such as the Army Corps of Engineers, conquering nature means paving it over with dams, highways, and airports, poisoning all the bothersome insects, killing off the wild animals that could frighten or attack people, filling in the swamps, chopping down the trees, and installing several chlorinated swimming pools where there was once a lake. True scientists who see the dependence of human life upon the intricate ecological web encompassing all living things in the soil, air, and water must speak out against the destruction being caused by applied science. But first there has to be a radical rethinking of the initial premise that the universe is something "out there" apart from us and hostile to us.

3. PREOCCUPATION WITH PROBLEMS OF CONFLICT. Probably 95 percent, and maybe even 99 percent, of social-science research concerns the analysis of human conflict. Political science studies conflicts of power, competition for values, zero-sum games, decision making as competition among individuals, and so forth. Sociology and social psychology study conflicts between the individual and organized society, between groups in society, between authority figures and the masses, and between nations. Psychology, too, is primarily concerned with individuals who are in conflict with society, and attempts to adjust such individ-

uals into the more normal pattern. Recent extrapolations from observations of aggression and territoriality in animals have reinforced the basic conflict-oriented viewpoint of social scientists. Moreover, the pattern of conflicts in society makes the daily headlines and creates demand for the output of social scientists. Nothing fascinates the reading public more than human conflict, whether between long-haired students and the National Guard, or between American soldiers and the Viet Cong, or between the Black Panthers and the F.B.I. We have "wars" on poverty, on rats in the ghettos, and on godless communism. There is black power, white power, soul power, and backlash power. The United Nations has become a forum for the power of invective, as has the Vice Presidency. Language itself has become conflict-charged; only those who use verbal violence are quoted in the daily press. And meanwhile commissions are established to study violence and conflict, and the scientific establishment encourages social scientists to devote their full efforts to the analysis of the root causes of human conflict.

These efforts are important, but if Spaceship Earth is a sinking ship, we should not devote too much time to the study of individual conflicts upon that ship. The human race cannot afford to squander its intellectual capital on intraspecies matters because the species itself is endangered. We cannot simply declare a moratorium on the poisoning of our air and water so that we will have time to straighten out crime, poverty, war, and injustice. It is imperative that we break away from the fascination of the study of human conflict and turn our attention to human survival in a deteriorating environment.

IV   What Can Be Done?

So far we have been examining physical trends and human perceptions. It is clear that, left to its own resources, political society will become increasingly repressive as environmental degradation becomes more and more visible. For great waves of fear will descend upon the nations of the world as portents of environmental destruction increase in frequency. This fear will be translated into calls for strong-man leadership. Given the pervasive democratic and egalitarian values, the political leadership will probably not do anything so rational as to curtail pollution, punish overpopulation, or reduce industrialization. Rather, the leadership may be expected to mollify the public by silencing dissenters. We might anticipate far greater invasions of privacy than we have had so far, control of communications, censorship, regimentation of working conditions and industrial production and distribution, withdrawal into national units and a breakdown of global trade and tourism, and a shift to plebiscite "democracy" instead of representative fixed-term democracy.

Social scientists have only limited tools and perhaps can do nothing to ward off these bleak prospects. But at least an effort should be made. We have to ask what social science can do.

It is clear, first of all, that preoccupation with intraspecies conflict cannot solve the external problem of the species in a degrading environment. It is less clear, though fairly likely, that a shift of studies to environmental psychology will have minimal value. The relation of man to his environment and the environmental stimuli affecting man are, of course, important aspects of research but might not yield much in the way of action programs. Indeed, the ultimate stimulus-response vision outlined by B. F. Skinner is the control of man by the manipulation of his environment, but the problem now is that the environment has had much too much manipulation already. The impact of science on the environment, which has so drastically shaped the life style of modern man, has been all too successful. Further work along these lines might work in the opposite direction from that of human survival.

What then should we study? The opposite side of the coin of conflict is cooperation. This is not the same as "conflict resolution," which, as social science has proceeded so far, is simply that little bit of analysis at the end which says that if the preceding conflicts are avoided there will be resolution and harmony. Rather, what is needed is an initial and pervasive focus upon cooperation itself. How do normal human beings cooperate with each other? (*Not:* How does an abnormal person "fit in" with society?) What are the factors in non-zero-sum games that are successful in getting people to work together? It is a trivial observation that if the earth were invaded by aliens from outer space, the human race probably would bury its intraspecies differences and unite together in the common aim of repelling the alien invaders. Our present environmental threat to survival is in the same category, but what will make human beings engage in a common-aim effort on the home front? Is perception of the problem sufficient? What kinds of perceptions—a television "special" on pollution or a "population war" between Honduras and El Salvador? Can perceptions ever be enough? How can we find common ground between vastly different human-value systems in the world? How can people be persuaded—and by whom—to give up their quest for "more" technology and more products of technology? Would it ever be possible to convince our society that killing a pelican or an eagle is a more serious crime than killing a human being? (In certain island cultures, killing an animal is a capital crime.) Where are people "vulnerable" to pleas of cooperation? And how can the political system be structured so as to elicit this cooperation?

Human beings clearly "get along" with each other in families, in communities, and in societies. But what are the dynamics of this cooperative process? To be sure we have to know about the exceptions—namely, conflict—in order to know about the norm. But we do know a great deal about conflict; it is the norm that we have overlooked. We not only have to study the norm, but we also have to find where it is susceptible to change. We have to see how people can be persuaded, moved, cajoled, or simply led to cooperate with each other in a historically unprecedented task of cosmic proportions—to change their values and life styles so as to make it possible for future generations to continue to inhabit this small green planet.

BERYL L. CROWE *

2

The Tragedy of the Commons Revisited

Major problems have neither technical nor political solutions; extensions in morality are not likely

There has developed in the contemporary natural sciences a recognition that there is a subset of problems, such as population, atomic war, and environmental corruption, for which there are no technical solutions.[1,2] There is also an increasing recognition among contemporary social scientists that there is a subset of problems, such as population, atomic war, environmental corruption, and the recovery of a livable urban environment, for which there are no current political solutions.[3] The thesis of this article is that the common area shared by these two subsets contains most of the critical problems that threaten the very existence of contemporary man.

The importance of this area has not been raised previously because of the very structure of modern society. This society, with its emphasis on differentiation and specialization, has led to the development of two insular scientific communities—the natural and the social— between which there is very little communication and a great deal of envy, suspicion, disdain, and competition for scarce resources. Indeed, these two communities more closely resemble tribes living in close geographic proximity on university campuses than they resemble the "scien-

* Professor Crowe is teaching at the Evergreen State College, Olympia, Washington. The article originally appeared in *Science*, 166, 3909, November 28, 1969. Copyright 1969 by the American Association for the Advancement of Science.
[1] G. Hardin, *Science* 162, 1243 (1968).
[2] J. B. Wiesner and H. F. York, *Sci. Amer.* 211 No. 4, 27 (1964).
[3] C. Woodbury, *Amer. J. Public Health* 45, 1 (1955); S. Marquis, *Amer. Behav. Sci.* 11, 11 (1968); W. H. Ferry, *Center Mag.* 2, 2 (1969).

tific culture" that C. P. Snow placed in contrast to and opposition to the "humanistic culture." [4]

Perhaps the major problems of modern society have, in large part, been allowed to develop and intensify through this structure of insularity and specialization because it serves both psychological and professional functions for both scientific communities. Under such conditions, the natural sciences can recognize that some problems are not technically soluble and relegate them to the nether land of politics, while the social sciences recognize that some problems have no current political solutions and then postpone a search for solutions while they wait for new technologies with which to attack the problem. Both sciences can thus avoid responsibility and protect their respective myths of competence and relevance, while they avoid having to face the awesome and awful possibility that each has independently isolated the same subset of problems and given them different names. Thus, both never have to face the consequences of their respective findings. Meanwhile, due to the specialization and insularity of modern society, man's most critical problems lie in limbo, while the specialists in problem-solving go on to less critical problems for which they can find technical or political solutions.

In this circumstance, one psychologically brave but professionally foolhardy soul, Garrett Hardin, has dared to cross the tribal boundaries in his article "The Tragedy of the Commons." In it, he gives vivid proof of the insularity of the two scientific tribes in at least two respects: first, his "rediscovery" of the tragedy was in part wasted effort, for the knowledge of this tragedy is so common in the social sciences that it has generated some fairly sophisticated mathematical models [5]; second, the recognition of the existence of a subset of problems for which science neither offers nor aspires to offer technical solutions is not likely, under the contemporary conditions of insularity, to gain wide currency in the social sciences. Like Hardin, I will attempt to avoid the psychological and professional benefits of this insularity by tracing some of the political and social implications of his proposed solution to the tragedy of the commons.

The commons is a fundamental social institution that has a history going back through our own colonial experience to a body of English common law which antidates the Roman conquest. That law recognized that in societies there are some environmental objects which have never been, and should never be, exclusively appropriated to any individual or

[4] C. P. Snow, *The Two Cultures and the Scientific Revolution* (Cambridge Univ. Press, New York, 1959).
[5] M. Olson, Jr., *The Logic of Collective Action* (Harvard Univ. Press, Cambridge, Mass., 1965).

group of individuals. In England the classic example of the commons is the pasturage set aside for public use, and the "tragedy of the commons" to which Hardin refers was a tragedy of overgrazing and lack of care and fertilization which resulted in erosion and underproduction so destructive that there developed in the late 19th century an enclosure movement. Hardin applies this social institution to other environmental objects such as water, atmosphere, and living space.

The cause of this tragedy is exposed by a very simple mathematical model, utilizing the concept of utility drawn from economics. Allowing the utilities to range between a positive value of 1 and a negative value of 1, we may ask, as did the individual English herdsman, what is the utility to me of adding one more animal to my herd that grazes on the commons? His answer is that the positive utility is near 1 and the negative utility is only a fraction of minus 1. Adding together the component partial utilities, the herdsman concludes that it is rational for him to add another animal to his herd, then another, and so on. The tragedy to which Hardin refers develops because the same rational conclusion is reached by each and every herdsman sharing the commons.

Assumptions Necessary to Avoid the Tragedy

In passing the technically insoluble problems over to the political and social realm for solution, Hardin has made three critical assumptions: (i) that there exists, or can be developed, a "criterion of judgment and a system of weighting . . ." that will "render the incommensurables . . . commensurable . . ." in real life; (ii) that, possessing this criterion of judgment, "coercion can be mutually agreed upon," and that the application of coercion to effect a solution to problems will be effective in modern society; and (iii) that the administrative system, supported by the criterion of judgment and access to coercion, can and will protect the commons from further desecration.

If all three of these assumptions were correct, the tragedy which Hardin has recognized would dissolve into a rather facile melodrama of setting up administrative agencies. I believe these three assumptions are so questionable in contemporary society that a tragedy remains in the full sense in which Hardin used the term. Under contemporary conditions, the subset of technically insoluble problems is also politically insoluble, and thus we witness a full-blown tragedy wherein "the essence of dramatic tragedy is not unhappiness. It resides in the remorseless working of things."

The remorseless working of things in modern society is the erosion of three social myths which form the basis for Hardin's assumptions, and this erosion is proceeding at such a swift rate that perhaps the myths can neither revitalize nor reformulate in time to prevent the "population bomb" from going off, or before an accelerating "pollution immersion," or perhaps even an "atomic fallout."

Eroding Myth of the Common Value System

Hardin is theoretically correct, from the point of view of the behavioral sciences, in his argument that "in real life incommensurables *are* commensurable." He is, moreover, on firm ground in his assertion that to fulfill this condition in real life, one needs only "a criterion of judgment and a system of weighting." In real life, however, values are the criteria of judgment, and the system of weighting is dependent upon the ranging of a number of conflicting values in a hierarchy. That such a system of values exists beyond the confines of the nation-state is hardly tenable. At this point in time one is more likely to find such a system of values within the boundaries of the nation-state. Moreover, the nation-state is the only political unit of sufficient dimension to find and enforce political solutions to Hardin's subset of "technically insoluble problems." It is on this political unit that we will fix our attention.

In America there existed, until very recently, a set of conditions which perhaps made the solution to Hardin's problem subset possible: we lived with the myth that we were "one people, indivisible. . . ." This myth postulated that we were the great "melting pot" of the world wherein the diverse cultural ores of Europe were poured into the crucible of the frontier experience to produce a new alloy—an American civilization. This new civilization was presumably united by a common value system that was democratic, equalitarian, and existing under universally enforceable rules contained in the Constitution and the Bill of Rights.

In the United States today, however, there is emerging a new set of behavior patterns which suggest that the myth is either dead or dying. Instead of believing and behaving in accordance with the myth, large sectors of the population are developing life-styles and value hierarchies that give contemporary Americans an appearance more closely analogous to the particularistic, primitive forms of "tribal" organizations living in geographic proximity than to that shining new alloy, the American civilization.

With respect to American politics, for example, it is increasingly evident that the 1960 election was the last election in the United States to be played out according to the rules of pluralistic politics in a two-party system. Certainly 1964 was, even in terms of voting behavior, a contest between the larger tribe that was still committed to the pluralistic model of compromise and accommodation within a winning coalition, and an emerging tribe that is best seen as a millennial revitalization movement directed against mass society—a movement so committed to the revitalization of old values that it would rather lose the election than compromise its values. Under such circumstances former real-life commensurables within the Republican Party suddenly became incommensurable.

In 1968 it was the Democratic Party's turn to suffer the degeneration of commensurables into incommensurables as both the Wallace tribe and the McCarthy tribe refused to play by the old rules of compromise, accommodations, and exchange of interests. Indeed, as one looks back on the 1968 election, there seems to be a common theme in both these camps—a theme of return to more simple and direct participation in decision-making that is only possible in the tribal setting. Yet, despite this similarity, both the Wallaceites and McCarthyites responded with a value perspective that ruled out compromise, and they both demanded a drastic change in the dimension in which politics is played. So firm were the value commitments in both of these tribes that neither (as was the case with the Goldwater forces in 1964) was willing to settle for a modicum of power that could accrue through the processes of compromise with the national party leadership.

Still another dimension of this radical change in behavior is to be seen in the black community where the main trend of the argument seems to be not in the direction of accommodation, compromise, and integration, but rather in the direction of fragmentation from the larger community, intransigence in the areas where black values and black culture are concerned, and the structuring of a new community of like-minded and like-colored people. But to all appearances even the concept of color is not enough to sustain commensurables in their emerging community as it fragments into religious nationalism, secular nationalism, integrationists, separationists, and so forth. Thus those problems which were commensurable, both interracial and intraracial, in the era of integration become incommensurable in the era of Black Nationalism.

Nor can the growth of commensurable views be seen in the contemporary youth movements. On most of the American campuses today there are at least ten tribes involved in "tribal wars" among themselves and against the "imperialistic" powers of those "over 30." Just to tick them off, without any attempt to be comprehensive, there are: the uptight protectors of the status quo who are looking for middle-class union

cards, the revitalization movements of the Young Americans for Freedom, the reformists of pluralism represented by the Young Democrats
and the Young Republicans, those committed to New Politics, the Students for a Democratic Society, the Yippies, the Flower Children, the
Black Students Union, and the Third World Liberation Front. The critical change in this instance is not the rise of new groups; this is expected
within the pluralistic model of politics. What is new are value positions
assumed by these groups which lead them to make demands, not as
points for bargaining and compromise with the opposition, but rather as
points which are "not negotiable." Hence, they consciously set the stage
for either confrontation or surrender, but not for rendering incommensurables commensurable.

Moving out of formalized politics and off the campus, we see the
remnants of the "hippie" movement, which show clear-cut tribal overtones in their commune movements. This movement has, moreover, already fragmented into an urban tribe which can talk of guerrilla warfare
against the city fathers, while another tribe finds accommodation to
urban life untenable without sacrificing its values and therefore moves
out to the "Hog Farm," "Morning Star," or "Big Sur." Both hippie tribes
have reduced the commensurables with the dominant WASP tribe to the
point at which one of the cities on the Monterey Peninsula felt sufficiently threatened to pass a city ordinance against sleeping in trees, and
the city of San Francisco passed a law against sitting on sidewalks.

Even among those who still adhere to the pluralistic middle-class
American image, we can observe an increasing demand for a change in
the dimension of life and politics that has disrupted the elementary social processes: the demand for neighborhood (tribal?) schools, control
over redevelopment projects, and autonomy in the setting and payment
of rents to slumlords. All of these trends are more suggestive of tribalism
than of the growth of the range of commensurables with respect to the
commons.

We are, moreover, rediscovering other kinds of tribes in some very
odd ways. For example, in the educational process, we have found that
one of our first and best empirical measures in terms both of validity
and reproducibility—the I.Q. test—is a much better measure of the existence of different linguistic tribes than it is a measure of "native
intellect." [6] In the elementary school, the different languages and different values of these diverse tribal children have even rendered the commensurables that obtained in the educational system suddenly incommensurable.

[6] G. A. Harrison et al., Human Biology (Oxford Univ. Press, New York, 1964), p.
292; W. W. Charters, Jr., in School Children in the Urban Slum (Free Press, New
York, 1967).

Nor are the empirical contradictions of the common value myth as new as one might suspect. For example, with respect to the urban environment, at least 7 years ago Scott Greer was arguing that the core city was sick and would remain sick until a basic sociological movement took place in our urban environment that would move all the middle classes to the suburbs and surrender the core city to the ". . . segregated, the insulted, and the injured." [7] This argument by Greer came at a time when most of us were still talking about compromise and accommodation of interests, and was based upon a perception that the life styles, values, and needs of these two groups were so disparate that a healthy, creative restructuring of life in the core city could not take place until pluralism had been replaced by what amounted to geographic or territorial tribalism; only when this occurred would urban incommensurables become commensurable.

Looking at a more recent analysis of the sickness of the core city, Wallace F. Smith has argued that the productive model of the city is no longer viable for the purposes of economic analysis.[8] Instead, he develops a model of the city as a site for leisure consumption, and then seems to suggest that the nature of this model is such that the city cannot regain its health because it cannot make decisions, and that it cannot make decisions because the leisure demands are value-based and, hence, do not admit of compromise and accommodation; consequently there is no way of deciding among these various value-oriented demands that are being made on the core city.

In looking for the cause of the erosion of the myth of a common value system, it seems to me that so long as our perceptions and knowledge of other groups were formed largely through the written media of communication, the American myth that we were a giant melting pot of equalitarians could be sustained. In such a perceptual field it is tenable, if not obvious, that men are motivated by interests. Interests can always be compromised and accommodated without undermining our very being by sacrificing values. Under the impact of the electronic media, however, this psychological distance has broken down and we now discover that these people with whom we could formerly compromise on interests are not, after all, really motivated by interests but by values. Their behavior in our very living room betrays a set of values, moreover, that are incompatible with our own, and consequently the compromises that we make are not those of contract but of culture. While the former are acceptable, any form of compromise on the latter is not a form of ra-

---

[7] S. Greer, *Governing the Metropolis* (Wiley, New York, 1962), p. 148.
[8] W. F. Smith, "The Class Struggle and the Disquieted City," a paper presented at the 1969 annual meeting of the Western Economic Association, Oregon State University, Corvallis.

tional behavior but is rather a clear case of either apostasy or heresy. Thus, we have arrived not at an age of accommodation but one of confrontation. In such an age "incommensurables" remain "incommensurable" in real life.

Erosion of the Myth of the Monopoly of Coercive Force

In the past, those who no longer subscribed to the values of the dominant culture were held in check by the myth that the state possessed a monopoly on coercive force. This myth has undergone continual erosion since the end of World War II owing to the success of the strategy of guerrilla warfare, as first revealed to the French in Indochina, and later conclusively demonstrated in Algeria. Suffering as we do from what Senator Fulbright has called "the arrogance of power," we have been extremely slow to learn the lesson in Vietnam, although we now realize that war is political and cannot be won by military means. It is apparent that the myth of the monopoly of coercive force as it was first qualified in the civil rights conflict in the South, then in our urban ghettos, next on the streets of Chicago, and now on our college campuses has lost its hold over the minds of Americans. The technology of guerrilla warfare has made it evident that, while the state can win battles, it cannot win wars of values. Coercive force which is centered in the modern state cannot be sustained in the face of the active resistance of some 10 percent of its population unless the state is willing to embark on a deliberate policy of genocide directed against the value-dissident groups. The factor that sustained the myth of coercive force in the past was the acceptance of a common value system. Whether the latter exists is questionable in the modern nation-state. But, even if most members of the nation-state remain united around a common value system which makes incommensurables for the majority commensurable, that majority is incapable of enforcing its decisions upon the minority in the face of the diminished coercive power of the governing body of the nation-state.

Erosion of the Myth of Administrators of the Commons

Hardin's thesis that the administrative arm of the state is capable of legislating temperance accords with current administrative theory in political science and touches on one of the concerns of that body of theory when he suggests that the ". . . great challenge facing us now is to invent the corrective feedbacks that are needed to keep the custodians honest."

Our best empirical answers to the question—*Quis custodiet ipsos custodes?*—"Who shall watch the watchers themselves?"—have shown fairly conclusively [9] that the decisions, orders, hearings, and press releases of the custodians of the commons, such as the Federal Communications Commission, the Interstate Commerce Commission, the Federal Trade Commission, and even the Bureau of Internal Revenue, give the large but unorganized groups in American society symbolic satisfaction and assurances. Yet, the actual day-to-day decisions and operations of these administrative agencies contribute, foster, aid, and indeed legitimate the special claims of small but highly organized groups to differential access to tangible resources which are extracted from the commons. This has been so well documented in the social sciences that the best answer to the question of who watches over the custodians of the commons is the regulated interests that make incursions on the commons.

Indeed, the process has been so widely commented upon that one writer has postulated a common life cycle for all attempts to develop regulatory policies.[10] This life cycle is launched by an outcry so widespread and demanding that it generates enough political force to bring about the establishment of a regulatory agency to insure the equitable, just, and rational distribution of the advantages among all holders of interest in the commons. This phase is followed by the symbolic reassurance of the offended as the agency goes into operation, developing a period of political quiescence among the great majority of those who hold a general but unorganized interest in the commons. Once this political quiescence has developed, the highly organized and specifically interested groups who wish to make incursions into the commons bring sufficient pressure to bear through other political processes to convert the agency to the protection and furthering of their interests. In the last phase, even staffing of the regulating agency is accomplished by drawing the agency administrators from the ranks of the regulated.

Thus, it would seem that, even with the existence of a common value system accompanied by a viable myth of the monopoly of coercive force, the prospects are very dim for saving the commons from differential exploitation or spoliation by the administrative devices in which Hardin places his hope. This being the case, the natural sciences may absolve themselves of responsibility for meeting the environmental challenges of the contemporary world by relegating those problems for

[9] M. Bernstein, *Regulating Business by Independent Commissions* (Princeton Univ. Press, Princeton, N.J., 1955); E. P. Herring, *Public Administration and the Public Interest* (McGraw-Hill, New York, 1936); E. M. Redford, *Administration of National Economic Control* (Macmillan, New York, 1952).
[10] M. Edelman, *The Symbolic Uses of Politics* (Univ. of Illinois Press, Urbana, 1964).

which there are no technical solutions to the political or social realm. This action will, however, make little contribution to the solution of the problem.

Are the Critical Problems of Modern Society Insoluble?

Earlier in this article I agreed that perhaps until very recently there existed a set of conditions which made the solution of Hardin's problem subset possible; now I suggest that the concession is questionable. There is evidence of structural as well as value problems which make comprehensive solutions impossible and these conditions have been present for some time.

For example, Aaron Wildavsky, in a comprehensive study of the budgetary process, has found that in the absence of a calculus for resolving "intrapersonal comparison of utilities," the governmental budgetary process proceeds by a calculus that is sequential and incremental rather than comprehensive. This being the case ". . . if one looks at politics as a process by which the government mobilizes resources to meet pressing problems" [11] the budget is the focus of these problem responses and the responses to problems in contemporary America are not the sort of comprehensive responses required to bring order to a disordered environment. Another example of the operation of this type of rationality is the American involvement in Vietnam; for, what is the policy of escalation but the policy of sequential incrementalism given a new Madison Avenue euphemism? The question facing us all is the question of whether incremental rationality is sufficient to deal with 20th-century problems.

The operational requirements of modern institutions makes incremental rationality the only viable form of decision-making, but this only raises the prior question of whether there are solutions to any of the major problems raised in modern society. It may well be that the emerging forms of tribal behavior noted in this article are the last hope of reducing political and social institutions to a level where incommensurables become commensurable in terms of values *and* in terms of comprehensive responses to problems. After all, in the history of man on earth we might well assume that the departure from the tribal experience is a short-run deviant experiment that failed. As we stand "on the eve of destruction," it may well be that the return to the face-to-face life in the small community unmediated by the electronic media is a very functional response in terms of the perpetuation of the species.

[11] A. Wildavsky, *The Politics of the Budgetary Process* (Little Brown, Boston, Mass., 1964).

There is, I believe, a significant sense in which the human environment is directly in conflict with the source of man's ascendancy among the other species of the earth. Man's evolutionary position hinges, not on specialization, but rather on generalized adaptability. Modern social and political institutions, however, hinge on specialized, sequential, incremental decision-making and not on generalized adaptability. This being the case, life in the nation-state will continue to require a singleness of purpose for success but in a very critical sense this singleness of purpose becomes a straightjacket that makes generalized adaptation impossible. Nowhere is this conflict more evident than in our urban centers where there has been a decline in the livability of the total environment that is almost directly proportionate to the rise of special purpose districts. Nowhere is this conflict between institutional singleness of purpose and the human dimension of the modern environment more evident than in the recent warning of S. Goran Lofroth, chairman of a committee studying pesticides for the Swedish National Research Council, that many breast-fed children ingest from their mother's milk "more than the recommended daily intake of DDT" [12] and should perhaps be switched to cow's milk because cows secrete only 2 to 10 percent of the DDT they ingest.

How Can Science Contribute to the Saving of the Commons?

It would seem that, despite the nearly remorseless working of things, science has some interim contributions to make to the alleviation of those problems of the commons which Hardin has pointed out.

These contributions can come at two levels.

1. Science can concentrate more of its attention on the development of technological responses which at once alleviate those problems and reward those people who no longer desecrate the commons. This approach would seem more likely to be successful than the ". . . fundamental extension in morality . . ." by administrative law; the engagement of interest seems to be a more reliable and consistent motivator of advantage-seeking groups than does administrative wrist-slapping or constituency pressure from the general public.

2. Science can perhaps, by using the widely proposed environmental monitoring systems, use them in such a way as to sustain a high level of "symbolic disassurance" among the holders of generalized interests in the commons—thus sustaining their political interest to a point where they would provide a constituency for the administrator other than

[12] Corvallis, *Gazette-Times*, 6 May 1969, p. 6.

those bent on denuding the commons. This latter approach would seem to be a first step toward the ". . . invention of the corrective feedbacks that are needed to keep custodians honest." This would require a major change in the behavior of science, however, for it could no longer rest content with development of the technology of monitoring and with turning the technology over to some new agency. Past administrative experience suggests that the use of technology to sustain a high level of "disassurance" among the general population would also require science to take up the role and the responsibility for maintaining, controlling, and disseminating the information.

Neither of these contributions to maintaining a habitable environment will be made by science unless there is a significant break in the insularity of the two scientific tribes. For if science must, in its own insularity, embark on the independent discovery of "the tragedy of the commons," along with the parameters that produce the tragedy, it may be too slow a process to save us from the total destruction of the planet. Just as important, however, science will, by pursuing such a course, divert its attention from the production of technical tools, information, and solutions which will contribute to the political and social solutions for the problems of the commons.

Because I remain very suspicious of the success of either demands or pleas for fundamental extensions in morality, I would suggest that such a conscious turning by both the social and the natural sciences is, at this time, in their immediate self-interest. As Michael Polanyi has pointed out, ". . . encircled today between the crude utilitarianism of the philistine and the ideological utilitarianism of the modern revolutionary movement, the love of pure science may falter and die." [13] The sciences, both social and natural, can function only in a very special intellectual environment that is neither universal or unchanging, and that environment is in jeopardy. The questions of humanistic relevance raised by the students at M.I.T., Stanford Research Institute, Berkeley, and wherever the headlines may carry us tomorrow, pose serious threats to the maintenance of that intellectual environment. However ill-founded *some* of the questions raised by the new generation may be, it behooves us to be ready with at least some collective, tentative answers —if only to maintain an environment in which both sciences will be allowed and fostered. This will not be accomplished so long as the social sciences continue to defer the most critical problems that face mankind to future technical advances, while the natural sciences continue to defer those same problems which are about to overwhelm all mankind to false expectations in the political realm.

[13] M. Polanyi, *Personal Knowledge* (Harper & Row, New York, 1964), p. 182.

HAROLD SPROUT *   **3**

The Environmental Crisis
in the Context of
American Politics

This discussion was addressed originally to a Conference (in March 1970) that included politicians, civil servants, business executives, professional conservationists, representatives of civic organizations, academic scholars, and students. At the Conference and since, many have tried to dismiss the environmental [1] crisis by branding it a "political fad" that will soon pass, and then business can return to normal.

The plain implication of this paper is that this is unlikely to occur. It is unlikely for the obvious reason that, in the absence of massive action to arrest and reverse the present ruinous trend, living conditions in America will progressively worsen, as indeed they have in the months since this paper was written. Unlike the spectre of nuclear war, to which people have adjusted as a speculative threat of a problematical catastrophe that might happen at some unspecified future time, the environmental crisis is here and now. It is a state of affairs that obtrudes pervasively, inescapably, and increasingly unpleasantly and in-

* Professor Sprout teaches at Princeton University. This paper was delivered at a Conference on "Ecology and Politics in America's Environmental Crisis," held at Princeton University in March 1970. Copyright 1970 by the Center of International Studies, Princeton University. Reproduced by permission of the author and the Center of International Studies.
[1] The word *environmental* is used here in the narrower sense of land, air, water, and other features of the physical habitat. When referring to urban squalor poverty, discrimination, and the like, I shall use the adjective *social*, even though such things are part of environment broadly defined.

juriously into the lives of everyone, old and young, rich and poor—none can escape.

Even so, there is no certainty, of course, that politicians, bureaucrats, business leaders, and citizens generally will react creatively, percipiently, wisely, or in time. But branding the environmental crisis a passing fad, or treating it so at the level of action, will not make it go away spontaneously, any more than poverty will vanish spontaneously, or than dying cities will renovate themselves spontaneously. Our chosen representatives may fail to act, or they may act ignorantly, meretriciously, even perversely; but we as citizens cannot escape the consequences of their actions.

Coming now to the issues with which the paper is specifically concerned, I begin by emphasizing the linkages between the environmental crisis, on the one hand, and growth of population and economic trends on the other.

In this country and nearly everywhere else in the world today, environmental deterioration is worst where human density is greatest. The problem here, as I see it, is not how to fit 250 to 300 million people into our deteriorating habitat. The problem is rather how to bring down the birth rate—soon!—in order that our children and grandchildren may inherit a land fit to live in.

Second, environmental deterioration to date has kept pace with the rise of our gross national product. Nearly everyone still subscribes to the expectation of endless economic expansion. Yet few face the environmental consequences of indefinitely consuming resources and piling up goods at the rate of the past twenty years or so. In any case, if continuing economic expansion for a while longer is not to worsen progressively our environmental crisis, it seems certain that there must be massive changes both in what is produced, how it is produced, how it is consumed, and what is done with the residual wastes. It is difficult to avoid the conclusion that such changes will entail comparably major changes in the values that we are wont to call the American "way of life." And I suggest that most of these changes are going to be decidedly unpalatable, especially to the more affluent members of our society.

This brings me to the issue of public attitudes toward the environmental crisis. Here I take off from the truism that what matters in the making of policies is not how conditions actually are, but how these are perceived by those who participate in the process. Applied to the environmental crisis, this distinction is between conditions *as profes-*

sional ecologists and other relevant experts declare these to be, and as nonexpert law-makers and private citizens believe them to be.

This distinction becomes especially important when the ultimate effects of a current situation are not immediately obvious. Such is notably the case with environmental pollutions. For example, adverse effects of poisoned air on health may not become fully evident for ten to twenty years or more.

Plainly, 99-plus percent of the American people (including most elected law-makers) have little or no expert knowledge of ecological cycles, ecosystems, or the ramifying consequences of environmental changes. These 99-plus percent are about as ill-equipped to assess the longer-range effects of foul air, polluted water, denuded land, ravaged wildlife, as they would be to describe the mechanisms of a space-rocket. But however limited their ecological knowledge, citizens have votes. And their elected representatives determine priorities, levy taxes, and allocate scarce resources.

There is a well-known tendency in America to dismiss expert predictions as unproved conjectures. This tendency is especially strong if the policy implications threaten vested interests and cherished freedoms and amenities. Thus, the first question to ask about the political context of our environmental crisis is: *How is this crisis perceived by politicians and citizens generally?* Is there a widespread sense of peril? If so, is it sufficient to sustain restrictive and very costly courses of action?

I think we may take it for granted that most Americans are at least intermittently and unpleasantly aware of smog, polluted water, excessive noise, rising mountains of debris, and other evidence of our deteriorating habitat.

Opinion polls indicate that a majority favor doing something about it. One notes, in particular, that environmental quality is becoming a serious concern of young people all over the country. Some observers assert that public opinion is "forcing the pace" for remedial actions.

However, we have little basis as yet for predicting how much Americans are willing to pay for a cleaner and more salubrious environment. How will they react when they begin to feel the pinch in their accustomed style of life? How will they respond to higher taxes and higher prices that will certainly accompany significant environmental programs? *My impression is that most people are reluctant even to talk about such an unpalatable prospect.*

Put this another way: It is doubtful if any but the tiniest minority —chiefly professional ecologists and dedicated lay conservationists— believe as yet that conditions are sufficiently menacing to justify drastic remedies. It is still more doubtful if any substantial number of Americans believe the experts who insist that continuation of present trends could render the earth uninhabitable within two or three generations. *Such a possibility is simply beyond the comprehension of most people.*

In sum, there is clearly a spreading awareness of environmental deterioration. There is apparently a widespread and growing desire to do something. But I can find little evidence that any large number of Americans are ready as yet to pay a high personal price to achieve environmental goals. And it is notorious that important agencies of government, strongly supported by influential bodies of citizens, cling tenaciously to ongoing programs and new projects—for example, in air transport, among others—that promise to make conditions worse rather than better.

This assessment may be too pessimistic. I hope it is. But I am inclined to believe that it comes close to the actual state of affairs, upon which we are trying to build environmental programs today.

Moreover, this is only half of the picture. *Environmental imperatives are competing with other massive demands on scarce resources.* Available goods and services are never sufficient to cover demands in any society. But I can think of no time (except possibly the final months of World War II) when the gap between demands and disposable resources in America has been so wide as it has become today. For this reason, it is needful to examine environmental programs within the context of a larger American crisis—one that has been aptly called the *crisis of priorities.*

This larger crisis has many roots. But three are chiefly responsible for its intractability as well as centrality in American politics today. One of these is the *size and inflexibility of the military budget.* The second is the *rising demand for action to arrest environmental deterioration.* The third is a concomitant *massive rise in demands for a cluster of social needs,* associated with poverty, the cities, and other urgent social problems. These competing claims on resources at the disposal of government at various levels—Federal, State and local—are indicated in the diagram on the facing page.

The size of the military budget is notorious. In 1960 the military departments received approximately 50 percent of all monies disbursed through the federal government. By 1969, the total dollar expenditures of those departments had risen from $38 billion to $77 billion. Much of this increase was for the war in Vietnam. Some of it was inflation of prices largely attributable to the war.

During the 1960s, the percentage of federal expenditures allocated to the military establishment declined slightly. But at the end of the

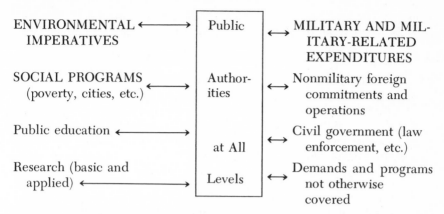

decade it still amounted to 45 percent of the federal budget. Recent decisions promise some further reduction of military spending—but how much remains to be seen.

It has been repeatedly asserted that federal spending for military purposes should be further reduced; some claim by as much as 50 percent. It is argued that such a reduction could be achieved without any real loss of security. This is, of course, debatable. *But it is not debatable that the government lacks adequate procedures for weighing prudentially the demands of the military establishment against the rising and proliferating needs of the civil society.*

Hitherto, the absence of prudential allocation procedures has worked mainly to the advantage of the military establishment. In the changing context of American politics, it may work increasingly in the opposite direction. In any case, given a taxing system as rigid as ours has become, the huge military budget is an obvious and attractive alternative source of the massive funds needed for domestic civilian purposes—both for environmental and for social programs.

There is some tendency on the part of ecologists and conservationists generally to assume that a cleaner and more healthful environment is a universal value. This is manifestly so from a physiological standpoint. But it is by no means so from a political perspective.

Environmental values are strongly identified with the higher income classes—notably those in the top 20 percent who receive over 40 percent of all distributed income; and perhaps most of the next 20 percent who receive nearly a quarter of all distributed income.

From the standpoint of the less affluent, environmental values rank somewhat lower. They tend to be regarded as luxuries until more elemental needs are satisfied. This is repeatedly asserted by those who speak for the poor and near-poor: for example, for the bottom 20 percent who receive less than 5 percent of distributed income; and more broadly, the lowest 40 percent whose total take is only 16 percent.

When exhorted about the virtues of clean air, pure water, noise abatement, unlittered landscape, and the rest, they are often unimpressed. Their perspective is summed up tersely by Whitney Young:

> People live in blighted housing, can't find decent jobs, send their kids to second-rate schools, die too soon because they can't afford doctors, and the cities they live in are sinking under the weight of countless unresolved problems of poverty and discrimination.
>
> That's where our national attention should be focussed. The war on pollution is one that should be waged after the war on poverty is won. Common sense calls for reasonable national priorities and not for inventing new causes whose main appeal seems to be in their potential for copping out and ignoring the most dangerous and most pressing of our problems. (From *Trenton Evening Times*, Feb. 16, 1970.)

There was a time—not so long ago—when the millions whose cause Whitney Young and others are defending constituted the "invisible poor." They were invisible in the sense that those who ruled paid scant attention to their needs, and did next to nothing to alleviate their condition. The poor were ignorant and unorganized. They had little or no effective access to the government that ruled ostensibly on their behalf. They were, in effect, aliens in the society of which they were nominal members.

It is not news that times have changed. Those who speak for the poor and near-poor can make their demands heard. And these demands are more often heeded than formerly—thanks in part to leadership and organization. But their rising political potential springs also from another source. That is their tightening grip on essential services in our easily disrupted urban society. What this might portend was fleetingly revealed in the sanitation workers' strike of 1967 in New York City. It was revealed again in the more recent firemen's strike in Gary. It was starkly evident in the chaos produced in a single day by the police strike in Montreal.

In short, demands on behalf of the less affluent parts of our society are acquiring a political muscle that makes them increasingly formidable claimants in the competition for scarce resources. And most of their spokesmen, I repeat, do not put environmental values first. Specifically, I am suggesting that *any program for spending large sums for cleaner air, water, and the rest is likely to run into grave political trouble if these values are put ahead of comparable outlays to eradicate poverty and the conditions and consequences of poverty.*

So far as I am aware, no one has yet offered a carefully researched estimate of the overall cost of repairing a century and more of environmental exploitation and neglect. Or how much it will cost to prevent further serious deterioration. Conservative guesses run to "tens of billions of dollars annually," as noted in the pre-Conference statement of "issues and alternatives." Furthermore, estimates of cost are escalating as more is learned about the magnitude and technical complexities of the problems that confront us.

A salient feature of the present situation is the simultaneous peaking of demands for social and for environmental reform. Combined these demands present a picture of needed future outlays for the domestic society that may be more nearly comparable to the cost of World War II than of the war in Vietnam. Demands of this magnitude would present formidable difficulties in any circumstances. They appear even more formidable when viewed in the light of the overall crisis of priorities.

I have said something about the size and inflexibility of the military budget. But there are still other, if lesser, claimants for scarce resources. These include the modernizing countries which have come to depend upon us for economic and technical assistance—and in whose political future we profess to have a vital interest. There are demands for further research and sorties into outer space, for supersonic air transports, and other expensive projects on the scientific and engineering frontiers. There are escalating demands for more police and stronger law enforcement generally, and for many other things deemed essential by politically influential segments of our national community.

This peaking of demands and costs in nearly every sector of public expenditure bedevils policymaking at all levels of government. Plainly, we are in for radical changes of priorities. But what changes?

Some, though perhaps a diminishing number, continue to give highest priority to military power on a scale sufficient to sustain most of the vast and scattered commitments built up around the world during the past generation. From any standpoint, military defense is a vital concern. Whether fighting wars in Asia or other distant places is essential to defense is hotly debated. One thing seems certain, however. *Barring drastic changes in the international climate, such questions will no longer be decided without more regard for the impact of military commitments on our domestic society and habitat.*

Specifically, the environmental and social crises present major challenges to previous modes of determining the size of military budgets. The growing strength of these challenges is a new factor in American politics.

Respected voices in our midst are even insisting that continued neglect of the environment will leave us nothing worth defending. One of these, George Stewart (eminent Princeton graduate and dedicated conservationist) asks starkly: ". . . who dares his death willingly to defend a garbage dump?" (From *Not So Rich As You Think*, p. 1. Houghton Mifflin, 1967).

Some spokesmen for the poor and for our cities level on the military budget still more savagely. One of these is Robert Heilbroner. He says: "Demilitarization of the nation's budget" is "necessary to restore American society to life. Politically, economically—even militarily—this budget is a disaster for America. It has sucked into the service of fear and death the energies and resources desperately needed for hope and life." ("Priorities for the Seventies," *Saturday Review*, Jan. 3, 1970.)

Obviously, there can be no quick or clean solution to this many-sided dispute over priorities. Massive changes in the allocation of resources could not be carried out overnight, or even in a year or two. They will be especially difficult within a political system so bureaucratized and rigid as ours has become. Equally obviously, the domestic crisis is not going to subside, simply by being ignored. Neglect here—whether benign or malevolent—can only make things worse. Nor will palliative remedies cure our environmental malaise. Yet palliatives and promises are about all that the politicians have given us to date.

Reduced to elementals, there appear to be three ways to mobilize resources on the scale needed to check environmental deterioration and provide adequately for future protection and maintenance. One way is to reduce much more drastically the allocations to military-related purposes. A second is to provide more revenue by raising taxes. A third way is to push some or most of the cost onto private business with the certainty that much of it will be passed along to consumers in higher prices for automobiles, power, food, newspapers, and nearly everything else.

The present strategy in Washington seems to *favor the third, reject the second*, and *resort to the first as sparingly as possible*. This strategy is accompanied by apparently sincere efforts to liquidate the Vietnam war, to reduce other commitments overseas, and to reach a more comprehensive detente with the Russians. But it is also accompanied by severe curtailment of ongoing and promised social programs.

This strategy has obvious limitations. It is likely to free only a small fraction of the resources required to check the worsening environmental crisis. Cutbacks of social programs and prospect of higher consumer prices are likely to intensify the opposition of those who give first priority to poverty, the cities, and social services in general. Moreover, as indicated in the pre-Conference statement, financing environmental programs through the market place is as inequitable to citizens of low income as are the regressive sales taxes upon which most of our States depend so heavily. For reasons previously discussed, stiffened opposition from the social sector could seriously blunt the thrust of any environmental program.

Other strategies may be lurking in the wings. What might happen, for instance, if a legislative coalition should take form between those who are carrying torches for social and for environmental reform? Would not the obvious basis for such a coalition be to mobilize support for a more drastic assault on the military budget?

Consider another proposal, reported recently in the press. The essence of this proposal is about as follows: Tie income tax rates to military spending. Cover any increase by an appropriate surtax. On the other hand, tie support of domestic programs to the Gross National Product. That is to say, give such programs the full benefit of increased revenue resulting from rise of the GNP. (Reported by Max Frankel, *The New York Times*, February 26, 1970.) This is an ingenious scheme. But what odds would you give on the chance of mobilizing Congressional approval for it? Moreover, it may be doubted whether it would come anywhere near to generating resources needed even for environmental programs alone—not to mention the comparable needs for poverty, education, and the cities.

It would be easy to close on a note of pessimism. To do so would be to ignore much in the picture that is more encouraging. Not since the Japanese attack on Pearl Harbor has any public issue received such massive support in all the news media, local as well as national. Restoration of environmental quality has become a concern of students that may approach in scale and intensity their opposition to the war in Vietnam. More and more politicians are finding it a congenial issue. The President and numerous Governors have spoken out strongly, as have leading members of Congress and State legislatures. Larger sums have already been allocated than one could reasonably have anticipated ten years ago. Civic organizations of many kinds are supporting the cause in scores if not hundreds of communities across the country. Increasingly, some of the most influential leaders of industry are identifying with the demand for a cleaner and more healthful environment.

A few, chiefly some of the more gross polluters, speak bitterly as if the environmental crisis were a synthetic fad manufactured by fanatics. But it is notable how relatively few such vocal dissenters there are, and how mildly they complain—at least in public.

One can cast up the account to date, and demur that all this is far from enough. And this is clearly so. But considering the rigidity and inertia of our political system, the diversity and magnitude of rising demands on disposable resources, and the traditional exploitive American attitudes toward the earth and its subhuman inhabitants, one may conclude that what has been accomplished thus far represents a stronger beginning than might have been expected even as recently as three or four years ago.

PUBLIC OPINION

The study of public opinion and the environment is intrinsically concerned with such topics as:

1. What are the attitudes of different publics on problems of pollution, conservation, population growth, and the like?
2. Will the environment issue be an enduring one that will continue to arouse the public in the 1970s?
3. What are some of the reasons underlying increased public interest in the environment?

One series of questions relevant to both the articles in this section concerns the relationships between elite and mass. How do elites influence the public with regard to the environment issue? What is the feedback from public opinion and interest to elite behavior? The first article, by Miss Trop and the editor, concentrates upon the mass public and its relationship to the political elite. The second article, by Maloney and Slovonsky, focuses upon the behavior of a communications elite—newspaper editors. Newspaper editors were polled about their treatment of environment-related events, about groups involved in local conflict over pollution issues, and about the future of "the environment" as a newsworthy public issue.

CECILE TROP
LESLIE L. ROOS, JR.

4

Public Opinion
and the Environment *

Until recently the conservation movement has been a relatively small coalition of groups directed toward the preservation and protection of the nation's natural resources. Over the last few years a series of events has served to move this environmental issue into the political arena. In 1965, President Johnson, through political actions and speeches, helped increase public concern about the environment.[1] Publicized attention resulting from the politicalization of the issue has successively stimulated higher levels of concern, priority, and commitment to seeking a cure for environmental ills. Finally, constituent pressure upon representatives has helped influence them towards supporting environmental legislation.

Although this recent and rapid growth of public concern over the environmental crisis has been widely discussed, there have been no attempts to analyze systematically the phenomenon within the American political framework. Through a detailed investigation of the reciprocal influences between public opinion and elite behavior, the future of the environmental issue might be better ascertained. Through the direct observation of Congressional activities over a ten year period—legislation, appropriations, and authorizations—an effort can be made to measure elite behavior. Public opinion polls can be used to help determine the direction of public interest and the nature of the attitudes, as well as

* This research has been aided by N.I.H. grant IRO3MH 19055–01 to the junior author. This article was prepared for this volume.
[1] Murray Edelman, *The Symbolic Use of Politics* (Urbana: University of Illinois Press, 1964), p. 172.

differences in preferences between the various subgroups of the population.[2]

The environmental issue provides an excellent case study of the development of an important public policy issue. In this paper, an effort is made to evaluate both public preferences and institutional responses. As is usual in such an endeavor, it is most difficult to specify the direction of causality. Leaders seem to have influenced the masses, while changing public opinion has put new pressures on elected representatives. Various events and shifts in political activity are intermingled temporally, making it almost impossible to use the time sequence of events to untangle the causal linkages.

Over the last decade, those sectors of the population demonstrating the most concern about and commitment to the environment have been the affluent (income over $10,000 a year), the college educated, the suburbanite, and the younger generation. The poor, the black, and those with only a grade-school education have been least likely to care about improving environmental quality. For these latter groups deleterious living conditions have combined with a lack of knowledge about the problem's significance, a lack of awareness of its effect on their own lives, and a perception of other problems as having a higher priority to produce a low level of expectation and concern in regard to the natural environment.[3] In the South, the comparatively low level of industrialization and a traditional orientation toward "states' rights" have led to a lesser concern for environmental problems, and a distaste for expanding the role of the federal government to solve these problems.

Concern about environment quality and willingness to accept an increase in total living expenses to finance environmental programs can be further analyzed. Over the decade studied differences between the answers of middle- and upper-income respondents have decreased while those between lower- and middle-income Americans have increased. A similar pattern was noted when education was substituted for income. In 1969 as in 1965, suburbanites were most willing to accept an additional financial burden, but the gap between those living in towns and in cities compared with those living in suburbia seems to have increased in the last few years.

The only public opinion data available for any aspect of the environment in the early 1960s were compiled by the Michigan Survey Re-

[2] Eva Mueller, "Public Attitudes Toward Fiscal Programs," in Fremont J. Lyden and Ernest G. Miller, eds., *Planning, Programming, Budgeting* (Chicago: Markham), p. 63.
[3] See, for example, "Public Attitudes Regarding Environmental Improvement," *Congressional Record, Dec. 20, 1969* (Washington, D.C.: U.S. Government Printing Office), p. E10941.

search Center in 1960–1961.[4] The Center's study was designed to evaluate public attitudes toward major government programs. One item in the survey coded "parks, recreation facilities" identified the major environmental programs receiving government attention up to that time. Forty-eight percent of the sample was satisfied with the level of government expenditures for these programs, while 27 percent desired an increase and 15 percent a decrease in the allocation for them. When additional taxation was mentioned, only 7 percent of the respondents remained interested in increasing the expenditures for parks and recreational facilities.

The respondents' low level of desire to increase finances for parks and recreational facilities suggests a lack of commitment to the major environmental programs of the early 1960s.[5] Of the legislation enacted between 1960 and 1964, twice as much was related to the procurement of additional parks and recreational facilities as to all other environmental programs combined. The lack of public interest in these other programs corresponded with the absence of political attention before 1965. The education and welfare programs, which received some attention in the 1960 presidential contests, also received the most survey support for increased expenditures and higher taxes. An examination of the 1964 political party platforms reveals that only the Democratic Party gave the environment brief attention, emphasizing conservation of the nation's natural resources and the expansion of recreational facilities. The Republican platform did not mention the environment.

During the early 1960s activity directed toward improving the quality of the environment was at a minimum. In 1960 the Izaak Walton League attempted to acquaint the public with the existence of an environmental crisis by nationally sponsoring "Clean Air Week." In the same year a New Jersey citizen's group campaigned for legislation to ban all air pollution, proposing that, "no person shall cause, suffer, allow or permit to be emitted into the outdoor atmosphere substances in quantities which shall result in air pollution."[6] Neither group received significant popular support. Congress enacted several relatively minor pollution control bills in the early 1960s: The Water Pollution Control Act

---

[4] Mueller, op. cit.

[5] On the other hand, Caldwell has argued that willingness to be taxed for the support of parks and recreational facilities did not provide a fair measure of the population's commitment to environmental quality programs (Lynton K. Caldwell, "Environmental Factors in Public Health Policy—A Retrospective Look," paper presented at the Conference on Arctic Health, Fairbanks, Alaska, May 12–14, 1970, p. 13).

[6] John Rodman, "Public Opinion on Air and Water Pollution in the 1960's" (Unpublished manuscript, Northwestern University, 1970), p. 3.

Amendment (1960), a bill extending the Air Pollution Control Act (1961), the Air Pollution Control Act (1962), and the Clean Air Act (1963).

The fact that publicity about the pollution problem has been present as early as 1960 without stimulating mass support emphasizes the influence political sources have had in bringing the environmental issue to the fore of public concern. *The New York Times* printed between 60 and 90 articles annually through 1964 on air and water pollution, and approximately 150 a year on all forms of pollution combined.[7] Typically these articles were descriptive in nature, making no demands for civic or legislative action. In 1965, the year in which former President Johnson proclaimed the beautification of our surroundings as a national goal, the number of articles published by *The New York Times* on air and water pollution more than doubled the 1964 figures with the total number of articles on the pollution topic increasing to 350. Of the major environmental legislation in 1965, four laws related to improving the esthetics of our natural surroundings. One of these, the Highway Beautification Act, directly accomplished this goal, while at least three others, the Water Quality Act, the Water Resources Act, and the Rural Water Sewage Act, did so through attempting better control of pollution.

In August, 1965, a Harris poll sought to determine how concerned Americans were over eleven different issue-areas.[8] Forty-three percent of the national sample often felt concern for the environmental issue, "pollution of rivers and streams." In the same year the American Institute of Public Opinion conducted a survey asking: "Which *three* of these national problems (shown on a card) would you like to see the government devote most of its attention to in the next year or two?" Only 17 percent and 3 percent of the respondents ranked "reducing air and water pollution" and "beautify America," the representative environmental programs, highest in priority. These low levels of priority are understandable; in 1965 the environmental issue was a recent entrant into the political arena and had to compete with problems that had been receiving both public and political attention for some time (education, crime, unemployment, and poverty). The 43 percent of the Harris survey sample reporting concern about water pollution seems to have been the first manifestation of the public's response to the call for a cleaner environment.

In 1966, the number of pollution-related articles published in *The*

---

[7] *Ibid.*
[8] "America's Concerns: The Harris Survey—Affluent America Still Concerned," *Congressional Record*, Aug. 18, 1965 (Washington, D.C.: U.S. Government Printing Office), p. 19753.

New York Times increased almost two-thirds over the 1965 level.[9] Conservationists successfully campaigned for public support to thwart the construction of two dams in canyons adjacent to the Grand Canyon National Park. Advertisements in *The New York Times* and in *The Washington Post* had instructed readers to write to their congressmen and to their executive branch offices to voice their opposition to the proposal. Senator Thomas B. Kuchel claimed on July 15, 1966, that these publicity efforts had generated one of the largest letter-writing campaigns he had ever seen.[10]

Congress also legislated for the acquisition of five major park and recreational areas, the Clean Water Restoration Act, the Clean Air Act, and—for the first time—two major oil pollution bills and ten bills regulating permissible motor emissions that year. One of the latter bills required the installation of pollution control devices on all new 1968 automobiles manufactured for use in the United States, a suggestion the Secretary of Health, Education, and Welfare had fruitlessly recommended to Congress in 1960.

In April 1967, former President Johnson sent a memo on the environment to the related federal departments announcing both that the control of pollution had become a matter of the highest national priority and that the fight against air pollution in particular would be strengthened. A Harris poll published that month indicated greater public support for federal control over pollution than over any other domestic program (1/2), while a large minority (1/3) were satisfied with the government's current level of involvement.[11]

The Air Pollution Control Act was enacted in 1967. Fifty-three percent of a 1967 sample mentioned "some or a lot" of air pollution, but a broad segment of the population (44 percent) felt that there was "little or none." [12] An examination of the population breakdown explains this rather unremarkable level of awareness. Over 70 percent of urban residents, as opposed to slightly over 30 percent of the residents of towns and rural localities, felt there was "some or a lot" of air pollution. Because areas with the densest populations also have been those with the most visible pollution problems, a higher level of awareness should have been expected from the residents of these areas.

Respondents demonstrated both a knowledge of air pollution sources and a skepticism about what was being done to control it. The performance of local industry received the highest positive rating (29

[9] Rodman, *op. cit.*, p. 10.
[10] *Congressional Record*, Senate (July 15, 1966), p. 15854.
[11] *Congressional Quarterly Weekly* (Washington, D.C.: Congressional Quarterly Service, May 5, 1967), p. 723.
[12] *Congressional Record Appendix* (July 25–October 2, 1967), p. 3763.

percent), followed in descending order by the federal government, local government, state government, the average citizen, and automobile manufacturers (21 percent). Motor vehicle exhaust and industrial fumes were perceived by 45 percent and 40 percent of the respondents, respectively, as the most prominent air polluters.

The strength of the public's desire for air pollution relief was measured by its willingness to be taxed for it. On the national level 44 percent of the population was willing to accept $15 a year or more in increased taxes to meet the costs of a pollution abatement program. This compares favorably with the percentage feeling that there was "some or a lot" of pollution (53 percent), with the percentage wanting the federal government to expand its control over pollution (50 percent), and with the 1960 percentage supporting increased taxes (7 percent). These findings suggest that the status of the pollution issue had risen in terms of public awareness, priority, and commitment.

Opinion polls indicate that by 1968 approximately 50 percent of the public had developed some interest in preserving environmental quality. The 1968 Democratic Party platform devoted one section to "environment, conservation, and natural resources," discussing recreation, waste disposal, conservation, agriculture, wildlife, clean water, and clean air programs. The Republican Party platform acknowledged in one sentence the existence of an air and water pollution problem and the need for its correction. Although pollution control was frequently mentioned by both parties, the Vietnam war received paramount political priority throughout the entire campaign period. The number of articles published in *The New York Times* decreased from 580 to 300, the lowest number printed since before 1965.[13] Only two major pollution control bills were passed during this period: the Water Rights Act and the Water Quality Improvement Act.

The passage of bills devoted to the conservation of natural areas may have stimulated *The Christian Science Monitor* study on public attitudes toward national park policy.[14] Respondents to this survey were generally willing to make personal sacrifices to preserve the quality of the park system and the natural state of the wilderness. They agreed on a need to increase users fees, to limit the stay of individual park visitors in order to prevent overcrowding, to control the speed limit of automobiles, to limit highway construction, and in many cases to substitute public transportation for automobiles in order to alleviate traffic congestion.

Neither in his 1969 State of the Union Message nor in a subse-

[13] Rodman, *op. cit.*, p. 10.
[14] Robert Cahn, *Will Success Spoil the National Parks?* (Boston: Christian Science Publishing Society, 1968), pp. 48–53.

quent message to Congress outlining preferred legislation did President Nixon mention environmental improvement. A far reaching attack on deteriorating conditions would have been contrary to his primary economic objective of holding back on government expenditures to help combat inflation. But during 1969 the strength of public opinion appears to have reached a level almost compelling both Congress and the President to address themselves to increasing demands for a better environment.[15] Congress enacted many important environmental bills in 1969, one of which established the President's Environmental Quality Council.

In 1969 the American Institute of Public Opinion conducted two surveys for the National Wildlife Federation.[16] Fifty-one percent of one sample were "deeply concerned," and 35 percent "somewhat concerned," about the deterioration of the nation's natural surroundings. Fifty-two percent of the other sample thought that present environmental quality programs had not been receiving substantial attention and support from the government, while 5 percent thought that they had been receiving too much, and 22 percent believed they had been receiving the correct amount. Fifty-one percent of the respondents were willing to pay a small amount (such as $10.00 or less) to improve environmental quality. Though not directly comparable with the previous questionnaires, these data represent the highest level of concern and commitment expressed thus far towards the environment.

Forty-five percent of one sample thought that the effects of certain highly toxic chemical pesticides were detrimental to the environment, while only 9 percent believed that the continued use of these chemicals had a good effect. A plurality of rural inhabitants, those who would be expected to benefit most from the use of pesticides, felt that they had a bad effect on the environment, while 12 percent said that they had a good effect.

Air and water pollution were perceived by 36 percent and 32 percent of the respondents, respectively, as the most pressing environmental problems. But only 29 percent mentioned that air and water pollution had affected their enjoyment of their lives. People with incomes over $10,000 (43 percent), those in suburbia (43 percent), and the college-educated (42 percent), tended to feel that air and water pollution were personally affecting them.

[15] The number of articles printed in *The New York Times* recovered the losses of the election year, suggesting a full recovery in treatment of the issue by the media. Rodman, *op. cit.*, p. 10.
[16] "Public Attitudes Regarding Environmental Improvement," *op. cit.* and "The United States Public Considers Its Environment" (Princeton: American Institute of Public Opinion, Feb. 1969).

The surveys attempted to discern the respondents' willingness to be taxed to finance environmental programs. Sixty-five percent of the national sample rejected a $200 a year increase in family expenditures for environmental improvement programs while 22 percent indicated a willingness to accept it. This figure represented an 18 percent increase over the number willing to pay $100 or more in a survey conducted one year earlier. The highest sum for which a majority (55 percent of the public) was willing to be taxed was $20.[17]

Two separate samples were used to determine public attitudes about current spending priorities. One group was handed a card listing ten federal programs and the percentage of the annual federal budget spent on each. The other group was given the same card but was not informed of current budget allocations. This technique permitted a comparison that might be indicative of the potential effects of further public education. The majority of both samples preferred less federal spending on international affairs, the space program, and national defense. The public was ambivalent about spending increases for commerce and transportation, health, labor and welfare, and agriculture. The focus was upon increased expenditures for domestic concerns: education, natural resources, veterans' benefits, housing, and community development.

With an awareness of budget program expenditures, 97 percent of the population was willing to reduce funds from another federal program to finance that of the environment. Those with information on current government appropriations were in favor of more spending on natural resources (from 62 to 68 percent) and less on national defense (from 55 to 61 percent). Substantial majorities of the college educated, the suburbanites, those with incomes over $10,000, and people under 30 years of age favored more federal money for natural resources (between 62 and 68 percent) and less on national defense (between 55 and 61 percent). Strong majorities of the college educated, the suburbanites, those with incomes over $10,000, and people under 30 years of age favored more federal money for natural resources. The least support among respondents with knowledge of current appropriations came from blacks (35 percent), from people who had not gone to high school (49 percent), and from those with annual incomes under $5,000 (53 percent). Seventy-one percent of the college educated chose the defense budget, while 62 percent of the blacks and 53 percent of those without high school education selected the space program, as a source of money for natural re-

[17] Respondents were also asked about assisting electric companies in financing the costs of pollution control devices. Only 14 percent were willing to accept an increase of $2.00 a month and 28 percent, an increase of $1.00 monthly, to improve our natural surroundings.

sources. Respondents under 30 years of age were most inclined to draw money from defense and international affairs.

Time series data suggest substantial changes between 1965 and 1970. Ninety percent of the respondents to a 1970 survey mentioned being concerned about water pollution; this represented a substantial increase over the 1965 public response of 43 percent to the question of whether or not the public felt concern "often" or "sometimes" about such pollution.[18] Fifty-three percent of another 1970 sample rated "reducing the pollution of air and water" an issue of the highest priority; this was a 36 percent increase over the 1965 level of concern.[19]

Fortune magazine administered an opinion poll to the chief executives of the nation's largest corporations in February 1970.[20] Business leaders seemed to feel that financial risks precluded their taking the initiative in establishing pollution control programs necessary for environmental protection. Executives expressed the desire for the federal government to step up its regulatory activities (57 percent) and to intervene and set national standards for all industries (53 percent). Fifty-nine percent of the sample believed that tax credits would be the most effective means of implementing pollution control devices. "Passing on costs to the consumer" was expressed as being the least effective means of achieving this end by 47 percent of the respondents. Fifty-eight percent of the businessmen planned to cut into company earnings rather than employ this alternative, but a sizable minority (24 percent) were in favor of passing the increased expenditures for control programs to the consumer.

These executives rated pollution as the fifth most important national concern (following tax reform, health care, the Vietnam war, and law and order), but they continued to perceive their primary responsibility as maximizing corporate profits. Although 60 percent of the respondents considered pollution an issue of "high priority," seven out of ten did not feel that it directly affected their own or their families' health. More than one-half of the sample favored research expenditure to develop a pollution-free engine to replace the internal combustion engine and eight-tenths supported population control. But about 60 percent also advocated financing of the SST, a notorious atmospheric polluter.

In the 1969 survey, executives claimed they would accept

[18] *Congressional Quarterly Weekly Report* (Washington, D.C.: Congressional Quarterly Service, February 27, 1970), p. 650.
[19] George Gallup, "United States Sets Top Domestic Priorities" (Princeton: American Institute of Public Opinion, May 14, 1970).
[20] "What Business Thinks: Fortune 500—Yankelovich Survey," *Fortune* (81, 2, February 1970), pp. 91–98, 118–119, 171–172.

"inhibiting the introduction of a new product" (84 percent), "foregoing an increase in production" (86 percent), and "reducing profits" (85 percent), in order to protect the quality of the environment. At the time this survey was administered, business reported having 81 percent more pollution control programs than five years before. Seven-tenths of the respondents mentioned company participation in pollution control activities, 44 percent of these claiming to have a pollution abatement budget. This latter figure includes those industries which have not needed pollution abatement budgets (banks, insurance companies, and so forth). The increase in pollution abatement programs may be related to more government-sponsored control activities, but its significance is offset by the fact that most of the executives' antipollution budgets have been less than 3 percent of their companies' annual capital outlay over the last five years.

Industrial leaders consider the public responsible for a substantial amount of the environmental deterioration and believe the public should share the responsibility of controlling pollution. They have been hesitant to initiate antipollution programs that might require passing part of the cost on to the consumer; businessmen fear decreased sales and competition from industries not initiating such programs.

Both the public and industrial elites have articulated a desire for more federal pollution control activity. But the question of "who pays?" is a central one. Business leaders believe that the public could compel Congress to impose heavy restraints upon industry, but doubt whether the average citizen is aware of the financial burden imposed by stringent pollution control programs. One executive noted that:

> We have got into the habit of putting productivity increase into wages and fringe benefits. The public has to be told that if we are to clean up the air, the water, etc; this is going to cost money, and probably going to mean that from here out we are going to divert increased productivity to improving the quality of life rather than the quantity of possessions.[21]

The public seems to feel that the federal government should get involved, but as of 1970 consumers were not willing to make major sacrifices to finance environmental quality programs. Clearly there is some contradiction here; federal involvement is unlikely to be "free" for the taxpaying public. Such contradictions are not unusual. Phillip E. Converse has contended that moving from elite sources of belief downward on an information scale:

[21] *Ibid.*, p. 118.

. . . the contextual grasp of "standard" political belief systems fades out very rapidly. . . . Increasingly simpler forms of information about "what goes with what" . . . turn up missing. The net result is that constraint declines across the universe of idea-elements, and that the range of relevant belief systems becomes narrower and narrower.[22]

The recently acquired interest in the environment has compelled politicians to respond to what is perceived as significant public concern. The recent political success of conservation groups is linked to their image as speaking for significant sectors of the public. The rapid growth of such groups over the last ten years may have influenced their perception. In one decade nationwide enrollment in the Sierra Club has risen from 15,000 to approximately 85,000; in the East, membership has expanded from 750 to 19,000.[23]

The government has responded to public demands with increased legislation and appropriations for environmental improvement programs. But there appears to have been more talk about what needs to be done than there has been meaningful political activity. Few high priority programs have received smaller appropriations than those designated for natural resources. Both the authorizations and the appropriations for major environmental quality programs have increased since their inception. On the other hand, there have been wide gaps between the sums authorized for these programs and the final amounts appropriated. It has not been unusual for environmental expenditures to have been even less than the amounts appropriated for them. With the exception of a few 1970 programs, the gap between authorizations and appropriations has steadily increased.

Although offering some encouragement, political activity regarding the environment has been inadequate. The passage of legislation has not insured its financial support or effectiveness. Given the current level of political and public concern in the issue and the symbolic nature of legislative activity, the future of the issue is uncertain. Edelman has suggested that:

The intensity of an interest in a particular objective is lessened in the degree that there is (1) constitutional, statutory, or administrative action dedicating "the state" to achieving the objective, and (2) frequent renewed ritualistic assertion, overt or implicit, that the objective is being achieved.[24]

[22] Phillip E. Converse, "The Nature of Belief Systems in Mass Publics," in David E. Apter, *The Ideology of Discontent* (New York: Crowell-Collier, 1964) p. 213.
[23] *Congressional Quarterly Almanac* (Washington, D.C.: Congressional Quarterly Service, Jan. 30, 1970), p. 282.
[24] Edelman, *op. cit.*, p. 164.

Both of these prerequisites are being fulfilled. In 1965, President Johnson dedicated the nation to environmental quality. Campaign oratory has centered upon the inadequacies of present programs while Congress has been enacting large quantities of environment-related legislation to strengthen constituency support. But, after symbolic legislation is passed, new programs seem to be administered with the purpose of preventing further deterioration rather than improving environmental quality. Former Secretary of Interior Hickel indicated what environmental programs can expect from the Nixon Administration "no spending" policies:

> Now I believe that it should be the duty and responsibility of the new Secretary of the Interior to continue these programs established by Congress. I believe we should devote a period of time to the consolidation of the gains that have been made and to a reassessment of our long range objectives.[25]

The public seems to reach a tolerance threshold with any political controversy; then the issue fades from the public mind. Knowledge acquired by elites tends to increase the stability of their beliefs, but mass opinion often shifts in response to dramatic, visible problems. Despite publicity about the environment, in 1969 only 29 percent of the population reported that air and water pollution affected their personal enjoyment of their lives.

Current public concern and commitment may not be enough to insure a sensitive legislative response to environmental needs. Concern for the environment must be internalized into personal and national value systems; such a process is time-consuming and at least partially dependent upon formal education. Because more immediate action is necessary, measures must be taken to institutionalize the government's responsibility for the health of the environment while the political momentum still exists. A constitutional amendment such as that introduced by Senator Gaylord Nelson declaring it an "inalienable right" of every American to have a decent environment would be the first step in this direction.

[25] Richard A. Cooley and Geoffrey Wandesforde-Smith, *Congress and the Environment* (Seattle: University of Washington Press, 1970), p. xvi–xvii.

JOHN C. MALONEY
LYNN SLOVONSKY*

The Pollution Issue:
A Survey of
Editorial Judgments

As the 1970s begin, the issue of environmental quality control has taken its place near the top of the list of public concerns. President Nixon's claim that the war on pollution *must* be won in the coming decade has given the pollution story a new urgency, and politicians of both parties—on the federal, state, and local levels—have seized the issue. People of varying philosophies and groups ranging from the old conservationists to the new conservationists are rallying to the cause. "The antipollution fight shows signs of becoming one of the most powerful grass-roots movements of recent decades," says John S. Gillen, managing editor of the *Philadelphia Inquirer.*

According to an urban journalism center review, major magazine stories on pollution, on environment, or on human ecology increased nearly sixfold between 1955 and 1965. Coverage of pollution-related news in newspapers and magazines and on radio and television has continued to increase dramatically since that time. But mere coverage of the issue by the mass media is not enough to assure any progress toward overcoming the pollution problem. The challenge, according to the variety of authorities, including Dr. Carl W. Bruch of the Food and Drug Administration, is to involve the public in making the very crucial decisions affecting the quality of life throughout the nation.

In a report prepared for the Brookings Institution while he was on leave from FDA ("Voluntary Private Behavior as a Means to Reduce Consumer Health Hazards and Environmental Pollution"), Dr. Bruch

* Professor Maloney teaches at Northwestern University. Mr. Slovonsky teaches at University of Illinois, Urbana. This article was prepared for this volume.

insisted that regulatory processes must be converted into an open forum. He asserts that efforts to reduce pollution should not be left to the discretion of the agencies and industries, meeting behind closed doors, but that "the public must be heard to supply persuasion for voluntary action." In his opinion, "an agency doing the best possible job to defend health, safety and security should welcome outside review, encourage vigorous debate over its actions and generate a public consensus as to what future direction control efforts should take."

Many newspaper editors agree with Bruch's position, and businessmen and civic leaders who are often themselves the targets of environmental cleanup campaigns will often concur in these views. In Chicago the Commonwealth Edison Company recently withdrew its request for an approval to delay compliance with the city's ban against burning high-sulfur coal. One Chicago paper commented that "the power of aroused public opinion has seldom had a better demonstration than in the decision by Commonwealth Edison Company to move farther and faster toward eliminating its share of Chicago's air pollution." The president of the utility, in a press conference, agreed: "I think that public pressure, widely expressed, has accelerated our program."

The Special Role of the Press

But the role of the press as a molder and shaper of public opinion on such issues is not always clear. The pollution issue has many technical, economic, and political ramifications, and while many people oppose pollution as a matter of principle, they may oppose it for very different reasons or on the basis of very different kinds of understanding. Many of the solutions that have been proposed in the war on pollution are considered drastic by some and absolutely repulsive to others. Some charge that the issue is a smoke screen to divert student interest from the problems of war and race. Others fear that it will be a vehicle for an irresponsible sort of radical revolution. Still others think it is just a fad or a soon-to-be-forgotten political football.

Because the issue is complex, and because experts do not always agree, there appears to be more than ample opportunity for the public to become confused rather than enlightened in ways that would be conducive to a "public consensus." As columnist Sydney J. Harris has put it, the movement itself may succumb to "fractionation." This is likely when "everybody wants a piece of the action and nobody is left to direct and control the action as a whole. It is the way people build empires and destroy movements."

A 1967 HEW task force, in assaying the role of the mass media in the upcoming war on pollution, put it this way: "Under the prevailing categorical approach, the public's attention is being competed for by information programs relating specifically to single environmental health problems—air pollution, solid-waste management, injury control, and others. To a marked degree, the task force believes, this tends to overwhelm the receiving public with an array of problem-related information at the expense of a more constructive awareness of the interrelationships between environmental problems and goals."[1]

Generalizations from Earlier Mass Media Research

The concerns of the HEW task force, no doubt, grew out of a study of mass-media handling of earlier issues of the same general sort. More than 20 years ago Bernard Berelson warned that "effects upon the audience do not follow directly from and in correspondence with the intent of the communicator or the content of the communication. The predisposition of the reader or the listener are deeply involved in the situation, and may operate to block or modify the intended effect or even to set up a boomerang." In viewing the apparent mass-media effects upon public opinion, he noted that the media may overwhelm at least a portion of the audience and promote a sense of apathy "simply through the presentation of the magnitude, the diversity and the complexity" of an issue. But he also suggested that the presentation of facts, rather than exhortation, could have the greatest positive effect upon public attitudes or understanding, and that "the communications media are most effective when their reportorial and interpretive contents are in congruence."[2]

Sociologists' theories of information diffusion imply that the mass media shape public opinions and behaviors by (1) making people aware of the issues, (2) making them interested in or curious about them, (3) providing information that will permit the audience to evaluate the issue in the light of their own interests and outlooks. In specific instances where citizen actions are to be taken the media may additionally (4) induce action at a particular time or place (for example, with a get-out-the-vote effort) if people are already aware of, interested in, and informed about the issues. Finally, the media may function (5) to rein-

[1] Department of Health, Education, and Welfare, *A Strategy For Livable Environment* (Washington, D.C.: U.S. Government Printing Office, June 1967).
[2] Bernard Berelson, "Communications and Public Opinion" in *Communication Modern Society* (Wilbur Schramm, Ed.), (Urbana: University of Illinois Press, 1948).

force attitudes or understanding by reminding people of certain facts, in addition to "minding" them in the first place.

Most communication theorists agree that the mass media are seldom responsible, all by themselves, for significant change in public opinion. Word-of-mouth communication and group action are likely to play key roles in later stages of opinion formation. The media are less likely to affect public opinion, in other words, when there are no community organizations involved in the issue at the grass-roots level to encourage conversation and action (or to make news for the media to report in the first place).

One particular study of a pollution-related issue provides an example of the way in which too much public interest or curiosity, unaccompanied by *clarifying* media coverage, can simply lead to greater anxiety without leading to an informed citizen response. The issue in question was the radiation fallout controversy of the early 1960s. At the time, public opinion researchers reported that the radiation fallout problem was perceived by much of the public as devastating and

> . . . when in addition there is basic conflict among scientists to whom one looks for authoritative clarification, it is a small wonder that no reduction of anxiety was found despite knowledge, media exposures, etc. It is reasonable to assume that where such a conflict among authorities quoted in the mass media exists, the finding of this study would probably be substantiated regardless of the subject matter under consideration, provided such were perceived by the mass media audience as a basic threat in the face of which they are completely helpless.[3]

It is not the purpose of this informal report to review all of the considerable body of research literature (or academic speculations) concerning mass-media effects upon public opinions about social issues. These few examples from that literature may serve to illustrate some of the bases for our own present concerns about press coverage of the war on pollution.

Purpose of Our Survey of Editorial Judgments

Without preconceived opinions about specific formats or formulas for the "right" kind or the "wrong" kind of press coverage, we assume that effective press coverage *can* lead to the kind of informed citizen

[3] S. Kraus, R. Mehling, and Elaine El-Assal, "Mass Media and the Fallout Controversy," *Public Opinion Quarterly* (Summer 1963).

participation that Dr. Carl Bruch seeks. At the same time, ineffective coverage may well lead to polluting public opinion itself with a futile anxiety. That is to say that the wrong kind of coverage could create a crisis of confidence in mankind's ability to survive—what some have called the pollution-problem problem.

Before proposing any detailed research of the issue, we wanted to know what newspaper editors themselves were thinking and doing, or planning to do, about pollution coverage. Are editors convinced that the war on pollution *is* a major news story for the 1970s? If so, how are they staffing the pollution beat and how much coverage are they giving the story? What are the best news sources about pollution? How does the story vary from one community to another? Are there many communities where the press and grass-roots organizations are both trying to inform the public about the problems of environmental degradation? What advice does the editor experienced in handling this story have to offer to those who are now turning attention to it for the first time?

In order to answer these questions, we compiled a list of 118 editors in 75 urban areas that the Federal Air Pollution Administration had designated as high (air) pollution areas. A three-page questionnaire was mailed to these men on February 6, 1970; a follow-up reminder letter went out on February 6 to those who had been unable to respond before that time. The information reported here is based upon replies from 56 of these editors, whose papers ranged in size from the New York *Daily News* (circ. 2,102,655) to the *Edinburg* (Texas) *Daily Review* (circ. 3,-890).[4]

Survey Findings

All but one of our respondents agreed that the environmental pollution story will be one of the biggest news stories of the 1970s, though a few of them doubted that it really should be.

[4] We have no adequate way of appraising the "nonresponse bias" in our replies. Editors are busy people and many of them must have regarded our request for help as an unwarranted nuisance. Some who have done little to cover the pollution story may have felt that it would adversely reflect upon themselves to answer the questions. Others probably have little or no interest in press coverage of the pollution story, one way or the other. Thus, editors who did reply probably give us an "over-representation" of those seriously concerned about pollution and interested in its coverage. We do not, in any case, offer these findings as being representative of the views of all editors, or of all editors in highly polluted areas. We do think that those who cooperated helped us a great deal to understand the issues and to build a much better base of understanding for further study of the issue.

Reasons for Emphasis on Pollution Coverage

More than half of the respondents indicated that pollution would be a big news story in the coming decade because of the attention already given to it and the already developed levels of public interest.

One editor referred to this as "the bandwagon instinct, the herd psychology of the media," and a few suggested, as the studies cited above have suggested, that the story could easily get *too much* of the wrong kind of coverage. Robert C. Notson, publisher of the *Portland Oregonian*, remarked in this connection that "there may be some danger that we could move from a position of indifference to one of hysteria on the subject."

Others felt that the story would be a big one in the earliest years of the 1970s, but that it would not last out the decade. A Chicago managing editor observed that "if history is any indication, the environmental push won't retain its steam through the decade. The movement may last through the 1972 elections."

Many editors felt that the story will be treated importantly simply because the pollution problem has become such a threat to the life of mankind. The fact that everyone is affected by pollution (or that it affects people's lives in so many different ways) makes pollution a big story in many editors' minds. The fact that this is becoming, or has become, a major political issue with the government and that large sums of money are involved was not overlooked in the replies.

A number of editors felt that pollution will be a big story because it has attracted the attention of, and fired the imaginations of, young people, and several noted that it is one issue that encompasses the inter-

Table 1 Reasons for Believing Pollution Will Be a Big Story in the 1970s

	Number of Times Mentioned
Publicity already given subject / existing public interest	28
Seriousness of pollution problem / threat to environment	17
Everyone affected / people affected so many ways	14
Will be big political issue	13
Government involvement / Presidential involvement	7
Young people are or will be active or interested	6
Issue can pull people together	5
Complexities or conflicts which will surround issue	4
Economic issue / lots of money involved	4

est of the right and the left, the young and the old, the hawks and the doves.

One editor felt that the war on pollution will attract major press coverage because "it is such a simple story" and a story about which everyone is sure to be agreed. But a more commonly expressed notion was the contrary view that it will be a big story because the issue is so complex and so likely to breed dissent and conflict once people begin to understand what is really at stake. As one editor put it, the pollution story will be big news because "conflict is always news."

Echoing the sentiments of Kraus, *et al.*,[5] the *Buffalo Evening News* editors noted: "As the pollution fever rises, so does the fragmentation and proliferation of information. One goal of newspaper coverage on a regular basis should be to put the war on pollution in perspective, restating the goals and aims and the progress that is being made in the newspaper's region." Edward H. Miller of Allentown, Pa., Call-Chronicle Newspapers, is among those who feel that "a serious knowledge gap" already exists.

Kurt Luedtke, assistant executive editor of the *Detroit Free Press*, mentioned most of the things that others had indicated could make this a big story in the period ahead. "The people are ready for it," said Luedtke. "Pressures to turn our eyes away from Viet Nam and the moon and back to the grave problems of our own nation and cities have been building for several years. The movement attracts followers because it is a ground on which we can come together—young and old, right and left. Coincident with the turn of the decade, the approaching 200th anniversary (of the U.S.), and borne by futurism, the Big E will certainly be a prime political and substantive issue in the decade ahead."

The greatest concern with the pollution problem was most often expressed by editors from highly industrialized urban centers like Detroit, where the pollution problem is most serious. But even the editors from less seriously affected areas show a concern. "We have problems of air and water pollution, but they are minor in comparison with the problems facing many areas," wrote Howard C. Cleavinger, managing editor of the *Spokane Daily Chronicle*. "Our situation in the Spokane area is retrievable. Our challenge is to control pollution before it becomes an uncontrollable monster."

Amount of Coverage in January

In order to sample a single time period that would be the same for all papers, our questionnaire asked editors to report on their pollu-

[5] *Op. cit.*

tion coverage in January. "Why January?", asked one editor. "It's the dead of winter here." Nonetheless, the survey did turn up a significant amount of daily and special coverage in January, a month that included, among other things, pronouncements on pollution by the President.

Two newspapers, *Chicago Today* and the *Texarkana Gazette*, submitted tear sheets showing that they had run stories, editorials, and feature columns relating to pollution almost every day of the month. On January 11 the *Detroit Free Press* published a 12-page special section entitled "1970's: The Peril and the Promise." They have had requests for more than 117,000 reprints.

In January the *Providence Evening Bulletin* ran a five-part, staff-written series entitled, "The Air We Breathe." Each part began with a story and picture on page one and continued with a full page of related material inside. The headline on the first article—across the top of page one—set the theme for the series: "Air Cleanup Drive at Snail's Pace in R.I." Joseph Ungaro, the *Bulletin's* managing editor, reported that a similar series on water pollution is in the works.

The Washington *Evening Star* ran a seven-part series in January and, in response to many requests, reprinted the series in a booklet entitled, "A World in Danger." The articles "examine what man has done to his world, and what we can do to save it."

In all, more than one-fifth of our respondents ran series of varying lengths on pollution during January. *The Philadelphia Bulletin* ran a special color page.

As one might expect, the larger newspapers, with the manpower to handle such assignments, tended to run the most page-one pollution stories and editorials in January. The average number of such stories by large (circ. 58,000 or more), small (circ. 58,000 or less), and all reporting newspapers is summarized in Table 2.

This is not to say that the newspaper giants have had a sharp edge in pioneering the pollution story coverage. Harry Hamm, editor of the *Wheeling News-Register,* reports that his paper's attack in the 1950s led to the adoption of a city air-pollution control ordinance.

Table 2   Emphasis on Pollution Coverage in January 1970

	Average Number of Stories Run		
	Large Papers	Small Papers	Combined Average
Page-One local stories	6.6	2.8	4.6
Page-One wire stories	3.6	4.0	3.8
Editorials	5.8	3.2	4.5

The "new interest (in pollution) being stirred nationally is old hat to Ironton-area residents," according to Dan Martin, managing editor of the *Ironton* (Ohio) *Tribune.* "We're glad that he [the President] and the federal government are finally joining the battle that communities like Ironton have been waging for years."

The *Toledo Blade* submitted a copy of its edition of May 23, 1965, which included a page-one start of a seven-part series on water pollution, four additional articles, and a map in the "Behind the News" section, as well as a cover story in the Sunday magazine.

E. J. Paxton, Jr., of the *Paducah* (Ky.) *Sun-Democrat,* described the war on pollution as a "continuing war" and indicated that "we will continue to give all of the leadership and encouragement we can, as we have done for more than 30 years." In Easton, Pennsylvania, the *Easton Express* has been campaigning against industrial pollution in the eastern Pennsylvania-New Jersey area for several years, and the tangible results of its efforts have been commended by the county medical society.

Staffing the Pollution Beat

Of the 26 large newspapers that returned our questionnaire, 22 had reporters regularly assigned to the pollution beat, 8 on a full-time basis. Nine of 30 smaller papers have reporters covering pollution on a part-time basis, and three other smaller papers are planning to make regular pollution beat assignments.

Major coverage efforts often require several people, either regularly or temporarily, assigned to pollution. For example, the 12-page *Detroit Free Press* section mentioned above was prepared by a special editor and three reporters who cover different aspects of pollution on a part-time basis. They worked for six months to produce the 19 stories in this section.

The *Chicago Tribune,* which has won acclaim for its "Save Our Lake" campaign (launched in 1967), is among the larger newspapers in the nation which have named full-time environment editors.

Part-time pollution reporters divide their time between environmental problems and other beats such as government, industry, transportation, planning, science, public health, medicine, outdoors, and consumer news. These companion assignments probably indicate something about the paper's orientation toward pollution. If pollution is viewed primarily as a threat to hunting and fishing, it can be naturally paired with an outdoors assignment. If it is seen as a political issue, it ties in naturally with covering governmental assignments. If it is seen as an urban problem, its coverage complements a transportation, planning, or a public health assignment, and so on.

Prior experience in reporting government or urban affairs, or a background in science and an investigative ability, is frequently seen as a qualification for environment reporting. Luedtke of the *Free Press* says: "Because the public's level of awareness and comprehension of environmental questions is growing rapidly, reporters can no longer approach the subject without their own solid understanding of the issues. Basic understanding of principles of scientific investigation, of ecology and the technology of pollution-abatement equipment is essential to intelligent coverage in this area. Unless the reporter can write from that kind of background, the newspaper will lose the respect of both industry and enforcement agencies. Its role as a leader will have been demolished."

Pollution News Sources

When asked to rank seven different sources in terms of their overall value as pollution news sources, the editors collectively ranked wire services highest and the Weather Bureau lowest. However, there was a marked difference between the larger and smaller papers in their reliance upon different news sources. The larger papers ranked local and state government agencies, "other" sources (for example, civic groups and universities), and federal agencies ahead of the wire services.[6]

Table 3   Editors' Ranking of Pollution News Sources

| | Average Rank Assigned Source* | | |
	Large Papers	Small Papers	Combined Average
Wire service	3.6	1.7	2.5
State government agencies	2.9	2.9	2.9
Local government agencies	2.1	3.7	2.9
Other sources (civic groups, universities, etc.)	3.2	3.6	3.4
Federal agencies (not Weather Bureau)	3.4	4.1	3.7
Utilities or other industries	5.0	4.8	4.9
Weather Bureau	5.9	5.4	5.6

* The highest rank, indicating greatest importance, was 1; the lowest rank was 7, assigned to any single source by a single editor.

[6] The greater reliance of smaller papers upon wire services also shows up in their greater likelihood of using wire service stories for page-one pollution coverage. See Table 3.

Pollution as a Local Problem

It is clear from our survey that "the pollution problem" consists of many different problems that vary considerably from one area to another. In many cases the problem is specifically defined by the nature of local industry (steel mills, paper mills, cement plants, coal mining operations, or nuclear power plants). Many editors mentioned local problems of lake or river pollution or certain geographic conditions (such as valleys that trap polluted air). Editors from New York and Philadelphia mentioned special solid-waste disposal problems. Runoff from cattle feedlots into the Missouri River is a problem at Kansas City. The burning of debris by loggers poses a problem for Portland, Oregon.

All but a few of our respondents were able to mention local groups that were active in the fight against pollution. Most often these were citizens groups, either those especially organized to fight pollution or those who had taken on the pollution fight as a special project. City, county, and state governments were often mentioned as being most active in opposing pollution locally, and where universities or colleges were present (especially in middle-sized areas) these institutions and their student groups were often mentioned. The editors' own newspapers were mentioned about one-fifth of the time as being among the most, if not the most, potent local sources of institutional opposition to pollution.

In terms of specific organizations, the League of Women Voters and the Izaak Walton League received the most frequent mention. Chambers of Commerce or other business or industrial groups received a comparable mention (from 7 of the 56 respondents). Tuberculosis associations and the Sierra Club each received mention twice.

News-Handling Judgments

In reviewing questionnaire returns, we were especially interested in looking for evidence of what one of our associates has referred to as editorial "behavior models" with regard to the pollution issue.[7]

Editors of two of the smaller newspapers from opposite ends of the nation called for objectivity and a cautiously balanced approach:

[7] John DeMott has described the *political model* that casts the newspaper in the role of the "Fourth Branch of Government" (to use Douglass Cater's term); the *commercial model*, which aims to make the newspaper popular reading matter; the *professional model*, which presumably calls for reflecting current events as "objective and impartial intelligence"; the *clerical model*, "somewhat like the old-time hell-fire and brimstone preacher [aimed at] showing his neighbors the error of their ways and taking the hide off the community's most notorious sinners"; and so on. (John DeMott, "Behavior Models for The Editor," *Nieman Reports*, December 1969, pp. 21–24.)

Be constructive—not particularly anti-industry or particularly in bed with the radicals on the other end of the spectrum—but politically interested and responsible.

We insist that when charges are made, the firms or agencies involved be given space in the same story or on the same page to answer so that no distorted picture results.

A Texas editor carries this note of caution a step further:

The role of the media is to inform the public of what the problem is and how it might be cured. Another role in the near future will be to keep the pollution thinking on the right track. Seems to me that the pendulum is swinging and it might well go too far before all of the pollution kick is over with.

Other editors from smaller urban areas favored a more aggressive stance:

The mass media must be more than a professional observer of the pollution problem. They must get emotionally involved and pattern their coverage of the problems accordingly.

Seek out and expose the sources of pollution without fear of economic or political pressure.

This more aggressive orientation may also be found among editors of the larger urban areas, two of whom say:

There is one addition to the standard role of the newspapers that we have adopted . . . advocacy. This means we judge and write the news from a clearly understood point of view that progress toward environmental cleanup is good, and stalling on that road is bad.

Let the polluters know that their offenses against the public will be treated like any other stories about law violators.

The following pleas for advocacy also stress factual analysis:

If it weren't for the mass media, who would be alerting the public to the dangers of pollution? The media have a two-fold job: Tell the factual story of pollution and what it can mean to our way of life; explain to readers and listeners how their local, state and federal governments can do something if they are harried into it.

The editorial page should keep up the pressure by pinpointing major problems, holding the performance of public agencies and private industry up to the light and helping the public to concentrate its energies in the most productive manner. Editorials also should sift out the realities from the political rhetoric that is pouring forth. In its news columns, the paper should stay alert for new threats to the environment and keep close tabs on what actually is being done to clean up the air, water, etc. The rising tide of public concern should be reported wherever it surfaces."

In a way that reminds us of the debate about the dangers of coverage that is too fragmented or specific versus the dangers of vague over-generalizations, one editor had this to say:

Focus on individual problems. General articles with no specific target seem unlikely to accomplish anything.

A Chicago editor was among the many calling for focused attention on specific polluters and a continuous monitoring of government action:

Stress the damage pollution causes to people and the quality of their lives. Identify the polluters. Analyze the kind of job government is doing.

In a special question regarding editorial judgment, the editors were asked how they played the December 29, 1969, speech by Professor Barry Commoner at a meeting of the American Association for Advancement of Science in Boston. In this speech, Commoner proclaimed that man may have only 30 years left on Earth if he doesn't do something massive about pollution and starvation. The story appeared in almost half of the responding newspapers. Three-fourths—26 of 34—of the editors who were aware of having received the story ran it. Fifteen editors said they did not receive the story, and nine either said they didn't know if they had received the story or did not answer the question.

Of the 26 papers that ran the story, 12 played it on page one or otherwise gave it special treatment (such as on a section page or feature page). Several of the 14 other papers played it big on inside pages. The top play was given by a Chicago paper, which ran a 15-inch story by its science editor over the roof on page one under an 8-column banner, "Scientist Fears End of Man in 30 Years."

Two editors said that their failure to print the Commoner story was a regrettable oversight, and one, whose paper had carried it as an 8-inch story under a 2-column headline on page 2, said, "it should have been played page one."

But other editors defended their judgment in not running the story, although it had come to their attention. Some said it was "old hat" or that Commoner had failed to document his case. Douglas Turner of the *Buffalo Courier-Express,* which has taken a very strong antipollution stance, remarked: "We did not use it. . . . We have long since passed the stage where we need canned wire material on pollution. The story is the type of unsupportable 'scare' article which does much to instill mistrust of the press and concerned scientists." [8]

Some Ideas for Fellow Editors

Our questionnaires turned up a few ideas which have produced very positive effects, at least in some of the larger urban areas. They may be worthy of consideration by editors in other communities. One of these is the publication of an "environmental hot line" directory, telling readers where to complain about various types of pollution. This has produced a heavy response in Philadelphia, and *The Philadelphia Bulletin* plans to reprint the "hot line" at least once a month.

Only a handful of the responding papers indicated that they regularly report, on either a year-round or seasonal basis, local pollution data such as sulfur dioxide concentration in the air or water pollution levels at beaches. In most cases the information is not available. In other cases it is used in news stories when pollution levels are high. The latter approach has produced very marked results in St. Louis, where the Globe-Democrat ran a page-one lead story last August headed "Smog Buildup Here Termed Peril to Life." [9]

As noted earlier, various newspaper series and editorial campaigns on pollution have attracted widespread interest, and many editors plan to increase such efforts. In a number of areas this has stimulated public demand for stricter enforcement of antipollution regulations and has stirred industries to move faster in their own efforts to fight pollution.

---

[8] This reminds us of a recent *Science* magazine article in which a scientist was exhorting other scientists to use every opportunity in their pollution-related public relations to maximize "symbolic disassurance." We take that to be a call for scaring hell out of people, and one cannot help but wonder whether the editor quoted here is not making a good point in this connection.

[9] More than one editor has found that such stories are subject to challenge by city fathers whose civic pride may be wounded by such coverage. Last November when Mayor Daley of Chicago accused the news media of exaggerating the danger of smog that hung over the city for a week, he obtained a letter from the Federal Air Pollution Control Administration stating that dangerous levels of pollution had not been reached. The Department of Air Pollution Control, which had released the original data, was subsequently taken over by a new city Department of Environmental Control.

Conclusion

Judging from the experiences of editors who have been battling to control the quality of our environment, the task is not an easy one. The problems are complex. The specifics of the problem vary from one area to another. As debates about pollution standards, abatement procedures, health hazards, and social costs develop, many news media will find it difficult to assign sufficiently knowledgeable reporters to the pollution beat.

Many questions remain unanswered about ideal strategies (or even whether there are ideal strategies) for covering this issue. Many editors see the need to abdicate a simple position of neutrality and to take the lead in the war on pollution.

Many have stressed the importance of highlighting local issues and relating environmental problems to the individual, but the universality of the situation (what the young refer to as a need for a new "ecological ethos" or a general truce with nature) should not be overlooked. We're all in this together. As George F. Kennan wrote recently in proposing the creation of an international environmental agency, "the entire ecology of the planet is not arranged in national compartments; and whoever interferes with it seriously anywhere is doing something that is almost invariably of serious concern to the international community at large."

Editors seem to agree that the press has the responsibility for putting the problem in perspective and providing the public with a forum for serious discussion that appeals to reason and avoids hysteria.

Our survey confirms impressions from earlier studies, cited in the introduction of this report, that the editor's intention to contribute to citizen enlightenment may not be enough. Facts must be presented clearly; apparent contradictions must be resolved as best they can be, and the paper's own stance on the issue must be congruent with the facts as they are presented. There is evidence that in many instances this obligation is being met and the public interest is being stimulated.

"The god of public opinion, though unknown and unknowable, does exist," says columnist Joseph Kraft. "However difficult to measure, there is such a thing as a national mood, a climate of ideas that makes certain things acceptable—and others not." Though doubts still exist as to the extent of the illness of the environment, definitive proof might not be available until the autopsy. Most of our respondents would agree that problems of the environment merit the best editorial judgments that can be brought to bear upon them . . . now.

PART THREE

NEW INSTITUTIONS

How are shifts of public attitudes accepted into the political process and selectively filtered through governmental structures? Lynton Caldwell, one of the foremost proponents of government structural adjustment to meet environmental problems, notes in "Achieving Environmental Quality: Is Our Present Governmental Organization Adequate?" that "the present organization of government as it relates to the natural environment was created largely by and for the natural resources industries. . . ." He believes present institutions to be inadequate for dealing with environmental change and that new environmental legislation should be enacted to remedy this situation.

While for many years Caldwell and others have advocated a national environmental policy, it was not until January 1970, that "The National Environmental Policy Act" was promulgated. This Act, broad in scope, recognized the need to ensure the harmony of man and his environment, particularly by resolving the problems accompanying population growth, urbanization, technological advance, and resource exploitation. It states that the environmental consequences of government actions must be explicitly evaluated to ensure that economic and technical considerations are not the sole determinants of government policy, as they have often been in the past. Such evaluations are to be reported to the Council on Environmental Quality established in the executive branch to oversee government activities that relate to the environment.

Since this structural adjustment and statement of concern have been only recently enacted, the extent to which they will be implemented remains to be seen; it is the implementation of enacted legislation by government agencies that is the truest measure of their concern with the environment. Recently, for example, when seeking an appropriation of $290 million for supersonic transport, the Department of Transportation responded only minimally to complaints about prospective environmental hazards associated with the anticipated use of 500 such planes; the Department of Transportation's appropriation was for but two prototypes whose pollution would add only marginally to that caused by existing subsonic aircraft. In noting the marginal environmental effects of the two planes the agency was certainly acting within the letter of the law, but it was definitely not complying with its spirit. The desire to retain United States commercial air supremacy was apparently more important to departmental policy makers than a quiet, clean environment.

Despite this ill omen for future implementation, the passage of Public Law 91-190 may open a legal channel for redress of environmental grievances by making possible the suing of federal agencies to ensure true compliance with the reporting provisions of this legislation. In this way, greater access to the political system has been granted by the National Environmental Policy Act of 1970 to that segment of the public intensely concerned with the maintenance of environmental quality.

LYNTON K. CALDWELL *   6

Achieving Environmental Quality: Is Our Present Governmental Organization Adequate?

The question posed in the title is easily answered, and the answer is "No." More difficult is the explanation of how and why governmental organization poorly serves the environmental needs of man. Even more difficult is the answer to the questions that logically follow: What changes in governmental organization are necessary for the wise use of the human environment and how are these changes to be obtained?

To declare unequivocally that governmental organization is adequate to serve the environmental needs of man implies a criterion for adequacy. The test of adequacy is based upon a definition of the task. If one accepts the proposition that the protection and enhancement of the human environment is, or should be, a governmental function, then the performance of government may be compared with the objectives and an appraisal of adequacy may be made. But if one does not believe that responsibility for the condition of the human environment is or can be a governmental responsibility, the question of adequacy becomes irrelevant. Therefore, if one declares governmental organization to be inadequate for environmental management, he is obliged to explain how it is inadequate, and to do this he must also explain why.

The consideration that is basic to all discussion regarding public and governmental responsibility for the environment is man's relationship to the natural world. This relationship is complex and varied in de-

* Professor Caldwell is teaching at Indiana University. This paper was presented at the 13th National Conference of the U. S. National Commission for UNESCO, November 23–25, 1969, San Francisco, California.

tail. No two men, for example, have precisely the same environment, nor [do they] interact with their environments in precisely the same way. But there are certain generalities that hold true for all men in relation to all environments. These generalities comprise the environmental parameters for human health, happiness, and survival. They may be described as mankind's planetary life-support system. This system is an integral part of the larger natural system that encompasses the entire living world and which is called the "biosphere."

The elements of man's natural life-support system are familiar, but their relationship to one another and to man's well being are not adequately understood. In everyday language the major environmental elements are air, water, soil, sunlight, and other living things. Man's parameters include his adaptive capabilities and his ranges of tolerance for temperature, noise, light, crowding, and isolation. Space exploration has provided more exact descriptions of these parameters, but much more needs to be known regarding their implications for man's interrelationships with Earth. This knowledge is needed because man is now altering the state of all the elements of his environment and the consequences of his action are proving to be disastrous as well as advantageous.

Scientific knowledge and technology have enabled man to change the state of his environment, but as yet they have been of little help in using the environment wisely and safely. The sciences most directly relevant to this assistance are environmental biology and ecology, and these sciences have been undervalued and under-supported in the scientific community and by society-at-large. This neglect may be in part attributed to the human tendency to take its environment for granted; literally to assume the biosphere to be a gift to man from God or nature. Before the growth of science and science-based technology, man could live in relative safety with this belief. As long as his numbers were few and his technology simple he could live like his fellow animals in a state of dynamic balance with his environment. By the beginning of the 20th century, however, the relationship of human society to the natural world was radically changed. It is this changed relationship that is basic to the question of the adequacy of governmental organization for the management of man's environmental relationships.

The Vulnerability of Nations

The thesis of organizational inadequacy rests upon the following premise. Through scientific knowledge and technology, human impact upon the planetary life-support system or biosphere is being stressed beyond the point of safety. The quality of man's natural environment is being steadily and rapidly impaired throughout the entire world, including the upper atmosphere, the depths of the sea, and the once remote polar regions. The major factors in this threatening stress are the sheer numbers and mobility of people and the impact of their technology. During the past century the human species has preempted almost every habitable area of the Earth, and nearly all other animal and plant life now exists by human sufferance. The Earth that was once almost limitless in relation to the numbers and needs of man has suddenly become limited and increasingly small in relation to the demands of man. Within hardly more than a generation, man's traditional perception of his relationship to the natural world has become false and hence unsound and dangerous as a premise for action.

In the past the world was wide; endless seas, trackless deserts, impenetrable forests, boundless plains were practical illusions. Man could act as if the world were infinite so long as his numbers and impact were relatively slight. The capacity of the world for self-renewal was vast in relation to the stress of man upon it. And so modern man busied himself occupying the Earth and subduing it to his purposes. To assist this enterprise he organized governments that would not only maintain civil society, but would help him get what he wanted from nature. Modern industrial man came to perceive the world as a limitless storehouse of natural wealth, or "natural resources." The concept of the biosphere was neither articulated nor understood. The physical unity of the Earth was accepted as an obvious but unconsequential fact. Preoccupied with farming, mining, lumbering, city building, manufacturing, and disposing of waste residuals, human society paid little attention to the resulting transformation of its own environmental condition. But not long ago there came a day when perceptive men looked around themselves and discovered that they had changed the open-space world of all past history into the closed-space world of the spaceship. Perhaps the first public official to express this new awareness was United States Ambassador to the United Nations, Adlai Stevenson. In his final address to the Economic and Social Council of the United Nations he described man's new condition, using the now familiar imagery of Spaceship Earth: He said, "We travel together, passengers on a little spaceship, dependent on its vulnerable resources of air and soil; all committed for our safety to its security and peace; preserved from annihilation only by the care, the work, and I will say the love we give our fragile craft." [1]

The spaceship image is equally valid for nations and for the world as a whole. It symbolized the finite character of the world and its re-

[1] U.N. Economic and Social Council, *Official Records*, *39th Session*, 30 June–31 July, 1965, p. 90, Paragraph 42.

sources, and the necessity for protecting and maintaining its regenerative capabilities as an unavoidable price of human survival. Implicit in the spaceship idiom are concepts of carrying capacity, recycling of resources, articulation of sub-systems and total system, and continuous systems maintenance. These are not concepts which governmental or international organizations have been designed to implement. The structures of law and public institutions have evolved on the basis of assumptions and objectives that, whatever their validity in the past, cannot be relied upon to cope with the environmental problems of the present and future. Because man has not heretofore recognized a problem in the relationship of society to its total environment, he has not organized his public institutions to deal with it. On the contrary, the human tendency to concentrate on immediate material objectives and to ignore the broader context of action has led to a structuring of government that is actually dysfunctional to environmental policy and control.

The social mechanism for establishing the rules and procedures under which men use natural resources and the environment has been government, organized juridically through national states and now supplemented by international agencies. National jurisdiction has been largely geographically defined. Now, however, human mobility and technological impact upon the total terrestrial biosphere tend increasingly to alter the conditions of the planet beyond the unilateral control of governments. Popular recognition of the limited ability of any nation to protect its people from the effects of global ecological disaster has led to such developments as the nuclear test ban treaty, the treaty for the peaceful use of outer-space, and growing worldwide concern over pesticides, the pollution of the oceans, manipulation of climatic conditions, and the destruction of the varied flora, fauna, and landscapes of the natural world. The incapacity of isolated nations to guard against ecological disaster from beyond national boundaries has led to calls for international action to safeguard the biosphere. At national levels, environmental quality is becoming a major political issue. At all political levels, the condition and management of the environment has become controversial. This is because the harmful effects of environmental overstress are being felt, but more people perceive their relationship to the Earth as it has been in the past than understand why this relationship has changed. Dissatisfaction grows with the declining quality of the environment, but consensus on remedial measures has been slow to develop.

We can now summarize the inadequacy of governmental and international organization for environmental policy. The machinery of government has not been designed for environmental policy; it is in fact largely dysfunctional for environmental protection and management, having been intended, insofar as any specific intention was evident, to assist the exploitation or development of discrete resources with minimal regard to the full range of environmental interrelationships or consequences. The impact of science and technology on the environment has increasingly stressed its capacities for renewal and led to ecosystems and species extinction and to ecological degradation. In response to these and greater impending threats, perceptive men have called for a new set of national and international policies for the protection and management of the environment. But traditional assumptions still widely prevail. To men to whom Spaceship Earth is *merely* a poetic abstraction, and whose faith is placed in the unlimited beneficence of nature and the technological ingenuity of man, there is no environmental crisis. To men whose economic interests depend or appear to depend upon the exploitation of the environment, the prospect of public intervention on behalf of long-range ecological considerations is threatening. Because the present structure of public affairs tends to favor traditional policies toward the environment, attempts to reorganize government to cope more effectively with environmental issues is correctly perceived as an attack upon those policies themselves and hence also upon their beneficiaries. Organized blocs of resource users and economic development interests resist the imposition of new policies and controls aimed at guiding or restraining their use of the environment. Issues are therefore joined between (a) those users of the environment who wish to proceed along traditional lines or to invoke technology to offset the exhaustion and impairment of nature and (b) the advocates of the political-economy of Spaceship Earth. The new outlook sees need for the dynamism of the economy to be internalized toward qualitative goals and for new types of organization, national and international, that can serve man's material needs without endangering his health, happiness, and survival on Earth.

Organization and Public Policy

In government, as in nature, form tends to follow function. But when the objectives of government change in response to the exigencies of society, the forms often prove resistant and restrain the exercise of new functions. Governmental organization in the United States is characterized by a large number and variety of adaptations and improvisations to enable old forms of government to meet new public needs. The traditional structure of American government, although malleable and adaptable in its broad constitutional outline, has become obsolete in detail. Specific, incremental changes have been made in the federal executive branch and in state and local governments. Some of these innovations, such as the federal Department of Transportation, or the Hahn plan for restructuring local government in Virginia along regional lines, are, in principle, moves toward a more rational and realistic organization of public affairs. Yet, for the most part, reform lags far behind events. The gap between public needs and organizational response is steadily growing wider. A crisis of institutional inadequacy is upon us, but few people in or out of government understand its seriousness or what it implies for the effort to cope with man's environmental problems.

Pessimistic appraisal of our practical capability to cope with environmental problems has been influenced by the generally negative results of inter-departmental and inter-governmental coordinative efforts. Because of public apathy and the entrenched interests of governmental agencies and their clients in Congress and throughout the country, fundamental administrative reorganization is very difficult to obtain. Even though the general interest may no longer be served by a narrowly programmed governmental agency, its beneficiaries are alert to the defense of their special interests. The natural resources use and development interests of the country are not generally dissatisfied with the present state of governmental organization. They may be critical of public policies that restrict their use of resources, but they would be even more displeased at the prospect of a reorganization in which the agency that administered their particular resource, and with which common perceptions and understandings had developed, was replaced by or subordinated to an agency oriented primarily to environmental and ecological considerations. The present organization of government, as it relates to the natural environment, was created largely by and for the natural resources industries, including agriculture. Efforts to reorganize government for environmental quality purposes therefore encounter a phalanx of opposition from well-organized economic interests whose past influence with congressmen and federal executives is a matter of record.

For more than half a century, appeals have been made for a more coherent and coordinated administration of natural resources policy. The argument for new approaches to public responsibility for the environment draws upon similar reasoning—that responsible and effective public administration requires a more coherent organization. But the environmental quality appeal has two great advantages over its conservationist predecessor.

First, the environmental quality movement is evolving an organizing concept and philosophy that could provide the catalyst that earlier efforts never obtained. The advocates for a coordinated approach to natural resources policy found great difficulty in articulating a positive, substantive goal for their efforts. Although an objective of environmental quality was latent in their arguments, the actual discourse tended toward elimination of competition, duplication, and cross-purpose action among the agencies. The politically sterile "economy and efficiency" objective of their reorganization efforts had little public appeal. The dissimilarities in the specific economic problems of management among specific natural resources made their coordination somewhat like an effort to coordinate the varieties of goods on supermarket shelves. In contrast, the environmental issue, especially in its Spaceship Earth context, provides a more coherent view of life and society from which public policies might be deduced and around which governmental organization might be restructured.

The *second* advantage of the environmental quality movement is that the complex and often synergistic character of many environmental problems is forcing new forms of administrative action. For example, the problems of environmental pollution and waste disposal are interlinked in many ways. Initial efforts to deal with these problems as if they were discrete has followed traditional approaches to natural resources problems, and they have been hardly more successful. It is becoming ever more apparent to informed observers that new public agencies must be invented if society is to cope with the environmental problems of the space age. Creative thought is being given to the development of total systems for the management of water and waste residuals in urban communities. The aerospace industry has technical capabilities that are being applied to the planning of new approaches to this formidable problem that is literally threatening to overwhelm many American communities. It is probable that many of the new organizational approaches to environmental quality management will involve partnerships among governmental, quasi-governmental, and nongovernmental agencies working together in coordinated systems that are "total" in relation to their tasks. But before this can happen, some fundamental changes in the popular attitudes and political behavior of Americans will have to occur. These changes, however, may be forced by the extremely unpleasant nature of impending events in urban ecology.

At this point in time, circumstances and people being as they are, the greatest immediate public need is for an explicit national policy for the environment and a high-level advocate to give the policy practical meaning and to make it widely visible. To obtain this objective, more than thirty-five bills have been introduced into the 91st Congress. Bills have been passed in the Senate and the House of Representatives, but as of the date of this writing none have been enacted. These bills, and particularly Title I of Senate Bill 1075, declare a national commitment to a policy of environmental quality. The enactment of one of these bills would mark a first step toward the establishment of environmental administration as a major responsibility of government. A strong bill will not easily be enacted unless assisted by some sudden, alarming, critical event in the environment that stampedes the Congress into action. After enactment, the process of implementation will be rugged. A high-level national council on the environment is needed not only to assist the growth of public understanding that is essential to the effectiveness of environmental quality efforts, but also to enable the United States to cooperate with rapidly developing international efforts to cope with growing threats to the quality and viability of the world environment.

7

Public Law Establishing the Council on Environmental Quality *

Public Law 91–190
91st Congress, S. 1075
January 1, 1970

An Act

To establish a national policy for the environment, to provide for the establishment of a Council on Environmental Quality, and for other purposes.

Be it enacted by the Senate and House of Representatives of the United States of America in Congress assembled, That this Act may be cited as the "National Environmental Policy Act of 1969".

Purpose

Sec. 2. The purposes of this Act are: To declare a national policy which will encourage productive and enjoyable harmony between man and his environment; to promote efforts which will prevent or eliminate damage to the environment and biosphere and stimulate the health and welfare of man; to enrich the understanding of the ecological systems and natural resources important to the Nation; and to establish a Council on Environmental Quality.

* United States Government Printing Office publication 37–139.

Title I

Declaration of National Environmental Policy

Sec. 101. (a) The Congress, recognizing the profound impact of man's activity on the interrelations of all components of the natural environment, particularly the profound influences of population growth, high-density urbanization, industrial expansion, resource exploitation, and new and expanding technological advances and recognizing further the critical importance of restoring and maintaining environmental quality to the overall welfare and development of man, declares that it is the continuing policy of the Federal Government, in cooperation with State and local governments, and other concerned public and private organizations, to use all practicable means and measures, including financial and technical assistance, in a manner calculated to foster and promote the general welfare, to create and maintain conditions under which man and nature can exist in productive harmony, and fulfill the social, economic, and other requirements of present and future generations of Americans.

(b) In order to carry out the policy set forth in this Act, it is the continuing responsibility of the Federal Government to use all practicable means, consistent with other essential considerations of national policy, to improve and coordinate Federal plans, functions, programs, and resources to the end that the Nation may—

(1) fulfill the responsibilities of each generation as trustee of the environment for succeeding generations;

(2) assure for all Americans safe, healthful, productive, and esthetically and culturally pleasing surroundings;

(3) attain the widest range of beneficial uses of the environment without degradation, risk to health or safety, or other undesirable and unintended consequences;

(4) preserve important historic, cultural, and natural aspects of our national heritage, and maintain, wherever possible, an environment which supports diversity and variety of individual choice;

(5) achieve a balance between population and resource use which will permit high standards of living and a wide sharing of life's amenities; and

(6) enhance the quality of renewable resources and approach the maximum attainable recycling of depletable resources.

(c) The Congress recognizes that each person should enjoy a healthful environment and that each person has a responsibility to contribute to the preservation and enhancement of the environment.

Sec. 102. The Congress authorizes and directs that, to the fullest extent possible: (1) the policies, regulations, and public laws of the United States shall be interpreted and administered in accordance with the policies set forth in this Act, and (2) all agencies of the Federal Government shall—

(A) utilize a systematic, interdisciplinary approach which will insure the integrated use of the natural and social sciences and the environmental design arts in planning and in decisionmaking which may have an impact on man's environment;

(B) identify and develop methods and procedures, in consultation with the Council on Environmental Quality established by title II of this Act, which will insure that presently unquantified environmental amenities and values may be given appropriate consideration in decisionmaking along with economic and technical considerations;

(C) include in every recommendation or report on proposals for legislation and other major Federal actions significantly affecting the quality of the human environment, a detailed statement by the responsible official on—

(i) the environmental impact of the proposed action,
(ii) any adverse environmental effects which cannot be avoided should the proposal be implemented,
(iii) alternatives to the proposed action,
(iv) the relationship between local short-term uses of man's environment and the maintenance and enhancement of long-term productivity, and
(v) any irreversible and irretrievable commitments of resources which would be involved in the proposed action should it be implemented.

Prior to making any detailed statement, the responsible Federal official shall consult with and obtain the comments of any Federal agency which has jurisdiction by law or special expertise with respect to any environmental impact involved. Copies of such statement and the comments and views of the appropriate Federal, State, and local agencies, which are authorized to develop and enforce environmental standards, shall be made available to the President, the Council on Environmental Quality and to the public as provided by section 552 of title 5, United States Code, and shall accompany the proposal through the existing agency review processes;

(D) study, develop, and describe appropriate alternatives to recommended courses of action in any proposal which involves unresolved conflicts concerning alternative uses of available resources;

(E) recognize the worldwide and long-range character of environmental problems and, where consistent with the foreign policy of the United States, lend appropriate support to initiatives, resolutions, and programs designed to maximize international cooperation in anticipating and preventing a decline in the quality of mankind's world environment;

(F) make available to States, counties, municipalities, institutions, and individuals, advice and information useful in restoring, maintaining, and enhancing the quality of the environment;

(G) initiate and utilize ecological information in the planning and development of resource-oriented projects; and

(H) assist the Council on Environmental Quality established by title II of this Act.

Sec. 103. All agencies of the Federal Government shall review their present statutory authority, administrative regulations, and current policies and procedures for the purpose of determining whether there are any deficiencies or inconsistencies therein which prohibit full compliance with the purposes and provisions of this Act and shall propose to the President not later than July 1, 1971, such measures as may be necessary to bring their authority and policies into conformity with the intent, purposes, and procedures set forth in this Act.

Sec. 104. Nothing in Section 102 or 103 shall in any way affect the specific statutory obligations of any Federal agency (1) to comply with criteria or standards of environmental quality, (2) to coordinate or consult with any other Federal or State agency, or (3) to act, or refrain from acting contingent upon the recommendations or certification of any other Federal or State agency.

Sec. 105. The policies and goals set forth in this Act are supplementary to those set forth in existing authorizations of Federal agencies.

Title II

Council on Environmental Quality

Sec. 201. The President shall transmit to the Congress annually beginning July 1, 1970, an Environmental Quality Report (herein after referred to as the "report") which shall set forth (1) the status and condition of the major natural, manmade, or altered environmental classes of the Nation, including, but not limited to, the air, the aquatic, including marine, estuarine, and fresh water, and the terrestrial environment, including, but not limited to, the forest, dryland, wetland, range, urban, suburban, and rural environment; (2) current and foreseeable trends in the quality, management and utilization of such environments and the effects of those trends on the social, economic, and other requirements of the Nation; (3) the adequacy of available natural resources for fulfilling human and economic requirements of the Nation in the light of expected population pressures; (4) a review of the programs and activities (including regulatory activities) of the Federal Government, the State and local governments, and nongovernmental entities or individuals, with particular reference to their effect on the environment and on the conservation, development and utilization of natural resources; and (5) a program for remedying the deficiencies of existing programs and activities, together with recommendations for legislation.

Sec. 202. There is created in the Executive Office of the President a Council on Environmental Quality (hereinafter referred to as the "Council"). The Council shall be composed of three members who shall be appointed by the President to serve at his pleasure, by and with the advice and consent of the Senate. The President shall designate one of the members of the Council to serve as Chairman. Each member shall be a person who, as a result of his training, experience, and attainments, is exceptionally well qualified to analyze and interpret environmental trends and information of all kinds; to appraise programs and activities of the Federal Government in the light of the policy set forth in title I of this Act; to be conscious of and responsive to the scientific, economic, social, esthetic, and cultural needs and interests of the Nation; and to formulate and recommend national policies to promote the improvement of the quality of the environment.

Sec. 203. The Council may employ such officers and employees as may be necessary to carry out its functions under this Act. In addition, the Council may employ and fix the compensation of such experts and consultants as may be necessary for the carrying out of its functions under this Act, in accordance with section 3109 of title 5, United States Code (but without regard to the last sentence thereof).

Sec. 204. It shall be the duty and function of the Council—

(1) to assist and advise the President in the preparation of the Environmental Quality Report required by section 201;

(2) to gather timely and authoritative information concerning the conditions and trends in the quality of the environment both current and prospective, to analyze and interpret such information for the purpose of determining whether such conditions and trends are interfering, or are likely to interfere, with the achievement of the policy set forth in title I of this Act, and to compile and submit to the President studies relating to such conditions and trends;

(3) to review and appraise the various programs and activities of the Federal Government in the light of the policy set forth in title I of

this Act for the purpose of determining the extent to which such programs and activities are contributing to the achievement of such policy, and to make recommendations to the President with respect thereto;

(4) to develop and recommend to the President national policies to foster and promote the improvement of environmental quality to meet the conservation, social, economic, health, and other requirements and goals of the Nation;

(5) to conduct investigations, studies, surveys, research, and analyses relating to ecological systems and environmental quality;

(6) to document and define changes in the natural environment, including the plant and animal systems, and to accumulate necessary data and other information for a continuing analysis of these changes or trends and an interpretation of their underlying causes;

(7) to report at least once each year to the President on the state and condition of the environment; and

(8) to make and furnish such studies, reports thereon, and recommendations with respect to matters of policy and legislation as the President may request.

Sec. **205.**   In exercising its powers, functions, and duties under this Act, the Council shall—

(1) consult with the Citizens' Advisory Committee on Environmental Quality established by Executive Order numbered 11472, dated May 29, 1969, and with such representatives of science, industry, agriculture, labor, conservation organizations, State and local governments and other groups, as it deems advisable; and

(2) utilize, to the fullest extent possible, the services, facilities, and information (including statistical information) of public and private agencies and organizations, and individuals, in order that duplication of effort and expense may be avoided, thus assuring that the Council's activities will not unnecessarily overlap or conflict with similar activities authorized by law and performed by established agencies.

Sec. **206.**   Members of the Council shall serve full time and the Chairman of the Council shall be compensated at the rate provided for Level II of the Executive Schedule Pay Rates (5 U.S.C. 5313). The other members of the Council shall be compensated at the rate provided for Level IV of the Executive Schedule Pay Rates (5 U.S.C. 5315).

Sec. **207.**   There are authorized to be appropriated to carry out the provisions of this Act not to exceed $300,000 for fiscal year 1970, $700,000 for fiscal year 1971, and $1,000,000 for each fiscal year thereafter.

Approved January 1, 1970.

Legislative History

HOUSE REPORTS: No. 91–378, 91–378, pt. 2, accompanyng H. R. 12549
    (Comm. on Merchant Marine & Fisheries) and 91–765
    (Comm. of Conference).
SENATE REPORT No. 91–296 (Comm. on Interior & Insular Affairs).
CONGRESSIONAL RECORD, Vol. 115 (1969):
    July 10: Considered and passed Senate.
    Sept. 23: Considered and passed House, amended, in lieu of H. R. 12549.
    Oct. 8: Senate disagreed to House amendments; agreed to conference.
    Dec. 20: Senate agreed to conference report.
    Dec. 22: House agreed to conference report.

PART FOUR

POLITICS AND THE BUREAUCRACY

The need for organizational restructuring and interagency coordination has been discussed in terms of increasing access for particular publics intensely concerned with the environment. In the articles in this part, such changes are discussed in the context of organization and decision-making theory.

Daniel Grant, in "Carrots, Sticks, and Consensus," speaks of the obstacles to innovation within bureaucratic structures. Grant notes that fragmented authority within and conflict between agencies and governments can often militate against the achievement of desired social goals. To overcome such problems, he believes a "sense of mission" is needed. Grant sees a potential for change, provided (1) the proper leadership can be developed, (2) conservation groups can ally with related interest groups, (3) political ground rules that strengthen the power of anticonservation groups are changed, and (4) metropolitan or state consensuses are mobilized to overcome local inaction, while national consensuses help override state inaction.

Norman Wengert, in "Perennial Problems of Federal Coordination," observes that interagency conflict is often the product of the desire for bureaucratic self-preservation, and that the technological biases of individual actors often contribute to such conflicts. He notes that coordination of government programs, rather than being an integral component of policy formation, is usually an afterthought. Programs are invariably established on an ad hoc, "problem-solving" basis that is the antithesis of a well-developed planning approach.

While our present policy-making and organizational structure appears to be woefully inadequate, caution must be exercised in any future reorganizational efforts. Future structures should provide a more effective means for evaluating alternative policies and generating more useful government programs, but devising such structures is obviously both controversial and difficult.

DANIEL R. GRANT *   # 8

Carrots, Sticks,
and Consensus

What present or emerging interests or attitudes in and out of
government influence public action on such environment-
affecting issues as urban planning, pollution control, management of public lands, wildlife conservation, and industrial location? Upon what basis and to what extent can agreement on public environmental policy be developed among these interests?
What are the apparently irreconcilable conflicts, and how may
these conflicts be reduced or resolved, or in some sense made
constructive?

Daniel R. Grant finds that the basic political problems implicit in these questions do not differ fundamentally from those
encountered in other changes in the *status quo,* as in school districts, racial segregation, or metropolitan government. After analyzing the viewpoints of a number of political scientists and
urban planners on the prospects for more effective public control over environmental change, he takes a moderate position in
favor of stronger governmental and national leadership. "The
national government," he writes, "holds the key to most of the
issues of shaping the physical environment." Thus the road to
consensus at state, local, and personal-interest levels of interaction may be (paradoxically from some viewpoints) via the national level.

* Dr. Grant is president of Ouachita Baptist University in Arkadelphia,
Arkansas. This article originally appeared in *Environmental Studies—Papers
on the Politics of Public Administration of Man—Environment Relationships,* 4 volumes, Lynton K. Caldwell, editor (Bloomington, Ind.: Institute
of Public Administration, Indiana University, 1967).

The American's relationship to his natural environment is characterized by some strange paradoxes. He is filled with great pride for his heroic conquest of the vast New World wilderness during the past four centuries, and yet he finds himself a conscience-stricken member of movements to salvage or restore parts of this wilderness to its original state. He takes great pride in a free enterprise system which has permitted property owners to use their land and resources as they please, and yet he finds himself actively involved in urban renewal programs committed to declaring certain land to be "wrongly used," acquiring the land through government condemnation, and putting it to "right use." Again, he is filled with pride for a miraculous technology that has brought him closer than ever before in history to being able to control the hostile elements of his physical environment, and yet he probably lives in one of the 220 metropolitan areas which seem to be fighting losing battles against an environment characterized by slums, smoke, filth, ugliness, traffic congestion, and a scarcity of open space and parks. Probably no other subject has called forth more prophets of gloom and pessimism than the spreading blight in the environment of the American metropolis.

Just as the blessings of American geography have contributed greatly to our prosperity, they may well have led us, as Irish and Prothro suggest, "to accept our good fortune without thinking about how to sustain it." [1] The problem of conservation, which was dramatized by Theodore Roosevelt more than a half-century ago, is still with us, but it is being given new life and meaning by the swelling tide of such forces as industrial dispersion, the mass automobile market, the relentless centrifugal spread of suburbanism over vast areas of rural land, and a host of other pressures related to the population explosion and technological change. It is the political implications of these rapid changes taking place in our natural environment to which these essays are addressed. More specifically, this essay is concerned with the nature and significance of the political process by which man seeks to control the utility and beauty of his natural environment, and with how this process may change in the future. Such an analysis should be of assistance to those seeking to discover or to broaden the basis for consensus among groups with conflicting interests on environmental issues, but it is not the purpose here either to advocate change or to defend the *status quo.*

---

[1] Marian D. Irish and James W. Prothro, *The Politics of American Democracy* (2nd ed.); (Englewood Cliffs, N. J.: Prentice-Hall, 1962), p. 25.

The Clash of Interests on Environmental Issues

Conservation in the abstract may be placed alongside patriotism, motherhood, and the home as something generally agreed upon as virtuous and of great value. Even when made a bit more specific by referring to "the conservation of natural resources," or "the renewal of the natural environment," popular consensus on its desirability is not difficult to obtain. But when efforts are made to translate the ideals of environmental conservation or renewal into concrete legislative and administrative action, popular consensus seems almost inevitably to melt away in the heat of battles between opposing interests.

The alignment of interest groups and the intensity of their conflict on environmental issues vary considerably, depending upon subject, time, circumstance, and many other factors. The efforts of national and state governments to preserve the natural beauty along the new interstate highways by controlling the erection of billboards have met with strong, and in many cases successful, opposition from a variety of lobbyists for billboard and hotel-motel interests. Principal among these have been the Outdoor Advertising Association, Roadside Business Association, American Hotel and Motel Association, American Motor Hotel Association, National Restaurant Association, and the Brotherhood of Painters, Decorators and Paper Hangers of America (AFL-CIO).[2] Chief supporters for billboard control legislation have been garden clubs, park-planning and wildlife preservation groups, and the American Automobile Association.

The history of congressional efforts to establish the National Wilderness Preservation System, beginning as early as 1949, illustrates very clearly the array of conflicting interests which fight to oppose or support such a new public policy proposal. The bill to place more than eight million acres of federally owned land permanently in a wilderness system, and to provide the ground rules for the addition of close to 60 million additional acres, was supported by conservationist groups generally. It was opposed by a variety of commercial interests, primarily Western mining, grazing, lumber, and recreation interest groups who charged that it would "lock up" lands, preventing future natural resource development and "violating the federal principle of multiple use of resources which provide for a co-ordinated program of economic activities and conservation projects."[3] With strong administration support

---

[2] See *Congressional Quarterly Almanac*, 1963, p. 461. For a good summary of the politics of natural resource conservation and development, see Norman Wengert's *Natural Resources and the Political Struggle* (New York: Random House, 1955).
[3] *Congressional Quarterly Almanac*, 1962, p. 455.

and following major concessions to some of the opposition groups, the wilderness bill became a law in 1964.

A somewhat different type of alignment and conflict took place in the mid-1950s over the Bureau of Reclamation proposal to build Echo Park Dam in Dinosaur National Monument as a part of the Upper Colorado River Storage Project. The issue for the "conservationists" who got involved in this battle was in many ways similar to that of the wilderness bill, namely, whether or not to preserve our primeval wilderness. Yet they were on the defensive rather than the offensive in this conflict, and their opponents were not the same, being primarily the powerful Western groups genuinely interested in developing the water resources so vital to them. The Bureau supporters made strong claims of representing the long-range public interest by irrigating vast areas of arid land and supplying more power for industrial development. Actually, both sides favored water development as such, but the conservationists looked upon the Echo Park Dam proposal as a possible forerunner of many other invasions of national parks and monuments. The conservationists were treated rather cavalierly by some congressmen as "nature lovers" in the early stages of the controversy, but it soon became clear that they not only had a considerable array of talent and influence, but that they had potential allies among Easterners who opposed high-cost irrigation projects in Western states and among Californians who believed that they stood to gain more water if the Colorado River were uncontrolled rather than controlled. The result was the defeat of the Upper Colorado River project in both the 1954 and 1955 sessions of Congress and a decision by its backers to eliminate Echo Park Dam from the bill to be pushed in 1956.[4]

Environmental issues relating to recreation policies of government provide a wide spectrum of types of conflicting interests, and many of these are described in a 1962 study by Morton Grodzins.[5] Organized groups supporting an expansion of public recreational facilities have long criticized such agencies as the U.S. Army Corps of Engineers and the Bureau of Reclamation for giving short shrift to recreation interests in determining land use at reservoir sites. Similarly, prime federal targets of criticism by recreation and conservation specialists and support-

[4] For a brief account of interest group alignments in this case, see Clay P. Malick, "The Dinosaurs Go to Washington," *The Colorado Quarterly*, V (Summer, 1956), pp. 26–37. A more detailed account is given by Owen Stratton and Phillip Sirotkin, *The Echo Park Controversy*, Inter-University Case Program (University, Alabama: University of Alabama Press, 1959).

[5] Morton Grodzins, "The Many American Governments and Outdoor Recreation," in The Outdoor Recreation Resources Review Commission, *Study Report 22, Trends in American Living and Outdoor Recreation* (Washington, D.C.: U.S. Government Printing Office, 1962).

ers have been the Forest Service and the Bureau of Land Management for their large-scale opening up of the public domain for a variety of commercial purposes. The conflict has become more intensified in recent years as both recreation and commercial lumbering have experienced a strong upsurge in activity and growth pains. This is not to say that all commercial uses of public land are incompatible with recreational use, for some types are compatible, but *full* development of one purpose tends to result in decreased utilization of the other in most cases. Grodzins concluded that "commercial pressures on the Forest Service are immense and well organized" and that "large gains in the recreation use of the national forests depend upon concerted public efforts in support of that use." [6]

Some of the conflicts in environmental issues exist between different levels of government, as when federal efforts to develop a grant-in-aid program for purchase of park land failed on several occasions because "the State park boys were not sold." [7] Still other conflicts exist within a single governmental level, such as the relationship between the National Park and Forest Services, which has varied through the years from one of cool indifference to warm enmity. At the state level the greatest cleavage of interest may be found between the park personnel and the fish and wildlife officials, and generally between the more "pure" recreation workers and those whose work includes more diversified objectives in the management of land and water resources.

Finally, some recreational policy conflicts are not so much an alignment of recreational versus nonrecreational interests as they are inherent conflicts between short-run and long-run recreational goals. The seemingly clear focus of the National Park Service on recreation has a built-in ambiguity because of its twofold task of conserving scenery and natural beauty for the enjoyment of future generations, while *also* making them available to millions of people for current enjoyment. It has become increasingly clear that current enjoyment of park resources on holiday weekends by the mobile masses can threaten the natural scene with overuse and destruction.

The determination of policies for the management of public land is thus no simple matter involving only rational decisions concerning what is right and just. Neither is it one big clash of interests concerning one major policy controversy. It involves many controversies, both large and small, on many different questions, including the following: (1) What goals shall be given priority in the development of water resources?; How much consideration should be given to claims for low-cost electric

[6] *Ibid.*, p. 11.
[7] *Ibid.*, p. 37.

power, navigation, flood control, irrigation of rural areas, water supply for urban areas, promotion of the interests of fishermen and other sportsmen, and provision of sites for industrial location? (2) To what extent should grazing privileges on public land be granted cattle and sheep operators? Have such privileges resulted in ruinous overgrazing, as conservationists claim, or have federal agencies overprotected tremendous areas of valuable grasslands, as Western stockmen contend? (3) To what extent should mineral rights on public land be granted to private developers? Are federal restrictions on the granting of oil, gas, and mineral leases essential to prevent abuse, erosion, and eventual destruction of the land, as conservationists argue, or are they serious barriers to necessary industrial development, as private interests claim? (4) To what extent should the timber on public lands be made available to the lumbering industry for cutting? Should federal timber lands be turned over to the states, as often advocated by lumbermen, or would this result in stripping the forests, as claimed by the conservationists? (5) As the modern pressures of urban congestion and increased leisure time continue to grow, how much weight should be given to current recreation demands for public land use in competition with commercial and other public demands for the same land? These and many other questions are a part of the increasingly complex clash of interests on environmental control issues.

There is one other type of environmental issue or, more accurately, "cluster of issues," which should be included in this brief inventory of conflicting interests. This is the rather overwhelming array of issues and interests involved in the problem of shaping the urban and metropolitan physical environment. Although this subject is often excluded from the more traditional discussions of conservation, it may well cut across the most important conservation problems of the future. Charles Press and others who have criticized the familiar "efficiency and economy" definition of the "metropolitan problem" argue for a "conservation approach" to the metropolitan problem. By this definition the metropolitan problem, like that in the natural resource field, "is that of *conserving resources for human uses;* in this case those resources created by a metropolitan environment." [8]

Some writers are rather pessimistic about the prospects for conserving the resources of the metropolitan environment, at least to the extent that conscious political effort at planning is involved. Banfield and Wilson have said that "the most fundamental problem of the central cities and of the older suburbs—one that constitutes a life-and-death cri-

[8] Charles Press, "Research on the Metropolis: Foundation for Conservation," *Public Administration Review*, XXII (Spring, 1962), p. 91.

sis for them—[the spread of blight and lower class slums] . . . cannot
be 'solved' or even much relieved, by government action at any level." [9]
In this they agree with the clear implication of Raymond Vernon's appraisal of the major forces (primarily economic) shaping the environmental development of the New York metropolitan region.[10] They conclude gloomily:

> The forces that are at work—especially changes in technology, in
> location of industry and population, and in consumer tastes and incomes
> —are all largely beyond the control of government in a free society.
> Given these restraints, the future of the cities is probably beyond the
> reach of policy.[11]

Others are not so pessimistic. Robert A. Wood in his *1400
Governments* does not accept the assumption that economic facts will
inevitably control metropolitan development, and he argues that a metropolitan policy would control and guide some of the forces which are
often thought to be impersonal and unchangeable.[12] Scott Greer and
David Minar also disagree with the proposition that urban development
is beyond the reach of public policy, pointing out that the political side
of urban development and redevelopment is inescapable and that, in the
urban scene, "the only encompassing organization is the political community. . . ." [13]

Whether optimism or pessimism is the justifiable view, there can
be little doubt about the existence of conflicting interests concerning efforts to shape the urban environment. Early goals of housing and slum
clearance, with their strong orientation toward improving the residential
living environment for low-income families, have been virtually pushed
into the background by newer goals of reviving decaying central business districts and industrial areas, unsnarling congested traffic patterns,
saving open space, and fighting pollution of water and air. Even though
the earlier residential emphasis in public programs has now diminished,
William Grigsby contends that:

> The most perplexing problems and crucial issues involving the
> physical environment of our metropolitan areas are still, today, residen-

---

[9] Edward C. Banfield and James Q. Wilson, *City Politics* (Cambridge: Harvard University Press, 1963), p. 344.
[10] *The Myth and Reality of Our Urban Problems* (Cambridge: Harvard University
and M.I.T. Joint Center for Urban Studies, 1962).
[11] Banfield and Wilson, *loc. cit.*
[12] Harvard University Press, 1961.
[13] Scott Greer and David W. Minar, "The Political Side of Urban Development and
Redevelopment," *The Annals of the American Academy of Political and Social Science*, 352 (March, 1964), p. 73.

tial in nature. This is explained partly by the simple fact that housing is by far the largest consumer of urban land. It is equally true, however, that approaches to many nonresidential problems, such as those involving transportation, central business districts, and open space, are determined to an important degree by conditions and preferences in the housing market. Most important, . . . there is widespread disagreement over housing goals. Fundamental differences regarding both residential development and residential renewal exist between federal and local government, city and suburb, and even planner and consumer.[14]

Much of the change in emphasis of urban renewal programs appears to be a shift away from policies which have met with strong opposition, such as that of private real estate interests against extensive government ownership and operation of housing. Even the trend toward more business-oriented goals of urban renewal, such as expressways, downtown malls, civic plazas, auditoriums, airports, and convention facilities, is handicapped by disagreement between national and local business leaders on how to finance such programs. The national Chamber of Commerce has traditionally stood on principle against urban renewal programs financed by federal funds, but many of the local community campaigns to sell urban renewal programs are headed by local Chamber of Commerce secretaries and leaders. As might have been expected, predominantly business-oriented urban renewal programs have begun to meet with strong opposition from spokesmen for those interests once served by the greater emphasis on low-rent housing. Some resent urban renewal as, in effect, "Negro removal" programs. It is at this point that deep conflicts between central cities and suburbs become obvious, with the higher-income suburb quite willing to segregate its housing problems from those of the lower-income core city and quite unwilling to accept the principles of city-suburban interdependence in the problem of housing.

City planners generally are in agreement on the importance of taking the area-wide view of city-suburban development, but this agreement does not extend to their views on "urban form" goals. For example, it has become rather common among some city planners since World War II to deplore the suburban residential "sprawl." Their arguments are too well-known to mention here, but it is worth noting that they actually seem to be more concerned over these "slurbs" than they are over slums. This may well represent the majority position among city planners, but there seems to be a growing body of dissenting opinions to the effect that "sprawl" is not necessarily synonymous with bad urban de-

[14] William G. Grigsby, "Housing and Slum Clearance: Elusive Goals," *The Annals of the American Academy of Political and Social Science*, 352 (March, 1964), p. 108.

sign and may well have important advantages over compaction of cities with its multi-family residential construction. Dissenters are also being found who disagree with the implicit assumption of many city planners that the suburban residential pattern of "thousands of little boxes" on separate lots is a kind of conspiracy of developers and the F.H.A. foisted on unwilling customers. In actuality, numerous surveys have made it clear that two-thirds to three-fourths of American families prefer the detached single-family house.[15] Yet as sprawl continues and disagreement on planning goals continues, the current trend does seem to be toward greater residential compaction of cities.

Politics of Stasis Versus Politics of Change

Against this imposing backdrop of conflicting interests, two questions suggest themselves: (1) What is the political process by which particular interests are translated (or *not* translated) into public policy? and; (2) What are the means, if any, by which the basis for consensus among these conflicting groups might be broadened? The first question is in one sense almost as broad as the whole field of political science, but it is posed here in a much more limited context. More specifically, the question involves what our knowledge of the political process can tell us about the difficulties we experience in achieving public control of environmental change or nonchange.

Stacked Cards for the Status Quo

One of the first principles of politics is that "the cards are stacked against the innovator," as Lockard expresses it.[16] Proponents of change must run the gauntlet of formal and informal obstacles which are found in our governmental system. The formal obstacles to the adoption of new policies are numerous and well-known, with such devices as separation of powers, federalism, vetoes, two-thirds majority requirements, and other checks and balances making almost inevitable a lag between the growth of environmental problems and the formulation of relevant public policies. Greer and Minar have described very well the effects of governmental fragmentation upon urban renewal as follows:

Urban renewal is limited by the dichotomy of public and private control, tension between federal and municipal agencies, division of

[15] *Ibid.*, p. 115.
[16] Duane Lockard, *The Politics of State and Local Government* (New York: Macmillan, 1963), p. 143.

power between different federal agencies, and fragmentation of power at
the local community level. . . .

Out of this diffusion of power and dilution of responsibility comes
a curious rigidity, not a rigidity of program but a rigidity of process that
enervates program. . . . It is as though policy must follow an open road
full of ruts and chuckholes, with hairpin curves and false crossroads to
confuse the trip. But not only is the road itself difficult, the country is
also filled with hostile tribes that may come out of the hills at any step of
the way. If one but counts the veto groups that can snipe at public programs or confront them head on in full battle dress, he may wonder if
any program can negotiate the journey successfully. . . . Any one or
combination of these may develop the power to revise, delay, obfuscate,
or forbid action. . . . It safeguards stasis.[17]

Concerning the impact of fragmentation on metropolitan area development, Greer and Minar are even more specific:

At the metropolitan level, the multitude of jurisdictions—cities,
towns, suburbs, special districts, counties, and even states—makes any
over-all planning of the city a farce. . . . The central city-suburb schisms
turn urban renewal into a holy war to recapture the suburban, white,
middle class—a war the central city is doomed to lose—and distract attention from the major clientele of the central city: the working class, the
ethnics, the disprivileged.[18]

Imposing as these formal legal obstacles to innovation may seem,
there are informal social and psychological obstacles to change which
may ultimately be more important. There is an intangible power which
might be called "community equilibrium," which is exceedingly difficult
to upset because of a strong tendency by the general public to be suspicious of proposed changes in the existing order. It is not so much a de-
votion to the conditions of the *status quo* as it is a combination of apathy and fear of the unknown. Sayre and Kaufman confirm these
"tendencies toward stasis" in their observations on the politics of New
York City, pointing out that change is looked upon as a risk venture involving possible loss of money, power, and prestige by those participat-
ing. Officials tend to be unwilling to "stick their necks out" or to lead a
fight down the "tortuous path" of change.[19]

Additional support for the proposition that major policy innovations are rare, indeed, comes from Charles E. Lindblom's criticism of the

[17] Greer and Minar, *op. cit.*, pp. 62, 65, and 67.
[18] *Ibid.*, p. 67.
[19] Wallace S. Sayre and Herbert Kaufman, *Governing New York City* (New York:
Russell Sage Foundation, 1960), pp. 716–719.

"rational-comprehensive" models of administrative decision-making. Lindblom suggests and defends a model of policy and decision making by "muddling through," that is, by considering only incremental or limited changes which build closely on the past experience.[20] Great emphasis is placed upon the value of agreement and administration by consent, and upon maximizing security by making relatively small degrees of policy change. In a more recent publication, co-authored by Lindblom and David Braybrooke, "muddling through" is given the more sophisticated title of "the strategy of disjointed incrementalism," but the message is still a strong bias in favor of the *status quo*.[21]

Can the Pattern of Stasis Be Broken?

With so many obvious drags on public policy, how are innovative policies and programs which actually break new ground ever adopted and carried out? Is it sheer accident that down through history we have a sprinkling of "star performances" by our policy makers—such as an Alaska Purchase, a Tennessee Valley Authority, a Marshall Plan, or radical new metropolitan governments in Miami and Nashville? These and others which could be mentioned are hardly examples of the "muddle through" model of policy making, and Braybrooke and Lindblom admit that the model has serious limitations when applied to revolutionary and utopian situations, as well as to wars, revolutions, crises, and "grand opportunities." [22] These exceptions cover a considerable span of situations where presumably the "politics of stasis" is not so strong. In addition, the Lindblom model has been criticized for assuming the existence of three essential preconditions which in actuality seldom exist. They are (1) generally satisfactory results of present policies, (2) continuity in the nature of the problems, and (3) continuity in the available means for dealing with the problems.[23]

Mere incremental change is not possible when there are no past policies, such as for some of the depression problems in the 1930s. Nor is it possible when national values change and past policies simply must be abandoned, as in the case of segregation policies. Changes in knowledge can lead to drastic policy changes, whether in the fields of health, education, air transportation, space research and development, or televi-

[20] Charles E. Lindblom, "The Science of 'Muddling Through,'" *Public Administration Review*, XIX (Spring, 1959), pp. 79–88.
[21] David Braybrooke and Charles E. Lindblom, *A Strategy of Decision: Policy Evaluation as a Social Process* (New York: Free Press of Glencoe, 1963).
[22] *Ibid.*, p. 78.
[23] Yehezkel Dror, "Muddling Through—'Science' or Inertia?", *Public Administration Review*, XXIV (September, 1964), pp. 153–157.

sion, and many would add that such policy changes not only can but *must* take place. Morton Kaplan suggests that "muddling through" with incremental decisions may well "promote internal adjustment and consensus to the detriment of long-term stability. While many would not agree, there is at least some logic in the argument that this [resistance to major change] is, indeed, the process by means of which most civilizations collapse." [24]

The pattern of stasis can be broken, according to Lockard, if the motivation or sense of mission is strong enough to provide the necessary stimulus to action. He points out that there "is a tendency to overlook the importance of this intangible source of motivation—this sense of mission that changes torpor to temper. Motivation by way of excitement and a sense of community is often ignored by those who attribute improvements, if such they be, to change in the form or structure of government." [25] Robert Dahl makes it clear that a considerable amount of unused "slack" power is available in most community political systems, simply awaiting the time or circumstance when it may be called into use by proper stimulation. He describes these "resources" as follows:

> Very few people seem to exploit their resources to the limit in order to influence political officials; even political officials often have resources available to them which they do not fully use. But precisely because of the existence of these slack resources, a great many significant, abrupt, short run changes in the distribution of influence can be brought about; for whenever some one in the community begins to exploit his available and hitherto unused resources much more fully and efficiently than before, he gains markedly in influence. [26]

The *potentiality* for major changes in policy seems to be indisputable, even without formal change in the structure of government, but the *likelihood* of such changes is hedged in by the requirement of the right combination of forces and circumstances—a relatively rare occurrence. It is too a consideration of these requisites for major changes in public policy on environmental issues, and an appraisal of the prospects for achieving such, that we now turn.

[24] See his review of Braybrooke and Lindblom, *op. cit.*, in *The Annals of the American Academy of Political and Social Science*, 352 (March, 1964), p. 189. [The phrase within the brackets is not a part of the quotation.]
[25] Lockard, *op. cit.*, p. 146.
[26] Robert Dahl, "The Analysis of Influence in Local Communities," in Charles Adrian (ed.), *Social Science and Community Action* (East Lansing: Michigan State University, Institute for Community Development and Services, 1960), p. 36.

Carrots, Sticks, and Consensus on Shaping the Environment

As Greer and Minar suggest, "whatever paths to action we find, they will be paths that lead through the perils of democratic procedure," [27] which simply means that all changes must be accomplished in a setting of politics. Therefore, if conservationists are to secure the kinds of changes in public policy considered desirable, they must work to improve their techniques and methods of political action, and more particularly, of consensus mobilization. The following list of possible methods of securing major changes in public policy is by no means exhaustive; the categories of political action overlap in some respects, and it is possible only to comment briefly on each one. They should be suggestive, however, of the more likely methods of accomplishing policy innovations.

1. *Effective Exploitation of a Crisis Situation*

Probably nothing opens the door for policy change more surely than a crisis or catastrophe of some kind. The Galveston tidal wave provided the stimulus for a radical new form of government for that city shortly after the turn of the century. The unusual conditions of national economic crisis during the 1930s helped to make it possible to neutralize the many normally antagonistic interest groups and to establish the Tennessee Valley Authority. It took a jolting political crisis for the city of Miami, when the people almost voted to abolish the city, to lead to a dramatic experiment in two-tiered metropolitan government for Dade County. A strong contribution to the establishment of a single metropolitan government for Nashville and Davidson County in 1962 was a growing suburban sewer crisis with thousands of septic tanks located in poorly suited soil. The degree of proper timing of proposals by conservationists through effective exploitation of environmental crises will undoubtedly determine the course of much future public policy.

2. *Developing Leadership and Enthusiasm in an Apathetic Conservationist Majority*

Many conservation issues are lost because the large apathetic majority which mildly favors conservation or environmental control is defeated by the enthusiasm, leadership, and cohesion of fairly small interest groups. The prime requisite for effective public policies concerning environmental development and control is a strong will on the part

[27] Greer and Minar, *op. cit.*, p. 70.

of the people to control the environment. As Connery and Leach express it, "the greatest need in the cities today is not water or sewers, or wider streets, or more schools, or housing, important as they are. What is needed most is drive, organization, and leadership." [28] The kind of vision which George Washington had of the city of Washington, which Thomas Jefferson had of the University of Virginia, and which Theodore Roosevelt had of a national park system, is the kind of vision and leadership which could make a tremendous difference in shaping the American environment in the next century.

3. Establishing Alliances of Conservation Groups with Related Interest Groups

In a political system as pluralistic as ours it should be obvious that few interest groups can afford the luxury of "going it alone." Conservationists are no exception and could well afford to develop not only dependable coalitions of interests to deal with certain types of issues, but also a broader base for the "conservation interest" generally. For example, as mentioned earlier, the idea of "conservation of metropolitan area resources" is not basically different from the traditionally more rural concept of natural resource conservation, and the merger of these natural allies should strengthen the hand of both. Additional political strength could be garnered if the various separate urban interest groups would recognize that the physical environment of the city—consisting of roads, public buildings and grounds, pipe lines, parks, factories, and houses—is indivisible. Should they find ways of working together on environmental control, it might be surprising to see the resulting array of political influence.

4. Research and Education Aimed at Significant Opposition "Publics"

It is easy to become cynical about the value of research and education as a practical means of changing the values, or at least the behavior, of groups opposing conservationist policies. Rational arguments often seem to hold little sway over organized economic interests fighting for economic survival and, indeed, who is to say which arguments are more rational? Nevertheless, the broad goal of controlling the environment for the greatest good of the greatest number has an impressive case to make, and few would deny that the job of research and edu-

[28] Robert H. Connery and Richard H. Leach, *The Federal Government and Metropolitan Areas* (Cambridge: Harvard University Press, 1960), p. 238.

cation on its behalf could be vastly improved. The hope for success of this technique of political action is more realistically placed in long-run, rather than in short-run decisions. Short-run disagreements *can* be transformed into long-run consensus by "getting the facts to the masses."

5. Changing the "Ground Rules" which Have Strengthened the Power of Anti-Conservation Groups

As simply a matter of strategy, some "ground rules" for public policy making have tended to strengthen the hand of commercial interests favoring fewer controls over the exploitation of natural resources. The federal system, for example, with its emphasis on states' rights, has made it more difficult to secure adoption of uniform national regulations to protect natural resources and has put states in the awkward position of trying to regulate a big industrial duck in a little state pond. With broader interpretation of the commerce power by the Supreme Court, this particular ground rule no longer provides the protection from national regulation that it once did. Representation formulas that guarantee rural domination of legislatures have had the effect of placing the control of urban development into unsympathetic or indifferent hands. *Baker v. Carr* has paved the way for drastic changes in this ground rule. Other restrictive instances could be cited in state constitutional provisions which handicap the adoption of new state and local environmental control measures.

6. Changing the Stakes (*Carrots-and-Sticks*) Involved in the Conflict

Perhaps the best example of an organized interest group accomplishing the seemingly impossible by means of judicious use of the carrot-and-stick approach has been the school consolidation movement in the United States. When it is considered that nothing was more sacred than the little red schoolhouse operated by the small school district, and yet literally thousands of these districts have been merged into larger ones, the political method used is certainly worth noting by conservation interest groups. Obviously, years and even decades of educational groundwork had to be laid, but the heart of the administrative technique has been a state-aid formula rigged to reward consolidated school districts and/or punish those which did not consolidate. Such a device is now in use in connection with billboard regulation on the interstate highways in a very mild form, and would seem to be an appropriate device for use in other environmental control issues. A part of the usefulness of the "carrot" is the fact that it is sometimes easier to secure legislative passage of a reward for compliance than of a punishment for noncompliance.

7. Metropolitan or State Consensus as a Means of Overriding Local Conflict or Inaction

In those circumstances when small segments of a metropolitan area seemed to be locked in hopeless conflict over environmental policy questions, present practice seems to be simply to allow anarchy to reign in many of these situations. Conservationists have traditionally had better luck at higher levels than at lower ones, so there is good reason to believe that it would be possible from time to time to secure consensus (or near consensus) at the metropolitan or state level when a stalemate exists at a local level. At present, however, the absence of a metropolitan policy for virtually all metropolitan areas makes "metropolitan consensus" a meaningless term so far as actual policy making is concerned. The issue of metropolitan area fragmentation versus integration is "old hat" by now, but so has been the school consolidation issue for decades. Fragmented attempts to regulate metropolitan growth and development have no more chance for success than does state regulation of interstate commerce, and yet we have talked ourselves into accepting the impossibility of establishing area-wide metropolitan governments. Suffice it to say here that urban environmental controls would be far more feasible if such governments did exist. In their absence, Greer and Minar suggest that "the state seems to be the most promising organizational lever to break the urban log jam." They add that "among the side effects of vitalizing state power would be the bringing of the hinterlands into proper focus in their relationships with the urban system." [29]

8. National Consensus as a Means of Overriding State and Local Conflict or Inaction

The most common "last resort" device, and in many cases the most effective one available to groups desiring policy innovation, is to secure at the national level what proves to be impossible at the state or local level of government. Lack of consensus on environmental policy within particular states or localities is not necessarily the end of the political road for a particular policy, even when there seems to be an irreconcilable conflict of interests. If a national consensus or near consensus can be mobilized, opposition groups within states or localities may thus

[29] Greer and Minar, op. cit., p. 71.

be by-passed. Actually, the influence of *private* national organizations on local and state policies, in addition to that of national *governmental* bodies, is becoming increasingly important. Banfield and Wilson state that locally influential activists, such as the press, civic associations, and lay civic leadership, are increasingly taking their general policy lines on the "agenda of city government" from executives of national foundations, federal agencies, and from such national bodies as the International City Managers' Association, National Municipal League, National Association of Housing and Redevelopment Officials, and the American Institute of Planners.[30]

In the case of recreation Lowdon Wingo predicts that "local and regional planning for leisure activities will increasingly require a broad national context." He adds that "such a context can be usefully developed through the evolution of a new policy role at the federal level. . . ."[31] Even a casual reader of articles analyzing the problems of resource development and control is aware of the tendency of most to conclude with a statement of the ultimate necessity for greater coordination, stimulation, and control at the national level. Space does not permit cataloging them here.

This writer shares the opinion that the national government holds the key to most of the issues of shaping the physical environment, and that more and more the critical question is becoming whether or not it is possible to achieve *national* consensus on a given issue.[32] If this is possible, a local community's or state's "irreconcilable conflict" of interests may become less and less important and certainly will no longer constitute an absolute veto. President Johnson's Message on Natural Beauty submitted to Congress in 1965, calling for an era of "new conservation," included many suggestions of federal carrots-and-sticks for broadening the basis for consensus on environmental issues.

[30] Banfield and Wilson, *op. cit.*, p. 334.

[31] Lowdon Wingo, Jr., "Recreation and Urban Development: A Policy Perspective," *The Annals of the American Academy of Political and Social Science*, 352 (March, 1964), p. 137.

[32] A note should be added concerning the word "consensus," which has been used rather loosely without definition in this discussion. A definition of unanimous agreement or even of near unanimity is certainly not suited to its usage in this context. The word has been used very generally with the intention of connoting a "comfortable majority" which is sufficiently broad so that opposition groups see little immediate chance to overturn it. In the sense of unanimous consensus of views, government by consensus is an impossibility.

NORMAN WENGERT*

9

Perennial Problems
of Federal Coordination

What has been learned from past efforts to obtain more effective coordination of environment-shaping policies at the federal level? What are the critical points of federal coordination and how is the balance of interests in environmental policy weighted at each of these points? Can the responsibility of the federal government for nationwide environmental policy be clarified and strengthened? If not, what alternative structuring of national policy making may be feasible or desirable?

Until recently, federal actions in which environmental effects have been explicitly recognized have been largely incidental to the management of natural resources in land, water, minerals, forests, soils, or wildlife. Natural resources policies have evolved, each in its own way, often for reasons (and in relation to client interests) that tended to disregard the unity of the natural environment. The environment is a unity, but resources are discrete—hence a problem of coordination arises when an effort is made to reconcile resource-centered programs and agencies with comprehensive environmental goals. The problem of coordination is further complicated by the circumstance that a physical entity such as a river, a forest, or a sea coast may constitute a number of different resources that cannot be exploited simultaneously in equal measure. To place incompatible objectives and conflicting goals in an environment as contrasted with re-

* Professor Wengert, J. D., Ph. D., is professor of political science at Colorado State University in Fort Collins, Colorado. This article originally appeared in *Environmental Studies—Papers on the Politics of Public Administration of Man—Environment Relationships*, 4 volumes, Lynton K. Caldwell, editor (Bloomington, Ind.: Institute of Public Administration, Indiana University, 1967).

sources context may help to force a fuller consideration of the issues and values involved in any major environment-affecting decision. But as Norman Wengert points out, an environmental focus will not make the conflicts go away. The problem of coordination *is* perennial and it is basically a political problem.

Coordination of public programs dealing with or affecting many different facets of the environment superficially, at least, would seem to leave much to be desired. In many cases, little or no coordination is apparent, separate programs going their separate ways. In other cases coordination is only *pro forma* and superficial. Often those planning and conducting particular programs with obvious interrelationships have not consulted together, and in many cases programs dealing with similar or related problems may be seeking different and even conflicting goals or objectives. The pluralism of our society has been projected to government activities.

But while pluralism in the private sector is often rationalized as desirable since it encourages diversity, and in the economic sphere is an essential part of the market place, in the public sector pluralism is castigated as reflecting inefficiency, duplication, lack of coordination, and waste. Having four different supermarkets on the four corners of two intersecting main streets is good business; having four post offices similarly located is likely to be regarded as evidence of bureaucratic bumbling or pork barrel politics.

In the 1930s national planning was advanced as the means of rationalizing government efforts and bringing about more effective coordination of governmental administration as well as of public goals. But since World War II the idea of comprehensive national planning in the United States has had few advocates. At the same time both the volume and scope of public activities have increased, and with this increase has come an increased feeling that more effective coordination of public programs is imperative.

Impediments to Coordination

But coordination is no simple process, although the word rolls easily off the lips of organization and management specialists and government critics. There are, first of all, a number of difficult intellectual and psychological problems involved in seeking better program coordination which raise the question of how much coordination is possible. One of these is the problem of span of attention. While in one sense everything is ultimately related to everything else in a continuous web, government administrators can at any one time deal only with a very limited range of obviously interrelated factors.

A narrow span of attention is reinforced, moreover, by the lack of data on causes and effects, on reactions and consequences. It is one thing to know that the construction of an expressway through a city is likely to have *some* effect on the economy, the sociology, and the politics of the city. It is quite another matter of tremendously greater difficulty to identify *in advance* the specific consequences of such construction and to act with such knowledge in mind.

Coordination of activities with respect to the future is particularly difficult because the character of that future is so uncertain and so many factors will shape that future. Even the best bureaucracy has only a clouded crystal ball, although the hindsight of critics is always 20/20 vision. Because the future is indefinite, comprehensive coordination attempts frequently flounder on the shoals of differing premises, conflicting values, and speculations about things to come. Differing modes of thought and differing perceptions of reality make whole-hearted coordination virtually impossible.

These and similar psychological barriers to coordination are paralleled by related administrative problems. One of the most pressing of these is *time*. Most agencies operate under time mandates which preclude very much effort being devoted to coordination. And in any case, given their program responsibilities, the possible scope of coordination is generally restricted to subject matter over which there is no disagreement. Coordination at early planning or program formulation stages is usually not contemplated, often because the needs and opportunities for coordination have not been identified, and little staff time is allocated to this task. Moreover, it is just at this stage that fear over the possible loss of program control becomes very real. Later coordination among programs crystallized in the authority framework of particular agencies is much more difficult and hence of limited scope. In many cases, moreover, those working on particular programs in particular agencies are often ill-informed on what other agencies are doing or on how their activities might be interrelated.

These difficulties are compounded by the fact that institutions and techniques for program coordination and systematic exchange of program information are weak or nonexistent. In addition, the motivation for coordination is weak, partly because programs which would seem to be interrelated in effect or impact may in fact seek differing, even conflicting, goals, and may be supported by different clientele and interest configurations having little concern for consistency and coordination, particularly if this is likely to alter their influence on program content and administration. Although it may seem patent nonsense to a detached observer, irrigation interests, for example, have not been bothered by the fact that crops produced by subsidized water simply add to the surplus supply and increase the need for federal crop supports.

Jurisdiction and Coordination

Coordination and jurisdiction are obviously intimately interrelated. They suggest different facets of the same general situation, and this paper deals with both, since each provides a window for examining the role of the federal government in approaches to environmental problems. The need for coordination in part arises out of the fragmented character of jurisdiction. The fragmented jurisdiction, in turn, reflects the way in which government programs evolve, as well as patterns of authority and responsibility.

In one context, issues of jurisdiction (and hence of coordination) have traditionally been approached in terms of:

1. Conflicts between *different levels* of government;
2. Conflicts between *different agencies* of government; and
3. In a special sense, conflicts among *similar levels* of government (for example, interstate conflicts, intercounty conflicts, and intercity conflicts).

My concern is particularly with conflicts between agencies. At the same time, a few generalizations with respect to conflicts between levels will be useful, since more attention has been paid to this question in the literature and some insights may thus be provided as background for the main topic of this paper.

Conflicts between levels present the classic issue of federalism, now more frequently discussed under the rubric of "intergovernmental relations" and deeply involved in the so-called states' rights arguments.

Two points seem particularly important. The first is that throughout American history the arguments over relationships between levels of government in the federal system have often (one is tempted to say always) reflected a divergence between the overt and the covert objectives of those expressing a concern for these relationships. In recent times, for example, those deploring what they label "encroachments" of the federal government in areas of state responsibility have in many instances been seeking to preserve a society in which the Negro was, in fact, a second class citizen. Similarly, many of the criticisms of federal grants-in-aid have been based on the covert desire to cut federal spending and reduce federal income taxes rather than on the grant-in-aid procedures as such.

The second lesson from the literature on interlevel conflicts, which was well substantiated by the Anderson-Weidner studies in Minnesota,[1] and which was also subsequently corroborated by the investigations of the House Committee on Government Operations,[2] is that conflicts between levels among agencies dealing with similar program areas (for example, welfare, or agriculture or highways) are minimal. Thus Weidner has written:

> Administrative and legislative officials alike are of the opinion that the main clash of values occurs within a unit of government rather than between units. This is true even in regard to the issues arising from intergovernmental programs. The professional is especially prone to this point of view. . . .
>
> . . . As has already been emphasized, professionalism creates a powerful set of programmatic values the existence of which explains much of the behavior of professional and non-professional public officials in intergovernmental relations. But there is a larger point. To use the suggestive terminology of John M. Gaus, we are in an era of vastly increased physical and social technology, an era in which the catastrophies of war and depression can strike quickly. As a result, now programmatic values have been emphasized by those who want to take advantage of services that are now available because of the advances in physical and social technology and by those who demand governmental activities designed to lessen or avoid the ravages of wars and depressions. The technicians themselves have become attached to and encourage the creation of programmatic values. In such a situation, the cry of states' rights sounds a hollow note. . . .[3]

This is not to deny that sharp disputes may at times arise, but the cause of such disputes when they occur must be sought elsewhere than in traditional positions regarding federal-state relations. One source of dispute may involve professional differences as to how particular problems should be dealt with. Another and more pervasive source of dispute (though muted where professional or programmatic values dominate) lies in fundamental political questions of power. Here Lasswell's

[1] William Anderson (ed.), *Intergovernmental Relations in the U.S. as Observed in the State of Minnesota* (10 volumes; various dates, 1950–1958).

[2] Committee on Government Operations, House of Representatives, 85th Congress, 2nd Session, H. R. 2533, *Federal-State-Local Relations*, August 8, 1958.

[3] In Arthur W. Macmahon (ed.), *Federalism, Mature and Emergent* (New York: Doubleday & Company, 1955).

definition of politics comes to mind: the process that determines: "Who Gets What, When, How." [4]

This is not the place to explore the distribution of power as it affects problems of federal jurisdiction and coordination of federal programs. But it might be useful to identify in categorical fashion some of the factors that affect power struggles and in this way influence interagency coordination.

1. IDEOLOGY AND VALUES. Undoubtedly, participants in the power struggle may be contending for a particular view of society. They may be pro- or anti-governmental in orientation; they may have an almost infinite range of value positions, and they recognize that government action or inaction may be vital to those positions. To be sure, as has been noted elsewhere,[5] American politics is not strongly ideological in its orientation. But certainly some participants in the political struggle may be motivated by essentially ideological concerns.

2. COSTS AND BENEFITS. More often than not, the struggle for power involves a struggle over who will control the allocation of costs and the distribution of benefits flowing from government programs. In this connection, concern over control of access to points of decision in the legislative and administrative branches is of crucial importance. The relation of benefits to the re-election hopes of legislators is also relevant.

3. BUREAUCRATIC SELF-PRESERVATION. Power struggles to preserve bureaucratic advantages, such as agency size, budgets, and importance of programs, are not unusual. On the more positive side, struggles may involve the aggrandizement of power.[6]

4. TECHNOLOGICAL BIASES. These may involve the belief that certain specialists are better able to solve a particular range of problems. To technological biases should be added agency biases, which are often not distinguishable from technological biases (for example, conflicts between the U.S. Forest Service and the U.S. Park Service over which agency should play the larger role in providing recreation facilities).

[4] Harold Lasswell, *Politics: Who Gets What, When, How* (New York: McGraw-Hill, 1936).
[5] Norman Wengert, "The Ideological Basis of Conservation . . . Policies and Programs," *The Annals of the American Academy of Political and Social Science*, CCXLIV (November, 1962), pp. 65–75.
[6] As described in the so-called "Parkinson's Law." See also Philip M. Selznick, *TVA and the Grass Roots* (Berkeley: University of California Press, 1949), where the concept of "cooptation" is developed to describe the capture of an agency by the local power structure.

5. LEADERSHIP AND PERSONALITY FACTORS. This category opens
a Pandora's box, and yet it must be recognized that the personalities of
particular political and bureaucratic leaders have been important factors
in particular power struggles. The Soil Conservation–Agricultural Extension controversy of twenty-five years ago is unthinkable without a
Hugh Hammond Bennett. TVA would not have become a reality without the persistence of George Norris, and its direction would have been
much different had Arthur Morgan rather than David Lilienthal and
Harcourt Morgan won the power struggle in the 1936–1939 internal conflict.

Plural Programs

It has been a major premise of many studies of public management that government spawns agencies charged with the same or similar
tasks, and that hence a primary task of management improvement is
agency consolidation primarily through reorganization. This view, together with Presidential span of control problems, loomed large in the
recommendations of the 1937 President's Committee on Administrative
Management. It dominated the proposals of the first Hoover Commission and was not neglected by the second. Most recently the newly
adopted Michigan State Constitution mandated an organizational structure of "no more than twenty departments." In this view, the charge of
duplication is the call to battle; multiplicity of agencies is considered
prima-facie evidence of governmental inefficiency and waste. Little attention is paid to the political necessities out of which such multiplicity
developed, and the irreversibility of the original decisions is not considered. Yet pressures for better coordination, in fact, often arise only long
after agency programs have been authorized and work patterns and relationships established. Coordination is thus really an afterthought, and
for this very reason is often difficult to achieve except in a very superficial way.

A few comments on agency growth and program development
will help to illuminate this important point.

In many cases, to begin with, programs of one agency are usually
formulated separately and distinctly from those of other agencies, and
the need for coordination is rarely anticipated. Thus authorizing statutes
and the considerations that led to them pay little attention to coordination possibilities. Where the responsibilities of other agencies are identified as overlapping, attempts to distinguish become a part of the record.

But in most cases, only actual administration of particular programs indicates points of contact with other activities, and the need for coordination is identified after the fact. In addition, agency interests may broaden as those responsible for administration begin to recognize the logical necessities of including activities which were initially on the periphery of the original program. In other cases agency interests may shift through the accretion of many small decisions.

At the root of this situation, of course, is the dominance of the "problem-solving" approach in American public administration. "Problems" are manifested by concrete evidence of conflict, of instability, of articulated need, and the response of government is to seek programs and policies which will alleviate or do away with the assumed causes of the conflict and of the instability, and meet the need. It is typical of this pragmatic and often expedient approach that problems may be misidentified and solutions inappropriate. Problem-solving can become the antithesis of a planning approach. Very often it simply results in the squeaking wheel getting most of the grease. Yet it has been characteristic of the origins of most governmental programs, reflecting, among other things, the emphasis in our culture on techniques and technology and the low regard for the planner and generalist.

Two examples illuminate this pattern of program evolution. First, the expansion of the civil functions of the Corps of Army Engineers from navigation to comprehensive river basin engineering illustrates at many points the kinds of factors that shape an agency's program and often push it in directions in which it is initially reluctant to go. And second, the attention of the Department of Agriculture to problems of suburban land-use and its earlier interests in consumer problems illustrate a shift in focus arising partly from agency competence, partly from a dedication to public service, and partly from bureaucratic necessities.

In short, broadening interests may arise from many stimuli, such as research, problem analysis, administrative experience, developing technology, political pressures and bureaucratic behavior. But as this broadening occurs the potentials for program conflict increase and the need for coordination becomes more apparent.

One might argue that if programs were developed by means of systems analysis, points of intersection with other programs could be identified in advance. But these techniques are still very primitive. Moreover, their usefulness in anticipating points of interagency conflict and needs for coordination may also be limited because the definition of the system is the result of intellectual effort (it is not to be found in nature) and thus is likely to suffer from many of the same biases and influences which now make coordination so difficult. To illustrate: What is the system to be used for water planning? The watershed or the consuming market which may draw on several watersheds? [7]

To summarize, then, desires for logical neatness press in the direction of complete coordination and full program integration. The limitations of intellect, of time, of institutions, the divergence of values, and the politics of program decisions—all conspire to make plural programs and heterogeneous agencies inevitable. From these plural programs and heterogeneous agencies emerge problems of coordination—but also limitations on coordination.

Coordination at the Center

Many coordination efforts, with varying degrees of success, occur at the center in Washington. The more effective mechanisms for coordination are probably operative within a large department or agency, but even at this point the factors that make interagency coordination difficult are also at work. It has often been pointed out that departments like Interior or Health, Education, and Welfare represent a kind of federation of bureaus, each with its own authority base, its own program responsibilities, its own supporters and clienteles, its own program concepts and goals. Given the way in which component units evolved, similar centrifugal tendencies are apparent in the Housing and Home Finance Agency. And even in the Department of Agriculture, which in many respects is among the most effectively integrated departments in the federal government, many unresolved conflicts among component units may be identified.

In part, these observed conditions substantiate the point made earlier that initially instituted programs are of narrow scope and pose few issues of coordination. But as programs develop and administrative organization for their conduct grows, conflicts with other programs begin to be identified and the need for coordination becomes more apparent. But by this time the opportunity for coordination has, by the very fact of this development and growth, become very limited.

Within departments or agencies the secretary or agency head often does not have effective power to bring about complete coordination. He may not have the staff for this purpose or in many cases the staff (for example, assistant secretaries) come to their positions as hostages of inter-

---

[7] For a detailed analysis of this problem, see Harry Erlich and P. H. McGanhey, *Economic Evaluation of Water, Part II, Jurisdictional Considerations . . .* , (University of California: Water Resources Center, Contribution No. 42 [June, 1964]).

ests and clientele groups. Even where they are initially "free men," they soon find themselves seeking alliances and alignments in order to build a record of accomplishment. Moreover, attempts of secretaries or agency heads to build up staffs of their own have often run into political restrictions generated by hostile bureaus through their direct contacts with important congressmen.[8]

An important tool for coordination within the departments and agencies is the budget. Program budgeting has undoubtedly helped identify bureau objectives, but the process itself, presided over by the administrative assistant secretary (in the departments), is under such time pressure that only the more obvious conflicts can be given attention. The administrative assistant secretary, moreover, is a permanent civil servant whose loyalties may often be directed downward instead of to the secretary.

At the Presidential level the same pressures are at work in an even more intense fashion. The Bureau of the Budget is under time pressures which are compounded by the sheer size of the sums dealt with. Hence coordination must be on a very general level, and then only in those instances where conflicts appear obvious or have aroused political issues. The Bureau's questionnaire control is one such; another is the coordination of federal mapping efforts. Both of these are clearly on the periphery of major federal action, although each caused rather intense political and administrative problems when the controls were initiated.

In the background of the budget process as a control and coordination device are the realities of the appropriation process where special interests, local pressures, and program hobbles can easily upset the best administrative coordination, for at this point horsetrading and the pork barrel often dominate.

But what about coordination among agencies and programs, provided that institutional arrangements have been set up to permit this? Interagency committees (sometimes even at the subcabinet level) are the most frequently used devices. It must also be recognized that an unmeasurable but significant amount of coordination occurs informally, particularly among individuals with similar professional or program interests (for example, the foresters in the Bureau of Land Management and the foresters in the U.S. Forest Service). But voluntary coordination, whether formal or informal, has very definite limits. It cannot undermine the integrity of the agency nor that of the agency program. Its primary focus will thus be the exchange of information and intelligence. This is

[8] See John C. Honey and Norman Wengert, "Program Planning in the Department of the Interior, 1946–53," *Public Administration Review*, XIV (Summer, 1954), pp. 193–201, for an account of experiences in the Department of the Interior.

not unimportant, but it seems clear that fundamental conflicts in policy direction or program goals can usually not be dealt with on a voluntary basis, which can only result in a kind of "lowest common denominator" pattern of coordination, rather than the resolution of fundamental conflicts and differences.

Field Coordination

If coordination in Washington is severely limited, coordination in the field, both among the subunits of single departments and agencies and between departments and agencies, may provide more encouraging opportunities.

One device for internal coordination in a number of departments and agencies is the regional field committee, which, by meeting regularly, brings agency personnel into contact with one another and provides opportunities for collaboration and coordination. The record of coordination through such field arrangements has been encouraging for two reasons. First, programs are discussed at early stages of their development, when they are still relatively fluid so that points of potential conflict may often be identified and dealt with. Second, the situation or environment within which programs will be moving ahead is close at hand, and impacts and consequences can be considered at the points where action will occur. Without question the field perspective is more highly sensitive to concrete reality than the perspective of those operating at the center.

But, departmental or agency field committees also suffer from some of the limitations which are operative in Washington. Program rigidities —often embedded in statutes, administrative timidity, and clientele pressures—all may work to restrict the scope of field coordination, particularly when no mechanism for authoritative decisions has been provided. These comments made with respect to coordination within a department or agency would, of course, also apply with even greater force to attempts at coordination between or among departments and agencies. The various interagency committees dealing with resources program coordination in the field (for example, the several watershed committees) have impressive records of frustration and ineffectiveness.[9] This is not to say that such efforts should not be continued, but merely to recognize that coordination is at best difficult.

[9] See Irving K. Fox and Isabel Picken, *The Upstream-Downstream Controversy in the Arkansas-White-Red Basins Survey*, Inter-University Case Program (University, Alabama: University of Alabama Press, 1960).

What about the regional agency—the so-called TVA idea? The doctrine of the regional agency, as developed particularly by David E. Lilienthal and Gordon Clapp, placed great emphasis upon the role of the regional agency in developing resources of the region on a coordinated basis. But it must be admitted that the practices of the regional agency have been at considerable variance with the doctrine. The TVA statute was just not broad enough to permit, even in the heyday of its power, the assumption of leadership among federal resource development agencies operating in the Tennessee Valley, and where TVA could not persuade federal agencies to share or cede responsibilities, coordination was often minimal or nonexistent. As concepts of development began to stress the economic dimension rather than simply the development of physical resources, TVA interests tended to be ignored by other federal agencies. This is perhaps why today the TVA program is little more than a public power and river-channel water control program. TVA is still interested in the watersheds which make up the region, even as it is interested in the regional economy, but it is not in a position to do much about such broader concerns, nor even to exercise much leadership with respect to them. That the regional agency was a threat to regular federal resource agencies is apparent in the record of their opposition to proposals to expand this device,[10] and in the fact that the idea of the regional agency as a means for more effective coordination of federal programs is dead. It might also be noted that the regional river basin agency assumed the appropriateness of watershed boundaries for development and for coordination of governmental activities. Yet there is increasing reason to question whether the watershed makes sense except for a very limited range of activities. It has, however, the one strong feature of great political attractiveness, and this is that watershed boundaries are determined by God and do not permit the haggling over where to draw the lines which has always characterized the drawing of boundaries by men. Whether the ease of locating natural boundaries and the elimination of controversy over them compensates for their other incongruities is often questionable.

The Dilemmas of Coordination Standards

The fundamental problem of coordination, it seems to me, lies in the area of conflicting goals and purposes. If we accept Dewey's concept of many publics rather than one public, we must also recognize the plurality of values and goals. More than that, we must go on to recognize

[10] See Norman Wengert, *Valley of Tomorrow* (Knoxville, Tenn.: University of Tennessee, 1952), for references to some of these controversies.

that we really have very ineffective mechanisms for choosing among conflicting goals. Unquestionably, where choices must be made, the processes of politics become of primary significance, but the forces and factors involved in any particular decision must be identified on a case-by-case basis. Moreover, the market place analogy of expanding political resources like businessmen spend dollars is probably useful. But it must also be recognized that many forces support a pluralistic system in which integrative decisions are avoided even at the expense of program conflicts, incongruities, and inconsistencies.

Perhaps one of the most common examples of this tolerance for inconsistencies arises in the conflict between local and national interests. Most resource decisions, most development decisions (that is, most decisions of vital concern to the environment) are determined primarily on a local basis. The brilliant analysis of the Hells Canyon Dam controversy by Krutilla and Eckstein a decade ago answered the question whether a high dam or a low dam should be built on the Snake River, but it did not answer the question of whether federal investments should be made in the Pacific Northwest as compared to other regions.[11] Most cost-benefit studies, in fact, accept the geographic boundaries established in the proposal being analyzed and make no attempts at interregional comparisons. Yet from a national point of view the issue of where national investments might be most productive is important. With respect to irrigation investments, for example, the question is whether smaller investments in the Northeast or other regions might bring production increases equal to those anticipated from irrigation expenditures in the arid regions.

Many efforts to stress national rather than local interests may be frustrated because the system makes decisions based on the national interest, where this may be contrary to local interests, very difficult. The assumption that the sum of local benefits is the measure of national benefits is deeply embedded in our value system (without much worry about who pays the costs). Coordination is thus more often by addition than by integration. This is just another way of saying that pluralism rather than logical neatness remains the dominant characteristic of American governmental programs.

Environment as a Focus for Coordination

This description of the impediments to coordination is not meant to minimize the need for as much coordination as possible. Nor is

[11] John V. Krutilla and Otto Eckstein, *Multiple Purpose River Development* (Baltimore: The Johns Hopkins University Press, 1958).

it meant to discredit attempts to secure better and more effective coordination. Its purpose has been, rather, to present realistically the very substantial problems involved in coordination and perhaps to lay the groundwork for even greater effort in this direction. It cannot be assumed that the administrative machine operates without friction. The role and function of administrators is, in fact, primarily one of dealing with the points of friction, of providing "lubrication" so that achievement of public goals may be more effective.

Several years ago, Lynton K. Caldwell suggested that "environment" may provide a new focus for public policy, stating that "policy focus on environment in its fullest practicable sense would make more likely the consideration of all the major elements relevant to an environment-affecting decision." [12] With this statement I concur. The reasons why environmental coordination is often successful have already been alluded to. At the point where programs affect the environment, specialists can more readily comprehend how their several interests are related. They can see the consequences of their actions and often feel the need for supportive effort by others whose authority and responsibility complement their own.

The recognition of the opportunities for coordination arising out of a focus on the elements relevant to an environment-affecting decision has much in common with the doctrine of decentralization voiced by David Lilienthal in his *TVA: Democracy on the March*.[13] He, too, stressed the view that the concrete realities of action "at the grass roots" made far more effective interaction among specialists of differing types. To him, decentralization was an antidote for remote control which often rested on abstract generalizations inconsistent with real conditions of concern to the citizens. Lilienthal quoted de Tocqueville with approval: "However enlightened and however skillful a central power may be, it cannot of itself embrace all the details of the existence of a great nation." [14] A somewhat similar view was expressed by Mary Parker Follett in her approach to management situations. She, too, stressed the advantages which flow from attention to concrete realities as contrasted with abstract generalizations.

Unquestionably one of the difficulties with federal programs is that as formulated in Washington they must be highly generalized but then do not meet the specific needs of any particular area. One sometimes feels that the situation is not unlike the cavil that military uniforms are tailored to fit the average man and hence fit almost no one. The substan-

[12] Lynton K. Caldwell, "Environment: A New Focus for Public Policy?" *Public Administration Review*, XXIII (September, 1963), pp. 132–139.
[13] David E. Lilienthal, *TVA: Democracy on the March* (New York: Harper, 1944), esp. Chaps. 8 and 9.
[14] *Ibid.*, p. 149.

tial pressures to make federal programs nationally uniform are often rationalized on the specious basis that uniformity can be equated with equality of treatment. In fact, the failure to differentiate may reflect bureaucratic timidity more than anything else.

But environmental coordination is no panacea. It does not by any means solve many of the very difficult conceptual problems of coordination, and it does not eliminate, even though it may mitigate, the agency commitments and rigidities referred to earlier.

It is clear, for example, that a stress on environment does not solve the problem of environmental boundaries. If coordination is to take place on a less than national basis, some kind of areal limits have to be set. For many purposes the concepts of urban regionalists, who identify the center or nucleus and then do not worry too much about outer limits, may be useful. But at some points intersections must be dealt with. Historically the watershed has seemed a desirable region, but as has been indicated, for instance, consumption needs for water may be a more useful determinant of regional boundaries than water resources.

It seems clear, also, that an environmental focus may not significantly influence basic value orientations which so often lie at the heart of the coordination problem. The foresters have developed an attractive environmental concept, namely "multiple use," but a careful appraisal of the operational meaning of this term has indicated that it often obscures rather than solves value conflicts.[15]

Unquestionably, if one asked an industrial engineer, an economist, a sanitarian, a recreationist and a fisherman to state their views on the environmental standards applicable to a particular stream (and assuming they had some understanding of the impact of their standards), I am sure that many conflicts would become apparent. It is perhaps trite to stress that viewpoints and values may differ because of one's technological training, because of one's authority and responsibility, because of one's friendships and associations. Yet these differences will not dissolve because they are dealt with in environmental terms. It may be easier in some cases to secure *some* agreement in the context of a specific environment. But until we can agree on what is a tolerable, a productive, a pleasant, a beautiful environment, environmental coordination, too, will have its limits. Until angels govern men the task of politics will continue to be choosing from among alternate goals and differing objectives, often without any assurance that the choice made is really better than those rejected. This is the process of government; this is the essence of decision-making; this is the heart of the coordination problem.

[15] Outdoor Recreation Resources Review Commission, *Study Report 17: Multiple Use of Land and Water Areas* (Washington: U.S. Government Printing Office, 1962).

PART
FIVE
THE ROLE OF ANALYSIS

The awareness of the need to combat environmental pollution and resource mismanagement has produced a quest for systematic means of evaluating programs of various types. The articles in this part serve to suggest both uses and abuses of some of these methods of evaluation.

In his article entitled "Systems Politics and Systems Budgeting," Allen Schick seeks to juxtapose two modes of politics and budgeting and their respective consequences. He notes that in systems budgeting, outcomes are presumed to be unfavorable or "suboptimal" unless they undergo specific evaluation, whereas in process budgeting, outcomes are *assumed* to be favorable if the process from which they derive appears to be working properly. The "distinctive element" in systems budgeting is "the analysis of alternative opportunities, but in process budgeting it is the bargaining apparatus. . . ." Schick is basically correct in suggesting that the field of policy analysis is underdeveloped, and his disaffection with the outcomes of many federal domestic policies is widely shared. But it is doubtful that the process system is as much at fault and that systems budgeting is as much our savior as he appears to believe. As Schick admits, he is portraying the two processes in pure form and contends that in the "hybrid world" they "coexist." More importantly, Schick's taxonomy of the ills of process politics might also be applicable to systems politics. In this taxonomy he notes that collective values for the allocation of public goods do not prevail, production of goods with external costs may be stimulated rather than inhibited, income maldistribution occurs because of differences in the allocation of political power resulting from imperfect competition, manipulation of peoples' will can occur because people do not know their own true interests, and finally, immobilization of resources occurs due to structural impediments.

While most of the preceding analysis represents valid critiques of process politics (as portrayed by Truman, Lindblom, and Wildavsky), the same criticisms can be applied with almost equal rigor to systems politics. The perceptions and value systems of decision makers can have an enormous effect on their evaluative horizons and innovative capabilities, regardless of the prevailing system of decision making.[1] One might ask whether the indigent Appalachians mentioned by Schick as having been overlooked prior to 1960 would have been more visible if systems rather than process had been the prevailing budgetary and political procedure. Furthermore, the Eel River and Oakley Dam studies included in this part provide concrete evidence that the search for alternatives and the evaluation of information and allocation of priority weightings is constrained in large measure by the institutional and ideological loyalties of the evaluators. Advocates of particular programs may deliberately manipulate the data in an effort to present a stronger case. Citing another example, a Presidential task force is often appointed to explore particular issues in detail and to propose and discuss solutions to particular problems. While such groups are sometimes created so as to overcome prior "process" obstacles to such evaluations, the absence of governmental action on many of these task force proposals is an obvious example of the persisting shortcomings of process politics. Moreover, such inaction is an omen of the fate that may befall any attempts at innovation, no matter how clearly conceived and advantageous they may be.[2]

The second article in this part, by Dorfman and Jacoby, is a mathematical simulation of a politico-environmental problem; this paper clearly demonstrates the possible utility of mathematical models in the solution of problems of public policy. By presenting the reader with a wide range of possible solutions,

[1] The following comment by Bertram Gross is quite relevant in this regard: "Those willing to give (Secretary of Defense Robert S.) McNamara credit for a 'managerial revolution' . . . must ponder his role—and that of cost effectiveness analysis—in an Asiatic military operation of high costs, low effectiveness, and questionable wisdom." From "The New Systems Budgeting," in *Public Administration Review*, 29:2 (March–April 1969), p. 115.
[2] For a complementary critique of systems budgeting, see Aaron Wildavsky, "Rescuing Policy Analysis from PPBS," in *Public Administration Review* 29:2 (March–April 1969), pp. 189–202.

the authors implicitly recognize the spectrum of decisions that may evolve from a political process in which the allocation of political and economic influence can significantly alter the costs and benefits of particular decisions to affected parties. Moreover, by emphasizing the many assumptions that were necessary in their model, the authors highlight the extreme difficulties involved in reaching decisions of this nature and indicate some of the problems involved in the quantification of social costs and benefits.

The final two articles, by Hannon and Cannon and by Watkins, are empirical examples of how the use of a particular mode of analysis (benefit-cost analysis) does not necessarily lead to "more beneficial" outputs, and how the values of decision makers can alter relevant data so as to support, rather than evaluate, their predetermined means of attaining certain objectives. Thus the picture of benefit-cost analysis forwarded by Schick is contradicted by these conservationists. With respect to the Eel River project, the Corps of Engineers' favorable calculation of the benefit-cost ratio was generated by assumptions featuring maximization of possible benefits and minimization of possible costs; this was done *despite* previous construction and financial experiences suggesting that such calculations were truly unrealistic. Moreover, in neither case did the Corps of Engineers evaluate viable alternatives, nor did they give adequate weight to social and aesthetic values. In particular, with respect to the Eel River project, the evaluation of costs included a definite social judgment by white engineers of what the social function of Indians in the area should be, a judgment which might justifiably be considered "racist" by some.

As has been noted here, there are reasons for believing that systems budgeting and benefit-cost analysis are of limited applicability for many problems. Nonetheless, analytical tools are important. Although the Corps of Engineers' benefit-cost analyses are now being attacked with some sophistication, until recently no alternative methodologies seemed available. The article by Dorfman and Jacoby, and that by Caldwell, provide some rather different approaches. Dorfman and Jacoby explicitly contrast their model of public decisions with benefit-cost analysis, stressing that their work is "explicitly noncommital" with regard to the importance of the different political actors. The social evaluations implicit in benefit-cost analysis are bypassed in the Dorfman and Jacoby formulation.

The methodology used in the article by Caldwell—that of

interrupted time-series analysis—is of wide potential applicability for analyzing the effects of particular programs.[3] In interrupted time-series analysis, quasi-experimental logic is used in
an effort to distinguish real change from random effects. There
are a number of ways to apply this methodology to the study of
environmental problems. Caldwell uses interrupted time-series
analysis to see if abatement procedures had a significant effect
upon water pollution in the Gary, Indiana, area; similar techniques could help clarify other kinds of environmental issues.
For example, interrupted time-series analysis could be used to
see whether particular international agreements have helped
fisheries depleted by rampant competition.

The approaches discussed above provide some alternative
perspectives, but at least one final point should be made concerning the time scale used in the different analyses. Although
little work has been done on this subject, systematic analysis of
the long-term benefits associated with various alternative programs would be highly desirable. Such work would necessitate
devising better ways to analyze trade-offs among such disparate
things as pollution abatement programs, increasing the size of
national parks, and environment-oriented educational programs.
In line with the criticisms of benefit-cost analysis noted earlier,
the research should try to take account of long-term costs and
benefits. In this context, long-term might mean up to 50 years,
even though such a perspective adds to the difficulty of making
reasonable estimates.

[3] Donald T. Campbell, "Reforms as Experiments," *American Psychologist*
24:4 (April 1969), pp. 409–429.

ALLEN SCHICK *

10

Systems Politics
and Systems Budgeting

Change in budgeting means change in politics. Any doubts on this score ought to have been dispelled by Aaron Wildavsky's *The Politics of the Budgetary Process*. This implies that the arrival of planning-programming-budgeting [PPB], however brief its current run, heralds or reflects transformations in American political life. The politico-budgetary world is much different from what it was in 1965 when PPB was launched, and it probably will not be the same again. While PPB cannot claim parentage for many of the changes, neither can it be divorced from the ferments now sweeping the domestic political scene. Uniting the emergent changes in politics and budgeting is one of the popular metaphors of our times.[1] The central metaphor of the old politics and budgeting was *process;* the key metaphor of the new politics and budgeting is *systems.*[2]

With the process-systems dichotomy as the pivot, I will try to: (1) identify the distinctive and contrasting elements of old and new; (2) analyze the persistence of process politics and the challenge of systems politics; (3) assess the preparedness of politics and budgeting for the systems view; and (4) develop a taxonomy of political process deficiencies.

* Dr. Schick is affiliated with the Brookings Institution in Washington, D. C. His article originally appeared in the March/April 1969 issue of *Public Administration Review*.
[1] See Martin Landau, "On the Use of Metaphor in Political Analysis," 28 *Social Research*, 1961.
[2] Of course, there are other ways to view the changes currently unfolding. I use the systems concept because it unites study and practice and politics and budgeting.

Process and System

The salient feature of process politics is the activity by which bargains are struck and allocations negotiated—the so-called rules of the game and the strategies of the contestants. There is a presumption that if the process is working properly, the outcome will be favorable. Hence, there is no need for an explicit examination of outcomes; one can evaluate the process itself to determine its performance and desirability. The *sine qua non* of systems politics is the outcome, not the activity, but what results from it. Take away this component and you do not have a system.[3] In systems politics allocations are formally related to preferred outcomes or objectives. Its assumption is exactly contrary to that which undergirds the process approach: unless outcomes are evaluated specifically, the results will be suboptimal or undesirable.

In systems budgeting the distinctive element is the analysis of alternative opportunities, while in process budgeting it is the bargaining apparatus for determining public actions. (To avert a possible misunderstanding, let me note that process and system are portrayed in pure form. In the hybrid world, analysis and bargaining coexist.[4]) Contrary to some interpretations, neither approach requires or rejects a zero-based determination of government programs. Systems politics does not force an all-or-nothing choice. The alternatives are always at the margins, and the margins, like the increments in process politics, can be large or small—a one percent increase in the appropriation for a bureau or a billion dollars for a new Medicaid program.[5] The critical difference is that the increments are negotiated in bargains that neglect the outcomes, while the systems margins are determined via an analysis of outcomes. Nor does systems politics require that every program be compared to all others; programs can be divided into parts for the purpose of analysis and choice. This is the familiar methodology of suboptimization. But unlike the fragmented and piecemeal tactics of process politics in which the part stands alone, in a systems view the part always is viewed in

---

[3] It should be noted that systems politics and systems analysis are of much more modest proportions than "general systems theory" defined by Kenneth Boulding as the quest "for a body of systematic theoretical constructs which will discuss the general relationships of the empirical world." See Walter Buckley (ed.), *Modern Systems Research for the Behavioral Scientist* (Chicago: Aldine Publishing Company, 1968).

[4] See William M. Capron, "The Impact of Analysis on Bargaining in Government," presented to the 1966 Annual Meeting of the American Political Science Association.

[5] A hint of the closing of the gap between incrementalism and systems analysis is implicit in the latest version of Wildavsky's views, "Toward a Radical Incrementalism: A Proposal to Aid Congress in Reform of the Budgetary Process," in Alfred de-Grazia (ed.), *Congress: The First Branch of Government* (Garden City, N.Y.: Doubleday Anchor Books, 1967).

some relation to the whole. Systems politics does not require that everything be decided all at once or once and for all. Systems analysis is both serial and remedial, with iterative feeding back from means to ends.

In process politics the contestants tend to view the options from the perspectives of their established positions (existing legislation, last year's budget, the "base," etc.). Theirs is a retrospective bias. Budgeting is treated as the process of financing existing commitments and of creating some new commitments (the increments). Systems politics tends to have a prospective bias; budgeting is regarded as the allocation of money to attain some future value (the outcome or objective). This year's budget, in systems terms, is an installment in buying that future.

Because of its future orientation, systems budgeting is likely to induce somewhat larger annual budget shifts than might derive under process rules. But this does not mean a zigzag course of events, each successive budget disowning the previous allocations. All political life, whether process or systems, must achieve stability and continuity. Process politics accomplishes these through a chain of incremental adjustments; systems politics, by embracing a large number of years and values within its analytic frame.

In process politics the strategy is that of mobilizing interests, and in process budgeting of mobilizing funds. In systems politics and budgeting it is the allocation and rationing of values and resources among competing powers and claimants. Process politics (and budgeting), therefore, tends to favor the partisans such as agencies, bureaus, and interest groups, while systems politics (and budgeting) tends to favor the central allocators, especially the chief executive and the budget agency. Systems politics also can be used to bolster certain officials who have mixed mobilizing-rationing roles. A few department heads such as Robert McNamara have used systems budgeting in this fashion. But this is likely to occur only when top officials have mobilizing values that diverge from those of their subordinates.

Systems politics takes a relatively holistic view of objectives compared to the partial view associated with process politics. As many pluralists have asserted, the group process produces public objectives as derivatives or aggregates of the special, limited interests of the groups. Systems politics encompasses a broader range of public purposes, including some which cannot be extracted from or negotiated via the usual group interactions. But it would be erroneous to attribute to systems politics a global concern with objectives. That would tax the political system with an overload of calculation and conflict management. All politics has to work with limits on cognition and with the realities of multiple and conflicting objectives. To cope with these constraints, systems politics relies on the indispensable division of analytic and political labors furnished by group bargaining. Systems politics, in short, does not eschew group objectives, but it certainly is not confined to them.

The important facts of process budgeting have been portrayed in Aaron Wildavsky's *The Politics of the Budgetary Process*. Process budgeting is "incremental, fragmented, nonprogrammatic, and sequential." [6] There is a tendency to accept last year's budget as the base for next year's and to use an array of nonanalytic tactics to reduce the complexities and conflicts of budget making and to strengthen the opportunities of agencies to obtain funds. These tactics have stabilized into the rules and roles of bargaining that govern the incremental budget process. Although Wildavsky has underestimated the program content of traditional budgeting, he correctly observes that there is little explicit consideration of objectives and policies and almost no search for alternatives. The line-item method is one technical manifestation of process budgeting.

Systems budgeting is represented by the planning-programming-budgeting systems now being established in many government jurisdictions. While there are many versions of PPB and PPB is not the only appropriate expression of systems in budgeting, all PPB systems direct allocative choice to future outcomes, to the costs of achieving public objectives, and to alternative means of pursuit. The technology of PPB —the program memoranda, program and financial plans, and other federal documentation or the variant methods used in other jurisdictions— are of considerable relevance in the conversion of the systems idea into practice, but it is the concept of systems budgeting that overrides and ultimately must determine the techniques.

The Dominance of Process

The process school dominated American politics from the early 1950s through the mid-1960s. From David Truman's *The Governmental Process* (1951) through Wildavsky's justly praised budget study (1964) there prevailed the confidence that pluralist politics—particularly transactions among interest groups—produces favorable outcomes. For the most part, the politics of the period was practiced as described by the pluralists and incrementalists. The emphasis was on consensus and stability, on limiting the scope and intensity of conflict by allocating to each group its quota of public satisfactions. Change was gradual and piecemeal, with departures from the status quo limited by established

[6] Aaron Wildavsky, *The Politics of the Budgetary Process* (Boston: Little, Brown and Company, 1964), p. 136.

rules and by the actions of the "partisan mutual adjusters" who orchestrated the group process.[7] Despite their slavish lip service to Lasswell's formulation of politics as "who gets what, when, how," the pluralists gave scant attention to the outcomes of group interactions. One can search the vast pluralist literature and locate only scatterings of concern with "who gets what" from the power distribution in a community or from the established government policies. The pluralists were deterred from looking into such questions by their own focus on process.

Wildavsky's study is an excellent illustration of the pluralist methodology. After two lengthy chapters on "Calculations" and "Strategies" devoted to the partisan process of budget making, and with hardly a word about outcomes,[8] Wildavsky opens the next chapter with a strong rebuke to budget reformers:

> There is little or no realization among the reformers, however, that any effective change in budgetary relationships must necessarily alter the outcomes of the budgetary process. . . . proposed reforms inevitably contain important implications for the political system; that is, for the "who gets what" of governmental decisions.[9]

Yet nowhere in *The Politics* does the author evaluate "who gets what" from traditional budgeting. Instead, there is a *deus ex machina* faith in the goodness of the pluralist process:

> The process we have developed for dealing with interpersonal comparisons in government is not economic but political. Conflicts are resolved (under agreed upon rules) by translating different preferences through the political system into units called votes or into types of authority like a veto power.[10]

Why have the pluralists neglected to study the outcomes of their process? What inspired their awesome respect for the ability of that process to deliver the right results time and again? There are a number of explanations which manifest the potency and attractiveness of the pluralist view.

American political science is habituated to confidence in the for-

[7] The best statement of pluralist process for purposes of this paper is Charles E. Lindblom, *The Intelligence of Democracy* (Glencoe, N.Y.: The Free Press, 1965).
[8] While his work contains numerous illustrations and anecdotes, Wildavsky does not deal explicitly with which interests win or lose as a consequence of the budget process, or with the outcomes of the process; for example, with the question of whether people are well or poorly housed.
[9] Aaron Wildavsky, *The Politics of the Budgetary Process, op. cit.*, p. 127.
[10] *Ibid.*, p. 130.

mal relations among power holders. Just as the Constitution makers believed that government would be good (nontyrannical) if power were divided among the several branches, the pluralists have argued that government is good (responsible) because power is shared by many groups. A social checks and balances system has replaced the legal checks and balances as the "democratizing" process of government. The pluralists also have been swayed by the market model of economic competition. In the same way that the unseen hand of the market effectively and fairly regulates supply and demand, the interactions of competing groups yields the desired supply of political goods, and at the right price. Moreover, the proper functioning of both private and public markets hinges on the partisanship of the contestants. Social welfare is maximized by the self-interest of buyers and sellers, not by an attempt to calculate the general welfare. If either economic man or political man abandoned his partisan role, the expected result would be a misallocation of resources.

The pluralists were impressed by their "discovery" of interest groups. In the pluralist mind, not only do groups supplement the electoral process by providing additional channels of influence and information, they also compensate for some of the limitations of electoral politics, notably its inability to transmit unambiguous policy preferences (mandates) from voters to public officials or to accommodate differentials in the intensity of preferences. By virtue of the overlapping pattern of group identifications, interest groups also were esteemed as effective brakes on socioeconomic conflict. Accordingly, the pluralists came to regard the group process as the cornerstone of modern democratic government, possessing a representative capability superior to the voting process.

According to this pluralist interpretation, government is sometimes a representative of special interests (for example, a bureau advocating the interests of its clientele), and sometimes an arbiter of interests (for example, the budget bureau allocating the shares among the various agencies). But its role is not that of promoting some overarching public interest. Its job is to keep the process going, not to maximize some consistent set of policy objectives. Bureaucracies were considered faithful reflectors of group preferences; consequently, their growth to enormous power was not deemed a threat to norms of representation.

Once they were sold on the efficacy of interest groups, the pluralists stopped worrying about the ends of government. They were persuaded by a tautological, but nonetheless alluring, proof that the outcomes of the group process are satisfactory. If the bargain were not the right one, it would not have been made. Since it was made, it must be the right one. Unlike many economists who have become cognizant that market imperfections and limitations, such as external costs and benefits or imperfect competition, can produce unfavorable outcomes, most pluralists stayed solidly convinced group competition has no major defects.

The process approach offered a convenient escape from difficult value questions. A decisional system that focuses on the outcomes and objectives of public policy cannot avoid controversy over the ends of government, the definition of the public interest, and the allocation of core values such as power, wealth, and status. But the pluralists bypassed their matters by concentrating on the structure and rules for choice, not on the choices themselves. They purported to describe the political world as it is, neglecting the important normative implications of their model. The pluralists scrupulously avoided interpersonal comparisons and the equally troublesome question of whose values shall prevail. Instead, they took the actual distribution of values (and money) as Pareto optimal, that is, as the best that could be achieved without disadvantaging at least one group.

These political scientists, along with many others, assumed that politics is a giant positive sum game in which almost everyone comes out ahead. This perspective was inspired by the affluent mood of the period and by the "out of sight, out of mind" predicament of the poor. It had a powerful analog in the Keynesian model of economic growth and stabilization; if everyone benefits from economic development, it is hard to ask the question "development for what?" For verification of their interpretation, the pluralists resorted to a "failsafe" tautology. If there were any losers, surely they would have joined into groups to protect their interests. If a disadvantaged group had a great deal at stake, it would have been able to veto the proposed bargain or to demand compensation for its losses. The affluence, everyone wins presumptions removed any compulsion for an evaluation of policy outcomes; satisficing solutions would do. (Pareto solutions are, by definition, satisficing conditions, *modus vivendi* worked out to the satisfaction of those groups whose interests are involved.) Satisficing became a way of political life and a justification for the status quo, not merely a means of cutting down the cost of choice.[11] "Second best" became the preferred solution because the best would have required some agonizing reappraisal of policy and purpose, along with a renegotiation of delicate group relationships. More than a decade ago Robert C. Wood explained why

---

[11] When he introduced the concept, Simon's argument was "that men satisfice because they have not the wits to maximize. . . . If you have the wits to maximize, it is silly to satisfice." Herbert A. Simon, "The Decision-Making Schema: A Reply," *Public Administration Review* Winter 1958.

America was doing little to reconstruct her cities despite the warnings of reformers:

> Despite our predictions, disaster has not struck: urban government has continued to function, not well perhaps, but at least well enough to forestall catastrophe. Traffic continues to circulate; streets and sewers are built; water is provided; schools keep their doors open; and law and order generally prevail.[12]

It is only at the point of crisis that satisficing no longer is good enough and governments are compelled to reexamine what they are doing and where they are heading. But the crises that surround our public institutions today were remote, or at least underground, a few years ago.

Affluence enables winning groups to compensate their competitors. For this reason, log-rolling among interests was viewed as an efficient mechanism for negotiating side-payments. The quality of the "pork," in terms of some public interest criterion, was not taken into account— only the success of the groups in obtaining agreement. The fact that the groups consented to the exchange was taken as sufficient evidence of its utility. It is easy to understand that under conditions of scarcity the quality of the exchange would more likely be subjected to scrutiny. But these were not perceived as times of scarcity.

The pluralists emphasized the remedial features of incrementalism. A decision made today is provisional; it can be modified tomorrow. If this year's budget is deficient, corrections can be made next year. One need not search for the optimal outcome, nor need one attempt to take all factors into account before deciding. Some pluralists argued that better results can be achieved through a series of partial adjustments than through a systematic canvass of alternatives. The serial and remedial aspects of incremental politics were regarded as especially helpful in reducing the complexities and controversies involved in the negotiation of a $185 billion national budget.

The pluralists were impressed by the ability of the budgetary process to limit political and bureaucratic conflict. The annual competition over billions of dollars has the potential of generating explosive and divisive conflicts. The fact that this competition usually is waged peacefully and leaves few scars attests to the effectiveness of the traditional process. The pluralists tend to view anything that might broaden the scope of intensity of conflict as undesirable, and they believe that an explicit and systematic evaluation of public objectives, accompanied by empha-

---

[12] Robert C. Wood, "Metropolitan Government, 1975: An Extrapolation of Trends," 52 *American Political Science Review*, March 1958, p. 112.

sis on alternatives, trade-offs, and the outcomes of competitive resource allocations, will increase the level of conflict.

Finally, the pluralists looked at the American political scene and liked what they saw—abundance, growth, consensus, stability, satisfaction with the American way. (It should be remembered that the pluralist age followed a great depression and a great war.) Given these "success indicators," the pluralists readily assumed that the shares were being divided equitably and to the satisfaction of the citizenry. They saw no need to quicken the pace of change or to effect radical redistributions in political values. And, of course, they saw no need to question the entrenched politico-budgetary process or to reexamine the outcomes of that process.

In many ways, the political life of the times was a faithful image of the pluralist view. Political practice was geared to consensus, an avoidance of the big ideological issues. The economy was buoyant, the mood optimistic. Writing of "The Politics of Consensus in an Age of Affluence," Robert Lane identified this mood as a key to understanding the political behavior of the common man:

> Since everyone is "doing better" year by year, though with different rates of improvement, the stakes are not so much in terms of gain or loss, but in terms of size of gain—giving government more clearly the image of a rewarding rather than a punishing instrument.[13]

It was not a time for thinking about purposes or worrying about priorities. Perspectives did not extend much beyond this year and the next. There was great confidence in the capability of the political process to produce the right results. Muddling through was canonized as the American virtue. It was a time of governmental immobilism, capable neither of disowning the New Deal legacy nor of forging new directions in economic and social life. If there was an industrial-military-political cartel, it was outside the range of pluralist inquiry, above the middling levels of politics. If there were nonvoters, or apathetic voters, or uninformed voters, that all was good, for it cooled the level of political excitement and demonstrated the basic satisfactions with the process. If there were losers in American politics, there was no need for concern,

---

[13] Robert E. Lane, "The Politics of Consensus in an Age of Affluence," 59 *American Political Science Review*, December 1965, p. 893. For a fuller picture on the optimism of the common man in the 1950's, see Robert E. Lane, *Political Ideology: Why the American Common Man Believes What He Does* (Glencoe, N.Y.: The Free Press, 1962).

for they, too, could look to a better tomorrow when they would share in the political bargains.

The politicians practiced what the pluralists described.

The Systems Challenge

It is well known that the main impetus for PPB came from the new decisional technologies associated with economic and systems analysis, not from public administration or political science. Accordingly, it was possible for the government-wide introduction of PPB to occur at the time that the pluralist's bargaining model had reached its academic apogee, approximately one year after the publication of major works by Lindblom and Wildavsky. Yet a full appreciation of the sources and implications of systems politics and budgeting must take into account a wider range of influences and ferments. To move from process to systems requires at least the following: (1) dissatisfaction with the outcomes resulting from the established process and (2) confidence that better outcomes can be obtained via the systems approach.

The entry of economists into positions of political influence was important on both counts. Economists, unlike their political science brethren, were not committed to the established process. As they applied their specialized norms and perspectives to the political world, many economists became convinced that the process was inefficient and inequitable.[14] Moreover, economists already possessed sophisticated methodologies for examining outcomes: the positivist input-output models and the normative welfare economics concepts.

However, few political scientists qualified for the systems approach during the 1950s and 1960s. Rather than showing concern about political outcomes, they were preoccupied with celebrating an *ancien regime* that exhibited few signs of the traumas developing within.[15] There were some stirrings by men of prominence, but their work was premature or too late. David Easton did his first work on systems politics, but only in recent years have his input-output categories been filled with useful data.[16] On the normative side, Lasswell's call for a policy science, to

---

[14] More than anything else, this skeptical view of public spending prodded economists to be the leading sponsors of PPB.

[15] See Leo Strauss, "An Epilogue," in Herbert J. Storing (ed.), *Essays on the Scientific Study of Politics* (New York: Holt, Rinehart and Winston, 1962), p. 327. This caustic yet penetrating critique of the pluralist method was "buried" by the establishment.

[16] David Easton, *The Political System* (New York: Alfred A. Knopf Inc., 1953). See, also, his *A Systems Analysis of Political Life* (New York: John Wiley & Sons, 1965).

"enable the most efficient use of the manpower, facilities, and resources of the American people," [17] evoked a feeble response from his colleagues. (After all, if someone is convinced of the efficacy of the ongoing process, what incentive does he have to examine its outcomes?) A major methodological development has been the comparative study of state politics. Some scholars have taken advantage of the opportunities for multijurisdictional comparisons to correlate policy outcomes with certain economic and political characteristics.[18] Several of these studies call into question the pluralist assumption that the group process produces representative and desirable outcomes. Where these first methodological steps will lead is difficult to anticipate. Yet if it is true that researchers tend to follow their methodologies, the development of new systems techniques will have an impact on future conceptions of political reality. We might expect novel efforts to evaluate the performance of political systems and the quality of public policies. This is the forecast issued by Gabriel Almond in his 1968 Benedict Lectures at Boston University.[19] It is likely that when political scientists begin to probe policy outcomes, many will cast off the pretense of neutrality and take explicitly normative positions in evaluating the outcomes.[20]

More influential than the methods will be the level of dissatisfaction with political life. As more scholars become sensitive to politics in which there are losers and to a political world beset by scarcities, there will be a growing unwillingness to accept the process and its outcomes as given. In this connection, Michael Harrington's *The Other America* warrants notice because of the actions it provoked. For so many, the book was a revelation, bringing into sight and mind what long had been obscured by the pluralists' decision-making models. Its message was forthright: not everyone is protected and represented by the group mechanism. Not everyone benefits from the way politics works in the United States. There are unfavorable outcomes, and some of them are the results of the very processes and policies that have been established

[17] Harold D. Lasswell, "The Policy Orientation," in Daniel Lerner and Harold D. Lasswell (eds.), *The Policy Sciences* (Stanford: Stanford University Press, 1951), p. 3. The call for policy or systems analysis often is coupled with a comment on resource scarcity and the need for optimization.

[18] Thomas R. Dye, *Politics, Economics, and the Public: Policy Outcomes in the American States* (Chicago: Rand McNally, 1966); and Ira Sharkansky, *Spending in the American States* (Chicago: Rand McNally, 1968.

[19] Gabriel Almond, *Perspectives on Political Development*, Benedict Lectures on Political Philosophy, March 18–20, 1968, Boston University.

[20] In explaining why behavioral political scientists have emphasized process over content, Austin Ranney observes that many scholars "think that focusing on content is likely to lead to evaluations of present policies and exhortations for new ones," "The Study of Policy Content: A Framework for Choice," in *Items* (Washington, D.C.: Social Science Research Council, September 1968).

over the past 35 years. Once the spotlight was turned on outcomes, the weaknesses of the old processes became more conspicuous. Hence the search for new processes: community action, "maximum feasible participation," income guarantees, neighborhood cooperations, taking to the streets.

The systems mood became political reality when the President decided to "go public" with PPB. Viewed from the White House, what might have been some of the attractive features of PPB? During the initial part of his presidency, Lyndon Johnson displayed two characteristics that might have induced dissatisfaction with the pluralist processes: (1) a desire for involvement and initiative in program development and (2) an insistence on scrutinizing existing programs. Both characteristics required some modification in the rules of incremental choice; the first because it meant presidential rather than bureau leadership in program development; the second because it meant presidential rejection of the "preferred position" of last year's budget.

The traditional budget processes are unsuited for an active presidential role. In the usual bureaucratic pattern, budgetary power is located at the lower echelons, with successively higher levels having declining power and less involvement. By the time the budget reaches the President, most of the decisions have been made for him in the form of existing programs and incremental bureau claims. Barring unusual exertion, the President's impact is marginal, cutting some requests and adding some items of his own. PPB may have been perceived as a means of establishing the presidency earlier and more effectively in the making of budgetary and program policy. (No claim is made here that the President saw PPB as a vitalizer of his budgetary power or in a systems context. But the very arrival of PPB is strong evidence of high-level dissatisfaction with the status quo processes.)

Dissatisfaction is not enough to sway political leaders to underwrite an innovation. They also must have confidence that the new way is workable and desirable. This optimism was fueled by the Great Society mood. There was confidence in the ability of government to eradicate hard-core social and human problems, and in its ability to specify and reach long-range objectives. A few years earlier President Kennedy had predicted a moon landing in this decade; why not set concrete targets for a wide range of social endeavors? PPB was perceived as an effective apparatus for identifying legitimate national objectives and for measuring progress toward their attainment. PPB's objectives would be operational and reachable, politically appealing yet based on socioeconomic analysis, not just the expedients of politicians or the dreams of futurists. PPB's objectives would be presidential, marking the accomplishments of his administration.

The legislative explosion of the first Johnson years may have supplied another incentive. A President who was intensely concerned with building a program and legislative record was impelled to become an administrative innovator. This pattern parallels the course of New Deal politics. Following his unsurpassed legislative accomplishments, President Roosevelt appointed his Committee on Administrative Management and embarked on a battle for reorganization that was to culminate in the establishment of the Executive Office of the President and the growth of the budget function to its contemporary status. In both the New Deal and the Great Society, basic changes in program goals aggravated and exposed the organizational deficiencies rooted in the bureau-congressional committee-interest group axis that dominates the pluralists processes. There is reason to believe that the President viewed PPB as an opening prong in a major overhaul of federal organization, an expectation that was aborted by the Vietnam situation.

While economists and analysts have been credited and debited for PPB's debut, many hands and influences have been involved. One can even go back to the waning years of the Eisenhower Administration, to the commissions on national goals and purpose. These quests reflected disenchantment with the drift of the period, the lack of purpose or progression. As one expression of this temper, PPB has attracted both conservative and liberal sponsorship. The conservative version is based on the conviction that public outputs are not worth the private cost and that multiyear projections would disclose the ominous growth in government spending implicit in current policies. The motives of the liberals are more complex. They are confident that public objectives are worth the cost, but they also feel that existing programs are not producing optimal outcomes.[21]

Political Process Deficiencies

If systems politics is in step with the times, it is because the political process has been found wanting. The imperfections have produced unsatisfactory outcomes. But it would be senseless to discard the process because it is deficient: we can compensate for its weaknesses. This is what economists have done with the market.

The pluralist process is based on competition among interest groups. Its archetype is the economic model of competition among buyers and sellers. But the economists have come to reject a total reliance on

[21] Thus Governor Reagan has emphasized multi-year projections in his application of PPB in California government. A liberal's concept of PPB is suggested in Michael Harrington's *Toward A New Democratic Left* (New York: Macmillan, 1968).

the market's capability to allocate all resources efficiently or equitably. They have identified several classes of market limitations, the most important of which pertain to public goods and external costs and benefits. They also have identified certain characteristics of imperfect markets, in which competition is restricted, supply and demand are controlled or manipulated, and prices are administered. The pluralists still are in their *laissez faire* period. They attribute few faults to their political market. But the economic market supplies useful analogs for the appraisal of the political process. It is reasonable to expect that a political process which is modeled on market competition will exhibit many of the deficiencies of the economic market itself. Yet for many of the market defects and limitations, economists have looked to government for corrective action. Accordingly, the political process might reinforce rather than combat market inadequacies. As a first step toward conceiving a political process that is free of market-like defects, I propose to develop a taxonomy of political process deficiencies.

Public Goods

Goods that are available to all consumers, whether or not they pay for them, cannot be supplied efficiently by the private economy. For such public goods, nonmarket institutions, usually but not exclusively governmental, are used for determining how much should be provided.

In transferring the case of public goods from the private sector to the polity, economists assume that collective values will prevail. But the political process, as conceived by the pluralists, operates via competition. Is the process of political competition superior to, or different from, the process of market competition in deciding public goods issues? If government were to provide public goods on the basis of some public interest determinant—in terms of systems criteria—it might be superior to the market, for there would be a means of evaluating the social costs and benefits to the whole polity of an investment in national defense, space exploration, or other public goods. But when private group influences prevail, the result is that public goods are produced and distributed on the basis of private calculations. Perversely, something which economists regard as a public good, our pluralists regard as a private good. Take the case of defense. An economist would argue that we all receive, more or less, the same benefits. The pluralists would have to argue, however, that we do not benefit equally, for the defense establishment and military contractors get more out of defense spending than the rest of us do. Thus, while each of us is equally defended, we do not equally benefit from the production of defense.

Whether the supply of public goods will be distorted by the polity depends on the shape of group politics. When an influential group gains disproportionately from a public good, society may produce too much of it. Since we all gain some benefit from defense, we do not have the usual checks and balances that operate in the case of private goods. A swollen or misallocated defense budget may result. When the public good is promoted by a weak group, too little of the good might be produced. Perhaps this is what has hobbled the national movement for pure air. (Some pluralists now speak of two polities, one with the ordinary interplay of group interests, the other where the group process is subordinate.[22] The latter sector consists mainly of the national security and foreign policy areas which consume a huge portion of our public wealth and deal with the survival of this nation and the world.)

Externalities

A second class of allocative decisions which cannot be entrusted completely to the competitive market pertains to external costs and benefits. A classic case of an external cost is the discharge of pollutants into the air; the polluter does not pay for the social cost he engenders. An external benefit results when the beneficiary does not have to pay for another's largess. Some economists regard education as such a benefit because society benefits but does not pay for the investments I make in my own education. While the market can supply goods that carry external costs or benefits, it is not capable of producing them in the optimal quality or quantity. It would tend to overproduce goods that have external costs, and to underproduce those that provide external benefits.

Because of this market disability, the public sector gets the call. In the case of an external cost such as air pollution, the job of government would be to make the pollutor pay (through taxation, regulation, fines, or some other mode) so that his cost equals the social cost. For an external benefit such as education, government would require all members of the community to pay some share of the cost. But in a competitive polity, the group process might stimulate rather than inhibit the production of goods with external costs. After all, one of the aims of an interest group is to get others to pay for your benefits or to avoid paying your share of the costs. As a result, government can and does play Robin Hood in reverse, taking from the poor and giving to the rich. Urban renewal is a case in point. Government's fiscal and legal powers were used by developers to impose all sorts of costs on residents and shopkeepers

[22] Ex., Aaron Wildavsky, "The Two Presidencies," *Trans-Action*, December 1966, pp. 7–14.

in the renewal area. Sometimes powerful interests can engineer public policy to obtain rewards for imposing costs on the community. Thus we hear proposals to award tax credits to air polluters in order to motivate them to cease their harmful activity. Where there are external benefits, powerful beneficiaries may refuse to tax themselves for their gain.

Why doesn't the unseen hand of group competition keep everyone honest, making the polluter pay for the costs he imposes and society for the benefits it receives? The obvious answer is that not all interests are equally powerful. Polluters probably have better lobbies than city residents who breathe the air. And they use their political power to ratify, not to countermand, the edict of the market.

Income Distribution

Left to its own wills, the market will produce a distribution of income in which some have very much and some have very little. In a capitalist polity, we tend not to regard the possession of wealth as an evil, but we have become concerned about those who are poor. Hence the array of welfare programs that have grown over the past 35 years. Certainly these programs have resulted in a net redistribution of income in favor of low-income groups. But the results are not one-sided, as indicated by the regressive social security tax structure, the welfare problems, and some of the housing programs.

But the basic income distribution established by the market has not been greatly affected by public micropolicy. (Macropolicy, the stimulation of economic growth, definitely has had considerable impact on the numbers of people living below the poverty line.) The poor subsist under welfare; they also subsisted under the poor laws. Often the poor are denied the bootstraps that might enable them to rise above the poverty level. We rarely redistribute wealth by giving the poor money; instead we give them benefits in kind. These are woefully inefficient from an economic point of view (as the conservatives tell us) and woefully inadequate from a social viewpoint (as the liberals have discovered). Somehow, however, they are efficient and desirable from a political standpoint. There are several explanations for this anomaly (see the paragraphs below on imperfect competition and ideology). The main reason is that the poor lack not only money but political power as well. They cannot compete fully in political life because they lack money, status, self-confidence, political skill, and group and bureaucratic representation. Perhaps there can be no effective redistribution of income unless there is a concomitant redistribution of political power. But the established group structure is committed to the prevailing distribution of power because it is advantaged by that distribution, just as those who are economically potent tend to approve the market distribution of incomes. In order to achieve a meaningful redistribution of political resources, it might be necessary to challenge the group norms that undergird the political process, that is, to contest the legitimacy of the process itself.

Imperfect Competition

A market with few buyers and sellers will not produce the right outcomes; neither will a polity which is itself oligopolistic. The political process possesses the same tendencies toward concentration that drive competition from the market. In both instances there are advantages in bigness and in the ability to control resources. We have the Big Three in automobile production and the Big Two in political parties. While they are not interchangeable players, the robber baron and the boss had much in common, and so do the contemporary elites in business and government.[23] Powerful men have not been known to favor competition when competition does not favor them. In pluralist politics there is a special kind of market imperfection. Four-fifths of the population, according to most reckonings, is fairly affluent. When we speak of 30 or 40 million poor people, we tend to forget the political implications of the 160 or 170 million who are not poor. It is of great ideological import that the rise of pluralist politics coincided with the emergence of an advantaged majority and disadvantaged minority. At the very time the pluralists were celebrating minorities rule,[24] we had become a homogeneous majority of affluents. Under the guise of consensus, we had a new kind of tyranny of the majority—not a deliberate or invidious tyranny, but one of political incapability to deal with the interests of the minority. John K. Galbraith spelled out the economic and social implications in *The Affluent Society*.[25] As Mills argued, what passed for political competition were petty family quarrels, but the big issues went unchallenged.

How then have things begun to change in the cities and the ghettos? I would not leave altruism out of the answer, nor the efforts of activists and analysts who have warred against the established process and its stark outcomes. But the number one factor is that the poor and the

[23] It is not necessary, however, to accept Mills' view of interlocking military-industrial-political directorates to acknowledge the affinities in their behavior.
[24] The "minorities rule" phrase along with its theoretical elaboration is in Robert A. Dahl, *A Preface to Democratic Theory* (Chicago: University of Chicago Press, 1956).
[25] Much of Galbraith's thesis was misunderstood, and especially his comments on poverty.

blacks are becoming majorities in our inner cities, those strategic centers of communications and commerce that remain vital to suburban interests.

Not only did the affluence of the period create a new set of majority interests; it also turned would-be competitors into allies. As Galbraith has pointed out, countervailing power (which he carefully differentiates from pluralist competition) does not function well "when there is inflation or inflationary pressure on markets." [26] Unions can conspire with management to gain higher wages and to pass the cost on to consumers. In the political arena, interests can logroll and pass the cost on to taxpayers. Only under conditions of scarcity is competition an efficient allocator of resources. This is one important reason why systems politics converges with the politics of scarcity.

Ideology

According to the principles of competition, both economic man and political man know their own interests and fight for them against the competing interests of others. But one of the things a political process can do is to make people not know their own interests. In the market it is somewhat difficult to misdirect people; there is the profit motive and the relatively unambiguous price mechanism. In politics it's a lot easier; you use ideology to do the job. Any successful mode of political inquiry becomes a set of biases, encumbering its practitioners from viewing the world from some alternative perspective. Pluralism, more and more of us are willing to concede, became a statement of the way politics ought to be, not merely a descriptive summing up of the way it is. As political reality began to move from group pluralism to group conflict, many political scientists were debarred by their concepts from recognizing the changes that were occurring. Only the cumulative hammerings of urban, racial, fiscal, diplomatic, and military crises have uprooted growing numbers from their pluralists anchorage.

To study the workings of political interests, the pluralists refined the art and science of public opinion polling, asking citizens about every conceivable issue and reporting the results with statistical fidelity. They also studied power to communities to determine who participates in the making of decisions and which interests get their way. Both techniques assume that there are no ideological impediments to interest formation and expression. Two very different scholars, C. Wright Mills and Joseph

---

[26] John Kenneth Galbraith, *American Capitalism* (Boston: Houghton Mifflin Company, Sentry Edition, 1962), p. 128 ff.

Schumpeter, argued to the contrary. The Marxist thread in Mills leads to this statement:

> What men are interested in is not always what is to their interest; the troubles they are aware of are not always the ones that beset them . . . it is not only that men can be unconscious of their situations; they are often falsely conscious of them.[27]

Schumpeter took the view that the conditions of modern politics inevitably dull man's capacity to form a political will:

> Thus the typical citizen drops to a lower level of mental performance as soon as he enters the political field. He argues and analyzes in a way which he would readily recognize as infantile within the sphere of his real interests. . . . the will of the people is the product and not the motive power of the political process.[28]

Schumpeter anticipates and rejects the pluralist response that groups act as surrogates for individual interests, converting the ignorance of the voter into a powerful political asset, and possessing a collective intelligence that compensates for the citizen's lack of knowledge. But rather than serving as representatives of individual interests, groups "are able to fashion and, within very wide limits, even to create the will of the people. What we are confronted with in the analysis of political processes is largely not a genuine but a manufactured will." [29]

The community power studies often were exhaustive in their coverage, but they covered very little. Banfield was able to find only six controversies of citywide importance in the Chicago of 1957 and 1958, and none of them dealt with the guts of living in a mass urban environment. Apparently the political process already had dried up the wells of conflict, relegating the important things to what Bachrach and Baratz aptly termed "nondecisions." It is the "mobilization of biases," E. E. Schattschneider wrote in his last antipluralist work that determines the scope of political conflict.[30]

Ideology is one critical reason why people do not always know their own interests, why there are so few controversies. The political process socializes its citizens to accept certain norms and rules as legiti-

---

[27] C. Wright Mills, *White Collar* (New York: Galaxy Books, 1956), p. xix.
[28] Joseph A. Schumpeter, *Capitalism, Socialism and Democracy*, Third Edition (New York: Harper Torchbooks, 1962), pp. 262–263.
[29] *Ibid.*, p. 263.
[30] E. E. Schattschneider, *The Semisovereign People* (New York: Holt, Rinehart and Winston, 1960).

mate, not to be challenged or questioned. The myopics who have climbed the political socialization bandwagon (the successor to community power studies) look at the small things like who is Democratic and who is Republican, as if Tweedledee and Tweedledum made much difference, and all the time they neglect the big questions of the citizens' linkage to the polity.

"My chief objection," Christian Bay has said, "is not to a pluralist society but to a pluralist political theory." This theory "does not jibe with what political scientists *know* about the power of elites or the techniques of mass manipulation." [31] Under the cover of pluralism, elites flourished, but they were given new, deceptive titles: the active minority, opinion leaders, decision makers. Rarely were they identified in terms of the power they wielded or in terms of the gaps between mass and elite, powerful and powerless, manipulator and manipulated. All were given statistical equality and anonymity in the opinion polls.

The pluralists thought that their age was "The End of Ideology." Looking backward, we can see it as the triumph of an ideology—the ideology of pluralism. For pluralism became more a norm than a fact, the glorification of the bargain and the status quo, the sanctification of consensus and stability. Elite interests benefited from these norms; minority interests were constrained by them.

Immobility of Resources

Unlike water, economic resources such as labor and capital do not always flow to the right place. There can be barriers to their mobility. Unemployed miners remain in Appalachia and subsistence farmers on their farms. Bankers put their money downtown, not in Harlem where the interest rates are higher. One responsibility of government is to stimulate mobility via subsidies, loans, and regulatory devices.

There also can be immobility of political resources, by which I mean the failure of the political process to behave in response to numbers. For in a democratic polity, numbers (weighted for intensity of interest) is the key resource. Over the long run, this political resource tends to attract power. If Negroes move into a city and come to outnumber the whites, they ultimately will take over the elective offices, much as the Irish displaced the Yankees. But there are at least two kinds of impediments to the free flow of numbers—structural and ideological. All sorts of structural roadblocks stand in the way of interests which have

[31] Christian Bay, "Needs, Wants, and Political Legitimacy," *Canadian Journal of Political Science*, September 1968, p. 252.

the votes and want the power. Legislative apportionment, the committee system, parliamentary rules, seniority, federalism, the balkanization of metropolitan regions, bureaucratic patterns, election laws—whatever justification they may have, these structures have the potential of depriving interests of their just political fruits. Sometimes the structures are contrived for this purpose (gerrymandering, for instance); sometimes they evolve over many years of inaction (urban sprawl); sometimes they are abolished (as in the case of legislative malapportionment).

The second factor is a product of the incremental character of political choice. What economics writes off as sunk cost, politics rewards as a vested interest. The incremental ideology has the effect of immobilizing numbers because it protects status quo interests. Each incremental move forecloses additional opportunities, with the consequence that the iron grip of the past is tightened with each successive decision. Of the $180 billion in the budget, only a tiny fragment is actionable. A President who would war on poverty today has fewer options than Franklin Roosevelt had in his time. By the time the pluralist process reached its zenith, the political world was almost immobilized by the accumulation of previous commitments. (In his study of state expenditures, Ira Sharkansky shows that previous expenditures are an excellent predictor of current spending. For selected years between 1913 and 1965 he has computed the deviation between actual and incrementally predicted spending. For the years prior to 1957, an average of 22 states had a deviation of at least 15 percent. But for the years between 1957 and 1965, only seven states had a 15 percent deviation of actual from predicted spending.) [32] Lindblom was right. You can move far with incrementalism, but only in the direction in which you started.[33]

It is not surprising that Pareto norms became popular to some sophisticated pluralists. The economists' justification of the status quo had more appeal than their own "veto group" concept. By 1965 politics was a massive Pareto optimum. In politics the optimum almost always is what is; at least one person (or group) would be displeased by any proposed change. Every moment of the Vietnam war has been Pareto optimal; regardless of the political or military conditions, every moment was justifiable in terms of any alternative.[34]

[32] Ira Sharkansky, op. cit., Table III-8.
[33] See Charles E. Lindblom, A Strategy of Decision (Glencoe, N.Y.: The Free Press, 1963).
[34] In this light, it is understandable why public opinion polls fluctuated with Administration policy in Vietnam before the Tet crisis. Tet revealed some of the true outcomes of the war.

Representation

There is one kind of imperfection in the political process that has no market analogy. While the market is impelled by hidden levers, the polity is dependent on a representative mechanism, whether electoral, bureaucratic, or group. There is no other way to convert numbers and preferences democratically into policy. Many have written on the inadequacies of representation; the structural impediments mentioned above; the ignorance of the electorate and its limited "yes-no" vocabulary; the under- or over-representation of group interests; the tendency of group leaders to represent themselves rather than their members; the conspiratorial relationship between bureaucracies and their clienteles. The research of Nelson Polsby has added one more to this formidable inventory: the "institutionalization" of the House of Representatives (and, I suspect, of many other legislative bodies).[35]

It would take papers the length of this one to map all the blockages between citizens and their representatives. The sociopsychological studies of mass and elite call into question many critical aspects of voting and interest group theory. In sum, regarding all the modern institutions of representation, one can apply the characterization of Erich Fromm concerning the voting process:

> Between the act of voting and the most momentous high-level political decisions is a connection which is mysterious. One cannot say that there is none at all, nor can one say that the final decision is an outcome of the voter's will.[36]

The Status of Systems Budgeting

Just as the process strategies described by Wildavsky suited the politics of its times, so the systems vistas of PPB are in tune with the politics of its times. PPB is part of a larger movement of revision in political study and adjustment in political practice. But just as upheavals in political life have produced disorder and confusion, the new wave in budgeting has generated a good deal of costly disruption and obfuscation.

PPB has had a rough time these past few years. Confusion is widespread; results are meager. The publicity has outdistanced the perfor-

---

[35] See Nelson Polsby, "The Institutionalization of the U.S. House of Representatives," *American Political Science Review*, March 1968.
[36] Erich Fromm, *The Sane Society* (New York: Holt, Rinehart and Winston, Inc., 1955), p. 191.

mance by a wide margin. In the name of analysis, bureaus have produced reams of unsupported, irrelevant justification and description. As Schumpeter said of Marxism: it is preaching in the garb of analysis. Plans have been formulated without serious attention to objectives, resource constraints, and alternative opportunities. PPB's first years have been an exercise in technique. There have been the bulletins and the staffings, the program memoranda, and the program and financial plans. Those who have been apprehensive over possible threats to cherished political values can find no support for their fears in what has happened during these years. Those who had hoped that PPB would not succumb to the tyranny of technique can find much disappointment in what has happened. PPB's products have become its end-products. For so many practitioners, PPB is not some majestic scrutiny of objectives and opportunities, but going through the motions of doing a program structure, writing a program memorandum, of filling in the columns of a program and financial plan.

It is tempting to attribute PPB's difficulties to the manner in which it was introduced, for the implementation strategy has been faulty. But the decisive factor has been the prematurity of PPB.

The conceptual side of PPB presents something of a paradox. The important ideas are few in number and easy to understand. But they happen to run counter to the way American budgeting has been practiced for more than half a century. The concepts which took root in economics and planning will have to undergo considerable mutation before they can be successfully transplanted on political soil. PPB is an idea whose time has not quite come. It was introduced governmentwide before the requisite concepts, organizational capability, political conditions, informational resources, and techniques were adequately developed.[37] A decade ago, PPB was beyond reach; a decade or two hence, it, or some updated version, might be one of the conventions of budgeting. For the present, PPB must make do in a world it did not create and has not yet mastered.

It is hard to foretell PPB's exact course of development. Certainly there will be many PPB's arising out of the diverse roots and images of systems politics and budgeting, and also out of the diverse perceptions of budget participants and the diverse capabilities of governments. In a technical and methodological sense, there will be continual upgrading in the sophistication of systems budgeting. But there will be no revolutionary overthrow of process in politics. There is an understandable ten-

[37] These prematurities have been examined in Allen Schick, "PPB's First Years: Premature and Maturing" (Washington, D.C.: U.S. Bureau of the Budget, September 1968), mimeo.

dency in politics to rely on stable, consensual processes. The pluralists were right about many of their claims for the existing process, the way it reduces conflict and complexity. One can make much the same case for an established process which governs the relationships among competing interests. A permanent systems politics might mean permanent crisis, constant struggle over public ends and means.

I have indicated that the systems ferment is grounded in the conviction that the existing process produces unfavorable outcomes. If systems people had confidence in the process, it would make little sense to go through the costly and possibly divisive reappraisals involved in a systems analysis of objectives and alternatives. How, then, can we reconcile the tendency toward process equilibrium with the challenges to the established process? I think the answer is that systems politics will induce a revision in the process. The systems approach enables us to ascertain why the process yields imperfect outcomes. But like the market, we need not throw out the political process because it is deficient; we can compensate for its weaknesses. The task of systems politics is to correct for the defects by making adjustments in the process and by creating new institutions of power and choice. Optimally, the political process should have some gyroscopic capability to assess its outcomes rather than accept them on blind faith as the pluralists have. Budgeting will have a leading role in this readjustment because it is the closest thing politics has to a system for choice. The hybrid process that will emerge will be more responsive and efficient by virtue of the feedback from outcome to process.

ROBERT DORFMAN
HENRY D. JACOBY *

11

A Model of Public Decisions Illustrated by a Water Pollution Policy Problem

Merely corroborative detail, intended to give artistic verisimilitude to an otherwise bald and unconvincing narrative.

—W. S. Gilbert

Introduction

Governmental decisions may be approached from either a normative or a descriptive point of view. The normative approach accepts well-defined objectives for governmental undertakings and recommends specific policies and actions for attaining them. It will not be followed here. The descriptive approach accepts the facts of life, including the nature of governmental agencies and the purposes of diverse interest groups in the community, and attempts to provide insight into what will happen in the circumstances. That will be our approach.

Our method will be to construct a mathematical model of a political decision problem. The model will contain room for a great many data, ranging from the technological features of the problem that technical experts have to take into account, to the political objectives and pressures that responsible officials have to evaluate. One of the advantages that we claim for the model, indeed, is that it provides a systematic framework for assembling such diverse data.

From these data the model will produce, mechanically, some predictions about the outcome of the political decision process. These will not be unambiguous predictions like an astronomer's prediction of the

* Professors Dorfman and Jacoby teach at Harvard University. This article first appeared in Robert H. Haveman and Julius Margolis, eds., *Public Expenditures and Policy Analysis* (Chicago: Markham, 1970).

moment that an eclipse will take place. Rather, they will take the form
of stating a range of likely outcomes of the process, perhaps a fairly
wide range but still much more limited than all the decisions that might
be conceived of in advance. The power of a scientific theory, it has been
said, is measured not by what it asserts but by what it precludes. This
theory will preclude a great deal. Within the range of likely outcomes
the theory (or model) will provide some valuable information. It will
highlight the political alignments that make some of the outcomes more
likely than others and will indicate, rather specifically, the changes in
the configuration of political influence that will tend to shift the decision
from one outcome to another. Furthermore, it will express vividly just
how interests oppose and how different decisions affect the welfares of
different participants.

Concede, for the moment, that such a model is possible. Whether
this is so or not is for the sequel to determine. Then, surely, the practice
of politics should take it into account. (Note that we are being normative temporarily.) Any political decision should be made in the light of a
realistic assessment of its consequences, which requires a prediction of
how things, people, and political bodies will react to it. In the case of
water pollution control, for example, the federal government's policies
are implemented by the states and by river basin commissions; the
states and river basin commissions work through local agencies and authorities, individuals, and business firms. Any decision at the federal
level has to be based on a prediction about how the states and basin
commissions will respond to it; the states and basin authorities must
similarly predict the reactions of subordinate units and of the public at
large. Many other programs of federal and state agencies are similarly
affected by the responses of other governmental bodies. All legislation
that concerns the powers and composition of government agencies is influenced by predictions of how those provisions will influence the behavior of the agency. In short, a predictive model of political behavior can
help improve political decisions.

Constructing a predictive model of political decision processes is
an ambitious, indeed presumptuous, undertaking. In fact, there is such
good reason to believe that it cannot be done that we have construed
our main task to be to convince ourselves and the reader that it is possible. Our method of proof is what mathematicians call "constructive."
That is, rather than arguing the matter in the abstract we have considered a political decision problem taken from the field of water pollution
control (not a real problem, but one that catches the essence of real
problems) and have constructed a theoretical model that predicts the
outcome of the political decision process in that instance. This construc-

tion shows that such a model is a possibility and exhibits its main features. It does not show that this model is a practical tool of political analysis. That showing would be a major research undertaking. In order to show that this political model or any political model is empirically valid, it would be necessary to apply it to several real political decisions and to compare its predictions with the observed political behavior. This would be a laborious and expensive task, for it would necessitate ascertaining all the physical, technical, economic, and political data that the model requires and then performing elaborate computations. We have not undertaken this mammoth empirical enterprise (and not merely out of laziness). This large task is not worth undertaking unless the analytic model to be tested shows at least fair promise of success. A necessary preliminary to serious empirical testing is trial experimentation under favorable circumstances to see whether the model can be implemented in principle and whether it behaves sensibly. If the model passes the preliminary screening, then it pays to go further with it. This chapter reports on such a preliminary testing of our conceptual model of political decision. To carry out this test we have conceived an artificial basin with a pollution problem, known as the Bow River Valley. It is small, it is simple; but it could exist in the sense that it does not violate any known principles of hydrology, sanitary engineering, economics, or politics. We have populated this valley with a large industrial source of pollution, two moderate-sized cities and a recreation area, and placed it under the jurisdiction of a pollution control commission organized under the Clean Water Restoration Act of 1966. We have provided everyone concerned with such data and information as he might actually have under the circumstances and no more.[1] We have simplified the problem by suppressing much detail that would obscure the essential conflicts and issues that would arise. For example, we have reduced the specification of water quality to a single dimension, namely, dissolved oxygen concentration (DO), and we have limited our description of the waste content of the various municipal and industrial effluents to the number of pounds of biochemical oxygen demanding material (BOD) that they carry.[2] In addition, we have limited the powers of the regulatory authority essentially to a single decision, namely, regulation of level of treatment by each polluter. We have ignored hydrologic uncertainty and other probabilistic complications and have made any number of simplifying approximations to facilitate computation. In short, we have loaded the dice heavily in favor of the model, as is perhaps appropriate for a

[1] Or, anyway, not much more.
[2] The description of the problem necessarily involves some technical concepts, such as these. Most of them will be explained below.

preliminary test. The question is: can this problem be expressed by a formal analytic model, and if so, does the model provide sensible and useful insights?

The Test Problem

The situation which we shall use to try out our conceptual scheme is sketched in Figure 1.[3] As can be seen, the Bow River flows generally from north to south. It is a respectable stream with a flow of

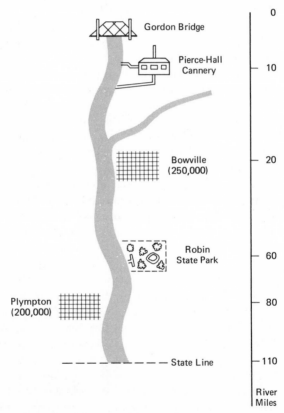

Figure 1. *Main features of the Bow River Valley*

[3] Professor Harold A. Thomas, Jr., acted as consulting engineer for this study. We are indebted to him for formulating and analyzing the hydrological and engineering aspects of our sample basin.

800 cfs during the summer months. But it is not a very high quality stream. Because of the residual waste from upstream cities, the river, as it passes under the Gordon Bridge, has a dissolved oxygen concentration of only 6.8 milligrams per liter (mg/l). Without the influence of effluent discharges upstream, one could expect the level of oxygen in the water to be near saturation (8.5 mg/l at summer water temperatures).

The northernmost installation in the region under consideration is the Pierce-Hall Cannery. This is a large but somewhat outmoded vegetable cannery with an annual production of slightly over 7 million equivalent cases a year, concentrated in the summer and autumn months. The cannery adds an ultimate BOD load of about one pound per case to the river, after primary treatment, to which it is already committed. The cannery is not very profitable. Its net operating revenues, allowing for the cost of primary waste treatment, are only about 7.5 percent of stockholders' equity. It employs about 800 workers, many of whom live in Bowville (pop. 250,000), ten miles downstream.

Bowville and the other riparian city, Plympton (pop. 200,000), are both fairly large centers supported by varied light manufacturing and commercial establishments serving the surrounding agricultural region. Both have waterfront parks of which they are proud, and Plympton in particular has some aspirations to being a tourist center because of its proximity to Robin State Park. Both cities discharge their wastes into the river after primary treatment. For simplicity, we shall assume that neither city anticipates that its population or its waste load will grow significantly in the foreseeable future. This simplification will save us from having to forecast growth rates and from having to consider the possibility of "building ahead of demand." In fact, it enables us to neglect all dynamic considerations.

Robin State Park, between Bowville and Plympton, has woodland recreational facilities. All concerned would like to develop its waterfront for boating, fishing, and if at all possible, swimming. The quality of the water does not permit those uses at present. The park is used by the inhabitants of both cities, by the neighboring farm population, and by some tourists and day-trippers from outside the valley. Everyone is agreed that the quality of the water in the neighborhood of the park should be improved.

Thirty miles below Plympton the river crosses a state line and flows out of our ken.

The current quality of the stream at critical points under low-flow conditions is shown in Figure 2. From just below Bowville down to the state line, water quality is very poor during summer droughts. For long stretches the river is anaerobic (i.e., the DO level falls to zero), and it is

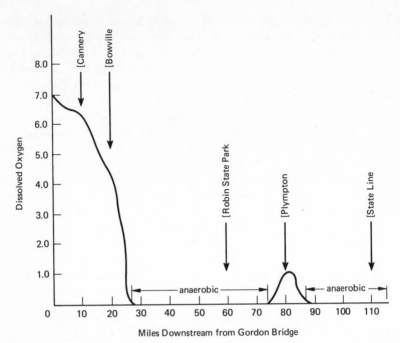

Figure 2. *Current water quality in the Bow River, summer drought conditions*

unfit for recreational or other use. In response to a generally felt need to improve the river, especially near the park, and in response to some pressure from the State Water Commission, the Bow Valley Water Pollution Control Commission has been established, with the editor of the *Bow Valley News* as chairman and membership drawn from the city councils of both cities and including the Deputy State Commissioner of Parks and Recreation.

The commission faces two crucial problems. The first is to determine the quality classification of the river which, for political reasons, must be the same from the Gordon Bridge to the state line.[4] The second problem is to decide on the levels of treatment to be required of the three sources of waste within its jurisdiction. The cost of the improvement in quality to each of the polluters is simply the cost of the treatment required of him. Each polluter would therefore like to have a low treatment requirement for himself, but sufficiently high ones for the others to permit the achievement of the quality standards for the stream classification that has been adopted. The standards are expressed entirely in terms of dissolved oxygen levels.

[4] Quality classifications will be explained more fully below.

Such are the decisions that we must analyze. But before considering how the commission as a body will act, we must see in more detail
how the problem looks from the point of view of each of the interested
parties.

The Pierce-Hall Cannery

The Pierce-Hall Cannery, located just 10 miles upstream from
Bowville, is a relatively large installation compared to other plants of
this type around the country: over the course of the 180-day canning
season the plant handles approximately 40,000 case equivalents per day
of a variety of fruits and vegetables. Most years gross sales amount to
around $25 million.

In response to mounting public concern for water quality, the
plant managers already have identified and incorporated some internal
process changes in order to reduce effluent volume and cut back on biological pollutants discharged into the Bow River, and they have installed primary treatment facilities in the form of screening and sedimentation equipment. Even after these changes, however, when the
plant is in full operation it discharges a waste stream of approximately
30 million gallons per day (mgd) which carries an ultimate biochemical
oxygen demand of 47,600 pounds per day.[5]

In order to reduce these waste flows further, Pierce-Hall would
have to install additional treatment facilities, and the plant manager has
already obtained preliminary estimates of the cost of different degrees of
improvement in effluent quality. These estimates are shown in Table 1.

As the table shows, 30 percent of the BOD in the Pierce-Hall effluent is removed in the firm's primary treatment plant. To accomplish
higher levels of BOD removal, the waste stream would be passed
through a tank where biological degradation—which in the absence of
treatment would occur in the stream itself—can take place under controlled conditions. The degree of purification can be varied over a wide
range by proper design of the plant. High degrees of BOD removal are
naturally more expensive than low.

From the wide range of possible choices, the engineering consultants to Pierce-Hall have provided two alternative secondary treatment
plant designs. The first, referred to rather loosely as a "low-efficiency

[5] In more detailed analyses of biochemical pollution, a distinction is made between
first-stage (or carbonaceous) and second-stage (or nitrogenous) BOD. For the purposes of this discussion, however, it is preferable to avoid the additional technical
discussion which this more complex specification would require. The original version
of this paper [5] did include consideration of the two-stage model of biochemical
degradation. [References in brackets may be found at the end of this article.]

Table 1 Cost of Additional Waste Treatment at Pierce-Hall Cannery

Type of Treatment	Percent° of BOD Removed	Additional Annual Cost ($/yr)	Additional Net Cost to Pierce-Hall ($/yr)	Additional Cost to Pierce-Hall Per % removed ($/yr/%)	Profit After Taxes ($/yr)
Primary (now in place)	30	0	0	0	375,000
Primary *plus* Low Efficiency Secondary	80	13,000	8,000	160	367,000
Primary *plus* High Efficiency Secondary	90	59,000	35,000	2,700	340,000
Primary *plus* High Efficiency Secondary *plus* Tertiary	95	159,000	95,000	12,000	280,000

° The figures shown are percentages of the *gross* waste load.

166

secondary" plant, would bring the total removal up to 80 percent of the original load. The total cost for the low-efficiency unit would be $13,000 per year as shown in the second column of Table 1. The second design, referred to (again rather loosely) as a "high-efficiency secondary" unit, would accomplish a greater total waste removal, 90 percent. The cost, however, is considerably greater as shown in column two of the table.

If it is necessary to subject the effluent from a high-efficiency plant to still further treatment, there is yet another set of processes, generally referred to as "tertiary treatment," which may be used. In effect, tertiary

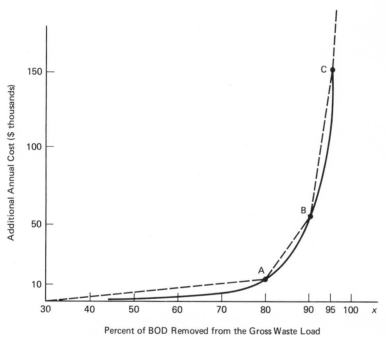

Figure 3. *Cost function for additional waste treatment at Pierce-Hall Cannery*

treatment is any process which reduces the waste contained in the effluent of a secondary unit, by such diverse and expensive methods as holding in stabilization ponds and adding special chemicals. One such design has been provided by Pierce-Hall's consultants. It would remove up to 95 percent of the firm's biochemical wastes. As may be seen in Table 1, tertiary treatment costs considerably more than "secondary" processes.

Of course the plants shown in Table 1 are only three of an infinite number of alternative designs. The curvilinear cost function in Figure 3 indicates the actual range of alternatives, with additional treatment cost stated as a function of the percentage removal of BOD from the gross waste load. Because the cannery already has primary treatment facilities, the zero point on the cost curve is at the 30 percent removal level. Since the data are so limited, we shall interpolate linearly between the data points provided by the consultants to estimate the cost of levels of removal other than 80, 90, and 95 percent. The resulting piecewise linear cost function is shown as a dashed line in the figure. For example, Figure 3 shows that a plant that brings total BOD removal up to 60 percent of the gross waste load would cost $7,800 per year.[6]

The net cost of waste treatment to Pierce-Hall is lower than this total cost because of the provisions of the corporation income tax code. Pierce-Hall's accountants have estimated that the net cost to the firm would be 6/10 of the total cost, and this latter figure is shown in the third column of the table. Column four presents the same information, expressed in terms of the net cost of each additional percent of waste removed from the plant's effluent. Thus, the figures in column four are the slopes of the piecewise linear cost function as sensed by Pierce-Hall management.

The firm's net operating revenues, after income taxes, are 1.5 percent of gross sales when primary treatment only is employed. This net profit amounts to approximately $375,000 a year, which is equivalent to 7.5 percent of the stockholders' equity. The firm is not a price leader and does not anticipate that it will be able to raise its prices appreciably even if a large increase in treatment costs is imposed. Neither does it know of any changes in its methods of processing that would enable it to reduce its waste load at the current scale of operations. Therefore any increase in treatment costs would have to come out of net profits. The estimated impact of different levels of treatment on net profits is also shown in Table 1. Notice that the effect is appreciable; the highest level of treatment would reduce annual profits by over 25 percent.

On the other hand, the management of Pierce-Hall is not adamantly opposed to improving the quality of the Bow River, even at some cost to themselves. As the major industrial polluter in this reach of the river, they recognize that they have some responsibility to users and inhabitants farther downstream. Besides, many of their employees live in Bowville and make use of Robin Park, so that improvement of the river will enhance the amenities available to the plant's workforce. Finally,

[6] Or from the table: $\dfrac{60-30}{80-30}(13{,}000)=\$7{,}800.$

the firm has some tentative plans for expanding by constructing a more modern plant on a site near Plympton. The efficiency of the branch plant would be greatly increased if the river near Plympton were of good enough quality to be tapped for washing water, which it is not at present. But the management also keeps in mind that it will not be able to raise the capital necessary for expansion if the return on the present equity falls below about 6 percent.

In short, the position of the Pierce-Hall management is a bit complicated. The prospect of improving the quality of the river is both a threat and an opportunity. They would like to see the river improved but do not feel that they can afford to contribute very much toward bringing improvement about.

Bowville

The city of Bowville, ten miles downstream from the cannery, is the second major source of pollution in the valley. The city receives better quality water than her downstream neighbors. According to the data in Figure 2, Bowville escapes the real pollution problems even during severe summer droughts. But the 250,000 inhabitants plus assorted light industries dump a heavy load of wastes into the river. Even after primary treatment, Bowville discharges 123,000 pounds of ultimate BOD into the river on an average summer day. The total volume of effluent discharged is about 51 mgd. This load, added to the cannery wastes, renders the river unsuitable for recreational use farther downstream.

In anticipation of the prospective discussions of pollution management in the valley, the mayor of Bowville requested his public works department to prepare estimates of what it would cost the city to install additional treatment facilities. Like the cannery, cost estimates were made for three different treatment plant designs, each removing a certain percentage of oxygen demanding wastes. These estimates are shown in Table 2.

Bowville would not have to bear the total cost of additional treatment unaided. Under the provisions of the Federal Water Pollution Control Act, Bowville could count on a federal grant in the amount of 50 percent of the construction cost of these facilities, and since capital cost is about half the total cost of waste treatment in this case, the citizens and local industries would have to bear only abou⁺ 75 percent of the total outlay. The adjusted costs are shown in the third column of Table 2. All these costs are based on the assumption of a twenty-year life of facilities and a 5 percent interest rate. As was true for the cannery, both the total costs of different degrees of waste removal and the

Table 2 Cost of Additional Waste Treatment at Bowville

Type of Treatment	Percent[*] of BOD Removed	Additional Annual Cost ($/yr)	Additional Cost to City ($/yr)	Additional Cost to City Per % removed ($/yr/%)	Addition to Property Tax Rate ($/thousand)
Primary (now in place)	30	0	0	0	0
Primary plus Low Efficiency Secondary	80	650,000	490,000	9,800	1.17
Primary plus High Efficiency Secondary	90	880,000	660,000	17,000	1.58
Primary plus High Efficiency Secondary plus Tertiary	95	2,520,000	1,890,000	246,000	4.52

[*] The figures shown are percentages of the *gross* waste load.

net costs to the city can be approximated by segmented linear cost curves of the type shown in Figure 3.

Table 2 shows also the estimated effect of the different levels of treatment on the property tax rate. These data are of particular interest to city officials and taxpayers. It is seen that the adoption of either high- or low-efficiency secondary treatment would have only a moderate effect on the property tax rate. (It is now $63.50 per thousand assessed valuation.) Tertiary treatment is far more expensive and the city comptroller has expressed some alarm that it might be adopted. He points out that tax rates are bound to rise in any event, because of recent increases in teachers' and firemen's salaries, and that they are already higher than tax rates in Plympton, which competes with Bowville for new industries.[7]

It appears that Bowville would gain only moderately from improvement in the quality of the Bow River. Bowville Waterfront Park is already a fine facility, although under extreme drought conditions the beach must be closed to swimming. If the river were cleaned up, these incidents could be avoided. In addition, the entire valley would be made more attractive to tourists and vacationers and, if the improvement were sufficient to permit the development of water-based recreation at Robin State Park, the park would become far more useful to inhabitants of the city. This latter consideration is important. Bowville Waterfront Park is already so overcrowded that some thought has been given to condemning some adjacent warehouses in order to expand it. This would not be necessary if any substantial proportion of the users could be diverted to the state park.

Besides, the *Bow River News* has been running editorials like, "Restore the Bow River!" and, after droughts, "The Shame of Bow River Valley." So there is considerable pressure on Bowville to contribute its share to improving the river, provided that the cost is reasonable.

Plympton

The difference between Plympton and Bowville is the difference between upstream and downstream riparian residents everywhere. Bowville has good water in all but the worst drought years; Plympton expe-

---

[7] There are many ways for a city to finance waste treatment facilities other than by the property tax as we assume here. Alternative financing methods differ not only in the impact of a particular facility on the city budget and in the distribution of costs among households and business firms; they also affect the total amount of waste to be handled. For example, certain types of sewer fees offer an incentive for industries and commercial establishments to cut back on total waste by means of internal process changes, while financing by the property tax offers no such incentive.

riences poor river-quality conditions almost every summer. Bowville's wastes degrade the river for most of the distance that concerns us, including the waterfront at Plympton; Plympton's wastes discommode no one, affecting only the quality checkpoint at the southern outlet of the valley. Bowville can improve the quality of the river by subjecting its wastes to a higher level of treatment; Plympton is virtually helpless—it cannot even protect its own waterfront. The stage is set for the classic conflict between upstream and downstream users.

Plympton is slightly smaller than Bowville and generally less affluent. It also has a primary treatment plant. Its effluent volume is 43 mgd, containing after primary treatment 92,400 pounds of ultimate BOD.

Although Plympton has, in fact, little effect on the quality of the river in the region that concerns us, it must expect to bear its share of responsibility for cleaning up the river. Indeed, since the inhabitants of Plympton will be the major direct beneficiaries of improved quality in the river, this city is particularly eager to contribute what it can and put pressure on the more consequential users upstream. The cost data for treatment at Plympton are shown in Table 3, and these also can be expressed as a cost function of the type shown in Figure 3. If you compare these data with the cost table for Bowville, you will see that the dollars-and-cents cost of each level of treatment are lower for Plympton, because it is a smaller city, but the effect on the tax rate is greater. This is because Plympton is a poorer city and the value of taxable property per capita is lower there. Fiscal problems are generally harder for Plympton than for Bowville.

It is true, nevertheless, that Plympton is more eager to participate in a program of river quality improvement than Bowville is. They would like to develop recreational facilities on their own waterfront, which does not now conform to sanitary standards and is occasionally beset by riverine odors. They are more dependent than Bowville on tourism and are closer to the park. For all these reasons, the Plympton Chamber of Commerce is one of the leaders in the movement for improving the river.

Other Interested Parties

The cannery and the two cities are the principal defilers of the river and represent the interests of most of the people who are directly concerned. But there are other interests too, which have to be taken into account and which are likely to have considerable influence on any decisions about the river.

First, there is the federal government, which has an expressed in-

Table 3 Cost of Additional Waste Treatment at Plympton

Type of Treatment	Percent[a] of BOD Removed	Additional Annual Cost ($/yr)	Additional Cost to City ($/yr)	Additional Cost to City Per % removed ($/yr/%)	Addition to Property Tax Rate ($/thousand)
Primary (now in place)	30	0	0	0	0
Primary plus Low Efficiency Secondary	80	550,000	410,000	8,200	1.37
Primary plus High Efficiency Secondary	90	730,000	550,000	14,000	1.83
Primary plus High Efficiency Secondary plus Tertiary	95	2,110,000	1,580,000	206,000	5.27

[a] The figures shown are percentages of the *gross* waste load.

173

terest in protecting and improving the quality of all interstate waters, including the Bow. This national interest is implemented by the Federal Water Pollution Control Administration. The FWPCA administers the grant and incentive programs established under federal water quality legislation, and it can be expected to contribute generously to meeting the costs of increased levels of waste treatment undertaken by the two municipalities. The FWPCA also has some enforcement powers.

The FWPCA's interest in the particular decision taken by the commission is twofold. First, it is responsible for protecting the interests of all users farther downstream, so that it feels compelled to, and is empowered to, insist on a reasonable quality of water at the southern outlet from the valley. Specifically, the FWPCA has required that the river should meet Class C standards (as described below) at the state line. It should be noted that the FWPCA is the only participant with a direct concern for the quality of the water so far south. Second, the FWPCA has a generalized interest in the quality of American streams and in protecting our natural heritage, and thus will share the desires of the inhabitants of Bowville and Plympton for the quality of their waters and for the waterfront potential of the state park. It will, however, be less worried about the effect of increased treatment costs on local tax rates and more concerned with the national economic costs which different plans will imply. On balance, we can expect that the FWPCA will attempt to induce the commission to undertake a combination of stream classification and treatment requirements that will yield the maximum benefit-cost ratio from a national point of view—taking into account the economic cost of abatement measures and the national economic and social benefits of different degrees of improvement in stream quality.

The state government is also concerned, particularly through the State Water and Sanitation Commission, and the State Department of Parks and Recreation. The State Industrial Commission may take a hand, however, if the financial health of the cannery should be jeopardized by any proposal. On balance, the influence of the state agencies can be expected to be similar to that of the FWPCA except that the state will attach more importance to the quality of the water at Robin State Park and less to the quality at the state line.

There are, in addition, a variety of conservation and special interest groups, perhaps typified by a branch of the Izaak Walton League. Although they have little voting power, these groups make their influence felt through all the media of public communications, through any hearings or investigative procedures of the Bow Valley Water Pollution Control Commission, through participation in municipal politics, and even through direct representation on the commission.

All the groups mentioned in this subsection share a more keenly felt concern for the quality and usability of the river than for the cost of achieving high quality. For the purposes of our discussion, we shall lump them together and consider them to be represented adequately by the FWPCA.

Water Quality Standards

The first task before the Bow Valley Water Pollution Control Commission is to adopt a stream-use classification for the Bow River between Bowville and the southern outlet at the state line. The State Water and Sanitation Commission has promulgated a set of standards that prescribe the quality of water to be used for different purposes. Once the commission has adopted a use classification, all its subsequent regulations must conform to it; that is, they must be designed to assure water of quality at least as good as that specified in the state standard for water in the use class that has been adopted.

In actual practice stream standards cover many stream characteristics—dissolved oxygen, floating solids, color and turbidity, coliform bacteria, taste and odor, temperature, pH, radioactivity, and others. For simplicity of exposition and analysis, however, we shall pretend that the state standard specifies only one dimension of stream quality, namely, instream dissolved oxygen.[8]

The state water standards are accordingly assumed to divide streams into five use classes: A, B, C, D, and U. Class A waters are very nearly in their pristine state—almost unaffected by man. Waters classified U are essentially uninhabitable for fish life, unsuitable for most recreational activities, and offensive to the sight, taste, and smell. Classes B, C, and D identify intermediate conditions of quality, and associated with each is a specified level of stream use. The state standards[9] are specified in Table 4.

These standards must be met under the average minimum consecutive 7-day flow to be expected once in ten years: for the Bow River, this flow is 800 cfs. Under these low-flow conditions, the entire river below Bowville currently is below the quality specified for Class D waters: indeed, as shown in Figure 2, in many parts of the valley the stream goes anaerobic and is occasionally rather unpleasant to be near.

[8] Other pollutants that would be especially important in the sort of situation we are discussing include coliform bacteria (from municipal waste) and nutrients. We assume that the former is taken care of by chlorination (which is relatively cheap). Nutrients will not be discussed explicitly but deserve mention here because they are a source of increasing concern to water quality managers.
[9] Adapted from the Massachusetts standards.

Table 4   State Water Quality Standards

Use class	Minimum oxygen concentration° (mg/l)	Description
A Public water supplies	7	Character uniformly excellent.
B Bathing and contact recreational use	5	Suitable for water contact sports. Acceptable for public water supply with appropriate treatment. Suitable for agriculture, and certain industrial cooling and process uses; excellent fish and wildlife habitat; excellent aesthetic value.
C Boating and non- contact recreation	3.5	Habitat for wildlife and common food and game fishes indigenous to the region; certain industrial cooling and process uses; under some conditions acceptable for public water supply with appropriate treatment. Suitable for irrigation of crops used for consumption after cooking. Good aesthetic value.
D Minimum acceptable	2	Not objectionable; suitable for power, navigation, and certain industrial cooling and process uses.
U Unacceptable	<2	Below Class D standards. Likely to be offensive.

° Standards to be met under the minimum seven-day consecutive flow to be expected once in ten years.

It should be noted that the imposition of defined standards of quality, which is almost inevitable in framing administrative regulations,[10] transforms the decision problem in a fundamental way. In the absence of codified classifications, a DO concentration of 5.1 mg/l will be recognized as only imperceptibly safer and more pleasant for swimming than one of 4.9 mg/l. But once the higher concentration qualifies the river for a higher use classification, there is all the difference in the

[10] Examples range from the definition of Grade A fresh eggs to the occupancy and safety regulations in building and zoning codes.

world between them—one permits the river to be developed legally for water contact recreation; the other does not.

A fundamental discontinuity is thereby introduced into decisions that impinge on water quality. This will have important consequences for our analysis, as we shall see later.

Waste Discharge and Stream Quality

We have been using instream dissolved oxygen as an indicator of water quality and "biochemical oxygen demand," or BOD, as the measure of the pollution content of the effluent of the two cities and the cannery. Improvement in dissolved oxygen concentrations in the river can be obtained in a number of ways—e.g., artificial aerators or flow augmentation—but this example assumes the removal of oxygen demanding material at the waste source as the only management method available.

In our model, we shall use the simplest formulation of the relationship between waste loads and stream quality, based on the work of Streeter and Phelps which dates back over forty years.[11] According to the Streeter-Phelps model of stream quality, the effect of discharging BOD into a stream at any point is to reduce the dissolved oxygen in the water at all points downstream by amounts that are directly proportional to the amount of BOD inserted and that depend in a complicated way on the distance from the point of waste discharge to the downstream points and on the hydrology of the stream. The factor of proportionality between waste discharge and quality response will be denoted by d. The value of d depends on where along the river the waste is being discharged and where the water quality is measured. These data will be indicated by subscripts: i for the point of BOD discharge and j for the quality control point. Specifically, d_{ij} will denote the decrease in dissolved oxygen at point j (in milligrams per liter) caused by an increase of one lb/day in the amount of BOD discharged into point i. For example: at the present time the cannery is discharging 47,600 lb/day of BOD. A pound of waste material dumped at the cannery ($i=1$) reduces the dissolved oxygen concentration at Bowville ($j=2$) by .0000461 mg/l because $d_{12} = 0.0000461$. If the load from the cannery were cut by 40,000 lb/day, the concentration of dissolved oxygen at Bowville would increase by 40,000 × .0000461 or 1.84 mg/l.

---

[11] Only the most casual treatment of the technical aspects of water quality is offered here. A brief introduction to the topic is provided also by Kneese and Bower [8, pp. 13–29]; for details of wastewater engineering see Fair, Geyer, and Okun [6].

Table 5   Dissolved Oxygen Transfer Coefficients, d_{ij} (Increase in DO at j (mg / l) resulting from decrease of 1000 lb / day in BOD discharge at i.)

Discharge Point (i)	Check Point (j)				
	1 Cannery	2 Bowville	3 Robin Park	4 Plympton	5 State Line
1 Cannery	0.0	0.0461	0.0502	0.0333	0.0159
2 Bowville	—	0.0	0.0585	0.0414	0.0206
4 Plympton	—	—	—	0.0	0.0641
Miles from Gordon Bridge	10	20	60	80	110

The full set of d_{ij} values for the Bow River is given in Table 5. Furthermore, the effects of different waste sources on downstream quality are additive. For example, if both the cannery and Bowville reduce their waste discharges, then the impact of each reduction on water quality at the park can be calculated in the manner shown in the preceding paragraph, using appropriate values of d_{ij}. The overall quality improvement at the park will be the sum of the influences of the two abatement measures.

Model of the Bow Valley Water Pollution Control Commission

The tedious recital of data in the last section will be recognized as a small-scale replica of the docket of any proceeding concerned with the use and control of public waters. Data and considerations of the sort that we have described are amassed in the form of staff and consultant reports, briefs, submissions, affidavits, transcripts of public hearings, court records, judicial findings, rulings of administrative agencies, and so on. The task of the commission is to digest, assimilate, and ultimately evaluate this mass of data, argument, rhetoric, threat, and cajolery dealing with a mixture of technical, economic, legal, demographic, political, aesthetic, moral, and social considerations. We are now concerned with what can be said about the upshot of this task.

One kind of consideration that we have not yet mentioned is precisely what the commission is trying to achieve. If you ask them they will point to the preamble of their charter where they are instructed so to regulate and control the use of the Bow River between the Gordon Bridge and the state line, and the discharge of liquid and solid matter of any form whatsoever thereinto, as to assure the highest practicable quality of water between and including the aforementioned points and to conform to all applicable state and Federal laws and regulations.

That is a vague and high-minded directive, as is the nature of enabling legislation, and needs a great deal of interpretation before it can be used as a guide for either action or analysis. For example, what is meant by "the highest practicable quality of water?" The soundest interpretation of these directions, and the one that we shall adopt, seems to be that the commission is directed to enforce the highest quality of water that can be obtained without imposing undue burdens on anyone. But this interpretation is still vague and in need of further interpretation.

First, what is the "highest quality of water?" Water quality is a multidimensional concept. In a genuine instance, where many characteristics of water are taken into account, there are likely to be measures that will increase the dissolved oxygen concentration at the expense of increasing the amount of phosphates or other plant nutrients in the water. Would such a measure increase or reduce the quality of the water? The Bow River commission is spared this source of perplexity since we have assumed that it pays attention only to dissolved oxygen, but sufficient ambiguity remains. For, different improvement measures will have differential effects on the concentration of dissolved oxygen at different points in the river, and between two measures, one which makes a greater improvement at Plympton and one which makes its major improvement at the state park, it is difficult to say which improves the quality of the river more. Such questions must be decided, somehow, by the commission, and it is not likely that any answer will command the wholehearted assent of all interested parties.

Second, what are "undue burdens?" There is no point in trying to find synonyms for a concept that necessarily incorporates a large ingredient of judgment. Clearly, if a decision requires Pierce-Hall to shut down or to operate at an abnormally low rate of profit, it imposes an undue burden. Or if it requires Bowville to raise its tax rate to a level that is markedly out of line with taxes in Plympton or other competing towns, an undue burden has been imposed. Whether a burden is undue is a matter of judgment, and inherently vague. But the restriction is a genuine limitation on the powers of the commission nevertheless.

In practice the commission's range of discretion is circumscribed even more narrowly than this legal mandate requires. If it is to be effective the commission must secure the willing cooperation of the cities and industries under its jurisdiction; it cannot govern by blunt coercion. This means that it must issue regulations that all concerned will regard as reasonable and fair, and submit to without recourse to law or to higher political authority or to other forms of resistance. In our specific context, this means that the regulations must not endanger the current administrations of Bowville and Plympton if they agree to it, nor can any decision undermine the profitability of the cannery.

We shall refer to all these considerations as "political constraints." However the commission may interpret the objectives set forth vaguely in its charter, it must endeavor to attain them without violating any of the political constraints. In the early stages of consideration it will not be clear whether these constraints impose loose or stringent restrictions on the commission's scope for decision; all interested parties will endeavor to make them appear very stringent. At any rate, the first order of business before the commission is to find some policy that attains a minimum acceptable improvement in the river while respecting all these requirements.

It is highly unlikely that there will be only one such policy. Then a choice must be made among them and, as we have noted, the charter gives only a vague indication as to how this choice is to be made. Within the limits set by the political constraints, therefore, the decision will depend largely on the judgments of the individual commissioners as to where the interests of their constituents lie. These judgments are not likely to coincide. Therefore, the second order of business before the commission is one of pulling, hauling, and compromising to ascertain the decision that best reconciles the interests of all concerned.

Finally, of course, the decision must be technically feasible. If the commission decides to classify the river for Class C use, then it must require all polluters to take whatever measures are needed to bring the river up to this standard.

These, in general terms, are the outlines of the decision problem faced by the commission. This problem must now be formulated more exactly for purposes of further analysis.

Decision Variables, Costs, and
Technological Constraints

The first step in formulating the commission's problem precisely is to express the decisions open to it in numerical form. The first decision is the use classification of the river. It will be recalled from the description of the water quality standards that the effect of adopting any use class is to prescribe the minimum permissible amount of dissolved oxygen in the river. For example, if Class C use is adopted there must be at least 3.5 mg/l of dissolved oxygen in the river at all points. Let us then denote by Q the minimum permissible concentration of dissolved oxygen. Then the commission must, in effect, choose a value of Q, either 7, 5, 3.5, or 2, depending on the use class selected. In order to avoid having to consider the effects of the commission's decisions on users farther downstream, we impose that the dissolved oxygen concentration at the state line shall be 3.5 mg/l. This specification is regarded as outside the purview of the commission and will not be considered further.

The only other decisions that the commission has to make concern the level of treatment to be required of each polluter. These, too, can be expressed numerically. Each polluter has a range of possible treatment plant designs from which to choose; as illustrated in Figure 3, the more effective the waste removal, the higher the cost. The commission has to prescribe the degree of removal which each discharger must attain, or in more precise language, the percentage of BOD which must be removed from each of the polluters' waste outflows. These decisions can be expressed numerically as follows. First, assign identifying numbers to the three polluters: 1 will designate the Pierce-Hall Cannery, 2 will designate Bowville, and 4 will designate Plympton (number 3 denotes the state park, and no wastes are generated there). Then, introduce a set of variables, called x_i, where x_i denotes the percentage of BOD removed by polluter i from his effluent. Accordingly, the commission must decide on x_1, the percent removal to be required of the cannery; x_2, the percentage to be removed by Bowville; and x_4, the percentage to be removed by Plympton.

The decision on the x_i simultaneously determines the treatment cost that each polluter has to bear. The relationship is shown clearly in Figure 3. If $x_1 = 85$, the cannery will have to build the plant that lies halfway between points A and B in that figure, which will cost it $21,-500 a year—i.e., ½ (8,000 + 35,000). The simplest way to express mathematically the relationship between percent removal and cost is to introduce some auxiliary variables to represent the percentage of BOD removed in accordance with each segment of the broken-line cost curve. These auxiliary variables will be distinguished by appending a subscript. In the case of the cannery, x_{11} will denote the percentage of BOD removed by methods along the line-segment from the origin to point A; x_{12} will indicate how far along the segment AB the cannery is required to go, and x_{13} will show how far along the segment BC. Note that x_{11} cannot exceed 50, x_{12} cannot exceed 10, and x_{13} cannot exceed 5. The total amount of BOD removed is simply the amount removed by primary treatment plus the sum of the amounts indicated by the auxiliary variables. In the case of the cannery

$$x_1 = 30 + x_{11} + x_{12} + x_{13}. \tag{1}$$

If $x_1 = 85$, we shall have $x_{11} = 50$, $x_{12} = 5$, and $x_{13} = 0$.

The cost of any level of treatment, x_1, is determined by the corresponding values of the auxiliary variables and the costs of advancing along the line segments, which are given in the fourth column of Table 1. Numerically,

$$\text{Cost of achieving } x_1 = 160x_{11} + 2{,}700x_{12} + 12{,}000x_{13}.$$

For example,

$$\begin{aligned}
\text{Cost of achieving 85 percent removal} &= 8{,}000 + 13{,}500 + 0 \\
&= 21{,}500,
\end{aligned}$$

as we found before by simple interpolation.

The cost of achieving x_2 removal from Bowville's effluent and x_4 from Plympton's, can be computed by using analogous concepts and relationships. An important property of the cost curves is that, in the case of all three polluters, the cost of removing a unit of BOD increases as you move off one of the cost segments to the segment on its right in the diagram.

The commission's decision problem has now been reduced to the selection of four numbers: Q, which determines the use class of the river, and the three x_i ($i = 1$, 2, 4) which specify the levels of treatment required of all polluters. The decisions about these numbers are not all independent. Once Q has been chosen, the x_i are forced to be high enough so that the level of dissolved oxygen does not fall below Q mg/l at any point in the river. The relationship between the x_i and the concentration of dissolved oxygen at points downstream from polluter i was discussed above in the section on "Waste Discharge and Stream Quality." That analysis led to a set of coefficients, d_{ij}, that give the effect of a unit reduction in the oxygen demanding discharge of polluter i on the dissolved oxygen concentration at any downstream point j. Since the x_i determine the amount of oxygen demanding discharge by polluter i, there is an equation, in which the d_{ij} are the important coefficients, relating the x_i to the dissolved oxygen content of the water at any downstream point j. The x_i have to be chosen so that the dissolved oxygen at all points is at least as great as Q, except that at the state line it must be at least 3.5 mg/l irrespective of Q. There is one such equation for each of the quality checkpoints in the river, designated by $j = 2$ for Bowville,

$j = 3$ for Robin State Park, $j = 4$ for Plympton, and $j = 5$ for the state line. A typical equation of this group can be represented in the form[12]:

$$\sum_i d_{ij} L_i (x_i/100 - 0.3) \geqq Q - \overline{q}_j. \tag{2}$$

In this equation L_i is the gross BOD load (i.e., before primary treatment) generated by polluter i; d_{ij} is the transport coefficient expressing the effect of his load on point j downstream, and x_i is his percentage removal of BOD from his effluent. The summation on the left-hand side expresses the increase in dissolved oxygen concentration at point j resulting from the waste treatment in excess of primary employed by all polluters.

On the right-hand side, $\overline{q}_j$ is the dissolved oxygen concentration at point j when only primary treatment is used by all polluters. These are the numbers plotted in Figure 2. The right-hand side is then the increase in dissolved oxygen at point j required by the use classification corresponding to Q, and the entire inequality asserts that the x_i must be chosen large enough to achieve the required improvement at point j. There is, as we said, one such equation for each quality checkpoint. These equations typify the technological constraints confronted by the commission.

Political Constraints

Once the x_i have been chosen, the increases in treatment costs imposed on the polluters follow as we have seen. The formulas expressing the relationship of removal level to cost (as sensed by the individual polluter) are part of the model. In the sequel we shall frequently denote the cost imposed on polluter i by g_i.

The costs imposed on the FWPCA are somewhat special. In this model the FWPCA plays the role of the custodian of the overall national interest. Therefore, the cost of any pollution-abatement plan as perceived by the FWPCA is the full economic cost of the additional treatment, without any allowance for the effects of tax advantages and federal grants-in-aid. In other words, the FWPCA is taken to react to economic resource costs rather than to budgetary costs.

There are limits on the treatment costs that the commission can realistically impose on the polluters. As was mentioned above, the commission cannot impair Pierce-Hall's earning abilities excessively. This

---

[12] The constant 0.3 is subtracted from each x_i since this is the BOD reduction achieved under the basal condition of primary treatment by all polluters.

consideration can be expressed in the mathematical model by including a condition such as $g_1 \le$ \$50,000, which would prohibit any decision that cost Pierce-Hall more than \$50,000 a year.

A different kind of political constraint is illustrated by the role of the FWPCA. The FWPCA, together with associated state agencies, is charged with maintaining the quality of the nation's waterways. It is empowered to enforce minimum standards and, in the case of the Bow River, will not permit it to continue in its present Class U condition. This means that the commission's field of choice of use class is confined to Class D or better, or, in numerical terms to $Q \ge 2$ mg/l.

In this section and the preceding one we have introduced the political and technological constraints that the commission's decision must satisfy. Within the limits set by those constraints the commission will search for the best decision available to it. We now turn to the formulation of that search.

Pareto Admissibility

We now envisage the commission in the process of choosing among decisions that meet the technological and political requirements discussed above. This is largely a process of compromise: each commissioner balances in his mind the advantages and drawbacks to his constituents of the decisions that seem within the range of possibility, and argues for the one that he deems most favorable. When the various positions have been aired, he finally agrees to a decision if he feels that it will be acceptable to his constituents and that no more favorable decision to them is obtainable.

Even this very simple and obvious characterization of the deliberations contains important information, for it entails that no decision will be adopted if there is some alternative decision that is just as satisfactory to all interested parties and more satisfactory to some of them. Following the terminology of welfare economics, we call a decision *Pareto admissible* if it is not ruled out by the foregoing criterion, that is, if there does not exist a feasible alternative that is preferred by some interested parties and that is regarded as equally beneficial by all. The commission's decision will almost surely be Pareto admissible, for if an inadmissible decision were proposed, someone would point out an alternative that he preferred and that no one would object to. We must therefore consider how the preferences of the commissioners among various possible decisions are determined.

Every decision confers benefits on the participants by prescribing the quality of the water in the river, and imposes costs by requiring cer-

tain levels of waste treatment. Each commissioner bases his attitude toward a decision on a mental comparison of the benefits and costs that it
entails for the participants with whom he is most concerned, his constituents. The costs, of course, are a matter of dollars and cents. The benefits are not: they accrue largely in the form of amenities and facilities,
and the eradication of distasteful conditions. To render the two terms of
this balance comparable, we (and the commissioners, for that matter)
have to assign a monetary magnitude to the extent of the benefits. The
natural, and most useful, measure of benefits is "willingness to pay," that
is to say, the value of the benefits of any decision to any participant is
the greatest amount that he would be willing to pay to obtain them. We
shall call the greatest amount that any participant, say participant i,
would be willing to pay to obtain any decision his gross benefit from
that decision, to be abbreviated GB_i.

This conversion of benefits to a monetary magnitude may seem a
little strained. Yet it is done, and has to be done—usually very informally—all the time in the course of arriving at governmental decisions. For example, it would not be at all exceptional to have an exchange like the following at a public hearing on pollution abatement.
The Bowville Commissioner of Water and Sanitation is on the stand:

> Q. How much would it cost you to reduce your daily waste load
> by an additional two percent?
> A. About $27,000 a year, I think.
> Q. If you did that, we could assure swimmable water at Robin
> State Park. How would you folks feel about that?
> A. I can't answer for the City Council, but I would certainly sup-
> port that kind of proposal myself.

The commissioner from Bowville has made the monetary comparison
and has concluded that swimming facilities at the state park are worth
at least $27,000 a year to his city. Further questioning could elicit a
more precise estimate.

These gross benefit estimates are part of the basic data on which
the commissioner's judgments and the commission's decisions rest. We
shall have much more to say about them below. The costs of a decision
to participant i have already been denoted by g_i. The difference between gross benefits and costs, $GB_i - g_i$, will be called net benefits, or
NB_i for short. Net benefits of any decision may be positive, zero, or negative, depending on how the actual costs imposed by the decision compare with the amount that the participant is willing to pay for the corresponding benefit. The net benefits are the crucial quantities that de-

termine how the commissioners, individually and collectively, regard various possible decisions.

These concepts enable us to express some of the considerations we have encountered more formally and quantitatively. First, we have already noted that political considerations place a limit on how disadvantageous a decision can be from the point of view of any participant. The net advantages of a decision to participant i are measured by the corresponding value of NB_i. Thus we can express some of the political constraints by requiring that a decision satisfy

$$NB_i \geqq b_i,$$

for all participants i, where b_i (presumably negative) is an estimate of the smallest net benefit that can be imposed upon i without violating the guarantees of due process, or endangering the careers of i's representatives, or otherwise provoking vigorous refusal to cooperate.

Second, we can now express Pareto admissibility in quantitative terms. Call any particular Decision X and denote by $NB_i(X)$ the resultant net benefits to participant i. X is then a vector with four components, i.e., $X = [Q,\ x_1\ x_2\ x_4]$, specifying the use class of the river and the treatment levels required of the polluters. In this notation, Decision X is Pareto admissible if there does not exist any alternative permissible decision, say Y, for which $NB_i(Y) \geqq NB_i(X)$ for all participants i with strict inequality holding for some.

We have now formulated the main part of the commission's decision problem mathematically. Suppose, for the moment, that we had estimates of the $NB_i(X)$ for all decisions X within the realm of consideration. It is a purely mathematical task to determine whether any particular decision satisfies the technological constraints typified by equation (2). It is also, now, simply a matter of mathematics to ascertain whether the decision satisfies the political constraints. And finally, as we shall see below, straightforward mathematics can be used to determine whether a decision is Pareto admissible. In short, given the net benefit data and the technological properties of the system, we can compute mathematically the range of decisions that are likely candidates for adoption.

Three tasks remain before us: (1) to discuss the estimation of benefits, (2) to indicate how to compute Pareto-admissible decisions from these estimates, and (3) to consider how to evaluate the relative likelihoods of adoption of the different Pareto-admissible decisions.

Valuation of Benefits

One way to estimate the values of the benefits anticipated from different decisions is simply to ask representatives of interested parties, as in the colloquy excerpted above. This is an impracticable method for analytic purposes: there are too many questions to ask too many people, and not enough reason to expect thoughtful and candid answers. A better way is to infer from past behavior and other evidence how much the participants have shown themselves to be willing to pay for the advantages that would be offered by the decisions.

Every decision is a package deal, resulting in a bundle of consequences to each participant. For example, if the commission decides on Use Class C then Bowville will benefit in several ways, including, especially, the advantages of improved water at its own waterfront and improved facilities at the state park. To estimate the value of the package, therefore, we separate its components, estimate the value of each of them, and total up these values. The conditions under which this procedure is valid will be discussed below.

The task of estimating the value of a specific improvement to a restricted group of citizens is arduous but not novel. Several methods are well established. One method, especially useful for recreational facilities, is the "user-days" approach. Following this method, to find the value to Bowville residents of an improvement at Robin State Park, one begins by estimating the additional use of the park that Bowvillers would make if the improvement were installed. Then, one estimates the value of each day's use of the park by a Bowville resident, and multiplies the two estimates. The record of Bowville's past decisions provides the data for estimating the value of a single user-day at a recreational facility. It happens that Bowville's park and recreation budget amounts to $6 per capita. Park department records indicate that the average Bowville resident uses park or recreation facilities about 30 times a year. Thus the city of Bowville is paying $.20 per user-day for its citizens' use of public recreation facilities. This figure, together with a forecast of how Bowvillers will respond to improved water recreation at the park, provides an estimate of the value to Bowville of such an improvement.

Another method for valuing public improvements is the "alternative cost" procedure. This is applicable when the improvement meets a need that will be satisfied by other means if the improvement is not undertaken. In such a case the value of the improvement is the saving that it affords by rendering the alternative expenditure unnecessary. For example, we noted above that if Robin State Park is opened for swimming, Bowville will not have to expand its own waterfront park. This would avoid an expenditure estimated at $165,000 a year or, taking an average, each mg/l of improvement would save Bowville $33,000 a year.

Estimates of the value of improved water quality have been made from the viewpoints of Bowville and Plympton by these and other methods, and are recorded in Table 6. It will be noted that each city places a value on improvements at its own waterfront and also on improvements at the park. In addition, the value of an improvement, wherever it occurs, depends on whether the water has already attained a quality of 5 mg/l of dissolved oxygen, which meets the state standard for water contact use.

Table 6   Value of Unit Improvements in Water Quality
($ / yr per mg / l) °

| Place Improved | Current Water Quality (mg/l) | Value Perceived by Participant | | |
		Bowville	Plympton	FWPCA
Bowville waterfront	<5	100,000		100,000
	≥5	50,000		50,000
Plympton waterfront	<5		75,000	75,000
	≥5		25,000	25,000
Park	<5	33,000	30,000	94,500
	≥5	17,000	10,000	40,500

° Values valid only for qualities meeting Class D standards or higher.

The table also contains estimates of the value of unit improvements from the point of view of the FWPCA. The FWPCA is regarded, again, as the custodian of the public interest. Its valuation of the improvement of water quality at Bowville and Plympton is simply a reflection of the values placed by the inhabitants of those cities on the improvement of their own water. Some empirical support for this method of imputation can be found in the federal government's habit of making 50-50 matching grants-in-aid to encourage local improvement. The FWPCA's valuation of improvements at the park is the sum of the valuations of Bowville and Plympton with 50 percent added to allow for the social value of use of the park by local residents who do not live in the two cities and by outsiders.

This table enables us to calculate the benefits of any decision from the point of view of each participant, provided that it is valid simply to add up the benefits of the different components of the improvement package. For example, if decision X increases the DO concentration at Bowville (where it is now 4 mg/l) by 2 mg/l and at the park (where it is now virtually zero during summer droughts) by 3 mg/l, then its gross benefits to Bowville are

$$GB_2(X) = 100,000 + 50,000 + 3 \times 33,000 = 249,000.$$

If, in addition, the decision imposes on Bowville treatment costs of $390,000 a year, the net benefits are

$$NB_2(X) = 249,000 - 390,000 = -141,000.$$

These computations and the ones to be introduced below are facilitated greatly by the fact that both gross benefits and treatment costs are piecewise linear functions of the decision variables, i.e., the water qualities attained at various points and the treatment levels required. The coefficients of these functions are contained in Table 6 and in the treatment cost tables.

The calculation captures the major measurable benefits of improvement, but there are others. Most importantly, lifting the Bow River out of its current, nearly disgraceful, Class U condition confers a gain on each participant that cannot be evaluated quantitatively. Fortunately we do not have to assign a numerical magnitude to these benefits since they will be enjoyed under all the decisions within the range of possibility, and do not form any basis for choosing among decisions.

But this simple method of deriving gross and net benefits is not inevitably valid. One must ask: are we justified in breaking up the improvement package into its components, attaching a value to each component, adding up, and regarding the total as the value of the entire package? This is an old and classic question in economics. The answer is a qualified affirmative. The value of an entire package to any participant (in the sense of what he would be willing to pay to obtain it) is the sum of the values of its components, provided that (1) the components are neither substitutes for nor complementary goods of each other, and (2) the total value of the package, computed in this way, is not a significant proportion of the budget of the participant. We should consider these provisos in order.

For simple summation of the values of improvements at different points to be valid, the benefits from those improvements should not be interrelated. The benefits of improvements at different points would be interrelated if, for example, there were two state parks accessible to Plympton. For then, if a water-based recreational facility were created at one of them the citizens of Plympton would be less willing to contribute to the cost of developing the other. In that case, the value of improvements to one of the parks would depend upon the extent of development of the other; those improvements would be substitutable goods as far as Plympton is concerned. Another possibility would be for the quality of fishing at the park to be affected by the quality of water both at Bowville and at the park. Then, if the water were improved at Bowville, it would be more valuable than otherwise to improve the water at the park, because the impact on fishing would be greater. This is an instance of complementarity: improvements of water quality at Bowville would enhance the value of each unit of improvement at the park.

These considerations show that substitutability and complementarity invalidate, in opposite ways, the simple addition of the values of improvements at different points along the river. Whether or not such interactions occur in any instance depends on the circumstances, and particularly on the use that would be made by the participants of the improved water at different points. In the case of the Bow River it appears reasonable to neglect such interactions.

Moreover, if the value of the improvement package is an appreciable proportion of the annual budget of a participant, simple addition of the values of components will not be valid. This is because a participant would not be willing to pay as much for one component of a package if the cost of other components had already strained his budget as he would be willing to pay for it in isolation, without having other costs to bear.[13] This is a serious complication in principle. In our case, expenditures on water quality improvement are only a minor proportion of the total expenditures of any of the participants. We can, as a first approximation, ignore the effect of increasing budgetary drain on willingness to pay for still more improvement, but we shall have to stay alert to the possibilities for error that this approximation may lead to.

On these grounds, we feel justified in adding up the values of the components of an improvement package, with due caution, in order to estimate the value of the entire package to any participant, as we have done.

Finding the Likely Decisions

Matters now stand thus: we have expressed the commission's decision numerically (in fact, as a vector with four components) and have found the consequences of any decision to be fairly simple mathematical functions of the decision variables. Now we use these formulations to as-

---

[13] Note the similarity to the difficulties caused by the income effect of expenditure in the conventional theory of consumer behavior.

certain the Pareto-admissible decisions, for the commission's decision will surely be one of those.

Pareto-admissible decisions are found by creating and solving certain auxiliary problems. Suppose we choose any set of positive numbers, to be called w_i, one for each participant in the decision, and use them to form the weighted sum of net benefits:

$$\sum_i w_i NB_i(X).$$

Then if we set ourselves the problem of finding the Decision X that makes this sum as large as possible while conforming to all the technological and political constraints, we shall assuredly discover a Pareto-admissible decision. For if the solution to this problem, say Decision X, were not Pareto-admissible, then there would be another decision, say Y, for which $NB_i(Y) \geqslant NB_i(X)$ for all participants i, with strict inequality for some i, so that

$$\sum_i w_i NB_i(Y) > \sum_i w_i NB_i(X),$$

contradicting the assumption that Decision X solved the auxiliary problem. If the net benefit functions and the constraints are all piecewise-linear or linear, as in this example, this problem can be solved by linear programming. Otherwise more elaborate mathematics will be required.

Every time a set of weights w_i is selected and the corresponding auxiliary problem is solved, a Pareto-admissible decision is discovered. A different set of weights is likely to lead to a different decision, more favorable to the participants whose relative weights have been increased. By trying out a number of different sets of weights, we can map the range of Pareto-admissible decisions. We can also see how much the relative weights have to be changed in order to move the solution from one decision to another.

We predict, of course, that the ultimate decision will be one or another of the solutions discovered by solving the auxiliary problems with judiciously chosen weights. Just which of those decisions will be chosen we have no sure way of telling—even the members of the commission don't know that until their deliberations are finished—but we can narrow the range of uncertainty further by proper interpretation of the artificial weights just introduced. For they are not actually artificial or arbitrary; they are really measures of political weight or influence.

To see this, suppose that the commission had adopted Decision X, which is a solution to the auxiliary problem with weights w_i. Then the commission has revealed something about the bases of its judgments, namely, that it values benefits to participants 1 and 2 (for instance) in something like the ratio $w_1 : w_2$. That is, the commission has shown itself to be willing to reduce the net benefits to participant 1 by \$1 if by so doing it can increase the benefits to participant 2 by \$$w_1/w_2$ or more.

Some of the Pareto-admissible decisions will correspond to auxiliary problems with weights that diverge widely from any reasonable estimate of relative political influence. Those decisions can be ruled out; they are too favorable to participants with relatively little political influence, and not favorable enough to powerful participants. The remaining Pareto admissible decisions, those that correspond to auxiliary problems with plausible political weights, are likely candidates for adoption. This theory provides no way for narrowing the prediction beyond this point.

Now we can test the operational feasibility of this approach by applying it to the problem faced by the Bow Valley Water Pollution Control Commission.

Prediction of Likely Decisions

In the preceding section we showed how to construct a mathematical problem whose solution will be one of the Pareto-admissible decisions available to the Bow Valley Water Pollution Control Commission. Specifically, this problem is constructed by assigning political weights, w_i, to the various groups concerned and then finding the decision that maximizes the weighted sum of net benefits, denoted by $\Sigma\ w_i NB_i(X)$, while satisfying constraints and relationships that describe the technological connection between treatment undertaken and quality achieved, between treatment level and cost incurred, and so on. As we noted, all the relationships are linear or piecewise linear, so that this mathematical problem is a linear programming problem, which is very convenient for computational purposes. It may be necessary in other instances to resort to more complicated mathematical formulations, with consequent increase in the cost of calculation, but such complications would not be justified for our present illustrative purposes.

The linear programming problem that corresponds to our model has been coded for the SDS 940 Time Sharing System.[14]

In this section we shall perform the mathematical analysis of the pollution control commission's decision problem and interpret the results. This is done by setting up and solving a number of auxiliary problems, selecting political weights so as to be able to block out the main outlines of the range of possibilities. These results then serve as a basis for forecasting where within the range the ultimate decision is likely to fall.

[14] A full description of the linear programming model was presented in an appendix to the original version of this paper [5].

Table 7   Weight Allocations Used
to Explore Possible Decisions

Relative Weight Assigned to			
Pierce-Hall w_1	Bowville w_2	Plympton w_4	FWPCA w_5
0	0	0	1
3	1	3	3
3	3	1	3
3	3	3	1
1	3	3	3
4	1	4	1
1	4	1	4
4	4	1	1
1	1	4	4
1	4	4	1
1	5	3	1
1	3	5	1
1	6	2	1
1	2	6	1
1	1	7	1
1	7	1	1
7	1	1	1

In our exploration of Pareto-admissible decisions, the auxiliary problem was solved for seventeen different weight allocations. In discussing these weighting schemes, we shall use the notation $w = (w_1, w_2, w_4, w_5)$ to indicate a set of w_i in which Pierce-Hall receives a weight of w_1, Bowville receives w_2, Plympton gets w_4, and the FWPCA receives w_5. As shown in Table 7, our selection of weights ranges from a set that pays exclusive attention to the overall national interest as reflected by the FWPCA, $w = (0, 0, 0, 1)$, to sets that place major emphasis on the profitability of Pierce-Hall, $w = (7, 1, 1, 1)$, on the welfare of Bowville, $w = (1, 7, 1, 1)$, or on the interests of Plympton, $w = (1, 1, 7, 1)$. Intermediate weighting schemes, such as $w = (3, 3, 1, 3)$ and $w = (3, 1, 3, 3)$, place varying degrees of emphasis on the welfares of the two cities. For each set of influence weights there is an appropriate admissible decision available to the commission.

Notice that we have not conducted a systematic search among all possible sets of relative weights in order to exhaust the full range of admissible plans. We do not have any satisfactory method for doing this. Our approach has been to try a relatively small set of alternative weight distributions, chosen in such a way as to cover the plausible range of

circumstances. As a result, we probably have failed to detect a number
of Pareto-admissible decisions that correspond to political weightings
that we have not tried. Nevertheless, we believe that we have obtained
a fairly accurate depiction of the Pareto-admissible choices available to
the commission.

Of course, as mentioned earlier the commission is not completely
free in its selection of a quality management plan. No matter what the
allocation of political weights may be, the range of choice is limited by
the requirement, imposed by FWPCA and state regulations, that the
river be brought up to at least a Class D standard. To incorporate his
externally imposed limitation in the model, Q was set equal to the Class
D minimum (2.0 mg/l) for purposes of computation. As will be seen
below, this preliminary determination of Q does not prevent the commission from adopting a higher classification in its final decision. Accordingly, in the computations the value of Q corresponding to Class D
was inserted in the water quality constraints at Bowville, the state park,
and at Plympton; the minimum dissolved oxygen level at the southern
outlet of the valley was set at 3.5 mg/l regardless of the value of Q established upstream. With each of the quality constraints set at the
proper level, the model could be solved for the seventeen alternative
sets of influence weights. The resulting solutions provide the basic set of
admissible plans from which we shall draw our prediction of the commission's choice.

In addition to this basic set of decisions, there are other circumstances that are worth investigating. We assume that the commission
can choose any stream classification from D on up, but it is possible to
imagine situations where such a body might have less flexibility in this
choice. For example, political conditions external to the commission
might be such that Class D was essentially forbidden, and the choice of
stream class limited to C or above. Or the selection might be restricted
to Classes B or A, with C ruled out as well. In order to study the influence of this type of political constraint on the commission's range of
choice we repeated the calculations two additional times, once with Q
= 3.5 to identify the decisions admissible if Class C were the minimum
allowed, and once with Q = 5 to do the same for a Class B minimum.[15]

We also are interested in identifying the management plans that
would achieve the different stream quality classifications at the minimum economic cost. In order to determine the "least cost" plan to attain
each use class, we solved a revised version of the auxiliary problem,
using the (0, 0, 0, 1) weights but ignoring any benefits attached to in-

[15] Class A (Q = 7 mg/l or above) was found to be not attainable given the pollution
loads and treatment alternatives that we assumed earlier.

creased water quality. Because the FWPCA is presumed to take account of the national resource costs of alternative treatment plans, and the (0, 0, 0, 1) weights bring only the federal viewpoint into consideration, each of these solutions yielded the minimum cost plan to meet the requirements of the specified quality class. These plans serve as a basis for estimating the increase in economic cost incurred when the benefit evaluations estimated in Table 6 are taken into account.

The result of the computations under a minimum quality class of D was a set of nine Pareto-admissible choices. As will be seen shortly, it often happens that several weight allocations lead to the same decision; seven of our weighting schemes all led to Decision 10, for example. Under a minimum classification of C, the analysis recommended eight admissible choices, and under the requirement of Class B it recommended five. Some plans appeared in more than one of the three sets of computations. The total number of Pareto-admissible choices encountered under all the various conditions was fourteen. All are described in Table 8 in terms of the quality class attained and the treatment levels, x_i, assigned to each of the polluters. Each row of the table contains one of the four-component decision vectors, $X = [Q, x_1, x_2, x_4]$, introduced above. For convenience in presenting and interpreting the results, the decisions are numbered in order of their relative attractiveness to Bowville.

The effect of two of the decisions on the quality of the river is

Table 8   Decisions Recommended by the Analysis

Decision Number	Quality Class Achieved	Treatment Level in Terms of Percentage BOD Removal by		
		Cannery	Bowville	Plympton
1	D	95	50	67
2	D	90	52	67
3	D	80	55	67
4	C	95	65	61
5	D	90	66	61
6	C	90	67	61
7	C	80	70	60
8	B	95	80	54
9	B	94	80	54
10	C	90	80	55
11	B	90	81	54
12	C	80	80	56
13	B	80	85	54
14	B	90	90	51

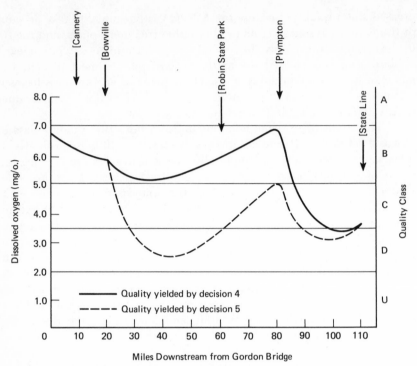

Figure 4. *Water quality in the Bow River under alternative decisions, summer drought conditions*

shown in Figure 4, which should be contrasted with the existing condition in Figure 2. Both Decisions 5 and 14 are included in the basic set of Pareto-admissible choices that results from solving the model with $Q = 2.0$. As the figure shows, Decision 5 fails to achieve 3.5 mg/l at the quality control point located at the state park, and thus is infeasible if the commission is required to attain Class C. Decision 14, which follows from a different set of political influence weights, achieves a higher water quality along almost the entire reach of river, and holds the oxygen concentration above 5.0 mg/l at all quality control points except the state line. If this decision is adopted, the river will be eligible for a B classification.

In the circumstances illustrated by Decision 14, the commission's freedom to select a use classification, within limits, becomes pertinent. Under the political weights that lead to that decision, so much importance is attached to the benefits of high quality that the optimal decision meets the standards for Class B, although the commission was empowered to select a use class as low as D. In these circumstances there are clear advantages to designating the river as Class B. It costs nothing, since this designation will not alter the levels of treatment required of any polluter. The announcement of a high use classification, by obligating the commission to the maintenance of high standards, qualifies the river for all the advantages appertaining thereto, such as public health certification of the Bow as a swimmable stream. Furthermore, though it might be difficult to enforce expensive levels of treatment that were so high that required quality standards were exceeded by a wide margin, those same levels would be easy to enforce if they were clearly necessitated by the officially adopted classification of the river.

For these reasons, the commission can be relied on to adopt the highest stream use classification that is compatible with the quality levels that result from the other components of its decision. Only this way can it realize the full benefit of the quality levels attained. If Decision 14 is adopted, then the commission will designate the Bow for Class B use. The other use classifications noted in Tables 8, 9, 10 and 11 were derived by similar reasoning.

Table 8 and Figure 4 indicate that there is considerable variation in the individual components of the different quality management plans, depending on the distribution of influence among the participants. Now let us see what political conditions are consistent with each of the admissible choices and compare the economic implications of the alternative outcomes. Table 9 shows the weight allocations that lead to each of the nine decisions that are admissible when the minimum classification the commission may assign is D. The table also shows the quality class actually achieved by each plan and the resultant net costs and benefits to each of the participants.

The net cost figures in Table 9 are straightforward; they are simply the additional outlays required to attain the treatment levels shown in Table 8. The net benefit data, on the other hand, merit further explanation. As mentioned earlier, our benefit estimates do not include all the advantages, achieved under all alternative decisions, associated with lifting the river out of its current Class U status. Therefore, they do not state in absolute terms how much benefit a participant derives from a decision. But if we compare the benefits received by any participant as a result of two different decisions, the unmeasured components of benefits will cancel out, and the difference between two estimates will be a meaningful measure of his comparative gains. That is to say, though $NB_i(X)$ is not a significant indicator of the benefits of decision X to par-

Table 9 Decisions Corresponding to Specified Weight Allocations under a Minimum Quality Classification of D

Weight Allocation	Decision Number	Quality Class Achieved	Net Cost ($ thousand/yr)				Net Benefits ($ thousand/yr)			
			Pierce-Hall	Bowville	Plympton	FWPCA	Pierce-Hall	Bowville	Plympton	FWPCA
1711 1621	1	D	95	201	302	829	−87	72	− 3	− 61
4411	2	D	35	217	302	750	−27	48	− 2	10
L.C.	3	D	8	250	301	746	0	0	0	0
3313 1531 1414	5	D	35	349	255	863	−27	− 38	160	101
1441 0001 3133 1144 1351 1333 3331	10	C	35	491	204	985	−27	−131	282	147
1261	11	B	35	512	199	1007	−27	−148	292	139
7111	12	C	8	491	214	953	0	−158	255	125
4141	13	B	8	568	198	1034	0	−219	294	97
1171	14	B	35	659	169	1162	−27	−279	348	36

"L.C." denotes least-cost plan for attaining specified quality.

ticipant i, the difference $NB_i(X) - NB_i(Y)$ does indicate how much better off he is under decision X than under decision Y.[16]

In the table, therefore, we have recorded the net benefits resulting from each choice in comparison with those that would result from one particular decision which is used as an arbitrary base point. For this purpose we use Decision 3, the least-cost plan to achieve Class D waters.

In order to illustrate the interpretation of Table 9, suppose that Bowville's interests are favored by employing the weighting scheme (1, 7, 1, 1). Then the table shows that Decision 1 is appropriate. This same decision is called for if the weight given Bowville's interests is reduced slightly and greater consideration accorded Plympton, as indicated by the weight allocation (1, 6, 2, 1). It will be noted that net benefits for Plympton, the cannery, and the FWPCA are all negative under Decision 1. This result should not be misinterpreted. In particular, it does not mean that all but Bowville will be worse off as a result of plan 1 than if the river were left in its current mediocre state. It only indicates that all but Bowville gain less from Decision 1 than from Decision 3. Other weight allocations, representing varying degrees of concern for the welfares of the four participants, lead to different quality management plans, as shown in the table.

Because the FWPCA is included as a participant in the decision process, it is possible to evaluate alternative plans from a national standpoint. In fact, benefit-cost analysis is a special case of this model in which exclusive weight is given to the representatives of the national interest. Using the (0, 0, 0, 1) weights, the model maximizes the excess of aggregate benefits from a national point of view over aggregate costs, disregarding sectional or specialized interest. Table 9 indicates that Decision 10 is appropriate under these weights, and scanning down the last column in the table it can be seen that this decision yields the greatest total of net benefits as the FWPCA would measure them. Decision 10, then, is the one that would be recommended by a conventional benefit-cost analysis.

It is also possible to evaluate from a national viewpoint the cost of yielding precedence to local interests. For example, if the cannery's interests are favored, as indicated by the (7, 1, 1, 1) weights, then national representatives would judge the result to involve a loss of $22,000 per year as compared with their preferred plan, for then the national net

[16] This is a familiar situation. To say that the temperature is 90° doesn't say how hot it is in any absolute sense, but only how hot it is compared with other temperatures all referred to the same arbitrary zero, 32° below the freezing point of water.

benefit would be $125,000 from Decision 12 as opposed to $147,000 from Decision 10.

It is also instructive to compare the different decisions with the least-cost plan to achieve Class D, Decision 3. Recall that Decision 3 is the decision that achieves Class D standards at the lowest possible national resource cost.[17] Column 7 of Table 9 shows that the minimum cost is $746,000 per year. When benefits are considered, and the political influence of the participants is taken into account, additional expenditure for waste treatment is warranted. In order to maximize national net benefits, for example, an additional $239,000 in national resource cost is required, as can be seen by comparing Decision 3 with Decision 10.

A striking characteristic of the model is that the same decision may be indicated by a wide variety of different weighting schemes. Decision 10 was recommended in response to seven of the weight allocations that were tried. This phenomenon has already been observed in connection with Decision 1, and there are three separate weight distributions that yield Decision 5. This is a consequence of the usual behavior of linear programming models.[18] For any given set of relative weights, the problem solution is likely to settle on a point where some element of incremental costs or benefits changes. Since there is a limited number of such points,[19] only a limited set of Pareto-admissible decisions will emerge, even though there is an infinite number of possible political weighting schemes.

In some circumstances, this characteristic of linear programming models leads to unrealistic and even ridiculous results. But in other circumstances, and this model is a case in point, it is realistic for the model not to incorporate a finer degree of discrimination than the institutional system that it analyzes is likely to display. In actuality, a commission or other political decision process is likely to focus attention on a few sensible possible decisions, corresponding to actions at which costs or benefits change markedly, and to make its selection from those. In this respect a linear programming model reflects institutional behavior.

The character of the relationships among the interested parties can be seen most clearly by studying some of the data from Table 9 in graphical form. In Figure 5, Bowville's net benefits are plotted against net benefits to Plympton for each of the decisions; cannery net benefits

[17] In fact, Decision 3 is itself Pareto admissible, though not for any of the weight allocations in the range we have used in this analysis. For example, Decision 3 is the recommended plan under the weights $w = (6.0, 3.0, 0.5, 0.5)$.
[18] For an instructive discussion of the technical peculiarities of linear models see Baumol and Bushnell [2].
[19] In our problem, for example, incremental costs change at the breakpoints of the individual polluters' treatment cost functions. As shown in Table 6, marginal benefits to each of the participants change at DO levels of 5.0 mg/l.

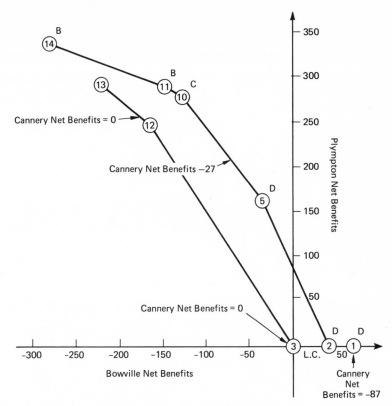

Figure 5. *Net benefits to the three polluters under decisions admissible if the minimum quality classification is D*

also are noted. By drawing connecting lines between those admissible decision points that have like values of benefits to the cannery, we can trace out a set of frontiers that indicate the maximum net benefit that can be provided to Plympton, given particular levels of net benefits to Bowville and to Pierce-Hall.[20] Three frontiers are discernible in the figure. The most obvious includes decision points 2, 5, 10, 11, and 14, and involves net benefits to the cannery of −$27,000 per year. A second is made up of Decisions 3, 12, and 13, yielding zero net benefits to the cannery. The third is a frontier in a technical sense, although it consists of a single point defined by Decision 1; cannery benefits are −$87,000 per year.

[20] There is another dimension—net benefits to the FWPCA—that is not shown in the figure. The pertinent data are in Table 9.

The connecting lines in Figure 5 are analogous to what economists would call "utility-possibility frontiers." For an elaboration of this device, see F. M. Bator [1].

The conflict of interests among the three polluters is easily seen in Figure 5. The classic upstream-downstream rivalry is evident in the relationship between Bowville and Plympton. Thirteen of our seventeen weight allocations lead to some point on the contour where the Pierce-Hall Cannery is receiving net benefits of −$27,000 per year, and along this contour the tradeoff between the interests of the two cities is particularly clear. There is conflict between the cannery and the two cities as well. Given sufficient weight, Pierce-Hall can maintain the treatment level assigned to it under the least-cost plan, and receive zero net benefit as a consequence. If the cannery dominates, $w = (7, 1, 1, 1)$, it achieves this by Decision 12. If its influence is shared with the downstream city, $w = (4, 1, 4, 1)$, Pierce-Hall maintains its preferred position, but more at the expense of Bowville than of Plympton as indicated by Decision 13. On the other hand, if Bowville dominates, $w = (1, 7, 1, 1)$, the resultant Decision 1 forces the cannery to its highest possible treatment level and imposes a net benefit of −$87,000 per year on Pierce-Hall.

Table 9 and Figure 5 summarize the Pareto-admissible choices when the only restriction on the commission's action is that the river must be brought up to at least Class D. We can prepare similar displays that indicate what happens to the range of choice if external political conditions constrain the choice to some higher use class. If the commission is forbidden the use of D classification, for example, the set of admissible choices changes to those shown in Table 10. Decisions 1, 2, 3, and 5 are no longer available because they fail to meet Class C standards, and they are replaced by three new decisions which were not Pareto admissible when Class D was allowed. The weight allocations that before called for Decisions 1, 2, or 5 now lead to either 4 or 6, and Decision 7 becomes the appropriate least-cost plan.[21] Decisions 10, 11, 12, 13, and 14 yielded waters of Class C or better even when such high classification was not required, and so they appear again in Table 10.

These results are also shown in the top half of Figure 6, which is drawn to the same scale and with reference to the same origin as Figure 5. As a comparison of Figures 5 and 6 will show, the range of choice open to the commission is reduced by the imposition of a higher minimum quality level.

If the commission's discretion is further limited, to the point where it can only consider plans that yield a Class B stream, then the range of choice is even more restricted. Five Pareto admissible decisions that are open to the commission under this condition are presented in Table 11

[21] Decision 7 is Pareto admissible under the weights (6.0, 3.0, 0.5, 0.5), as was Decision 3.

Table 10 Decisions Corresponding to Specified Weight Allocations under a Minimum Quality Classification of C

Weight Allocation	Decision Number	Quality Class Achieved	Net Cost ($ thousand/yr)				Net Benefits ($ thousand/yr)			
			Pierce-Hall	Bowville	Plympton	FWPCA	Pierce-Hall	Bowville	Plympton	FWPCA
1711, 1621	4	C	95	344	251	952	−87	− 21	169	34
4411, 3313, 1414, 1531	6	C	35	360	251	873	−27	− 45	170	105
L.C.	7	C	8	393	249	869	0	− 94	171	94
1441, 0001, 3133, 1144, 1351, 1333, 3331	10	C	35	491	204	985	−27	−131	282	147
1261	11	B	35	512	199	1007	−27	−148	292	139
7111	12	C	8	491	214	953	0	−158	255	125
4141	13	B	8	568	198	1034	0	−219	294	97
1171	14	B	35	659	169	1162	−27	−279	348	36

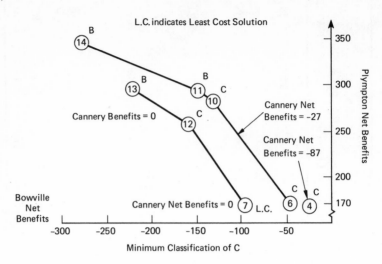

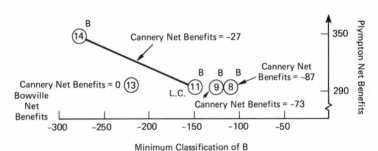

Figure 6. *Net benefits to the three polluters under decisions admissible if the minimum quality classification is C or B*

and in the lower half of Figure 6. Only Decisions 11, 13, and 14 remain from the earlier sets of admissible choices. Most of the weight allocations that formerly led to Decision 10 now result in Decision 11, and 11 also turns out to be the least costly plan that attains Class B. Two new plans previously inadmissible, Decisions 8 and 9, appear as options available to the commission.

Up to this point we have explored the range of admissible choice and have blocked out the conditions that would lead to the adoption of each of the different quality management plans. Now we can apply these results in predicting the outcome of the commission's delibera-

Table 11 Decisions Corresponding to Specified Weight Allocations under a Minimum Quality Classification of B

Weight Allocation	Decision Number	Quality Class Achieved	Net Cost ($ thousand/yr)				Net Benefits ($ thousand/yr)			
			Pierce-Hall	Bowville	Plympton	FWPCA	Pierce-Hall	Bowville	Plympton	FWPCA
1711, 1621	8	B	95	487	200	1074	−87	−115	292	80
1441, 1531	9	B	81	491	200	1056	−73	−121	292	96
4411, 3313, 0001, 3133, 1144, 1351, 1333, 3331, 1261	11	B	35	512	199	1007	−27	−148	292	139
7111	13	B	8	568	198	1034	0	−219	294	97
4141, 1171	14	B	35	659	169	1162	−27	−279	348	36

tions. We have already argued that the commission will select one of the Pareto-admissible choices discovered using the linear programming model. By supplementing these results with reasonable judgments concerning the influence of each of the participants, we can identify the plans that are most likely to be selected.

Part of the information we need for prediction is available in Table 9. The first column of the table shows the weight allocations that lead to each of the admissible choices under a minimum classification of D, where each set of weights is a shorthand expression for the distribution of political influence among the participants as they impinge upon the commission's decision on the matter at hand. To these data we add our knowledge of the political facts of life in the Bow River Valley. If we can judge some of the weight allocations as more likely to be experienced than others, then we can make similar judgments regarding the decisions they call for.

For example, it seems highly unlikely that the interest of a single industrial firm, such as the Pierce-Hall Cannery, would weigh many times more heavily than those of cities of 200,000 or more population, or that such a firm would be far more influential than the FWPCA in this type of situation. We should, therefore, say that the political condition described by the (7, 1, 1, 1) weights has a very low probability of coming about, and as a consequence that Decision 12 has only a low probability of being adopted.[22]

By the same token, since Bowville and Plympton are roughly the same size, we should not expect one to be able to command a great deal more consideration from the commission than the other. There may be some difference in the political pressures they can bring to bear, but it seems reasonable to place a low probability on any settlement that implies favoring Bowville seven, four, or even three times as much as Plympton. Even this simple political judgment gives us a basis for excluding Decision 1, which implies a willingness to increase Plympton's costs by $3 in order to save Bowville $1, or Decision 2, which similarly overrides Plympton's interests in favor of those of Bowville and the cannery. We also should not expect that Decisions 11, 13, or 14 will be

[22] There are many sets of weights besides $w = (7, 1, 1, 1)$ that would recommend Decision 12, though our analysis has not revealed them. In fact, the weight distributions form a continuum; for each Pareto admissible decision discovered by the model there is a range of relative weights within the continuum that would lead to that same decision. The probability that a particular decision will be taken is the probability that the actual distribution of political influence will fall within the range of political weight allocations that lead to that decision. If we were to explore in detail the boundaries of the range of influence weights that recommend Decision 12, we should expect to find that all allocations within the range give the cannery the preponderant influence in determining the outcome.

taken, because these are appropriate only if Plympton has a great influence, either alone or in cooperation with the cannery.

That leaves Decisions 5 and 10 as likely candidates for adoption. Decision 5 is called for under more plausible conditions than the plans discussed above. We discovered three different weight allocations that indicate Decision 5; all attribute heavier weight to Bowville than to Plympton. Because Plympton has suffered most among the riparian residents of the valley from the effects of river pollution, and its citizens are greatly concerned with the water quality issue, we should not expect that the downstream city would be dominated by all other interests, $w = (3, 3, 1, 3)$ or by Bowville and the FWPCA $w = (1, 4, 1, 4)$. On the other hand, it is conceivable that the two cities together would carry a great influence, but that Bowville would come out stronger than Plympton, $w = (1, 5, 3, 1)$, and therefore Decision 5 has some chance of being adopted.

The most likely choice, however, is Decision 10. It seems reasonable to expect that both of the cities will be influential in the commission, but that they will roughly balance each other at points of conflict as indicated by the $(1, 4, 4, 1)$ weights. It is conceivable that the FWPCA might carry weight roughly equivalent to that of each of the cities, $w = (1, 3, 3, 3)$. It is also possible that the cannery would be as influential as the cities, and that the FWPCA would play a lesser role, $w = (3, 3, 3, 1)$. Thus a whole region of weights that give heavy, and roughly equal, influence to the two cities leads to Decision 10. If either city can command an edge on this issue, it is likely to be Plympton, $w = (1, 5, 3, 1)$, simply because the city officials are more concerned with this question than their upstream counterparts, as noted above, and they will work harder in trying to influence the commission.

All together, then, it seems that the probability that the actual distribution of political weight will fall somewhere in the range appropriate to Decision 10 is higher than that for any other admissible decision. On this basis we should predict that the commission will adopt Class C, and that it will bring the river quality up to the required standard by imposing the treatment requirements for Decision 10 shown in Table 8. But Decision 5 is also a real possibility.

Our prediction would not be substantially changed if state and federal regulations were to forbid adoption of Class D. Even with a Class D minimum, the commission is expected to adopt Class C by Decision 10. If the minimum is raised to Class C, this same plan is still the most likely, with Decision 6 a real but less likely possibility.

Under normal circumstances, we should not expect the commission to be forbidden all but the B classification. If a regulatory body is to manage water quality effectively, it cannot have its hands completely tied on the question of use classification, and generally some flexibility is granted by federal and state regulations. Furthermore, in this particular case federal representatives have no incentive to try to enforce a minimum classification of B, for their preferred choice, Decision 10, is not admissible under this restriction. If, for some reason, the commission were restricted to a B classification, the political judgment and reasoning utilized above when applied to the data in Table 11, would lead to a prediction of Decision 11 as the most likely choice.

The application of the model together with very plausible judgments concerning the balance of political considerations have thus led us to forecast a very restricted range of possible outcomes of the commission's decision process. Of course, this very concrete upshot emerged from the analysis of a single, highly simplified example. Whether equally concrete conclusions can be expected in other instances merits further consideration.

Conclusions

Appraisal of the Test

At the very outset we raised the question of whether a complicated problem of governmental decisionmaking, in which the interests of influential groups were in conflict, could be expressed as a formal model and could be analyzed fruitfully in those terms. This entire discussion has been devoted to casting light on that issue by applying the model to a hypothetical case especially devised for the purpose. In the interests of clarity and economy, the test problem was highly simplified. It did, however, incorporate many of the salient features of real water pollution control problems. There were a variety of hydrologic, technical, social, political, and economic issues to formulate and to worry about. There were deep-seated conflicts of interest among the participants, and no obvious way to make everybody happy. Some of the data were very elusive. Nevertheless the model was implemented, and it produced intelligible results.

The model also provided a useful way to manage the diverse kinds of data that were pertinent to the decision. One especially helpful aspect of the model was its ability to incorporate not only data on aggregate costs and benefits but on costs and benefits as sensed by the individual participants as well. Federal and state tax laws and special grant programs surely have an influence on quality management plans, and the model provided a way to include those considerations in the analysis.

Of necessity, we dealt with information of widely varying quality. Some data—such as how much participants would be willing to pay to be free of occasional noxious odors and how the weight of political influence was distributed among the participants—were not observable at all; some, such as valuations of improved recreational opportunities, could be evaluated only tentatively and with difficulty; the best data, such as costs of waste treatment, were only fragmentary. This is a fair approximation of the situation actually faced by a pollution control commission. One of the advantages of the model was that it provided a way to coordinate such data as were available, and a method of analyzing the way that different assumptions would affect the set of plans likely to be adopted by the commission.

On this last point, our sample results proved highly informative. Even our limited selection of weight allocations allowed us to explore the set of plans that would be adopted under extremes of imbalance in the consideration given to the different participants. We found, of course, that there was conflict among the participants and that, in general, the greater the political weight the individual had, the greater were his net benefits. This is no profound discovery; it is only common sense, or perhaps tautology, that as the political influence of any participant grows he will be able to wangle decisions more to his liking at the expense of the others. But the analysis has quantified and sharpened this vague and obvious perception, and has shown concretely how the response to a change in influence is likely to be implemented and how it will effect the welfares of the individual participants.

Our results also provided a framework within which we could utilize reasonable political judgments to arrive at a prediction of the outcome of the decision process. Without performing the analysis, we should not have been able to guess what the different decisions would look like or to foresee which set of political circumstances would favor the adoption of one or another of the Pareto-admissible plans. It is not that the analysis can provide any new knowledge of the political situation; on this score we are ultimately limited by the previous experience and political sensitivity that we bring to the problem. But the model results did allow us to combine what judgments we may possess with data on the physical alternatives available and on the relative importance of different aspects of the problem, as viewed by the individual participants in the decision process. As a result, we were able to learn about the physical and economic factors and the political influences that make some outcomes more or less likely than others.

The analysis also taught us something about the commission itself.

We have seen how its actions are likely to be influenced if more or less stringent quality requirements are imposed from the outside. In a similar way we could have analyzed the effects of other changes in external conditions. For example, one of the assumptions in our example was that the commission had no authority to tax and to offer grants-in-aid. Our results show, however, that there are circumstances under which such powers would be very useful. Consider the situation that arises if Bowville and the FWPCA carry little influence in the commission so that the (4, 1, 4, 1) weights turn out, in fact, to be appropriate. Table 9 indicates that Decision 13 will be taken under these circumstances. It happens, however, that a shift from 13 to Decision 11 would maintain the same quality class and leave Plympton essentially unaffected, yet the change would save Bowville over $2 for every dollar that it cost the cannery. If fiscal expedients were available, the wasteful Decision 13 would never be adopted: the commission could tax Bowville and use the proceeds to reduce the financial burden on the cannery. In this way the technically efficient Decision 11 could be implemented without imposing any financial hardship, to everybody's benefit. The value of such authority, though it might have been suspect, could not have been established without invoking a model that brings out the economic consequences of the technical peculiarities of the river that make the cannery the strategic site for treating waste.

This finding illustrates that our concept of Pareto admissibility is relative. It depends heavily on the range of decisions that are assumed to be technically and legally practicable. Change those assumptions, and the Pareto-admissible set changes correspondingly. Thus the model can be used to estimate the value of changing either the technical possibilities available (by research) or the legal possibilities permissible (by legislation), by comparing the Pareto-admissible sets that correspond to alternative assumptions. Among the legal possibilities that merit consideration are the power to tax and make grants, the authority to impose effluent charges, and the authority to operate regional treatment facilities. All of these are issues now being debated earnestly in the several water pollution control commissions that are currently operative.

Applicability of the Model

Like any model, this one depends on numerous assumptions and can be applied only to circumstances that correspond fairly well to the assumptions. The fundamental assumption in this model is that a water pollution control commission, like any other government agency, is responsive to the wishes of its constituency. This seems highly reasonable.

By being responsive an agency reduces its exposure to complaints, litigation, and animosity, builds its reputation for efficiency and fairmindedness, accumulates political support and influence, and fosters cooperative attitudes among the people with whom it must deal. In short, it gains the consent of the governed, which is an essential prerequisite of effective government. In keeping with this assumption we have portrayed the Bow Valley Water Pollution Control Commission as consulting continually with its constituents and as endeavoring to formulate a plan that will be as agreeable to them, individually, as possible. Any government agency or commission that acts according to this simple principle will arrive at one or another of the decisions that we have called Pareto admissible.

The kind of analysis that follows from this assumption stands in contrast to the approach used in much of the literature, which rests on the postulate that government agencies endeavor to achieve some overarching goals which typically are called "the general welfare" or "the national interest." Such an agency, if such there be, would be unresponsive to the sectional or special interests of its constituents. There is much empirical evidence that agencies in fact behave predominantly as we have assumed. See, for example, the work of Matthew Holden [7].°

Furthermore, the institutional arrangements that are employed by water pollution control agencies in order to be responsive to their constituents are frequently similar to those used by the Bow Valley Water Pollution Control Commission. This is no coincidence. We have modeled our commission in the image of some established pollution control commissions. The Delaware River Basin Commission (DRBC) is made up of the governors of the four states through which the Delaware flows, plus a representative of the federal government, just as the Bow Valley Water Pollution Control Commission is made up of representatives from the municipalities and industries located along the river. The Ohio River Valley Water Sanitation Commission (ORSANCO) has a similar constitution.

The formal composition of the commission is not essential, however. What is essential is an anxious concern for the interests and responses of the people who are affected by the commission's decisions. Direct representation is one expedient for assuring this concern. A more fundamental expedient is the maintenance of intimate contact with the constituency by both informal consultations and formal conferences and public hearings before any important decision is made. Both the DRBC and the ORSANCO follow such procedures, as does the Bow Valley Water Pollution Control Commission. Indeed, the federal legislation

° References in brackets may be found at the end of this chapter.

that provides the charter for all the newer commissions requires elaborate consultations. The requirement to conduct public hearings at which all affected "interstate agencies, states, municipalities and industries involved" can present their cases, is stressed repeatedly in the federal laws. Operating practice, so far as we have been able to discern it, sincerely implements these requirements. In these respects the Bow Valley Water Pollution Control Commission appears to be a fair replica of the pollution control agencies now in existence.

A subsidiary assumption that we made was that the constituency of the Bow Valley Water Pollution Control Commission consists entirely of local residents except for a generalized public interest represented by the FWPCA. This characteristic is by no means universal, even in the field of water pollution control. For example, the Water Quality Act of 1965 gave primary responsibility for regulating the use of interstate waters to "State water pollution control agencies," which are simply departments of the state governments. Now the range of interest groups represented on the State Water Commission is quite different from those that we have envisaged the Bow Valley Water Pollution Control Commission as being responsive to. Therefore, if the problems of the Bow Valley were brought before the State Water Commission instead of the Bow Valley Water Pollution Control Commission, the decision might well be affected. It would remain true that in any proceeding before the State commission concerning the regulation of the Bow River, the parties with predominant interest and the ones that would exert the greatest pressure and influence on the decision would be precisely the ones that we have considered. But the political influence weights would be likely to be changed: purely local and sectoral interests would have smaller leverage for asserting their claims, while statewide and national interests would be likely to gain greater recognition. One of the useful applications of the model is to incorporate such variations in the constitution of decisionmaking authorities and to assist in forming judgments about their consequences.

Next, there are a number of specialized assumptions that were made purely to keep the computations simple and tractable. They concern the policy instruments considered, the technical aspects of waste management and water quality, the question of uncertainty, and the problem of growth in municipal and industrial waste loads. We can review each one of these four aspects in turn and give a brief indication of some of the limitations of the sample case we have used.

The first and most important of these simplifying assumptions was the narrow range of discretion permitted the Bow Valley Water Pollution Control Commission. Many actual commissions have a scarcely wider range of authority but, as we noted above, additional powers and privileges can permit superior decisions (in the Pareto-admissible sense) and some authorities have them. Additional policy instruments can be incorporated into the model, but only at the cost of some increase in complexity.

By means of a second set of assumptions, we vastly simplified the technological and hydrologic aspects of the problem. In particular, we utilized a highly simplified description of the biochemical composition of municipal and industrial sewage and of the technology of waste treatment. We ignored altogether such waste management methods as manufacturing process change and wastewater recirculation. In addition, we reduced water quality standards to a single dimension, dissolved oxygen, and built our analysis on the simplest available formulation of waste transport and decay. The model can be revised to incorporate more adequate assumptions about these aspects of pollution control, but then the problem solution and interpretation will be more difficult than in our case. For example, in the reformulation it may not be possible to maintain certain convenient mathematical properties (such as linearity) that were built into the Bow Valley example.

A third way we reduced the difficulty of the analysis was by ignoring the unpredictability and variability of streamflows, gross waste loads, treatment plant performance, and all of the other aspects of uncertainty that are vexatious parts of most real decision problems. There are decision models, of course, that incorporate these complications, and they are invariably far more elaborate than ours. To introduce uncertainty in its manifold aspects we should have to modify our model along well-established lines. To have done so in the present application would have been to obscure its main intent, which was to test the feasibility of comprehending both political and technical considerations in a model of a governmental decision process.

In our fourth area of simplification, we evaded dynamical considerations by assuming that neither the towns nor the cannery were expected to grow, and that no new industries were likely to be established along the river. The possibility of growth presents serious analytic difficulties of its own. Any satisfactory method for dealing with them could most likely be built into our model, but we have not allowed our attention to be distracted by this separate, important, and difficult analytic problem.

Finally, we must admit to having ignored two important features of the political decision process. One is the influence of logrolling, pressure politics, and side-payments of all sorts. There are pressures, threats, and inducements that Bowville can use to persuade the cannery to acquiesce in a decision that would otherwise be unacceptable, and vice versa. Even Bowville and Plympton, though their interests in the treatment of the river are almost diametrically opposed, can bargain a bit out in the corridor: if Plympton will moderate her demands for waste treatment, Bowville will be more agreeable in sharing the burden of maintaining the county roads. Such bargaining is an essential part of practical politics. It can shift the outcome of the decision process from one Pareto-admissible decision to another. Thus it can influence where in the range of likely outcomes the ultimate decision will come to fall. It reinforces the finding that our prediction is a range rather than a point. But such side bargaining will not push the decision outside the Pareto-admissible range.

Our other political simplification is, in principle, more fundamental. We assumed that each of the participants had a firm and immutable evaluation of the consequences of every decision for his own welfare. This assumption was contained in our estimation of the values attached by the participants to increments in water quality at different points in the river, and in our treatment of those evaluations as unchanged throughout the decision process. In fact, a significant feature of any group decision process is the attempt by each participant to persuade the others to alter their psychological evaluations so that they are more in line with his. The representatives of Plympton and the Izaak Walton League will emphasize the benefits to everyone of high quality water throughout the river and, in fact, will urge it as a moral imperative. The representatives of the cannery will point out that the prosperity of the entire basin depends on the economical use of the waste-absorption potential of the river. To the extent that this rhetoric is not in vain it will succeed in causing some of the participants to change their subjective valuations of the importance of improvements in water quality. It will make our Table 6 invalid.

How serious is this difficulty? This is a significant and open question, fundamental to the understanding of the political process. Perusal of the histories of ORSANCO and the DRBC suggests, however, that when specific decisions are being debated, most of the rhetoric is ineffectual, that people want at the end much what they wanted at the beginning, and that the operative aspect of the bargaining process is a reconciliation of the pressures that the different interest groups have been able to mobilize.[23]

---

[23] For an instructive account of the issues faced by ORSANCO and their resolution see Cleary [3].

Comparison with Current Practice

The prevalent method for analyzing public policy decisions of the sort dealt with here is benefit-cost analysis. Superficially, benefit-cost analysis applies to the government sector the calculus of profit and loss that is used in business decisions. Its popularity is at least partly a response to the businesslike ethic that prevails in our culture. But its contrast with the approach here advocated is, in fact, more profound than the question of whether the government should follow businesslike practices. It is really a reflection of the most ancient cleavage in the tradition of political philosophy.

One great school of political philosophy views a government as the leader of its people, responsible for defining the goals of its citizens and formulating their social standards, preferably under the wise guidance of a philosopher-king or benevolent despot. The other great school sees the government as the corporate embodiment of its people, serving their communal interests and carrying out their wishes, preferably as expressed in direct (nowadays, participatory) democracy.

Traditionally these two views have been advanced as norms, as expressions of what governments ought to be. But they deserve also to be taken seriously as expressions of how governments actually behave. Examples of both governmental leadership and responsiveness are easy to find. ORSANCO, which provides the best documented experience in the water pollution area, thanks to Cleary, was established in response to public demand (i.e., the demand of a few leading private citizens who mobilized widespread support) and went on to exercise a good deal of leadership and initiative of its own. It did so, however, less by pursuing its own goals than by undertaking a series of educational activities that increased its constituents' awareness of the importance of abating the pollution in the Ohio.

We cannot pursue here the rather ill-defined issue of leadership versus responsiveness. In practice, government agencies appear to mix the two in varying proportions, with responsiveness preponderating except for transitory episodes, usually at the highest levels of government.[24]

Benefit-cost analysis is, however, an expression of the leadership role of government. A benefit-cost formula is a tool for evaluating the desirability of different undertakings by the government's standards. This has long been recognized, though not so frequently articulated. For example, one of the chronic conundrums in benefit-cost analysis is the choice of the rate of discount to be used in evaluating deferred benefits

[24] Truman [12] presents a full-dress analysis of governmental responsiveness.

and costs. This rate, selected by agency officials or expert consultants, represents the official evaluation of the relative importance of consequences that emerge at different dates. Similarly, the Flood Control Act of 1936 instructs agencies to compute benefit-cost ratios by adding up the benefits and costs of a project "to whomsoever they may accrue." The intent is to maintain neutrality, but the effect is to impose a judgment about the relative social importance of effects upon upstream users and downstream users, rich and poor, farmers and urbanites, and so on. All governmental undertakings redistribute income in some manner, as we have seen in the case of the Bow Valley.[25] Any evaluative formula must incorporate some appraisal of redistributive consequences, either implicitly or explicitly. A third example of the governmental evaluations built into benefit-cost analyses is provided by the problem of aggregating benefits, and costs, of different kinds. When the beneficial results are priced on economic markets, as is the case with irrigation water and hydroelectric power, the market prices are used. Otherwise prices representing social evaluations have to be found. Outdoor recreation benefits, for example, are frequently valued at $1.50 per user day, but some authorities insist that use by comparatively deprived urban dwellers should be assigned higher "merit" values.[26] Clearly, some values have to be used, and any values represent the judgment of the agency that adopts them. Finally, some consequences of government undertakings, which are deemed excessively difficult to evaluate, are simply omitted from benefit-cost calculations. This, too, represents an implicit governmental judgment, and one that has drawn much criticism.[27] In sum, there is no way out of it: a benefit-cost formula incorporates many judgments, implicit and explicit, of the relative importance of the numerous diverse consequences of the undertakings being evaluated. These judgments must be those of the agency doing the evaluation or its superiors in the governmental hierarchy.

In fundamental contrast to the benefit-cost approach, the analysis used here invokes no other evaluations than those of the people affected. It is explicitly noncommittal with respect to the relative importance or influence of the different participants; that is why it does not lead to an

[25] This problem is discussed more completely by Marglin [11, pp. 67ff.]. Marglin recommends that different values be assigned to different consequences, dependent on the beneficiary. For a full treatment of the theoretical significance of income redistribution see Little [9].
[26] Mack and Myers [10] is a careful analysis of the problem of evaluating recreational benefits from a social point of view. There is much additional literature, some cited by them.
[27] These criticisms are reviewed by Dorfman [4] and elsewhere in the volume in which it appears.

unambiguous prediction. It assembles the data from which those people and the agency concerned derive their decisions, but it does not presume that anyone has a formula for global social evaluation. Therefore it does not purport to recommend what should be done, but only to describe how actors in a political process interact to produce a decision.

This analysis cannot be regarded as an alternative, even in principle, to the decision-making methods actually used. But it can be of assistance in understanding and even facilitating those methods. Its advantage lies in its ability to sketch quickly and cheaply the range of alternative decisions that is worth considering. In our test case, with the data and a moderately fast computer at hand, between two and three minutes were required to determine the corresponding admissible decision. By varying the assumed data artfully, the main outlines of the entire range of admissible decisions were mapped out with about sixty repetitions of this quick computation.

Of course, the computations that would be required in a practical instance are of an entirely different order of magnitude from those encountered in this simple test. Contemplate any actual river basin. It would contain a half-dozen or more cities and towns, several dozen factories or other points of waste discharge, a mainstream, and a number of tributaries with complicated hydrology. In addition, many among our impressive list of simplifying assumptions would be inappropriate. Policy instruments besides the enforcement of a certain percentage waste removal at the source would be relevant, and a rich variety of alternative technologies of waste management would have to be considered. Our uni-dimensional measure of water quality would be considered inadequate, as would our simple specification of the relationship between waste discharge and stream condition. Provision for future growth in wastes would need to be introduced, along with some appropriate method of dealing with uncertainty. If all these complications were taken into account, the calculations would not only be much larger than those that we have encountered, but would be beyond the capacity of any computer now extant or envisaged.

These complexities, however, do not render mathematical analysis inapplicable. They do necessitate a good deal of simplification of the full richness of reality. Simplifying assumptions would have to be made about waste management options, though probably not as severe as the simplifications that we have indulged in. A water quality index of one or two dimensions would have to be introduced in place of the multidimensional specifications set forth in water quality standards documents. The hydrology would have to be simplified. The number of points of pollution would have to be reduced by consolidating groups of nearby

218   ROBERT DORFMAN AND HENRY D. JACOBY

installations into a single synthetic polluter. All these and other simplifications would have to be carried to the point where the calculation became manageable.

The result would be an inevitable loss in accuracy. But this necessity does not invalidate the method, for the relevant standard of
accuracy is not some unattainable ideal but the level of accuracy that is
attainable by alternative procedures. The truth is that the economic-hy-
drologic-biologic-political ecology of a live river basin in the full maj-
esty of its intricacy far transcends the capacity of any method of analysis
of decisionmaking available to man. All methods of decisionmaking require severe simplifications, as a perusal of the dockets of any water
control authority will establish. And, there is reason to believe, the simplifications required for mathematical analysis are less disabling than
the simplifications that are conventional in more informal procedures.
Only hard experience can determine how practical and helpful mathematical analyses will be in actual instances, but the fact that they must
invoke some serious simplifications is not *ipso facto* decisive.

References

[1] Bator, F. M., "The Simple Analytics of Welfare Maximization," *American Economic Review*, 47 (March 1957), pp. 22–59.
[2] Baumol, W. J., and R. C. Bushnell, "Error Produced by Linearization in
Mathematical Programming," *Econometrica*, 35 (July–October 1967),
pp. 447–471.
[3] Cleary, Edward J., *The ORSANCO Story—Water Quality Management
in the Ohio Valley under an Interstate Compact*. Baltimore: Johns Hopkins Press, 1967.
[4] Dorfman, R., "Introduction" in *Measuring Benefits of Government Investments*, R. Dorfman, ed. Washington: The Brookings Institution,
1965, pp. 1–11.
[5] Dorfman R., and H. D. Jacoby, "A Model of Public Decisions Illustrated
by a Water Pollution Policy Problem" in *The Analysis and Evaluation of
Public Expenditures: The PPB System*, submitted to the Subcommittee
on Economy in Government, U.S. Congress, Joint Economic Committee,
May 29, 1969.
[6] Fair, G. M., J. C. Geyer, and D. A. Okun, *Water and Wastewater Engineering*, Volume II. New York: John Wiley and Sons, 1968.
[7] Holden, Matthew, Jr., "Political Control as a Bargaining Process: An
Essay on Regulatory Decision-Making," pub. no. 9, Cornell University
Water Resources Center, October 1966.
[8] Kneese, A. V., and B. T. Bower, *Managing Water Quality: Economics,
Technology, Institutions*. Baltimore: Johns Hopkins Press, 1968.

[9] Little, I. M. D., *A Critique of Welfare Economics,* 2d ed. London: Oxford University Press, 1957.

[10] Mack. R. P., and S. Myers, "Outdoor Recreation" in *Measuring Benefits of Government Investments,* R. Dorfman, ed. Washington: The Brookings Institution, 1965, pp. 71–101.

[11] Marglin, S. A., "Objectives of Water Resource Development: A General Statement," *Design of Water-Resource Systems,* Arthur Maass, et al. Cambridge: Harvard University Press, 1962, Chapter 2.

[12] Truman, David B., *The Governmental Process: Political Interests and Public Opinion.* New York: Alfred A. Knopf, 1951.

BRUCE HANNON
JULIE CANNON *

12

The Corps Out-Engineered

The selection by Bruce Hannon and Julie Cannon and that
by T. H. Watkins (Article 13) are valuable in their "advocacy" treatment of some issues raised by Schick (Article 10).
The orientation of both articles is clear: The authors share an
ideological perspective which is most skeptical of the benefits
produced by large-scale development projects. Beyond this, the
authors severely criticize the assumptions and figures used in
the benefit-cost analysis forwarded by the Corps of Engineers.
Some of the general problems of benefit-cost analysis are
pointed up in these articles [1]:

1. Questions as to the appropriate size of the public discount rate
   (the interest rates used by the Corps)
2. Inadequate knowledge about the distributional impacts of public
   expenditures (what happens to the residents displaced by Corps
   projects?)
3. Implications of benefit-cost analysis when underemployed resources
   exist (what is the market for electricity generated by particular
   hydroelectric projects?)
4. Appropriate treatment of risk and uncertainty (what sorts of water
   and power resources will be available in 1990?)
5. Valuation of costs and benefits when government has multiple
   objectives in addition to economic efficiency (are there some
   areas which—regardless of economics—should remain untouched?)

* Mrs. Cannon is News Editor of the *Sierra Club Bulletin*. Professor Hannon
is teaching at University of Illinois, Urbana. This article originally appeared
in the August 1969 *Sierra Club Bulletin*, 54,8.
[1] This summary list has been taken, in part, from H. E. Dolenga, "Limits on
the Contribution of PPBS to Bureaucratic Organizational Effectiveness," unpublished paper, Northwestern University School of Management.

Thus, the sort of objective systematic analysis which Schick sees as possible and desirable has often been twisted in the Corps of Engineers' effort to justify projects that contribute to the prestige and power of the Corps. The Corps of Engineers is not unique in this regard; both public and private organizations—both those in favor of rapid development and those which are pro-environment—tend to do this. It is just that the Corps is one of the largest, most active organizations which uses benefit-cost analysis for its own advantage.

In the past two years the Midwest District of the Army Corps of Engineers shipped out a general and two colonels to points in Okinawa, Korea, and Vietnam. The top civilian was "promoted" to another area. Why? Many think the answer lies with a small band of midwestern conservationists who hounded the Corps through its complex technopolitical procedural maze and achieved an alternative to the midwestern district's favorite project, the revised Oakley Dam.

This confrontation was in the making years ago when settlers in Central Illinois first began plowing the nation's richest soil. In pre-pioneer days wide belts of trees flourished along Illinois rivers. As the years passed, the grain fields were pushed to the very edge of the river banks—except in a 1500-acre area along the Sangamon River. Here the primeval forest endured and a long forgotten ecology continued undisturbed.

The area is intact today through the farsightedness of a nineteenth century Horatio Alger and his philanthropist son. The father, Samuel Allerton, built a fortune in the livestock market, and, as his fortune grew, he invested in land. By 1900 he owned 40,000 acres, including the 19,000 acres of land in Piatt County, Illinois, that he willed to his son Robert.

Robert Allerton, in addition to administering the family properties, developed a deep interest in the fine arts. It was Robert who took the 1500 acres of black-soiled woodlands in the Sangamon Valley and fashioned one of the most beautiful estates in the Middle West. In the words of a University of Illinois publication: "Here, through the ministry of architecture, sculpture, and landscape design, he illustrated how art and nature may be blended for the delight and edification of man."

In developing the estate, Robert built a 20-room Georgian mansion, created a series of informal and formal gardens, and sowed the property with both originals and copies of some of the world's finest sculpture. In all his plans he considered the native Illinois landscape. His gardens, though some are based on foreign inspiration, feature native floral materials. And most of the 1500 acres, including the bottom lands that fringe the rambling Sangamon River, are covered by a forest that has been evolving undisturbed for 20,000 years.

In 1946 Robert Allerton donated the 1500-acre tract, including the mansion, to the University of Illinois to be used "as an educational and research center, as a forest and wildlife and plantlife reserve, as an example of landscape architecture, and as a public park." Along with the park, Allerton gave nearly 4000 acres of his farmland to provide a permanent income to care for the park.

The Corps Finds a Dam Site

As with a number of America's natural resources, this gift to the generations to come may not survive the present generation. The Army Corps of Engineers has proposed an Oakley Dam and Reservoir project that would flood more than 1000 acres of Allerton Park. In 1961 the Corps suggested a 49-foot high dam 12 miles downstream from Allerton Park on the Sangamon River. Its main reservoir ("conservation" pool) would be 621 feet above sea level and during flood periods would reach 645 feet above sea level. The conservation pool would not inundate Allerton, but the flood pool periodically would cover about 700 acres of the park. The purposes of this dam were water supply for the nearby city of Decatur, flood control, and recreation. In 1962 Congress authorized the project.

During 1965 and 1966 the Corps instituted several changes. The dam was hiked to 60 feet—keep in mind that here on the Illinois prairie every foot added to the height of the dam means another mile of inundated land behind the dam. The conservation pool level was increased to 636 feet and the flood level to 654 feet.

The Corps sought to raise the dam to cover several mistakes made in the 1961 project proposal: siltation was greater than what they had figured and the maximum flood on record was not the one whose statistics they had used initially. By adding a fourth purpose, low flow augmentation (sewage dilution) for Decatur, these mistakes were covered up and the volume of water was increased enough to take care of the errors as well as the low flow.

The increased volume of water would also take care of Allerton Park. Instead of a dam that would trespass on Allerton during flood conditions, the revised project provided a dam that would permanently inundate over 40 percent of the park.

In addition to the dam and reservoir, the Corps planned 100 miles of downstream channelization on the Sangamon River. The $18 million channel improvement would require that 2800 acres be cleared for flood releases from the Oakley project. Thus, a 100 foot wide spoil bank would dominate the cleared area for the entire 100 miles.

Then, in March of 1969, the Corps reported, that to meet Illinois' new water quality standards, the project had to be enlarged again. The conservation pool was set at an elevation of 641 feet, 20 feet higher than what was authorized by Congress, and the flood pool at 656 feet, 11 feet higher than originally planned. Allerton Park would be gradually split in two as the waters of the Sangamon spilled over the lowlands. Finally, when the reservoir filled, flooding 650 acres of the park, only the higher fragments of the park on either side of the former river would be above water.

Conservationists Mobilize

In 1967, when the public learned that the revised Oakley project would require bulldozing about 650 acres of Allerton for the conservation pool and the periodic flooding of another 300 acres, the Committee on Allerton Park was formed. A technically diverse group of conservationists—economists, lawyers, engineers, biologists, botanists, zoologists, and artists, they decided to try a new approach in dealing with the Corps. Instead of harping at the Corps for its well-known insensitivity to ecological and esthetic values, the Committee on Allerton met the Corps head-on at a professional level. They out-thought and out-engineered the Corps, proving that an alternate, cheaper, and more aesthetic means existed to solve the same problems that the revised Oakley dam was proposed to solve.

The Committee on Allerton Park criticized the Corps on the following grounds.

1. The Corps Was Incredibly Narrow in Its Exploration of Alternatives

The Committee presented a petition with 20,000 signatures (followed by one bearing 80,000) to Illinois Senators Dirksen and Percy and 22nd District Congressman Springer in December of 1967. The Illinois legislators responded by asking the Corps to restudy the project. In March 1969 the Corps released 12 alternatives to Oakley, including proposals for an alternate water supply and advanced waste treatment for Decatur.

While the Corps was doing its restudy, the Committee continued its investigations. The Committee found that the law states that storage and water releases are not to serve as a substitute for advance treatment or other means of controlling wastes at their sources. Yet the Corps had designated over 16 billion gallons (69 percent of the initial lake volume) in the Oakley reservoir for low-flow augmentation. In fact, prior to its restudy the Corps had not considered a much cheaper advanced sewage treatment plant as an alternative to dilution storage at Oakley.

Another alternative the Corps neglected until it made its restudy was using the underground Teays Aquifer as an alternate water supply for Decatur. In 1954 Decatur installed two wells in this underground river. The wells have a capacity of five million gallons per day, one-fourth of the city's total current need, but they have never been used. This underground water is free of nitrate pollution, an increasingly dangerous pollutant common to surface water supplies.

The conservationists also found the Corps' plan for downstream channelization illogical. The Corps had calculated the costs of channelizing the 100-mile section of river at $18 million. The Committee on Allerton found that the entire 67,000 acres of bottom land along the same river section—much of which never floods—could be purchased at about the same cost.

2.   The Corps Overstated Project Benefits and Frequently Understated Project Costs

The Committee on Allerton set its economists, engineers, and lawyers to work on each of the benefits claimed by the Corps for the Oakley project. The Committee's engineers reported that the Corps' claim of flood damage on the lower Sangamon was exaggerated by about 5 to 1, that crop losses occur about one year in 20, and that much of the flooded farmland is now in the federal idle-acres program. Flood damages on the Illinois River, relievable by a project at Oakley, were found to be exaggerated by about 2 to 1.

Recreation accounted for more than 30 percent of the supposed benefits, so the Committee on Allerton pulled together statistics on recreation in the vicinity of the Oakley project. Within 65 miles of the proposed reservoir there is a population of 1,051,343. In the same area there are 26,838 surface acres of public lakes and only 3,505 acres of public woodlands. Allerton Park, the only large tract, represents one-third of this woodland acreage. However, the Corps of Engineers ignored the aesthetic and scientific values that would be lost, using instead the standard commercial price of bottom lands.

Almost half of the recreation benefit was to come from swimming in the reservoir. Lake Decatur, also a Sangamon River reservoir, was intended for swimming too. However, Lake Decatur has been closed for several years because of silt and algae-ridden and often polluted water. Oakley, with its low-flow augmentation feature, would be particularly unattractive to swimmers because during the dry summer months the average drawdown would leave an extensive foul-odored mudflat throughout the Allerton Park bottom lands.

The Committee on Allerton discovered that the Corps' revised and expanded reservoir project would provide no additional water for Decatur. The original 621-foot conservation pool included 11,000-acre-feet of water for Decatur and the 636-foot conservation pool allotted Decatur the same number of acre-feet.

The Committee on Allerton also found that the Corps had overstated the benefits from low-flow augmentation. When the Corps decided to include dilution augmentation as a purpose in the multi-purpose reservoir, they found it difficult to determine a benefit figure. Thus, they turned to the least-cost alternative concept. They calculated the cost of a single-purpose dam to hold the necessary dilution water and then claimed the cost of this fictitious dam as the benefit for dilution.

Thus the Corps calculated a $24 million low-flow benefit figure— the cost of a single-purpose dam, and they determined that the cost of dilution as a part of a multi-purpose dam is about $10 million. In this way the Corps claimed a benefit-cost ratio for dilution storage of 2.4 to 1. The Allerton Committee engineers calculated the cost of advanced sewage treatment, which would negate the sewage dilution feature of the dam, at about $5 million. The Committee claims that sewage dilution is the real least-cost alternative, and that the actual benefit-cost ratio is about .5 to 1. However, the Corps does not customarily accept non-dam alternatives, because dam building is their business.

3. The Dam is Not Economically Justified at More Realistic Interest Rates

Congress recently set a new interest rate for computing costs on federally funded projects. Projects authorized before January 1, 1969, use the old 3¼ rate; those authorized after that date use the new 4⅝ percent interest rate, which is being raised. Despite the intensive 1969 project revisions, the Corps claims that the old 1962 authorization is still in effect. In this way the Corps is able to use the outdated rate, and they figure the revised project has a benefit-cost ratio of 1.3, or an average benefit of $13 for each $10 of estimated costs. However, if the new rate is used, the project has a benefit-cost ratio of about 1.1. And if the actual rate on government borrowing, which approaches 5¾ percent, is used, the project goes in the red.

4. The Corps Outstripped Its Initial Authorization

The Corps moved ahead—without additional authorization or public hearings—on the revised Oakley project. (These revisions required the purchase of 24,000 acres of land instead of the original 6,200 acres and an expenditure of $75 million instead of the original $29 million.) The Committee on Allerton repeatedly sought hearings on the revised project. But the Corps did not regard these changes as major, explaining that, "such advanced engineering and design almost always involves some refinements of the project."

The Committee on Allerton threatened the Corps with legal action if it would not make public the Army's regulations on public hearings. The Committee's lawyer contended these regulations are information in the public domain. After a year of requests for hearings, the regulations on how to apply for a hearing were finally released. A local governing body had to make the official request (one county and one city council then made such a request), and within three months hearings were held on 14 technical alternatives to the original project.

The Corps Retreats

For two years the Committee on Allerton has continued to check the Corps' data. The Committee's engineers, lawyers, and economists have scored against their Corps counterparts repeatedly. The Corps replaced three of its top people in an effort to meet this unusual challenge. But after two years of being severely drubbed on all its plans, the Corps turned the problem over to the State of Illinois. The State waterways engineers proposed a Waterway Alternative that was agreed to in May 1969 by the City of Decatur, the Board of Trustees of the University of Illinois, and the State of Illinois.

Key conservation victories in the Waterways Alternative are:

1. Allerton Park is protected from permanent flooding by a return to the originally proposed 621-foot conservation pool and by the development of a major storage capability on a nearby tributary of the Sangamon. During periods of flood, the discharge rate from the reservoir is to be adjusted to attain, as nearly as possible, the natural seasonal flooding conditions in the park.

2. Decatur is denied the use of the Sangamon River for sewage dilution, which means the city must turn to advanced sewage treatment.
3. A 22,500-acre recreational greenbelt is to be developed along the lower Sangamon River in lieu of the much more expensive and severely destructive proposed channel improvement.

The Waterways Alternative represents a defeat for the Corps, a defeat on technical grounds. To insure its gains the Committee on Allerton Park is urging that appropriations for Oakley in the nation's 1970 budget be made with the stipulation that capital expenditures be frozen until the Corps demonstrates the feasibility of and accepts the Waterways Alternative. The Committee considers the dam a compromise, and they have said, "If any larger or more destructive project is proposed, we shall be required to increase the already nation-wide opposition to the total project." A general and two colonels now in Asia know they can do it.

T. H. WATKINS *   13

Crisis on the Eel

A Short History of the Tall Dos Rios Dam

On the Middle Fork of the Eel River, 600 miles north of Los Angeles, the U.S. Army Corps of Engineers and the California Department of Water Resources want to build a dam. Its name would be Dos Rios, and it would be 730 feet high. Its purposes are defined by the Corps of Engineers as follows: to "reduce substantially future flood damages in the Eel River Basin; provide additional water supply to meet the State of California Water Project requirements which are required by about 1985; provide a potential for hydroelectric power; and meet the expanding public need for water oriented outdoor recreational opportunities." The entire project appears to be an enormous miscalculation.

I The Powers of Obfuscation

The dam would destroy one of the few living rivers left in California. It would flood Round Valley, the town of Covelo, the Round Valley Indian Reservation, more than 400 archeological sites, and 14,000 acres of agricultural land potentially worth over three million dollars annually. The dam will cost far more than the $398,000,000 projected by the Corps, and the project's annual cost may exceed any beneficial return by as much as 25 percent. Its water would be at least as expensive, and possibly more expensive, than water from any one of several alternate sources. Only 5 percent of the project is allocated to flood control. The dam is expected to produce only 4,800 kilowatts of hydroelectric power. Finally, the so-called "recreational opportunities" have the surrealistic quality of something out of *Alice in Wonderland*.

* T. H. Watkins, former editor of *The American West*, is a historian and conservation writer whose numerous articles and books include *The Grand Colorado: The Story of a River and Its Canyons*.

The project is facing some stiff competition. In addition to the Sierra Club, organizations and individuals who have expressed opposition or serious misgivings include the Mendocino County Board of Supervisors; the people of Cavelo; the Indians of the Round Valley Reservation; the Save the Eel River Association; California Tomorrow; State Senator Randolph Collier; the Mendocino County Farm Bureau; the State Department of Fish and Game; the Mendocino County Flood Control and Water Conservation District; the State Department of Parks and Recreation; and many state newspapers, among them the San Francisco *Chronicle* and the Sacramento *Bee*. The State Senate's nine-member Committee on Water Resources on February 6 of this year reversed its earlier 6 to 3 recommendation of the project to a 5 to 4 vote against it.

The Dos Rios Project, then, is neither popular nor realistic, but the Corps and the DWR, convinced of the infallibility of their logic and determined to have their way, are going to exert every ounce of their considerable muscle to obtain a go-ahead from the state.

The Corps of Engineers began eying the Eel River's development potential during the 1950s and received Congressional authorization for intensive studies of the region in 1956, following a period of particularly damaging floods. Expanded authorizations followed, and in 1964 the Corps received the support of the California Department of Water Resources. In December 1967 the Corps issued an *Interim Report* to the Army's Board of Engineers for Rivers and Harbors.

The *Report* called for a dam on the Middle Fork of the Eel three miles upstream from the town of Dos Rios—a "multiple-purpose" earth-fill dam to be the largest in California, with a reservoir capacity of 7,-600,000 acre-feet of water and an estimated total cost of $398,000,000. California itself would be obligated to contribute a minimum of $153,-000,000 to construct the Grindstone Diversion Tunnel 21 miles through the Coast Range to carry water to Grindstone Creek in Glenn County, and from there to the Sacramento Delta Pool and ultimately to Los Angeles and the Metropolitan Water District.

The *Report* justifies the whole proposal by invoking the familiar "benefit-cost ratio," a device of statistical legerdemain which pits the cost of the project against the benefits to be derived from the sale of water ($26,100,000 annually by the Corps' estimate), the savings in flood damage ($1,500,000), the sale of hydroelectric power ($210,000), and recreational uses of the reservoir ($1,210,000). Based on these figures, the benefit-cost ratio was calculated to be 1.9 to 1—$1.90 in benefits for every $1 of cost. This may seem to be a comforting figure, until the *Report* itself is scrutinized—as it was shortly after its appearance by Professor Gardner B. Brown, Jr., of the University of Washington Department of Economics, at the request of the Round Valley Conservation League.

Using the *Report's* own facts and statistical methods, Brown calculated a .6 to 1 benefit-cost ratio—$.60 in benefits for every $1 of cost. The actual cost of the Dos Rios Project, he said, was underestimated by at least 12 percent (adding $47,000,000 to the total), and the benefits were variously *over*-estimated: water supply benefits by more than 60 percent (an annual revenue loss of about $18,500,000), flood control benefits by 17 percent (a $260,000 loss), hydropower benefits by 20 percent (a $40,000 loss), and recreation benefits by 10 percent (a $120,000 loss).

The Corps replied to Brown's analysis of its *Report* on October 17, 1968, when Colonel Frank C. Boerger presented a 41-page "Statement" before a joint public hearing of the California Senate and Assembly Committees on Water Resources. Critics of the *Interim Report* were disposed of quickly: "In some of the testimony presented on the Dos Rios Project we have found that some facts have been introduced in a negative context so that it is not always clear that they are facts. . . ." After issuing this masterpiece of obfuscation, Colonel Boerger dismissed the ability of anyone but a Corps specialist to comprehend the mysterious institutional expertise compiled in the *Report*, implying that an economist like Gardner Brown has no business questioning the economics of dam building, mainly because he has never built a dam and couldn't possibly be expected to know what was going on.

"Judging from its response," Brown said in November, "the Corps of Engineers seems to be more concerned about justifying its original position than with making a genuine attempt to meet economically the water needs of Californians. Its reply, in my judgment, reflects an abrogation of public responsibility. . . . Through misquotation, selective omission, and other debating tricks, the Corps of Engineers has attempted to circumvent rather than confront the issues involved."

Those issues are large ones.

II Myths, Realities, and Credibility Gaps

Of the numerous cost underestimates—$47 million worth, or 12 percent of the project's actual construction costs—a few are the most glaring. The *Interim Report* has allowed only a 20 percent contingency for price inflation between 1967, when the project was first proposed, and 1980, the year it is expected to be completed, assuming no delays—but during the *past* 13 years, according to the Bureau of Reclamation, construction costs of similar projects have actually risen some 30 percent. Round Valley, the *Report* claims, can be purchased for $12,-200,000, even though the Corps' own ally, the Department of Water Resources, has admitted that it can't be had for less than $25,000,000.

The Corps based its interest payments for the dam on the proposition that it would take seven years to complete; again, the DWR expectation of nine years would seem to be more reasonable. And, as a final blow, President Lyndon Johnson, shortly before leaving office, proclaimed that the interest rate for projects such as Dos Rios should be raised from 3¼ percent to 4⅝ percent—which, according to the Corps' figures, would propel the interest and amortization costs from $14,900,000 to $21,000,000 a year. It remains to be seen what effect this change in interest rates will have on the project's attractiveness.

There is nothing new in all this. One study of the agency's past record has shown that the actual costs in 167 flood control projects have been as much as *double* those estimated by the Corps at the time they were authorized. "No private construction company could have remained in business with such a performance record," Gardner Brown pointed out, and while the economist prudently kept his under-estimate figure at 12 percent, a concerned taxpayer might wonder somewhat uneasily how close to 100 percent wrong the Corps might actually be in regard to Dos Rios.

It is when one contemplates the benefits that the Corps assumes will be forthcoming from the Dos Rios Project, however, that the whole argument for its existence breaks down. Only 5 percent of the project is allocated to flood control, even though the Corps has been waving this benefit in the taxpayers' eyes as if it were the main purpose of the dam. The dam's futility as a flood control device is indicated by the Mendocino County District Engineer's contention that had the Dos Rios dam been in existence during the great flood of 1964, the crest of the flood would have been lowered only two feet at the lower reaches of the river —from 30 feet to 28 feet. In any case, the dam would only provide standard flood control if it operated in conjunction with huge levees in the Eel River delta and a second large dam at English Ridge, which is still on the drafting boards. Finally, the *Report* assigns a flood control benefit to Round Valley itself—*which the dam will place under 300 feet of water.*

Only 1 percent of the project is allocated to hydropower benefits. Its 4,800 kilowatts of power would supply only 263 average homes— hardly enough to mention.

A little over 4 percent has been allocated to recreation uses, predicated on the Corps' assumption that the lake created by the dam, together with a proposed "Indian Museum," will draw upwards of 2,000,000 tourist visits a year—but what possible recreational delights could be provided by a lake whose surface level could fluctuate as much as 150 feet in either direction as Dos Rios water is stored, then flushed out during the summer through the Grindstone Diversion Tunnel? Moreover, while the Corps has claimed it will take only eight years to fill the lake, William Penn Mott, California's Director of Parks and Recreation, has said it will take from 10 to 35 years, and has said further that "the state was going to be adamant in its refusal to undertake recreation maintenance and operation under the Dos Rios Project," according to the Ukiah *Daily Journal*. Altogether, the Corps' cheerful prediction of a recreation benefit exceeding $1,000,000 a year seems overblown.

In the face of such facts, the *real* purpose of the Dos Rios dam is obvious. It is designed to be an enormous tub where water for use in other parts of the state is to be collected and distributed—again, a questionable "benefit."

The Corps claims a water benefit based on the delivery of 900,000 acre-feet of Dos Rios water annually to the California State Water Project, even though the *Report* itself only claimed 700,000 acre-feet and the DWR has stated that except during dry years Dos Rios will export no more than 250,000 acre-feet. This water, the Corps maintains, will be sold for $26.00 per acre-foot, a price it claims is sufficiently competitive to make Dos Rios water profitable and saleable. The price includes a $1 charge for transporting the water from Grindstone Creek to the Delta Pool, but the Corps has not included in its figures the additional cost of conveying the water from the Delta Pool to the terminus of the California Aqueduct ($46 per acre-foot), and from there to the principal purchaser, the Metropolitan Water District ($15 per acre-foot). These factors raise the *actual* price of Dos Rios water to $87 per acre-foot.

There is every reason in the world to believe that by 1985, or shortly thereafter, sufficient water from alternate sources is going to be available in Southern California at prices considerably cheaper than Dos Rios' $87. Desalinization of ocean water is the most dramatic potential alternative. Recent studies compiled by the U.S. Bureau of Reclamation to ascertain California water needs after 1980 (expected completion date of the Central Arizona Project) have determined that by 1995 it will be possible to produce, through the use of nuclear power, desalinated water for $32.00 per acre-foot. If a maximum of $20.00 per acre-foot is added for conveyance cost (maximum because the water can be produced locally) the potential price for desalinated water in 1995 will still be $35 less than that for Dos Rios water.

Other alternatives are noted in an August 1968 report by the DWR entitled *Present and Future Water Supply and Demand in the South Coast Area.* This report makes several flat statements that severely undermine the justification for Dos Rios. According to the figures used in this report, the present and future water supplies of Southern California are in good condition: "Contrary to general opinion that there would be a supplemental water demand by 1990, present and future supply is adequate to 2000. This ten-year difference has important economic consequences, since it means that investment in new importation facilities [including the High Dos Rios Dam] can be postponed 10 years longer than was anticipated." By 2020, Southern California's water demand, according to the DWR report, will be about 5,800,000 acre-feet annually, while the supply of available water will be about 5,432,000 acre-feet. The DWR says the deficiency of 368,000 acre-feet can be compensated by the utilization of one or all of several sources, none of them outside Southern California: (1) the increased use of existing ground water, which the report says amounts to 960,000 acre-feet per year; (2) the reclamation and re-cycling of 500,000 acre-feet of waste water; and (3) the transfer of some 500,000 acre-feet of unused entitlement water from the California Water Project into ground basin storage—all methods whose cost would be far below that involved in building a 730-foot dam and carrying water 600 miles from Dos Rios.

The ones who will pay the most for Dos Rios water are those who need it most—the taxpayers of Southern California. Not only will they have to pay most of the project's cost if it is approved, they will pay more for Dos Rios water than for desalinated water. Prices for water from the several alternate sources mentioned above vary, but are generally expected to be lower than Dos Rios'.

III Water, Land, and People

Money is money, but there are other values to be considered in regard to the Dos Rios Project, few of them measurable in greenbacks. A river would be destroyed. The dam would back water up in the canyons of the Middle Fork of the Eel for miles, and the flow of the main branch would be crippled.

The Eel is one of the few rivers in California with a summer steelhead run. The damage to fish life from the dam has already been admitted by the Corps, which proposes a hatchery to mitigate the loss of 8,000,000 chinook salmon eggs and 2,000,000 steelhead eggs. The Department of Fish and Game says this is not enough: such a hatchery would have to produce more than three times that number of eggs, given the salmon's uncommon sensitivity to disease and the inconsistent record of such hatcheries in the past. Similarly, the Corps proposes to mitigate the ecological losses resulting from the inundation of the river's canyons by purchasing 14,000 acres of land to replace wildlife habitat. Again, the Department of Fish and Game says this is not enough: at least 22,000 acres are needed. The fact of the matter is simple—the ecology of an entire region is going to be wiped out, to be replaced by a statistically convenient one-for-one land and salmon egg swap.

The Corps has been equally cavalier in its attitude toward the people most intimately involved in the project—the 1100 residents of Covelo and the 350 Indians of the Round Valley Reservation. The Corps proposes to rebuild the town of Covelo on a more convenient location, ignoring the fact that since the town's economy is inextricably tied to the agricultural pursuits of Round Valley, its very reason for existence will vanish with the valley's flooding. The Corps' treatment of Round Valley's Indians, moreover, has all the sinister overtones of the nineteenth century. It plans to pick them up wholesale and move them to a mountaintop reservation, where none of them have ever lived, exchanging two acres of mountainous land for every acre of valley land taken away. There, those who wish to continue subsistence farming may do so on plots of marginally arable land; others will be instructed in the maintenance and supervision of an Indian Museum where, among other things, genuine tourists may watch genuine Indians weaving genuine blankets.

The Indians, understandably, object. They are a people of pride and independence. They have done well living on the edges of the white man's hectic world, working with the farmers of the valley and retaining withal that sense of identity with the land around them that made the California Indian the most serenely natural being ever to inhabit the boundaries of the state. They consider the Corps' plan an insult, as they should. The Covelo Indian Council has described the proposal as a "disruption of heritage," and rejected it outright as being "unfair and unjust to the Covelo Indian Community." As a final insult, "Lake Dos Rios" would flood 400 ancient Indian burial sites, some that may be 9000 years old, a prospect loudly deplored by anthropologists and archeologists.

What is the price of a lost heritage, or of history aborted?

The Dos Rios Project is illogical, ruinously expensive, predictably obsolete, and brutally destructive. Its very proposal places the economic framework of the second phase of the California Water Project under suspicion.

"Continue until you get to the end, then stop," the Red Queen told Alice. It is time to stop the Corps of Engineers and the Department of

Water Resources, and the place to stop is Dos Rios, before the integrity of the whole North Coast region is violated piecemeal, from the Eel to the Klamath.

It can be done. It was done at Marble Canyon on the Colorado. Enough public pressure exerted on the California Legislature during its current session can block any state approval of Dos Rios and halt the grinding course of water resource development in California. The choice is simple enough: we either want an intelligent, economical, and genuinely workable plan for the solution to our water problems, or the most expensive and useless plumbing system in the history of the world.

TED CALDWELL, *
with the collaboration of
LESLIE L. ROOS, JR.

14

Voluntary Compliance
and Pollution Abatement[†]

The past few years have witnessed growing concern on the part
of the public at large, public agencies, and conservation groups for environmental factors and their implications for public policy. With respect
to Lake Michigan in particular, the experience of the accelerated eutrophication of Lake Erie has alarmed not only the conservation-minded
but laymen as well. The mass media have seized this issue, highlighting
many of the inherent dangers of continued abuse of this precious resource. Awakened public concern, along with that of the scientific community, has contributed substantially to a widespread campaign to
"Save Our Lake."

While such widespread public attention and concern can be beneficial, much more than slogans, bumper stickers, and media exposure is
required. The involved public agencies on the local, state, and federal
level have instituted programs designed to bring under control a deteriorating situation. On the local level, the city of Chicago in 1968 passed
a $35 million bond issue to improve and expand existing sewage treat-
ment facilities and to deal more adequately with the increasing necessity to enhance the water quality for domestic, recreational, and industrial use. The state of Illinois has enacted legislation to enforce
pollution abatement by both municipalities and industry. The federal
government, specifically under the aegis of the Department of Interior,
has functioned as a regulatory agent, testing water quality and enforcing
federal laws against the pollution of interstate navigable waters. One as-

* Mr. Caldwell is a doctoral candidate at Northwestern University. This article was
prepared for this volume.
† This research has been aided by N.I.H. grant 1R03MH 19055-01 to the collaborat-
ing author.

pect of these programs will be evaluated here, that is, attempts to curb industrial pollution. The implications of the findings will be further explored from the public policy perspective.

Background

Water pollution has been defined by the United States Department of Health, Education, and Welfare as

> . . . such contamination or other alteration of the physical, chemical, or biological properties of any body of water of a state, including change in temperature, taste, color, turbidity, or odors of the waters, or such discharge of any liquid, gaseous, solid, or radioactive or any other substance into any waters of the state which is likely to create nuisance or render such waters harmful, detrimental, or injurious to public health, safety or welfare or to domestic, commercial, industrial, agricultural, recreational, or other legitimate beneficial uses, or to livestock, wild animals, birds, fish or other aquatic life.[1]

While pollution adversely affects the ecosystem of all water sources, perhaps most adversely affected are lakes. Lakes are sedimentation basins and, if only natural effects are operative, their life span is relatively short in terms of geological time. The biological aging process of a lake is known as eutrophication. A lake biologically "dies" when it no longer supports balanced quantities of phytoplankton and zooplankton. Other stages precede the eutrophic stage of an inland body of water. When a lake is first formed, it is oliogotrophic and characterized by little or no sedimentation. There are few plants to produce the dissolved oxygen and furnish the food necessary to support zooplankton. Hence, an oliogotrophic lake supports no complex life forms.

Sedimentation builds gradually over time by siltation or runoff and by incremental buildups of nitrogenous- and phosphorous-rich nutrients from droppings of waterfowl and the like. These processes are conducive to increases in the content of totally dissolved solids circulated through the lake in a biocycle, indicating a trend toward the second stage, mesotrophy. As the proliferation of marine plants takes place, the sedimentation level rises. Marine plants photosynthesize, oxygenate the water, and produce phytoplankton, which fauna feed on. While marine plants and phytoplankton are necessary in the early eutrophic stage of the lake's existence, if they become too profuse, the ecosystem gives way

[1] *Proceedings, Conference on Pollution of Lake Michigan and Its Tributary Basin*, U.S. Department of the Interior, Vol. 4, February 5, 1968, p. 1887.

to oxygen-consuming simple organisms. A lake can become so dense
with phytoplankton that zooplankton cannot breathe; fish may be virtually crowded out in the plethora of food sources. This is the ultimate
stage of the eutrophic process. It is characterized by heavy sedimentation, a very rich biocycle, and conspicuous algae blooms.

Thus far, man's role in the eutrophication processes of lakes has
not been sufficiently emphasized, but it is most significant. For example,
it was not until 1905 that Chicago treated its sewage in any way prior to
its disposal into Lake Michigan.[2] Many smaller municipalities and town-
ships in the Great Lakes area still do not have a system for primary
raw-sewage treatment. Man's role extends beyond the biological sphere;
human activity is also posing a direct threat to the chemical balance of
lakes.

Technological and industrial advancement have compounded difficulties in the management and control of water resources. As is seen in
Table 1, the purification costs for the city of Chicago water supply have
steadily increased over the past decade. The marked increase for the period 1964–1965 reflects the installation of a second water-treatment
facility—the Chicago South Works. A significant factor in the overall increase has been the waste discharged into Lake Michigan by industries
operating in the greater Chicago area. Technical experts have estimated

Table 1   Water Purification Costs for Chicago 1960–1969

Year	Purification Costs	Annual Percentage Increase
1960	$2,900,000	
1961	3,055,000	0.05%
1962	3,279,000	0.07%
1963	3,575,000	0.08%
1964	5,001,000	0.28%
1965	6,642,000	0.24%
1966	7,872,000	0.15%
1967	8,516,000	0.07%
1968	8,936,000	0.05%
1969	9,865,000	0.08%

[2] Alfred Beeton, "Eutrophication of the Great Lakes," in George W. Cox, *Readings in Conservation Ecology* (New York: Appleton-Century-Crofts, 1969), pp. 492–507. Also included among these readings of relevance is Claire Sawyer, "Basic Concepts of Eutrophication," pp. 462–492.

Table 2   Pollutants Entering Lake Michigan

Pollutant	Principle Sources	Effect
Iron	Manufacturing. Industrial effluent	Mildly toxic. Rust damage to treatment facilities
Phenol compounds	Steel mills. Production ingredient in coke quenching	Adds acidity to water affecting taste
Oil and grease	Oil refineries, large manufacturers, steel companies	Prevent light from reaching aquatic plants. Odors
Cyanide	Steel mills	Poisonous to aquatic life. Toxic in moderate quantities
Suspended solids	Chemical, inorganic particles of unspecified nature	Turbidity
Total solids	Organic and inorganic particulate matter. Sewage outfall from municipalities and industry	Requires extensive treatment for removal. Turbidity

that as high as 40 percent of all pollution in Lake Michigan is directly attributable to this industrial activity.[3]

A partial listing of the contaminants is given in Table 2. These contaminants affect the odor and taste of the water. In addition to being harmful to the aquatic environment, foreign matter adversely changes the quality of the potable water supply. Increased industrial activity in the Chicago region has resulted in greater quantities of these pollutants, requiring more public funds to purify the principal water supply of the Lake Michigan region.

Policy Formulation and Public Goods

In addition to the harmful effects of pollution on the domestic water supply, problems of esthetics and conflicting demands for usage must be encompassed in public policy dealing with water resource management. Polluted waterways and lakes are esthetically unpleasant,

[3] Testimony of R.J. Schneider of the Federal Water Pollution Control Administration, *Proceedings, 1968 Conference*, Vol. 2, p. 459.

emitting foul odors and detracting significantly from the surrounding landscape. The existence of polluted waters all but preempts their use for recreational purposes. The situation demands policy that takes into consideration the long-range priorities of the social unit along with economic factors that aim at balancing preferences in the most equitable fashion.

Consistent with these aims, policy makers in various federal agencies have followed the lead of the Pentagon, which, under former Secretary Robert S. McNamara, first successfully utilized the systems approach to policy formulation and adopted the Planning-Programming-Budgeting System (PPBS). Basically, this involves formulating and choosing among alternative programs designed to accomplish the same or similar explicit objectives. Plans are generally formulated on the basis of five-year programs with mechanisms that can take broad program decisions, translate them into contingency options, and express them in budgetary terms.[4]

The cornerstones of PPBS are welfare economics and benefit-cost analysis. Benefit-cost analysis is a subsystem of welfare economics [5] in trying to guide public policy when market prices do not accurately reflect social value, or when no market exists from which to directly observe the community's valuation of the social marginal product.

Water resources and their allocation fall under the general rubric of public goods. Substantial government involvement in this sector has had the effect of taking many public goods out of the purely economic realm, where the marginal product and its distribution is determined by mechanisms related to the marketplace, and where benefits and costs of products are largely reflected in a system of prices.

Public goods can be broadly classified in two types: those related to survival, and those related to artificial needs based on increased prosperity. Often public goods requirements based on artificial needs cannot be met. This presents a problem of priorities. The United States has provided many survival needs at a zero price by having the federal government assume an allocative role. The problem of artificial needs has been approached by means of rules and institutions governing the relationships among individuals affected by the allocative decisions. One of these guidelines, which is widely accepted by policy makers, is a variation of Pareto optimality. That is, the marginal costs of additional units

[4] Murray L. Weidenbaum, "Program-Budgeting: Applying Economic Analysis to Government Expenditure Decisions," in Ira Sharkansky (ed.), *Policy Analysis in Political Science* (Chicago: Markham Publishing Co., 1970).

[5] John V. Krutilla, "Welfare Aspects of Benefits/Costs Analysis," in Stephen C. Smith and Emery N. Castle (eds.), *Economics and Public Policy in Water Resource Development* (Ames: Iowa State University Press, 1964), p. 23.

of the collective goods must be shared in exactly the same proportion as the additional benefits.[6] If marginal costs are shared in any other way, the amount of the collective good provided will be suboptimal.

The need for water reflects a general problem of survival, but by careful resource management and allocation, society should not be faced with any severe drought. Water resource policy can be approached in terms of conflicting demands in the urban setting for satisfaction of many collective needs. On the one hand, industry views waterways, lakes, and the like as an economically efficient means of disposing of their wastes. On the other hand, large and growing segments of society value water for recreational and esthetic purposes. It is principally in this context that public policy will be examined.

The system of balancing preferences gives insight into an evaluation of competing policy alternatives. This requires a determination whether or not those who benefit from a policy decision are those who actually bear the costs of implementing it. In the case of water utilization, industry is presently the beneficiary at virtually negligible cost.[7] The public, through taxation, bears the largest burden of the costs but fails to achieve much of a share of the returns in terms of clean water for recreational purposes.[8] Preferences for the latter objective have remained generally unarticulated, but the present beneficiaries have a vested interest in preserving the existing arrangements.

The size of the group seeking the satisfaction of a public good is important in practical terms. In general, the larger the group, the less perceptible is the contribution of any single group member and the higher is the probability that those paying for it will discontinue their payments. In such a case, high levels of organizational agreement are needed to assure that the goods will be provided. Buchanan has characterized this situation as the "free rider problem." [9]

Olson has delineated three factors that inhibit large groups from furthering their objectives [10]:

1. The larger the group, the smaller fraction any person in the group receives; hence incentives will be lacking and group benefits will be suboptimal.

[6] Mancur Olson, *The Logic of Collective Action* (Cambridge: Harvard University Press, 1965), pp. 10–14.
[7] F. J. Trelease, "The Concept of Reasonable Use and Beneficial Use in the Law of Surface Steams," in Smith and Castle, *op. cit.*, p. 402.
[8] Irving K. Fox, "Policy Problems in the Field of Water Resources," in Allen V. Kneese and Stephen C. Smith (eds.), *Water Research* (Baltimore: Johns Hopkins Press, 1966), p. 284.
[9] James Buchanan, *The Demand and Supply of Public Goods* (Chicago: Rand McNally, 1969), pp. 77–100.
[10] Olson, *op. cit.*, pp. 51–52.

2. The lesser the benefits to a small segment, the less likely they will be willing to pay the burden of providing even a small amount of the collective good.
3. The organizational costs for large groups are great and the opportunities for selective incentives, coercion, or positive rewards are lacking.

Small groups are more effective in taking action and in acting decisively. The larger groups cannot act in accordance with their common interests so long as group members are free to further their individual interests. Thus, large-group members will not subordinate individual interests for the attainment of a collective good.[11] Olson's propositions suggest that the large latent group favoring cleaner water is at a distinct disadvantage when opposed by industrial groups organized for the purpose of preserving their privileged position.

The analytical, pluralist political scientists such as Bentley and Truman have maintained that pressure groups have power more or less proportional to their numbers.[12] Banfield has carried these arguments further, characterizing influence as analogous to money in that it can be spent, saved, or invested. They seem to have implicit faith in this process as being a just determinant of social policy. Olson takes the pluralists to task for failing to consider the motive states of organized groups which may undercut the democratic vestiges of the group-pressure system. The cohesiveness of groups is a function of their individual and not collective economic interests, and therefore small groups have a distinct advantage over large groups in achieving their demands.[13] Business lobbies obtain much of their strength and support because they represent organizations performing some function in addition to lobbying.[14] Given this arrangement, economic-based lobbies inevitably will have influence disproportionate to their numbers. Business interests may prevail even when the public is aroused. If a constituency is vitally interested in a specific issue, the boundaries of congressional-decision latitude are very tight. The Congressman has no alternative but to act in accordance with the constituency if he hopes to be reelected.[15] Likewise, where publicly desirable legislation is manifest, lobbies can do little to effect substantive outcomes, but they can and do influence the details of the legislation. And these details are important. An overall perspective is provided by Edelman, who has concluded that few regulatory policies have been

[11] *Ibid.*, p. 54.
[12] *Ibid.*, pp. 121–132.
[13] *Ibid.*, p. 125.
[14] *Ibid.*, p. 132.
[15] Lester Milbrath, "The Impact of Lobbying on Government Decisions," in Sharkansky, (ed.), *op. cit.*, p. 361.

pursued unless they have proved to be acceptable to the regulated groups or served the interests of those groups.[16]

Large latent groups that are the beneficiaries of regulatory legislation may demonstrate political quiescence; their demands are often satiated with symbolic reassurances. The political manipulation of symbols allows existing policies that deny resources to large numbers to be pursued almost indefinitely. Indicative of symbolic legislation are widely acclaimed resource allocations that include nonoperational standards connoting balance or equity. They are successful because quiescent groups tend to read their own meaning into situations that are unclear or provocative of emotion. On the other hand, small organized groups with high information are capable of sustained demands and cannot be easily deluded with symbolic rewards.[17]

The budgetary process may also facilitate a continuation of present policies.[18] Policy is characteristically attained as a result of incremental changes. Incrementalism helps keep policy within the bounds of ponderability, allowing for concern with marginal benefits and marginal costs. But questions of divergent values are rarely addressed; the whole is seldom evaluated completely. Change in policy may not be rapid enough to deal adequately with changing conditions.[19] Policies evolving through such a process of limited comparisons are often embedded in law or custom. Thus the feasibility of innovative policies, especially in the area of water allocation and utilization, is not high.

Research Design

Recent attempts directed at better management of Lake Michigan's water resources have provided an almost natural experimental setting for the study of the efficacy of public pressures and voluntary com-

---

[16] Murray Edelman, *The Symbolic Uses of Politics* (Urbana: University of Illinois Press, 1964).

[17] *Ibid.*, p. 32.

[18] Charles Lindblom, *The Policy Making Process* (Englewood Cliffs, N.J.: Prentice-Hall, 1968).

[19] An excellent example is provided by the incident of April 1969 when the Bureau of the Budget refused to authorize an Administration plan that called for the allocation of $500 million to the Clean Water Bill. The Bureau's initial refusal was based on the incrementalist notion that so large an increase, a doubling over the previous year's authorization, could not be justified in view of the fact that not all the funds for the previous fiscal year had been appropriated. In spite of apparent need for vast sums of money to accomplish the objectives put forward in the relatively more ambitious Clean Water Bill, such institutional impediments regularly recur. In point of fact, the Bureau finally made a compromise and the necessary funds were forthcoming. *The New York Times*, April 4, 1969, p. 16.

pliance on the part of industry. In the past several years a series of conferences about pollution in the Lake Michigan area have been held in cooperation with the Federal Water Pollution Control Administration. One of the largest of these conferences was held in Chicago from January 31 to February 5, 1968. In addition to the public agencies within the states of Illinois, Indiana, Michigan, and Wisconsin, spokesmen for industry and conservation groups were represented. As Table 3 shows, business groups were well represented, particularly when their numbers are compared with the number of spokesmen for conservation groups such as the Izaak Walton League of Illinois and the League of Women Voters.

Table 3   Attendance at Four-State Water Conference °

Affiliation	Number
Bureaucrats (city, state, and federal)	304
Corporation and business interest spokesmen	236
Conservationists (including civic organizations)	129
Educational institutions	46
Politicians (elected officials and staffs)	39
Military (including Army Corps of Engineers)	11
No affiliation specified	18

° Source: 1968 Conference Proceedings, Chicago, Department of Interior, Volumes I–IV.

The single, most tangible output of the 1968 conference was the endorsement of a deadline date, December 31, 1968, which had been negotiated between Chicago-Gary industries and the regulatory agencies of Illinois and Indiana. Corporations located widely around the southern basin area of Lake Michigan were to comply with a timetable for construction of additional waste treatment facilities designed to enhance the water quality of the lake. The clear implication of the meeting was that concrete action should be taken to alleviate a deteriorating situation in the southern basin area, but no explicit sanctions for noncompliance were endorsed. The emphasis was upon voluntary compliance to bring about pollution abatement. Among those affected by the deadline date were six corporations operating in the vicinity of the Indiana Harbor Canal: United States Steel, South Works; Youngstown Sheet and Tube Company; Inland Steel Company; Cities Service Oil Company; Mobil Oil Company; and Sinclair Refining Company. At the time of the 1968 conference, many of the additional treatment facilities were under construction, and others had already been completed.

A technical committee of the Federal Water Pollution Control Administration (FWPCA) monitored compliance with the agreement. The committee's function was to record values of selected parameters indicating the level of biological and chemical pollution of Lake Michigan and its tributary basin. Fifteen stations were established at various locations scattered around the southern portion of the lake. Samples were taken irregularly, approximately once each week. Most of the sampling sites or stations were chosen because of their proximity to hypothesized sources of industrial pollution, while others were selected as control sites to determine the water quality in the absence of industrial waste. Under the auspices of the Department of Interior, the samples were analyzed for detection of excessive increases in the pollution indicators. If detected, personnel were dispatched to confront the source and a determination of violation and/or liability was made. These data were also aggregated by the federal agency in order to determine long term trends.

Data Collection

Data for this study were made available by the Great Lakes Region Office of the Department of the Interior. Here the sampling stations were chosen on the same rationale as that adopted by the FWPCA, that is, proximity to hypothesized sources and a control site. The stations for which data were collected were located at the mouth of the Indiana Harbor Canal; 2½ miles farther in the Canal; at the mouth of the Grand Calumet River; and in the channel flowing out of Wolf Lake, located on the Illinois—Indiana state line.

As Figure 1 indicates, the Indiana Harbor Canal is the site of extensive commercial activity. In addition to the many industrial plants operating in the vicinity, the shipping lanes in the canal are often congested. As a consequence, the canal is grossly polluted; the samples taken invariably exceed the criteria set by the public agencies for the maximum allowable pollution level. The site at the mouth of the canal registers the effluent discharge of Inland Steel Company and Youngstown Sheet and Tube Company, which are located approximately equidistant on either side of the sampling site. Further upstream, at the Dickey Road highway bridge over the canal, is the station that records the effluents of the major oil refineries in Gary, Indiana, operated by Mobil Oil Company, Sinclair Refining, and Cities Service Petroleum Company. The third station is located at the mouth of the Grand Calumet River, immediately adjacent to the north pierhead light. The flow is usually inland from the harbor to the river; since there is no industrial activity ac-

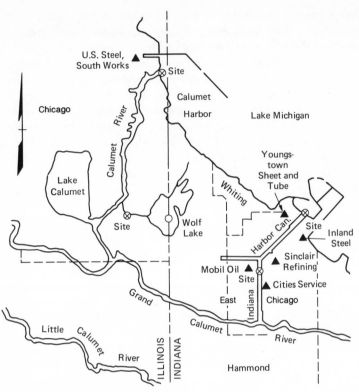

Figure 1. *Industries and sampling sites*

tually in the harbor, the pollution levels are not severe. However, the criteria for iron are not generally met at the river mouth because of the outfall from the U.S. Steel South Works plant, which frequently discolors the water and creates high turbidity in the entire area. This situation arises when the tidal ebbs correspond with the discharge from the U.S. Steel plant; iron shavings and the like are then carried into the harbor.

The fourth station monitors the quality of water leaving Wolf Lake; the quality at this outlet is generally good. This station was chosen as a control for measurements of industrial pollution. The function of control groups in experimental and quasi-experimental situations is to facilitate observation by isolating the experimental effect. Random assignment to a control or an experimental group is preferable, but the development of quasi-experimental designs allows for the relaxation of this requirement. For purposes of this study the three experimental sampling sites were taken to be identical with the exception of differences on the dependent variables—the particular pollutants being discharged.

The criteria for the pollution levels were codified by the Stream

Pollution Control Board of the State of Indiana, and the industries operating in the southern basin of Lake Michigan were advised that their effluent should be treated so as not to exceed the criteria set for the particular pollution parameters. Table 4 summarizes the maximum allowable pollution in the canal for the parameters investigated in this study. The maximum allowable levels vary somewhat among our sampling sites. The two parameters that were not quantified are considered to exceed acceptable levels when, by visual inspection, the water is obviously highly turbid or when oil and grease slicks appear on the water's surface.

Table 4   Criteria for Indiana Harbor Canal °

Pollutant	Maximum Allowable (mg/liter)
Iron	0.15
Phenol compounds	0.005
Oil and grease	No quantified criterion
Cyanide	1.00
Suspended solids	No quantified criterion
Total solids	275

° *Source:* Stream Pollution Control Board of the State of Indiana, effective June 13, 1967.

The data collected were in the form of semiannual means on the variables listed in Tables 2 and 4. Covered in this study are nine points in time, the first consisting of the mean values July to December 1965, and the last consisting of the mean values for July to December 1969. Every six months the Department of Interior publishes *Reports on the Water Quality of Lower Lake Michigan;* data for the two time periods in 1969 were aggregated at the Department's Chicago office.[20] Each time point represents an average of 20 samples taken approximately once a week for each six-month period.

Definitions and Operationalizations

Compliance is an elusive concept, subject to varying interpretations. The attempt here is to operationalize it in such a way that the outcome of the voluntary compliance schedule will be observable, and

[20] The authors wish to express their gratitude to Mr. David Kee of the Federal Water Pollution Control Administration, Chicago, for his assistance in making the data available.

that the performance or nonperformance of industries involved can be definitively assessed. Prior to 1968, individual arrangements were made through a series of informal bargaining sessions involving the regulatory public agencies and the several corporations representing the oil and steel industries. It was assumed that these sessions were undertaken in good faith on the part of all parties. If compliance, then, is defined in terms of improvements in the quality of industrial wastes discharged into the lake or its tributary basin within a specified period of time, its operationalization should reveal the extent of that good faith.[21]

The concept of compliance was operationalized by using the interrupted time-series model developed by Campbell.[22] Diagrammatically, the technique can be represented as:

$$0 \quad 0 \quad 0 \quad 0 \quad 0 \quad 0 \quad 0 \quad X \quad 0 \quad 0$$
$$1 \quad 2 \quad 3 \quad 4 \quad 5 \quad 6 \quad 7 \quad\quad 8 \quad 9$$

Observations 1 through 7 correspond to the semiannual means prior to December 31, 1968, and observations 8 and 9 to those after that date. The X indicates the intervention of the experimental treatment after which an evaluation is possible, contingent upon the rules outlined below. The chemical parameter values prior to the end of 1968 will be viewed as pretest scores, and those subsequent to that data as post-test. The assumptions of this quasi-experimental design are met with these data in that they have been aggregated along a continuous dimension that can be characterized as the dependent variable. If abrupt changes in this variable are attributable to a discrete event, that is, the voluntary compliance by the industries, this can be considered the independent or explanatory variable. Ideally, then, following the rendering of compliance, one would expect the post-test values to be significantly lower than the pretest values; the differences between them would be accounted for by the implementation of the compliance schedule, assuming plausible rival explanation for these differences can be eliminated by additional evidence. As of this writing the only evaluation carried out by the FWPCA has been on the rather weak "one-shot case study" of the pretest, post-test design.[23] The semiannual *Report*, dated August

[21] Thomas C. Schelling, "An Essay on Bargaining," in Polsby, Dentler, and Smith (eds.), *Politics and Social Life* (Boston: Houghton Mifflin, 1963), pp. 416–432. Schelling has noted it is a good bargaining tactic to incorporate a series of piecemeal bargains so that mutual expectations with regard to the prudence on the part of the bargaining partners will be revealed. The purpose then is to seek out and negotiate some minor items so that long-term good faith can be determined.
[22] Donald T. Campbell, "Reforms as Experiments," *American Psychologist*, 24 (1969), pp. 409–429.
[23] Donald T. Campbell and Julian C. Stanley, *Experimental and Quasi-Experimental Designs for Research* (Chicago: Rand McNally, 1966), p. 6.

1969, cited with respect to one of the experimental sampling stations included in this study: "There has been some improvement for some of the chemical parameters . . . although much progress was made, many of the recommended criteria were not met." [24]

From a quasi-experimental standpoint, a review of the inventory of threats to experimental validity will prove useful in efforts to identify plausible rival explanations to the attribution of success or failure of the treatment.

1. HISTORY. This refers to events between the pretest and post-test other than the treatment effect that might account for the change. A development over which the researcher has no control or data in this study was the extent of arrangements made with various industries by the public agencies. In this experiment it would be misleading to contend that the date for "substantially improving industrial effluent" was set uniformly and unambiguously.[25] At the conference held in January 1969, for example, the testimony of Perry Miller, superintendent of the Indiana Sanitary District, revealed that many exceptions and special concessions were granted to individual corporations; these concessions would affect the extent of their pollution during the crucial testing period. However, these arrangements were concerned exclusively with the installation of new facilities where none existed in the past, and not necessarily with improvements to existing facilities. In the case of U.S. Steel's Gary plant, extensions were granted to June 30, 1970, justified by "considerations of the complexity and magnitude of the job, the time required for site-preparation prior to construction of some facilities, and the availability of skilled labor in the area." [26] Apparently this arrangement was made just prior to the December 1968 deadline, and hence could have a confounding effect on the results of the experiment.

2. INSTABILITY. Campbell has cited instability of the measures involved in the experiment as a ubiquitous, plausible, rival hypothesis to attributing change to a discrete event. Instability refers principally to random shocks along the time series, which by definition occur in no cyclic pattern. Figures 2 and 3 illustrate how instability in the time series may be misconstrued when a one-shot case study is employed to determine the effectiveness of a treatment. When a larger number of obser-

[24] *Report on the Water Quality of Lower Lake Michigan,* Department of the Interior, August 1969.
[25] *Proceedings, 1965 Conference,* Vol. 1, p. 135.
[26] *Proceedings, 1969 Conference,* Vol. 2, p. 541.

Figure 2. *Hypothetical effect of compliance upon pollutants*

vations is taken into account, the change attributable to the treatment effect becomes confounded by the possibility that downward movement might be more accurately attributed to instability.

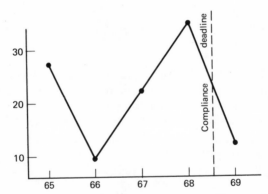

Figure 3. *Hypothetical effect of compliance upon pollutants (same data as in Figure 2 presented as part of an extended time series)*

In this study, the instability of the measures was largely the product of too few time points or observations.[27] The fundamental time-series model assumes that a proportion of periodic random shocks remains in the system to influence the movement of the system over time. Their influence on the series is not immediately dissipated but continues to

[27] Donald T. Campbell and Ross, H.L., "The Connecticut Crackdown on Speeding: Time-Series Data in Quasi-Experimental Analysis," *Law and Society Review* 3, 1 (1968), pp. 33–53.

work, although lessened on subsequent observations.[28] As will be readily apparent, with only nine observations it is conceivable that effects of a random shock in the first or second observation may hang over throughout the entire series.

Several methods of stabilizing the data were tried.[29] A revised moving average for two time points was employed because this approach eliminates cyclical and seasonal trends that may be anticipated with semiannual data, leaving the general trend along with random shocks due to nontrend related phenomenon.[30] But the data analysis depends upon the general trends and the shocks. Shocks around the compliance deadline reflect changes in the quality of industrial effluents, while the overall trend can be analyzed as the extent of sustaining improvements in the wastes discharged into the lake and the tributary basin.

The greatest disadvantage of the moving-averages method for stabilizing the data was that some of the data at the beginning and at the end of the series was lost. However, for the appropriate tests of significance, one time point in the post-test suffices. Additionally, the moving-averages method takes into account the values of all points in the series. Table 5 illustrates an example of the calculation. All data for all sampling stations were transformed in this way.

3. MATURATION. This refers to values of the parameters investigated which demonstrate fairly regular changes correlated with the passage of time. Maturation is distinguished from history in referring to processes rather than to discrete events. The general long-term trend of many pollution parameters can be attributed to maturation effects from the accretion of a richer biocycle and increasing eutrophication over time. In order to control for this threat to experimental validity, trend removal techniques are recommended to adjust for the extraneous source of variation due to aging. There are both methodological and substantive reasons for leaving long-term trend effects in the trans-

[28] Gene V. Glass, "Analysis of Data on the Connecticut Speeding Crackdown as a Time-series Quasi-Experiment," *Law and Society Review*, 3, 1 (1968), pp. 55–76.
[29] "Transformation," *New Encyclopedia of the Social Sciences* (New York: Macmillan, 1969), Vol. 16. In actuality, no truly satisfactory means to bring about data stability exists for semiannual data. One approach taken was the calculation of the means for the peaks and troughs, taking the differences between the means, and adding the mean difference to the troughs and subtracting it from the peaks. This did little in terms of reducing the variation in the data. A natural logarithm transformation was considered, but the log transform, while bringing the points closer together on the ends, preserves the ratio between the observations, therefore not reducing the variation.
[30] M. R. Spiegel, *Theory and Problems in Statistics* (New York: Schaum Publications, 1964) pp. 286–287.

Table 5   Oil and Grease (Indiana Harbor)

Date	Raw Data	Two-Season Moving Total	Two-Season Moving Average
2d–65	3.40		
1st–66	12.40	15.80	7.90
2d–66	6.20	18.60	9.30
1st–67	6.60	12.80	6.40
2d–67	10.40	17.00	8.50
1st–68	6.20	16.60	8.30
2d–68	5.90	12.10	6.05
1st–69	17.20	23.10	11.55
2d–69	12.10	29.30	14.65

formed data. As pointed out earlier, the aging process and the enriching biocycle refer primarily to organic pollutants and only marginally to the chemical properties of the water.

In addition to the methodological reason for leaving long-term trend effects in the transformed data, a substantive consideration must also prevail. This relates to the nature of the agreement reached between the industries and the public agencies that are calling for an enhancement of the water quality. We are interested in trends because compliance has been operationalized as reversal of the long-term trend.

Figure 4 illustrates how compliance might be construed pictorially. Assuming compliance, the long-term trend should reverse direction from sequential increments in pretest parameter values prior to the ini-

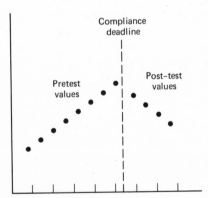

Figure 4. *Idealized relationship between compliance and values of pollution parameters*

tiation of the compliance schedule to sequential decrements subsequent to it.

4. TESTING. This refers to a change that may be caused by the initial measurement rather than the treatment. A great deal of publicity was given to the campaign against water pollution in the Chicago area. One of Chicago's largest metropolitan newspapers ran a series of articles in 1967, encouraging public action with regard to Lake Michigan. This does not actually pose a threat to the experimental validity. Since the objective was to elicit cooperation on the part of industry, the use of the mass media would be an effective tactic on the part of the public agencies to accomplish that objective.

5. INSTRUMENTATION. The measured change may be based on a change in the means of measuring rather than on the thing being measured. As has been noted by Campbell, the anticrime campaign during the term of Orlando Wilson as superintendent of police of the city of Chicago was deemed a success, although a changed bookkeeping technique made the records show a striking upsurge in recorded crimes during this period.[31] Fortunately, in this study, the measuring units have been uniform throughout the time periods covered. The samples taken by the FWPCA were all recorded in standard units, such as the number of milligrams per liter (mg/liter) of water sampled.

6. REGRESSION. If a group or unit was selected for treatment because it was extreme on some measure, statistical reasoning indicates that it will appear less extreme on subsequent tests even though the intervening treatment may be completely ineffectual. Campbell has argued that "moving along a time series, selecting points that are extraordinarily high, on the average, subsequent ones will be lower, less extreme, and closer to the general trend." [32] As was noted above, the industries were given three years before any evaluation of their long-term progress on reducing the amount of wastes discharged into the lake was made. No trends were established prior to the initiation of the program. The amount of lead time and the fact that the trends were not begun until June of 1965 tends to cancel out dramatic regression artifacts. In this study, regression artifacts do not pose serious threats to experimental validity.

[31] Campbell, *op. cit.*, p. 415.
[32] Campbell and Ross, *op. cit.*, p. 42.

Multiple Time Series

Of the four water-quality sampling stations chosen for this study, three served as experimental stations and one for purposes of control. The four stations were selected on the basis of overall comparability, but treatment effects differed—three sampling stations recorded chemical pollution parameters for corporations that were parties to the voluntary compliance schedule while the fourth was not. The assumption of equivalence on other extraneous factors was justified on the basis of the stations' geographical proximity and a multiple correlation coefficient of $R1.234 = 0.748$ for the mean water temperature values taken at all four stations over nine points in time.

However, the control station at Wolf Lake was subject to what could be called a diffusion effect. The Lever Brothers Company, which discharges its effluent into Wolf Lake, was not a party to the agreement, but was undoubtedly aware of the efforts of the public agencies to reduce industrial waste discharges. The overall trend in the values at the Wolf Lake station might be expected to decline over time if the management of the soap company voluntarily improved effluent quality without any intervention on the part of the public agencies.

Hypotheses and Data Analysis

The working hypothesis is that the voluntary compliance schedule was ineffectual in bringing about significant changes in the pollution levels for all experimental stations. The following hypotheses are offered as corollaries of the working hypothesis:

1. The pollution level for the monitoring station recording the outfall from two steel plants (Youngstown Sheet and Tube, and Inland Steel) will exceed all the other stations on all parameters.
2. The general trend will be marked by a gradual rise in all parameters.
3. Any appreciable reduction will be associated with phenomena other than those related to the voluntary compliance schedule.

Figures 5 through 12 represent several of the chemical parameters for the four sampling stations. The outfall from the two steel plants is plotted against the water-quality readings taken at the mouth of the Calumet River (which is partially influenced by U.S. Steel), and the outfall from the oil refineries is plotted against the values recorded at corresponding intervals on Wolf Lake.

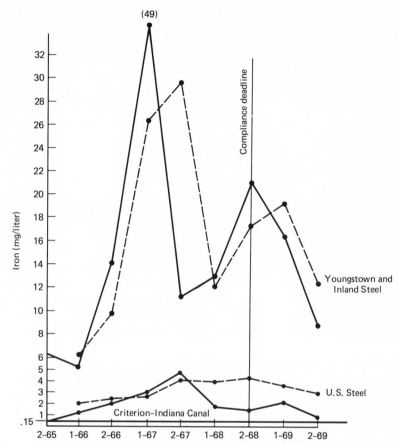

Figure 5. *Distribution of iron particles over time—steel plant outfalls (solid lines = raw data; broken lines = adjusted data)*

Figure 5 indicates that, subsequent to the treatment, some change in the quantity of iron particles was noted at the steel plant outfalls. But there has been great variation in this measure over the past few years. The change noted after the compliance deadline is not statistically significant.[33] In Figure 6 the trend line shows no appreciable

---

[33] The tests of significance were performed by use of a computer program written by Allan Pelowski. The single Mood test is calculated on the basis of the mean value and standard error of the pretest values establishing a confidence interval into which the next true or absolute value of the first observation in the post-test might be ex-

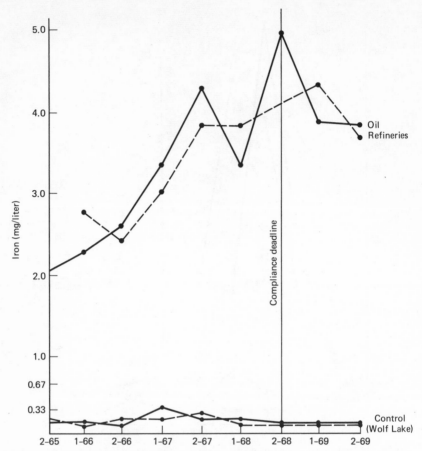

Figure 6. *Distribution of iron particles over time—oil refineries (solid lines = raw data; broken lines = adjusted data) NOTE: Criterion value for Indiana Canal was not scaled (.15 allowable)*

change after the compliance deadline; the Wolf Lake data show little variation in the small amounts of metal in that water.

pected to fall. Data transformation and trend removal generally reduces the standard error and thus narrows the interval in which deviation due to chance factors is likely. Due to the few number of observations in this pretest, however, a large standard error was present and could not be significantly reduced by trend removal techniques. For the steel-plant outfalls, the single Mood test of significance rendered a t value of 0.410 with five degrees of freedom. This value does not approach significance at the 0.10 level.

As seen in Figure 7, the phenolic compounds recorded at the site near the Youngstown and Inland Steel companies show a significant decrease in the second half of 1967.[34] Both plants installed settling basins, recirculation pumps, and naphthalene scrubbers in 1967. Large quantities of phenol, along with substantial amounts of ammonia and suspended solids, were removed from the effluent as a result of these installations.

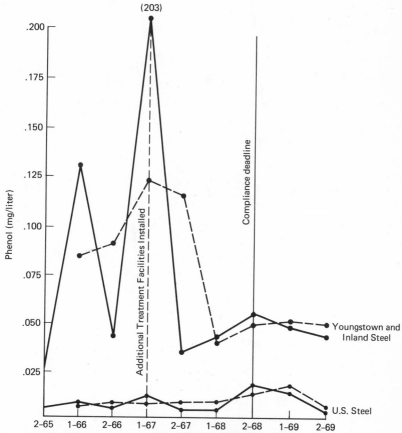

Figure 7. *Distribution of phenol over time—steel plant outfalls (solid lines = raw data; broken lines = adjusted data) NOTE: Criterion value for Indiana Canal was not scaled (.005 allowable)*

---

[34] The single Mood test produced a *t* score of 2.88; this was significant at the 0.05 level.

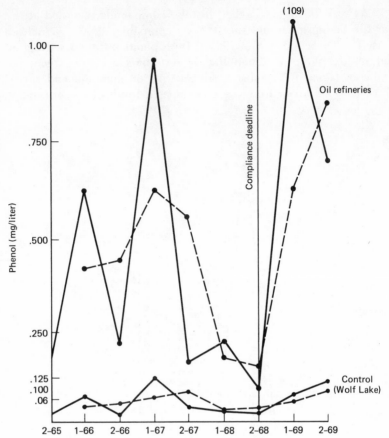

Figure 8. *Distribution of phenol over time—oil refineries (solid lines = raw data; broken lines = adjusted data) NOTE: Criterion value for Indiana Canal was not scaled (.005 allowable)*

Figure 8 provides data on phenol as monitored 2½ miles upstream from the steel plants on the Indiana Canal. This site should be monitoring the outfall from Mobil Oil, Cities Service, and Sinclair Refining plants. As graphed in Figure 8, there was a sharp rise in phenol in the vicinity of the oil refineries, which are not heavy users of acidic compounds. But the principal sources of phenol are the coke-quenching operations within the steel plants. Perhaps some dumping of this contaminant took place. This could have resulted from draining off the settling basins used to accumulate wastes over a period of several months. More complete information is necessary here.

The oil and grease trends sometimes behave erratically, owing to

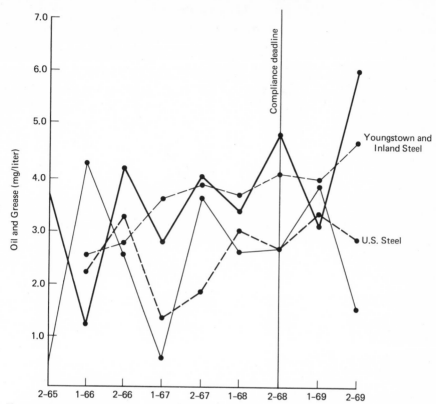

Figure 9. *Distribution of oil and grease over time—steel plant outfalls (solid lines = raw data; broken lines = adjusted data) NOTE: No quantified criterion exists*

infrequent oil slicks. These slicks can result from careless handling of petroleum products on shore, dumping or direct discharges from shipping vessels, tank ruptures, and the like. If the slicks are not treated or removed, they tend to break up. For prolonged periods of time, the surface of the water will be marked by the presence of an oily film, which may pose a grave fire hazard. Figure 9 shows a very perceptible upward trend in the oil parameter, as measured from the site near the outfalls from the two steel plants. The compliance schedule seems to have had virtually no effect. Figure 10 shows a sharp rise in oil pollutants from the three major oil refineries in the first half of 1969. A large oil slick resulting from a tank rupture at one of these refineries accounts for the dramatic increase in this parameter. The accident makes it impossible to determine the effects of the compliance schedule.

The cyanide reductions shown in Figures 11 and 12 are most encouraging. The results are statistically significant, and the upward trend illustrated in Figure 11 is reversed after the compliance deadline. Regression effect would appear ruled out as a plausible rival explanation. If a regression artifact were present, the observations subsequent to the peak reached in the second half of 1968 should fall near the series mean. But the last observation (using the adjusted data) is significantly below the mean. Similar results were obtained from the oil refinery data.

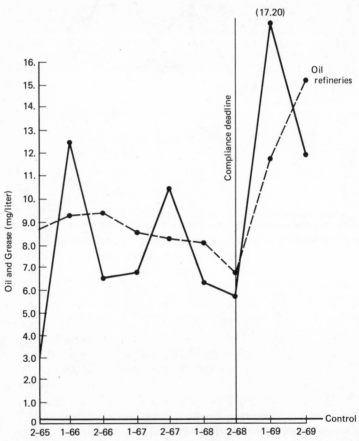

Figure 10. *Distribution of oil and grease over time—oil refineries (solid lines = raw data; broken lines = adjusted data) NOTE: No quantified criterion exists*

The data on the distribution of suspended solids were mixed. Improvements made in steel plant facilities near the end of 1967 brought about a temporary drop in levels of this pollutant, but these improvements were not long sustained. The oil refineries, on the other hand, seemed to show some improvement subsequent to the 1968 compliance deadline. But the changes were not sufficient to significantly "enhance the water quality of Lake Michigan's southern basin"; pollution from suspended solids merely returned to its 1965 level. Finally, an upward

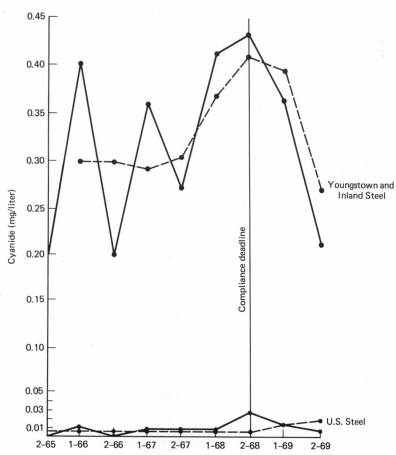

Figure 11. *Distribution of cyanide over time—steel plant outfalls (solid lines = raw data; broken lines = adjusted data) NOTE: Criterion value for Indiana Canal was not scaled (1.00 allowable)*

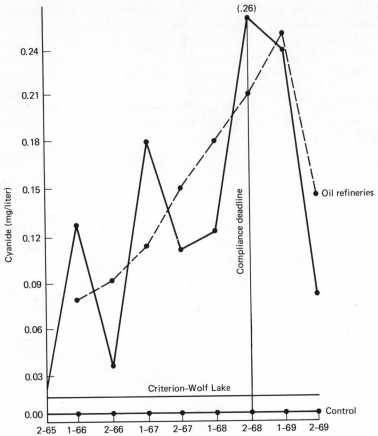

Figure 12. *Distribution of cyanide over time—oil refineries (solid lines =
raw data; broken lines = adjusted data) NOTE: Criterion value for
Indiana Canal was not scaled (1.00 allowable)*

deseasonalized trend was noted at the Wolf Lake control site. This
trend should be cause for concern, since until very recently the lake has
been enjoyed for water recreational purposes. Further increases are
clearly most undesirable.

The oil refineries also showed a sustained improvement in terms of
the quantity of total solids measured at the Indiana Harbor Canal site.
Nevertheless the values for total solids, which had reached a low point
of 240 mg/liter by the second half of 1969, were still substantially over
the criterion figure of 275 mg/liter. The voluntary compliance schedule

did not seem to have affected the steel companies' output of solid pollu-tants.

Discussion

Clearly, the most important results that seem to be attributable to the compliance agreement concern the reduction in cyanide in the steel companies' effluent. This was a most significant gain, but it should be noted that an earlier (1965) agreement with Inland Steel and Youngs-town Steel called for the total eradication of cyanide from their effluent. Although the upward trends were reversed after the 1968 deadline, total eradication was not achieved by the end of 1969. In fact, levels of cya-nide in the effluent of the steel companies were about the same in 1969 as in 1965 (about 0.15 parts per million of cyanide).

The hypotheses enumerated above have been for the most part confirmed. The working hypothesis, which posited the ineffectualness of the voluntary compliance schedule, was confirmed for four of the six pa-rameters tested, with the fifth parameter concerning the phenolic com-pounds somewhat in doubt. Corollary 1, hypothesizing that the highest pollution levels would be recorded from the outfall of the two steel plants, Youngstown and Inland, was confirmed also in four of the six pa-rameters tested. Corollary 2 hypothesized a gradual upward trend for all parameters. Of the 24 trends tested, the following tally resulted:

Upward	Downward	Irregular	Level
5	3	8	8

Corollary 3, which hypothesized that appreciable reductions would be associated with phenomena other than those related to the voluntary compliance schedule, was not confirmed. The three signifi-cantly downward trends apparently were related to industrial compli-ance.

In the latter part of 1968, the Great Lakes office of the FWPCA made a decision to extend the voluntary compliance schedule through December 1970. This involved working out piecemeal arrangements with individual corporations to make improvements in their treatment facilities; the public agencies would have recourse to litigation if the ar-rangements were abridged. The rationale was that the 1968 deadlines had been satisfactorily met. We believe that this was not a prudent deci-sion; for if the objective was to improve and enhance the waters of Lake

Michigan's southern basin, more strenuous policies should have been imposed. The governmental agencies have initiated programs to accomplish this objective, but better cooperation from industry is necessary.[35]

A comparison between the Ruhr Valley water pollution control scheme and the Lake Michigan experience may be instructive. The Ruhr Valley in Germany is one of the most densely populated, heavily industrialized areas of the world. It is slightly smaller than the state of Connecticut and consists of four different administrative districts. The waters and reservoirs in the valley support balanced quantities of marine flora and fauna and many species of water fowl. This was not always the case. In the late 1800s, pollution problems were acute, with industrial and mining wastes flowing through the valley along with household flotsam and jetsam and raw sewage. Water-borne disease was rampant.

By 1930 an association of six river authorities had been formed to investigate, plan, construct, operate, and replace all necessary installations for pollution abatement. The association accomplished its task with the help of public and private corporations (or persons) that polluted

---

[35] In the months immediately following the 1968 deadline, numerous suits and injunctions have been filed against polluters in the affected regions. A partial listing of this litigation follows:

Designated Source and Location:	Receiving Waters:	Action Taken:
Interlake Steel Company Riverdale, Illinois	Lower Calumet River	Suit filed by Metropolitan Sanitary District 10-69
U.S. Steel, South Works Chicago, Illinois	Lake Michigan, Calumet River	Suit filed by Illinois State's Attorney General 9-69
American Oil Company Whiting, Indiana	Lake Michigan	Suit filed by U.S. Justice Department, 2-18-70
Inland Steel Company East Chicago, Indiana	Indiana Harbor Canal	Suit filed by U.S. Justice Department, 2-18-70
Mobil Oil Company East Chicago, Indiana	Indiana Harbor Canal	Suit filed by U.S. Justice Department, 2-18-70
Youngstown Sheet & Tube Company (North Lagoon) East Chicago, Indiana	Indiana Harbor Canal	Suit filed by U.S. Justice Department, 2-18-70

Source: Great Lakes Region Office, Department of Interior, Chicago, Illinois. "Status of Compliance with Enforcement Conference Requirements," January 9, 1970 and subsequently updated.

or drew benefits from the improvements. It was financed by direct contribution in proportion to the distribution of those benefits and from taxes assessed on corporations for rectifying past damages. Assessments were made on the basis of corporate budgets; failure to meet the assessments resulted in litigation. Recalcitrants were subject not only to heavy fines but to imprisonment as well.

Effluent charges were assessed proportional to the quality and quantity of industrial discharge and were levied in proportion to the costs of abating the damage done. Detection was not on the basis of elaborate and frequent testing; such costs could not be justified. Rather, violators were reported on the basis of gross changes in water quality. This system was self-policing to the extent that the cost of damage caused by an undetected violation would be carried by everyone. Hence there was an inducement to report violations. The money saved by not policing or sampling went into research and development and applied treatment methods.

Of the maintenance costs of continued treatment, 45 percent was assessed to the Federal Water Works, which was allowed the largest representation in the policy-making assembly. Representation was proportional to the annual contribution, with one delegate allowed for each 1 percent of the budget. Representation was thus a right and not a privilege.[36]

Such an organizational framework is completely lacking in the case of Lake Michigan. Some of the reasons for this lack of organized effort are given here.

1. Public indifference. The pollution levels have yet to stir the public to the extent they are willing to defer their consumption habits for the long-range goal of improving the environment for future generations. This indifference is due in large part to the fact that potable water needs have been met in the past at practically no cost. Additionally, deleterious health problems arising from chronic water pollution have not affected the populace.
2. The funds necessary to curb water pollution alone could run as high as $1 billion a year over the next ten years,[37] and funds for pollution abatement must compete with other public demands.
3. Regulations and laws enacted in the past have been sorely wanting as far as bringing about successful enforcement. Symbolic rewards appear to be the norm for conservation efforts.

[36] Gordon Fair, "Pollution Abatement in the Ruhr District," in Henry Jarrett (ed.), *Comparisons in Resource Management* (Baltimore: Johns Hopkins Press, 1961), pp. 135–180.
[37] *The New York Times* editorial, October 17, 1969.

4. Political institutions are not fully responsive to the needs of the changing environment.

The four-state and federal government conference held in 1968 demonstrated the Lasswellian dictum that political demands articulated by organized groups probably have little relevance to social needs. Although the rhetoric went to the conservationists, the resources went to the industries. The speeches by industrial spokesmen applauded efforts to clean the water. Industry representatives claimed that they were doing their part to assist the public agencies accomplish the dual objectives of a cleaner environment and efficient resource management. But are these efforts appropriate or sufficient within the context of capabilities?

At virtually no cost, American industry has been afforded the use of public waterways for all phases of their production. Much of this use has served to deplete the supply of water available for other sources. Because of this, American industry is producing goods that may be underpriced, since the cost of their products does not adequately reflect the cost of the water inputs and outputs.[38] However, if some firms were put into a position where their costs of production were increased because of higher water costs, they might be forced out of business. Subsidies might be in order for these firms, but the subsidies to marginally productive firms need not be indefinite. Rather, they might only continue until such a time that the firm could alter its patterns of production.

Most water-polluting American industry is not marginal; included in the costs of production might be a modest assessment to be used to finance antipollution facilities.[39] Thus, water could become like all other factor inputs; when the cost of an input rises, business searches for ways to economize on it. Making the cost of water usage higher might prompt such a response.[40]

Management needs incentives to innovate. A 1959 industrial survey showed that the amount devoted to pollution control by such water-using industries as chemicals and paper totaled 0.2 percent of sales and 4.0 percent of sales, respectively.[41] Over the past ten years this percentage has undoubtedly increased, but the economic imperatives have

---

[38] John Breslaw, "Economics and Ecosystems," in Garrett De Bell, *The Environment Handbook* (New York: Ballantine Books, 1970).
[39] Blair T. Bower, "Economics of Industrial Water Utilization," in Kneese and Smith, *op. cit.,* p. 154.
[40] Kenneth Boulding, "Economics and Engineering," in H. Jarrett (ed.), *Environmental Quality in a Growing Economy* (Baltimore: Johns Hopkins, 1966).
[41] Bower, *op. cit.,* p. 155.

not been drastically altered.[42] Increased spending has not kept pace with the need. One way to stimulate such spending is to promote positive incentives (such as tax relief) for the construction of necessary waste treatment facilities. But the use of stronger governmental powers is more than justified by the need to rectify previous damages.[43]

The rapidly increasing demands for water recreation and an aesthetically pleasing environment call for a readjustment of resource allocations. The public spends vast sums of money on water-related recreation. People are willing to pay much more for waterfront property than for property located in a less pleasing setting. If accurate estimates could be made of those who would engage in water recreation and who would be willing to pay for the preservation of a scenic resource, the amounts would probably be quite large.[44]

If market conditions did prevail, industry clearly would lose its privilege of "free use." The market failure and subsequent government intervention should be used to reflect the maximum welfare.[45] The conclusion drawn here is that the price of water consumption and utilization should reflect the amount all users are willing to pay. By making the commodity more expensive, people might be encouraged to alter the practice of abusing this valuable resource.

[42] In a special survey taken by the American Iron and Steel Institute and released in August 1969, the following expenditures for water pollution control were given. Facilities placed in operation by iron and steel companies:

1966	$ 18,781,000
1967	54,652,000
1968	61,483,000
1969 and later	172,086,000 (expenditures authorized)

Unfortunately no data are given expressing the expenditures as percentages of sales or earnings.

[43] See the discussion by Hagevik in this volume [Article 18].

[44] Knetsch and Davis, "Comparison of Methods for Recreation Evaluation," in Castle and Smith, op. cit., p. 126.

[45] Davidson, Adams, and Seneca, "The Social Value of Water Recreational Facilities," in Kneese and Smith, op. cit., p. 186.

PART SIX

PROBLEMS OF CHANGE

How is change to be brought about? The current emphasis on environmental problems has resulted in the passage of new legislation and increasing public pressure upon individual companies seen as polluters. However, the factors which influence organizations to change their ways are rather hazy. In the absence of clear market controls, particular businesses may fight environmental-oriented legislation, complying only when political and legal avenues have been exhausted. Other businesses may announce their intent to help clean up the environment and initiate action in this regard with relatively little prodding on the part of the public, state and federal bureaucracies, or conservation groups.[1]

The readings in this part all emphasize influence and change, but different aspects are stressed. The Schiff article deals with the difficulties organizational members have in changing their ways of thinking. Particular value orientations may persist despite changed circumstances and new lines of evidence. Various factors are important in trying to explain a lack of organizational flexibility.

Previous research on innovative organizations has suggested that such variables as size, wealth, and availability of re-

[1] The confusion in this area is all too apparent. When leading industrialists were asked to evaluate the environmental performance of eight basic industries, only the electric utility industry was given reasonably high marks. This would undoubtedly come as a shock to the public in New York and Chicago, who have followed the wars waged by conservationists on Consolidated Edison and Commonwealth Edison. Robert S. Diamond, "What Business Thinks," *Fortune* (February, 1970), pp. 118–119.

sources are of critical importance.[2] Large rich organizations seem to be able to

1. give more flexibility to their personnel in developing new programs;
2. attract more specialized personnel;
3. provide free time for work on innovative material.

On the other hand, another study has suggested that the more profit-oriented an organization, the less innovative is its behavior.[3]

In addition to examining organization variables which might contribute to innovative behavior on the part of the organization, the innovative propensity of top-level management is also relevant. The factors which are related to the innovativeness of individuals have been more thoroughly researched. The following variables are considered important:

1. An individual's attitudes toward change
2. A cosmopolitan versus a local orientation
3. Individual competence and interests
4. The professional orientation of the individual
5. Individual opinion leadership.

An organization's overall resource level is likely to be related to an individual's ability to innovate. One study of innovation in the public health service found that when the level of resources was high, individual motivation played a substantial role in predicting innovative behavior, but that under conditions of resource scarcity, individual motivation was much less important.

The difficulty with innovation theory is that it was developed for circumstances where a procedural change was likely to bring some economic gain to the organization or individual undertaking the innovation. A change in an individual corpora-

---

[2] These organizational and individual variables are summarized from Lawrence B. Mohr, "Determinants of Innovation in Organizations," *American Political Science Review*, 63, 1 (March 1969) pp. 111–136. Research on businessmen's attitudes and behaviors has also found the variable of size to be crucial. See Raymond A. Bauer, Ithiel de Sola Pool, and Lewis A. Dexter, *American Business and Public Policy* (New York: Atherton Press, 1963).

[3] Martin M. Rosner, "Economic Determinants of Organizational Innovation," *Administrative Science Quarterly*, 12, 4 (March 1968), pp. 614–625.

tion's or sector's approach to the environment may result in a long-term social good, but this social good may come about at considerable cost to the organization which has changed its policies. The presence of such costs makes the innovation framework seem rather inappropriate.

A formulation which emphasizes compliance may be more relevant than one which stresses innovation. Organizations which molest the environment without concern for pollution control are under increasing pressure to comply with various statutes and regulations. The articles by Carter examine the changing status of conservation law; conservationists have been relatively successful in restraining some of the worst assaults upon the environment. But valuable as court suits may be, effective regulation and effective legislation provide the framework which makes it possible to protect the environment.

The articles by Hagevik and Vitullo-Martin present different approaches to problems of legislation and regulation. Hagevik believes incrementalism can result in significant changes, while Vitullo-Martin rejects the incremental approach for a more conflict-producing, radical strategy. Vitullo-Martin deemphasizes technical variables, while Hagevik stresses the importance of technical factors in generating the best, most workable regulations.

Studying change in terms of compliance and innovation is valuable, but one more theoretical approach might be mentioned here. Theory developed to handle the noneconomic behavior of business firms might prove useful, although no literature applying this theory to environmental problems is familiar to the editor. Cyert and March have suggested that a firm's allocation to noneconomic goals is subject to fluctuations both in organizational slack and in competitor's allocations.[4] Organizational slack is the disparity between the resources available to the organization and the payments required to keep various members inside the organization. Organizational slack represents a cushion for times of resource scarcity; during boom periods the organization may add frills, taking up the slack.

This concept of organizational slack is useful in a number of substantive areas. Hypotheses can be generated to deal with the differences among different sectors in the American economy and among enterprises within one economic sector. Organi-

[4] Richard M. Cyert and James G. March, *A Behavioral Theory of the Firm* (Englewood Cliffs, N.J.: Prentice-Hall, 1963).

zational slack may be measured in terms of the absolute and relative levels of resources available to an organization. Corporations might be more likely to exhibit a concern for the environment in good times than in bad times.

Resource levels may have an independent effect upon environment-oriented activities. The more successful corporations may have more long-range, conservation-oriented concerns; it may be that such relatively rich organizations are less motivated by the "quick buck" than are their less affluent counterparts.

Sensitivity to competitor's allocations also appears to be an important factor. Corporate managements seem to fear that their competitors will take unfair advantage if environment-protecting measures are adopted unilaterally. The corporate sense of social responsibility is pitted against the possibility of competitive disadvantage. This dilemma has tended to make corporations look favorably toward federal regulations which would be applicable to all companies in a given sector.

15

Innovation and Administrative Decision Making: The Conservation of Land Resources

Problems of organizational innovation have been examined from the perspectives of incentive management and limited cognition theory. This study, however, points to the significance of certain fundamental value orientations, often suprainstitutional, for an understanding of decision making. It examines the impact of an orientation toward change, shared by resource management agencies, upon biological science, resource economics, and administrative practices. It compares agency positions along a change spectrum to explain varying resistance to innovation. Possibilities for further research into the role of this variable in other substantive areas are advanced in a concluding evaluation of its significance for the study of innovation.

Ideology and Innovation [1]

Studies of organizational innovation have followed two main paths. Reflecting the influence of Barnard's inducements-contributions approach, some students have stressed the importance of effective incen-

* The late Professor Schiff taught at State University of New York at Stony Brook. This article first appeared in the June 1966 Administrative Science Quarterly, 11, 1.
[1] [Editor's Note: For author's acknowledgment of assistance by various co-workers and comments or sources provided by others, see original article in Administrative Science Quarterly.]

tive management.[2] Through the skilled use of explicit penalties and rewards, executives may enable organizations to maintain themselves in a
hazardous environment. Other students, aware of the significance of limitations on knowledge for a theory of administrative choice and search,
have focused on the phenomena of goal factoring, construction of
means-ends chains, subunit identifications, attention focus, and suboptimization or "satisficing." [3] Thus, administrators may simplify a complex
world by attending to only part of it at a time and by fixing their attention on proximate objectives and operational criteria.

Common to both viewpoints is a belief in the efficacy of purposeful
activity in organizational adaptation. Several students, however, have
expressed reservations. One found that organizations that deliberately
engineered changes failed to demonstrate marked superiority in adjus-
tive power.[4] Another proposed a theory of "natural selection" to reckon
capacity for survival, relying on random variations in organizational
forms and policy commitments.[5] This skeptical view of the administrator's ability to effect a deliberate adjustment of the organization may
well reflect a recognition of the many dimensions of organizational behavior that remain to be investigated. Pending isolation of these variables, reliance on chance to explain organizational fate is perhaps prudent even if it is not satisfying.

One variable that has not received sufficient attention in the
literature is the role of fundamental administrative outlooks or professional ideologies. Unfortunately, the very pervasiveness of these suprainstitutional orientations, reaching beyond the range of specific policies,[6]
has apparently led investigators to ignore them. Their almost metaphysi-
cal character is perhaps disconcerting to students seeking more manageable, analytical categories.

Despite the difficulties incident to a study of the role of administrative ideologies, however, it can be clearly demonstrated that at least
in the attitude of conservationists toward the treatment of land resources, ideology influenced organizational behavior and constrained innovative capability.

[2] Peter Clark and James Q. Wilson, Incentive Systems: A Theory of Organizations,
Administrative Science Quarterly, 6 (1961), p. 129.
[3] James March and Herbert Simon, *Organizations* (New York: Wiley, 1958); Richard
Cyert and James March, *A Behavioral Theory of the Firm* (Englewood Cliffs, N.J.:
Prentice-Hall, 1963).
[4] John McNulty, Organizational Change in Growing Enterprises, *Administrative Science Quarterly*, 7 (1962), p. 1.
[5] Herbert Kaufman, Organizational Theory and Political Theory, *American Political
Science Review*, 58 (1964), p. 13.
[6] Philip Selznick, *Leadership in Administration* (Chicago: Row, Peterson, 1957).

Past attempts at explaining institutional adaptation have correctly focused on the relationship between an organization and its environment.[7] By casting that relationship almost exclusively in objective terms, however, organization theorists have failed to take due account of subjective or ideological factors. In the prevailing view, administrative innovation, or goal succession, is determined by the environment. Janowitz has argued that present military thought and behavior patterns are traceable to changing technology.[8] Clark suggests that the orientations of service enterprises, such as the open-door college, are "determined to a large degree by context."[9] Economic theory, notes Dill, holds that the behavior of the firm is affected principally by the "offerings and demands of suppliers, customers, shareholders, competitors, unions, governments, and the like."[10]

As a consequence of this interpretation, organizational change is seen chiefly as a function of power or resource exchange. Several students have been attracted to a scheme which arrays organizations along a continuum describing varying degrees of environmental domination.[11] But power is itself partly a function of perception. The environment is filtered through layers of organizational ideology and traditions. Reality becomes relevant to organizational operations only when it is recognized.[12] This point has been implicitly noted in the literature. Blau and Scott proposed, for instance, that adaptation may occur if the environment supplies "*stimulating* challenges."[13] But the role of perception in mediating the environment-institution interface will never be assigned adequate weight as long as ideologies and fundamental value orienta-

[7] James D. Thompson and William J. McEwen, Organizational Goals and Environment, *American Sociological Review*, 23 (1958), 23–31.

[8] Morris Janowitz, *Sociology and the Military Establishment* (New York: Russell Sage Foundation, 1959), pp. 16–19.

[9] Burton R. Clark, *The Open Door College* (New York: McGraw-Hill, 1960), p. 175.

[10] William Dill, "Business Organizations," in James G. March (ed.), *Handbook of Organizations* (Chicago: Rand McNally, 1965), p. 1077.

[11] Thompson and McEwen, *op. cit.*; Sol Levine and Paul White, Exchange as a Conceptual Framework for the Study of Interorganizational Relationships, *Administrative Science Quarterly*, 5 (1961), 583–601. John Maniha and Charles Perrow, The Reluctant Organization and the Aggressive Environment, *Administrative Science Quarterly*, 10 (1965), 238–257. David Sills, *The Volunteers* (Glencoe, Ill.: Free Press, 1957).

[12] Edward Tiryakian, Existential Phenomenology and the Sociological Tradition, *American Sociological Review*, 30 (1965), 674–688; Alfred Schutz, *Collected Papers: The Problem of Social Reality*, ed. by Maurice Natanson (The Hague: Martinus Nijhoff, 1962); Brand Blanshard, Critical Reflections on Behaviorism, *Proceedings, American Philosophical Society*, 109 (1964), 22–28.

[13] Peter Blau and W. Richard Scott, *Formal Organizations* (San Francisco: Chandler, 1962), p. 231 (italics added).

tions are treated only as implications rather than as integral elements of analysis.[14]

To little attention has been given to examining the dialectical interaction between physical and ideational (values, ideas) phenomena, and to studying the persistent tension between reality and images of reality in various fields.[15] Such an inquiry might well address itself to a comparative study of the influence of ideology upon administrative innovation in activities ranging from control of the physical environment to intervention in socio-economic affairs. It would certainly be interesting to know whether adaptation is likely to come sooner in one area than in another. If it could be determined that ideology represents a significant variable, our understanding of the environment-domination continuum would be considerably improved.

It is not enough, in other words, merely to be aware that ideology plays some vague role or to treat perceptions as operating constraints, and then to proceed in an analysis along traditional lines. What is required is a continuing assessment of the constant interplay between organizations, ideology, and environment. Each component, and/or its parts, may be observed to undergo modification at varying rates. By examining ideological orientations, it may prove possible to ascertain which agencies, or their subunits, will innovate while others remain inactive and which will function at different times as ideological carriers furnishing strategic policy and behavioral cues to groups with related program obligations. Hopefully, concern with normative viewpoints will permit identification of those slight gradations in outlook that favor administrative adaptation. Conversely, this approach might allow analysts to specify alterations in that part of the environment most amenable to control in order to bring it into harmony with preferences believed worth preserving.

The present study had its origin as part of a larger effort to explain differences between Canada and the United States in their forest

---

[14] A special exception should be made for total institutions which, by restricting social contact with the outside world, internalize that world. Only in the case of these organizations did ideology appear to have immediate administrative relevance. *Cf.* Erving Goffman, "The Characteristics of Total Institutions" in Amitai Etzioni (ed.), *Complex Organizations: A Sociological Reader* (New York: Holt, Rinehart and Winston, 1961). See chapters by Cressey and Perrow in James G. March (ed.) *Handbook of Organizations* (Chicago: Rand McNally, 1965). Note inattention to ideological variable in Elihu Katz and S. N. Eisenstadt, Some Sociological Observations on the Response of Israeli Organizations to New Immigrants, *Administrative Science Quarterly* 5 (1960), 113–133.

[15] Arnold Rose, "The Relation of Theory and Method," in Llewellyn Gross (ed.), *Colliquium on Social Theory* (New York: Harper and Row, 1966); Tiryakian, *op. cit.*, p. 683.

research operations. Early in that investigation, it became apparent that American foresters had long held to a certain value orientation toward change. This orientation shaped their interpretation of the natural world, as well as their attitudes concerning resource economics and administrative management. This fundamental perspective was found to pervade not only the Forest Service but professional decision makers in other jurisdictions. The analysis which follows describes the chief components of the value orientation and then traces its impact upon forest, wildlife, park, and soil management. To underline the relevance of this normative commitment for administrative behavior, liberal use was made of material drawn from bureaucratic files and the technical literature of conservation.

Perspectives toward Change in the Conservation Movement

Central to conservationist thought was the concept of change in the natural and the social environment as a process characterized by such values as harmony, symmetry, continuity, and balance—values precious to all conservationists whether they favored preservation or development. Those who believed in preservation conceived of the natural order as permanent and unchanging, and argued that man should on no account interfere with the process of nature. Those who believed in development, however, deftly juggled both this static-mechanistic construct and an evolutionary-organic model of the universe to support their view that change was natural and that man ought to exercise initiative in manipulating the environment.

The preservationist attitude was represented in the outlook of the National Park Service, which saw its role as a mission to protect a changeless world from disfigurement by man. The developmental attitude was reflected in the outlook of the U.S. Forest Service, which believed that forests were a resource that nature intended to be harvested periodically as a crop. The conservationist change-spectrum, then, ranged only from a belief in a completely stable system to the view that nature underwent development at a predictable rate. Although the developmental view was partial to slow transformation, it could tolerate rapid changes, provided these proceeded at a uniform pace, or in a manner that is now modishly referred to as "steady-state dynamics." To be sure, developmentalists could accommodate silent revolutions—involving "small, nondiscernible steps or increments leading to a qualitative jump." [16] Even conflict, a concept integral to the organic model, was admissible as long as it was controlled and contained in the natural process. Alterations of a catastrophic kind (those requiring "a cataclysmic or critical event leading to a sudden change"),[17] however, utterly defied interpretation, except as the product of accid...tal disturbances.

Stochastic analysis—with its emphasis on statistical probability—offered an escape from the determinism of evolutionary thought, but the spontaneity, the "insecurity," which it posited could not serve as a base to a faith in the restoration of unity and order. Periods of crisis rarely inspire "slack" innovation.[18] The energies of the movement were guided by long-familiar paradigms; in search of continuities, it was apt to slight examination of discontinuities.

Scientific Basis of Conservationist Ideology

Conservationist arguments about the natural environment clearly indicate the difficulties they had in coping with the idea of catastrophic change in nature. They fancied a natural world which, before its defilement by "civilized man," was resplendent with primeval forests untouched by fire or the ax, graced by vast reaches of undisturbed grasslands, countless herds of animals and flocks of birds, pristine rivers rolling gently to the sea, and soils developed over eons of time. For many years, from the beginning of the movement in the late 19th century until recently, this image could claim scientific support. Equilibrium models —both static and dynamic—were considered valid descriptions of reality by most foresters, soil scientists, and plant and population ecologists.

Probably the most persuasive case for the stereotype of virginal America was made by the world-renowned plant ecologist, E. F. Clements, of the University of Nebraska, who first advanced his organismic idea of plant communities in 1904. Though proud of having formulated a "dynamic ecology," Clements placed highest value on the permanent plant community—"the climax." Whatever changes occurred following attainment of the climax stage were deemed to operate "within the fabric of the climax." [19] Thus, assuming a stable climate, climax plant asso-

[16] Kenneth Boulding, *The Organizational Revolution* (New York: Harper, 1953), pp. xxiv–xxv.

[17] Robert Chin, "The Utility of System Models and Development Models for Practitioners," in Warren Bennis, Kenneth Benne, Robert Chin (eds.), *The Planning of Change—Readings in the Applied Behavioral Sciences* (New York: Holt, Rinehart and Winston, 1961), pp. 209–210.

[18] R. M. Cyert and J. G. March, *op. cit.*, p. 279.

[19] John Weaver and Frederic E. Clements, *Plant Ecology* (2d ed., New York: McGraw-Hill, 1938), p. 80.

ciations would perpetuate themselves through time until they inevitably dominated the "natural landscape." Indeed, it was this stable condition which, according to Clements, had been encountered by Lewis and Clark when they traversed the "great climaxes from deciduous forest in the east through the vast expanse of prairie and plain to the majestic coniferous forest of the northwest." [20] Clements believed that the interest of forestry and grazing were best served by the maintenance of the natural climax.[21] Such advice could only have been proffered by one to whom all subclimaxes—earlier stages in the process of development to the climax—represented "imperfection." [22]

In stressing the pervasiveness of stability as a scientific fact and management norm, Clements minimized the effect of catastrophic forces. He believed that the natural incidence of fire was both infrequent and localized in its effects, except for the northern Rocky Mountains, where lightning strikes without rain were common.[23] Other "natural" catastrophes, Clements believed, were likewise limited in their duration and the extent of their consequences. Even at their maximum population levels, for example, bison and pronghorn antelope exerted "only a transient effect upon the [grass] climax." [24]

Clements went astray because he treated catastrophe as an exogenous variable operating upon a highly-integrated system. Ecological relationships are, in fact, more loose jointed. Catastrophe may properly be regarded as an integral feature of the natural environment. The most palpable example of the deficiency of Clements's reasoning is his misinterpretation of the significance of climatic extremes, such as those of temperature and precipitation. How telling it is of his equilibrium bias that he should have read stability into the effects of even this most erratic variable.

Forest Management

Despite the shortcomings of his theory, Clements was profoundly influential for many years. Only in 1955 could Frank Egler of The American Museum of Natural History say confidently that a revolution against the accepted interpretation was occurring:

[20] James Malin, *The Grassland of North America: Prolegomena to Its History* (Lawrence, Kansas: published by author, 1947), p. 125. See also Weaver and Clements, *op. cit.*, p. 92.
[21] Frederic Clements, "Climaxes, Succession and Conservation," in B. W. Allred and Edith Clements (eds.), *Dynamics of Vegetation* (New York: H. W. Wilson, 1949), p. 12.
[22] Frederic Clements, Plant Formations and Forest Types, *Proceedings, Society of American Foresters*, 4 (1909) p. 62.
[23] Frederic Clements, in *Dynamics of Vegetation, op. cit.*, p. 248.
[24] James Malin, *op. cit.*, p. 126.

> Much of traditional ecology is pretty well on the skids—going out—and
> it would be rather hard to find a strong and powerfully convinced, evan-
> gelistic ecologist, even though there are some who are thoroughly
> grounded in the old "plant succession to climax." [25]

In the period before it was fully repudiated, Clements's doctrine had a
pervasive influence on administrative decision making, not in changing
administrative thinking, but in providing a convincing rationale for
practices that had already become standard. It seemed to foresters that
Clements had provided irrefutable scientific verification for their experience. His systematic theory fit the view of the biological world that they
had previously only sensed and acted upon.

In most cases, foresters were not aware that they were applying
Clements's theory. Those who were did not question the theory because,
at least in some areas, the theory seemed to be confirmed by experience.
Particularly in temperate zones, where there was relatively little climatic instability, it was possible to believe that instability would be
damaging. Even where experience did not confirm the theory, foresters
seemed unwilling to challenge it. Thus, in the northern forests the evidence gathered by foresters themselves clearly indicated that extremes
of climate and natural catastrophe would sometimes have beneficial results. But some Canadian foresters persisted in arguing that since fire
was a destabilizing factor, it must be harmful. One Canadian research
forester, S. A. Mulloy, after admitting that fire had favored the regeneration of Newfoundland spruce, which were in competition with (less desirable) balsam fir, nevertheless went on to contend that fire increased
the severity of disease conditions by promoting instability.[26]

In the U.S., unlike Canada, the closer coalescence of theory and
woods experience makes it difficult to know whether ideology or practice was more important. Undeniably, their combined effect distorted
American foresters' perception of the nature of change and therefore
constrained them in policy questions on forest management. Under no
circumstances, foresters argued, should fire be regarded as a powerful
silvicultural ally. How irrational, reasoned Page Bunker (Alabama state
forester), to discern design in the acts of erratic, violent forces:

> To assume that such a violently destructive agent as fire could by a for-
> tuitous combination of circumstances be based upon the pine forests of a
> particular species for extended ages with such regularity and temper as

[25] Frank Egler, in William L. Thomas, Jr. (ed.), *Man's Role in Changing the Face of
the Earth* (Chicago: University of Chicago, 1957), p. 941.
[26] G. A. Mulloy, Silvicultural Problems of Our Balsam Fir—Spruce Type Forests, *Canadian Woodlands Review*, 1 (April 1930), p. 10.

to bring about adaptive changes rather than elimination must tax the credulity of even the most reckless theorist.[27]

Resistance to the idea that instability might be beneficial lingered on. Only in 1948 did a top-ranking U.S. Forest Service official, on an inspection tour of the Lake states, inform his colleagues that they had been guided by a thoroughly unrealistic assumption of natural stability:

> One outstanding impression I gained from my trip was that the new forests of the Lake States were undergoing very marked changes and that sites and vegetation were in anything but a static condition. . . . Up to date, it seems to me that our recommendations for the major types have assumed that forest conditions will remain fairly static; that jack pine might be expected to succeed jack pine under our recommendations; and that in red pine stands we should favor red pine reproduction. Perhaps my impression is wrong but it seemed to me that our own group was not particularly cognizant of the possible significance of these ecological changes, and that absence of recognition of their possible importance might eventually result in present recommendations being only of transitory value. This matter was touched upon in several discussions, and Eyre pointed out to me that the station [Lake States Forest Experiment Station] . . . had done a considerable amount of ecological research which had not been too productive.[28]

To claim that the Forest Service was bound to a completely static approach would overstate the case. A programmatic commitment to harvesting trees as a crop inclined it toward a modification, though not an abandonment of the ideal. Selective cutting, in contrast to block cutting, seemed to approximate "natural" logging, and so was approved.[29] But the Service was not prepared to employ fire, for that would have required a total rejection of its ideology.

Wildlife Management

Since the Forest Service was a kind of elite vanguard for the conservation movement, its attitudes permeated other resource agen-

[27] Page Bunker, quoted in Ashley L. Schiff, *Fire and Water: Scientific Heresy in the Forest Service* (Cambridge, Mass.: Harvard University, 1962), p. 36.
[28] Leonard Barrett, Lake States Inspection Report, May–June 1948, National Archives Box 1145, Record Group 95.
[29] Aldo Leopold, *Game Management* (New York: Scribner's, 1947), p. 397; Gifford Pinchot, *Breaking New Ground* (New York: Harcourt, Brace, 1947), p. 77. This may also explain in part Pinchot's defense of selective logging of Adirondack spruce, and the Service's enthusiastic interest in a similar cutting plan for Douglas fir in the 1930s. To be sure, the technique also furnished an excuse for highgrading (logging only profitable timber) in times of depressed markets.

cies.[30] At first, wildlife management thinking was influenced by theories of the balance of nature, which treated all population fluctuations as "unnatural," therefore undesirable.[31] This view was repudiated sooner in the wildlife field than in the field of forest management. Charles Elton —an early population ecologist—recognized that wildlife had an affinity for disturbed areas and that catastrophe sometimes had beneficial effects on plant and animal communities.[32] The theory was also rejected in the first large-scale private practice of game management, based on Herbert Stoddard's study of Georgia's quail preserves (1924–1928). Not unexpectedly, Stoddard's project was conducted under the auspices of the Biological Survey—predecessor of the Fish and Wildlife Service. Because the report recommended use of fire for habitat improvement, it met with Forest Service opposition. As Stoddard recalled:

> I rewrote the fire chapter five times in the attempt to get it cleared. Finally, seeing no course to pursue, I passed the word where I knew it would spread to the effect that the fire chapter, already sadly "watered down," would have to be cleared for publication or else I would resign and write a book on the subject that would *not be a compromise.* The sportsmen who had financed our study to the tune of over fifty thousand dollars included several of the most powerful men in the country, politically and financially; I knew they would back me to a man. . . . It was soon reluctantly cleared in the form it appeared in "The Bobwhite Quail" in 1931.[33]

Alerted to this valuable instrument for reversing the process of vegetative succession, wildlife management officials soon became avid proponents of controlled burning. By the early 1950s, they used fire extensively to improve waterfowl, muskrat, cattle, moose, and deer habitats.[34]

[30] In 1948, at 14 of the 23 institutions offering wildlife work, courses were organized under the forestry department. See Reuben Trippensee, *Wildlife Management* (New York: McGraw-Hill, 1948), p. 441. In his *Wildlife Management,* Trippensee frequently refers to the forestry profession as a model for wildlife management to emulate. Note influence of former forester Aldo Leopold in wildlife field. See Leonard Wing, *Practice of Wildlife Conservation* (New York: John Wiley, 1951).

[31] S. A. Forbes, On Some Interactions of Organisms, *Bulletin of the Illinois State Laboratory of Natural History,* 1 (1903), p. 15.

[32] Charles Elton, *Animal Ecology and Evolution* (Oxford: Oxford University, 1930).

[33] Herbert Stoddard, Use of Fire in Pine Forests and Game Lands of the Deep Southeast, Tall Timbers Research Station, Tallahassee, Florida, *Proceedings,* 1 (1962), 38–39.

[34] John J. Lynch, The Place of Burning in Management of the Gulf Coast Wildlife Refuges, *Journal of Wildlife Management,* 5 (1941). Also, Daniel Lay, Muskrat Investigations in Texas, *Journal of Wildlife Management,* 9 (1945). For a summary of previous literature, see William Longhurst, A. Starker Leopold, and Raymond Dasmann, *A Survey of California Deer Herds; Their Ranges and Management Problems* (California Fish and Game Bulletin No. 6 [Sacramento, Calif., 1952]).

Lately, the U.S. Forest Service has scheduled controlled burning operations to regenerate jack pine thickets in Michigan's Lower Peninsula. The object here is to produce breeding habitat indispensable for the Kirtland's warbler—a songbird endangered by the results of effective fire protection programs. Ironically, and apposite to our thesis, a prominent ornithologist, upon first confirming the warbler's nesting site, had suggested that fire might be the bird's worst enemy.[35] The tide has turned—the beneficial impact of catastrophe has become a subject appropriate for public discussion. Interior Secretary Stewart Udall told a recent resources gathering:

> Presently, we depend upon natural conditions, some of which approach the proportions of disasters, to keep the waterfowl habitat in balance. A hurricane strikes a coastal area and delivers large quantities of salt water into marsh areas decimating marsh vegetation and reducing it to what is called a "young" marsh. As time goes by, the marsh passes through various successions of plant life, becoming more and more attractive to waterfowl. Eventually it reaches a brackish "middle age"—its most attractive phase—and then, as the fresh water builds up, it loses its desirability to waterfowl. It is ready again for a hurricane, a flood, a burning, or some other kind of shock treatment.[36]

Park Management

The National Park Service, custodian of the nation's "crown jewels," long stood detached from controversies embroiling other resource agencies. Anxious to preserve primeval environments, it eagerly equated the notion of climax with the idea of "naturalness." Thus, the Park Service insisted in 1940:

> All areas are enhanced by the presence of natural forests. Removal of, damage to, or lack of forest materially reduces the value of any area, and natural undisturbed forest conditions have a greater appeal than artificially created or man-changed woodlands. . . . The climax types are . . . the very important forests which enhance the scenic and recreational values of the parks. . . . There are no forests in this nation that

---

[35] Harold Mayfield, *The Kirtland's Warbler* (Bloomfield Hills, Mich.: Cranbrook Institute of Science, 1960), p. 23. See U. S. Forest Service News Release for May 29, 1963. *Cf.* distorted story in National Wildlife Federation *Newsletter* of May 15, 1963.

[36] Department of the Interior News Release, October 16, 1964. See also relevant material in Joseph Linduska (ed.), *Waterfowl Tomorrow* (Washington: U.S. Department of the Interior, 1964).

deserve more intensive protection from fire, than those irreplaceable virgin stands.[37]

As recently as 1962, the Park Service still confused "natural" with unchangeable. A Service publication repeated that its mission was to manage "these properties so as to neutralize . . . all unnatural influences whether arising from unbalanced natural conditions and public use within, or whether invading the Parks from without." [38]

Unfortunately, the Park Service espoused a particularly inappropriate theory when it proclaimed the virtues of stability. Parks like Yosemite and Everglades contain attractions which owe their very existence to catastrophic forces. Without periodic burning to eradicate brush and competing vegetation, the giant sequoia would shortly find themselves displaced by more tolerant sugar pine and white fir. Unless Park managers reduced such accumulations of debris and plant material, even the normally fire-resistant sequoia might be consumed by holocausts.[39] Where in the past, Yosemite's Mariposa Grove had awed early visitors by its columns of widely spaced giants, later observers glimpsed dense thickets of young trees (but not Sequoia gigantea) obscuring the scenic vistas. The Service had been warned about these depressing developments. In 1930, a Park engineer advocated removal of this vegetation. Four years earlier, a Forest Service consultant came to the same conclusion, though he held fire responsible for destroying forest values.

Yosemite Superintendent Thompson (1934) carried out vista-clearing operations only to be censured by Washington for interfering with primeval conditions. In 1934, a Service biologist pointed out that fire protection in Sequoia communities should be regarded as unnatural. As with previous suggestions the Service failed to make a positive response. Nor did the agency ever undertake measures, e.g., control burning, to recapture the magnificence of Yosemite Valley carpeted with wildflowers—the sight of which had so impressed John Muir.[40]

[37] Department of the Interior, Forest Conservation on Lands Administered by the Department of the Interior (Washington: Department of the Interior, 1940), pp. 199–208.
[38] National Park Service, Comprehensive Natural History Research Program for the National Parks (Washington: National Park Service, 1962), p. 2.
[39] In this section I have relied heavily on Richard Hartesveldt, "The Effects of Human Impact upon Sequoia gigantea and its Environment in the Mariposa Grove, Yosemite National Park" (Ph.D. dissertation; Ann Arbor: University of Michigan, 1962). Also note Herbert Mason, Do We Want Sugar Pine?, Sierra Club Bulletin, 40 (1955). Mason observes that sugar pine is itself jeopardized by white fir and incense cedar displacement. Note recent changes in Park Service policy as reported by R. Hartesveldt, Fire Ecology of the Giant Sequoias, Natural History, 73 (1964).
[40] Advisory Board on Wildlife Management (Leopold Committee) to Secretary of the Interior, Wildlife Management in the National Parks, American Forests, 69 (1963).

Similarly, policy at the Everglades did not take account of the effects of catastrophe. Even before Egler noted the change in ecological theory, he took exception to the common position. He remarked that fires had been set by Indians ever since the late Pleistocene and that in the abnormal absence of fire—as well as of severe cold spells and hurricanes—hardwoods would invade pine forests.[41] Barely three years later, a young Park Service ecologist, William Robertson, extended Egler's view after observing lightning strikes. He reasoned that fires must have resulted from nonhuman causes:

> Up until two years ago or less the answer to the question "does natural fire occur in South Florida?" would have been "no." . . . . With the establishment (in 1951) of two fire lookout stations overlooking large sawgrass areas in Everglades National Park, it soon became evident that natural fires caused by lightning do occur frequently. Several fires were seen to start from observed lightning strikes in sawgrass and in true islands of the Everglades. . . . Some of these fires were extinguished by rain which accompanied the electrical storm, but among them are also some of the major fires in the history of Everglades National Park.[42]

On the basis of these findings, Robertson suggested tests of controlled burning. Initially, the Park Service reacted violently; the national parks, were "not the place in which to conduct management experiments," but it eventually granted permission.[43]

For failing to move aggressively towards a policy of dealing with these problems of a dynamic ecology, the Service was roundly condemned in the Leopold Report (1963) prepared by a panel of outstanding ecologists and wildlife management experts whose position reflected the dramatic shift in ecological thought. Administrators had been unable to accept this shift, perhaps because of commitments to clientele already influenced by the traditional approach. The panel sharply criticized the agency for its reluctance to undertake biotic management in order to preserve those features of primitive America of catastrophic origin.[44]

Leopold had earlier suggested tests of controlled burning in Yosemite. See California University Wildland Research Center, *Man, Fire and Chaparral* (Berkeley, Calif.: Wildland Research Center, 1961), p. 81. Note misleading statement in Park Service *Annual Report* for 1962, p. 94: "The invasions of meadows on the floor of Yosemite are natural but that those at higher elevations are caused by human interference."

[41] Frank Egler, Southeast Saline Everglades Vegetation and its Management, *Vegetatio*, 3 (1952).

[42] William B. Robertson, *A Survey of the Effects of Fire in Everglades National Park* (National Park Service, 1963).

[43] Memorandum from Acting Assistant Director Lou Garrison to Everglades Superintendent, February 25, 1955.

[44] Leopold Report; see note 30.

After a period of prolonged resistance, the Park Service now appears determined to heed its critics' advice. But critics are not confident that the Park Service has altogether altered its course. An assistant secretary of the interior recently reminded the agency that "to credit the Park Service with the Leopold Report is like crediting a collision at sea for a dramatic rescue effort—the captain of the offending ship is hardly likely to get a medal for making the rescue effort." [45]

Soil and Range Management

Alarmed by disrupted natural harmonies, soil conservationists long espoused a doctrine closely resembling that of the Park Service. Like the Park Service, the Soil Conservation Service laid catastrophe to human intervention in natural processes. Again, as with the Park Service, both its ideology and program obligations combined to make its theoretical interpretation of soil structure and development rigid and inflexible. Although the Soil Conservation Service advocated manipulatory practices designed to stabilize soils against erosion, it paid little thought to "productive potential, and none whatsoever to production functions." [46] In this respect, the action-oriented Soil Conservation Service differed from its research counterpart, the Soil Survey, which looked more favorably on agronomic techniques designed to raise soil productivity—a view supported by the state land-grant colleges.

C. F. Marbut, director of the Soil Survey, was the author of soil classification systems that reflected an organic, developmental bias; but he recognized their provisional nature. Marbut stood ready to discard theory which could not be supported by empirical observations and urged his subordinates to remain faithful to this standard. Consequently, soil scientists in the Soil Survey were themselves responsible for successive revisions of Marbut's formulations. Recognizing that Marbut had overemphasized virgin soils, and that he had understated the significance and pervasiveness of soil profile discontinuities produced by such forces as wind and fire, soil scientists have eliminated the misleading notion of "normal," "mature" soils as a basic feature of present classification systems. [47] Some even speculate that soil development "is more in-

[45] Remarks by Assistant Secretary of the Interior John A. Carver, Jr., to National Park Service Conference on Challenges, October 14, 1963. Another panel convened by the National Academy of Sciences at the request of the Secretary of the Interior strongly endorsed the Leopold Committee recommendations and urged a thorough revision of the agency's research operations.
[46] David Gardner, "The National Cooperative Soil Survey of the United States" (Ph.D. dissertation; Cambridge: Harvard University, 1958), p. 286.
[47] Charles Kellogg, Why A New System of Soil Classification?, Soil Science, 96 (1963), p. 4. John Retzer, Soil Formation and Classification of Forested Mountain Lands in the United States, Soil Science, 96, (1963), p. 69. See Charles Denny and

fluenced by the unusual than the usual." [48] Therefore, in contrast to the organic construct that Marbut adopted for his model, soil scientists are at present inclined to interpret the soil as an open physical system.[49]

It is important to observe that this shift was internally induced and that its roots can be traced back to the late 1920s. Certainly, neither Marbut nor his successor, Charles Kellogg, had the intense emotional (and bureaucratic) investment in the doctrine of soil maturity of H. H. Bennett (head of Soil Conservation Service). Marbut himself early expressed doubts about the advisability of using the word "mature" for a soil phase. He frankly conceded that the "identification of soils in such stages [evolution from youth to maturity], and the proof that such a development is taking place is a matter of interpretation rather than of observation by demonstration." [50] Whether Bennett fully understood or, indeed, cared about the theoretical implications of soil science, he found the theory of soil maturity a useful instrument to promote the cause of soil conservation.

The attitude of the Soil Conservation Service on catastrophe left it seriously exposed to the arguments of biologists, geographers, anthropologists, and historians, who perceived instability as the distinguishing feature of Great Plains existence. Whatever the particular factor responsible—drought, wind, fire, rodent and insect infestations, overgrazing by bison, pronghorn antelope, or mustangs—the fact of instability prior to the introduction of cattle could not be denied. Dust storms, gullying, and washing predated the advent of civilization. If culpability could be established, the blame would have to be broadly shouldered, reasoned critics of the Soil Conservation Service. Their dissenting views, most forcibly expressed by the historian James Malin, profoundly disturbed conservationists. Bernard De Voto was distressed by Malin's thesis.[51] What could possibly be more devastating to the natural environment than the havoc wreaked by herds of cattle? Conservationist thinking on range ecology was therefore shaped most directly by the de-

---

J. C. Goodlett, "*Surficial Geology and Geomorphology of Potter County, Pa.,*" Professional Paper No. 288, U.S Geological Survey, Washington, 1956. See also Earl Stephens, The Uprooting of Trees: A Forest Process, *Proceedings*, 20 (1956), Soil Science Society of America. Note comments by Charles Kellogg about disturbance to Harvard Forest soils by hurricanes in William L. Hutcheson, *Memorial Forest Bulletin* (New Brunswick, N.J.: Rutgers University, 1957), Vol. 1.

[48] Letter from soil scientist Walter Lyford (Harvard Forest) to author, October 30, 1963.

[49] James Malin, *op. cit.*, p. 53. Note import of this orientation for forestry in *Artificially Constructed Mounds Show Promise in Yellow Birch Regeneration* (Research Note LS-32, Lake States Forest Experiment Station, Madison, Wisconsin, 1963).

[50] *Life and World of C. F. Marbut* (Columbia, Missouri: Soil Science Society of America, 1942).

[51] I am grateful to Arthur A. Maass for this recorded reaction.

struction they ascribed to the hoofed beasts. Why search for other cul-
prits? Only recently has it been learned that many gullies in Wyoming,
apparently the product of the westward movement, are "in fact at least
pre-Columbian and may be several thousands of years old." [52] Where at
one time, soil conservationists from the Soil Conservation Service and
the Forest Service had automatically stigmatized graziers for causing ir-
reparable damage to the land, the tendency is now toward a more considered evaluation of the destructive effects of grazing animals. As a
former Forest Service officer cautioned: "A good many years ago, I stood
on the edge of a gully near Flagstaff with the late Lyle Watts, Chief of
the U.S. Forest Service. When the Chief asked how the gully had been
formed, a research forester standing by replied, 'overgrazing.' However,
after a more detailed look at the gully itself and a search of old maps, it
was found this gully coincided with the location of an old pioneer road
between Flagstaff and Cameron." [53]

Soil conservationists were not ready to lay aside their prejudices
and try to understand the actual impact of grazing on the range resource; their experimental designs merely incorporated their bias. A
range researcher has pointed to this theoretical blindspot:

> The effects of grazing, as they have usually been described, are almost
> entirely harmful. . . . One reason for this is that *overgrazing* has been
> studied a great deal more than *grazing*. Most references in the literature
> of range grazing are contrasts between overgrazing and complete protec-
> tion. The consequence of this is that we really know very little about
> grazing as an ecological influence.[54]

Believing as they did in the virginal stability of the grasslands (in their
climax form), administrators of the Soil Conservation Service were not
prepared to understand the catastrophic influences to which the grasslands had been periodically subjected or to appreciate the land's recu-
perative capabilities. Perhaps, like the Park and Forest Services, the Soil
Conservation Service was too devoted to its certitudes to wrestle with
the problems of uncertainty. So striking has been the transformation of
thinking in the resources field, however, that disturbance and catastrophe now rank high in the scientific programs of the resource agencies.[55]

[52] Luna Leopold, in Thomas, *op. cit.*, p. 739.
[53] Joseph Arnold, Crusade for Rangeland Restoration, *American Forests*, 69 (1963),
p. 28.
[54] Lincoln Ellison, "Role of Plant Succession in Range Improvement," in Howard
Sprague (ed.), *Grasslands* (A.A.A.S. Publication No. 53, Washington, D.C., 1959),
p. 307.
[55] *Research and Development on Natural Resources*, Office of Science and Technology (Washington: General Printing Office, 1963), p. 62.

Economic Basis of Conservationist Ideology

Just as the static nature of their scientific theory inhibited the conservationists' appreciation of change, so did their economic theory. Arguing from a fundamentalist perspective, conservationists blamed the market mechanism and consumer sovereignty for desecrating the land and imperiling national resources. In their search for a stable standard to guide policy decisions, they sought to avoid the capriciousness of the law of supply and demand. They therefore favored a calculation of the economic worth of resources in terms of their enduring physical quantities rather than according to their fluctuating market values. This antipathy to economics may well have reflected a sense of frustration in the face of the manifold uncertainties of a constantly changing economic order. Whatever the reason, it is clear that an aversion to the indeterminacies in the economic system made it difficult for conservationists to take adequate account of the consequences of technological change. The same attitude also influenced their dogmatic adherence to the concept of sustained yield and limited their efforts towards more diversified forest products.

In fairness to the conservationists, two points should be made. First, had they been disposed to seek the advice of nineteenth and early twentieth century economists on the role of technological advance, conservationists would not have received much enlightenment. At that time, economics, with its steady-state models, also assumed technology to be a constant. It could not conceive of technological progress except in the role of a *deus ex machina*.[56] Second, it should be noted that "economies of destruction," i.e., countries undergoing industrialization in which the extractive industries occupy the leading sector, are oriented toward primary producers rather than toward ultimate consumers. Secure in their position as suppliers of raw materials, these extractive industries were not very interested in technological research. Such efforts as were made "were the responsibility of the using industries. . . . Rarely did the raw material industry maintain elaborate research facilities. The shortage of raw materials meant that their users had to do their research homework."[57] To the extent that "vertical integration back to the resource" represented operational reality, economic structure thus seemed to confirm the validity of their fundamentalist bias.

[56] G. K. Goundrey, Economics and Conservation, *Canadian Journal of Economics and Political Science*, 26 (1960), p. 324. Harold J. Barnett and Chandler Morse, *Scarcity and Growth: The Economics of Natural Resource Availability* (Baltimore: Johns Hopkins, 1963).
[57] Anthony Scott, The Development of the Extractive Industries, *Canadian Journal of Economics and Political Science*, 28 (1962), 84–85.

But the classical economists were wrong; technological innovation was to prove of enormous significance. In an age of affluence, it is more obvious that whatever limitations may apply to our ability to exploit the environment, they are to be found in man, not in nature.[58] As Thomas Nolan (chief of Bureau of Mines) has noted, "We probably need to fear, not the exhaustion of our physical resources, but the dangers of inadequate or belated utilization of our intellectual resources. I hope we are currently rediscovering the need to practice this kind of conservation." [59]

A new recognition of the importance of scientific innovation to resource management came with the report in 1950 of the President's Materials Policy (Paley) Commission. Since then, students of resource policy have increasingly recognized that numerous "avenues of escape" from resource scarcity are available—scientific, social, economic, and political. Although ultimate limitations continue to be acknowledged, conservationists now have come to feel that they have a much wider scope for adjustment.

In addition to assuming that the stock of knowledge was limited, conservationists also posited a finite amount of resources, consisting of both exhaustible (stock) and reproducible (flow) supplies. Anxious to extend the life of existing inventories, they deemed unwise and wasteful any policies which would allow consumption of stock resources before all flow supplies had been utilized on a self-sustaining basis.[60] Physical limits were thought to restrict human productivity. But the assurance of continuity and stability of flow supplies relieved conservationists' anxieties. As late as 1955 at least, one writer clung to the belief that physical efficiency was still the primary relevant criterion. He could therefore erroneously argue, "It seems fortunate that our vital needs are met by flow resources." [61] The Forest Service, archadvocate of this view, specified it to mean that sustaining the yield of timber was the sacrosanct guide to management. This deceptively simple idea contemplated a cutting policy carefully adjusted to the life cycle of timber stands. Four questionable assumptions underlay this seemingly rational theory. According to forest economist Ernest Gould, these assumptions were stability, land scarcity, certainty, and a closed economy. The first hypothesis assumes "that a stable flow of forest products is required, ad infinitum. . . . Thus timber growth should ideally regulate wood use." The second hypothesis

[58] Barnett and Morse, op. cit., p. 264.
[59] Thomas Nolan, "The Inexhaustible Resource of Technology," in Henry Jarrett (ed.), Perspectives on Conservation (Baltimore: Johns Hopkins, 1958), p. 66.
[60] Barnett and Morse, op. cit., pp. 79–81. Also note dissenting opinion by Boulding in Thomas, op. cit., p. 248.
[61] Edward Price, Values and Concepts in Conservation, Annals, Association of American Geographers, 45 (1955), p. 69.

. . . takes the argument one step further and assumes that forest products are so scarce, relative to labor and capital, that land must be used with maximum efficiency. Growth should therefore be at or near the biological ceiling so that the largest amount of desirable products is grown on each acre. The certainty hypothesis states that production techniques, consumption patterns, and values are all known so that sustained yield can be planned five or ten decades in advance. If this seems too strong a statement, an alternative reading of this hypothesis would be that managers should act as though they had perfect knowledge, even though they may have some qualms about the future.[62]

The hypothesis of a closed economy indicates that "it is desirable for each operating unit, region, and country to equate internal consumption and production and ignore the possibilities of an outside supply of forest products and alternative uses for land, labor and capital." [63]

The sustained-yield approach, however, has been undermined by unanticipated developments. Instability of demand, raw material surpluses, uncertainty about the future, and an open economy, all have conspired to make unworkable this "first principle" of forest management. In many instances, forest liquidation and divergence of cut and growth may prove both economically and socially preferable to sustained yield. "Permanence and stability may create a false air of security," Gould recognized, "while really leading to obsolescence and irrelevance in an expanding economy." Furthermore, as with other resources, forest supplies can only be defined by known technology and by the criterion of economic feasibility. Inventories are of limited value in projecting prospective harvests, for they are "cast in a framework of static knowledge, products, techniques and institutions." [64] It is unreasonable to assume that industry will require logs at least 9–11 inches in diameter in the future. A dynamic economy continually assigns new meaning to the concept of "merchantable" stands. Perhaps the best justification for the periodic resources stock-taking is its self-denying power. By hastening adjustments in utilization, inventories vitiate the very assumptions on which they rest, so that their prognostic value—except for the immediate future—is severely limited. Inasmuch as present values and practices reflect estimates of future conditions, inventories that constitute the basis for calculation of sustained yield are also quite unsuitable as regulatory mechanisms. Most important, though the inventory may accelerate adaptation by forest-using industries in unanticipated ways, the sponsoring agency may fall captive to its own assumptions. If the in-

---

[62] Ernest Gould, Forestry and Recreation, *Harvard Forest Papers*, 6 (1962), 3–4.
[63] *Ibid.*, p. 4.
[64] Barnett and Morse, *op. cit.*, p. 228.

ventory orientation is a static one, agency policy developed in its defense may similarly be inclined toward rigidity. This result seems, in fact, to have characterized the Forest Service's position on sustained yield. After pressing Congress to pass the Sustained Yield Act of 1944, and after setting up a few units to promote this objective, the Service became disillusioned with the idea. Despite serious misgivings, however, the agency approved a unit for the Flagstaff area.[65]

The assumptions on which the sustained-yield concept rested help to explain the Service's orientation in the forest products field as well. Preoccupied with the problem of growing trees to avoid expected wood scarcity, the Service tended to over-economize on its product. In the face of threatened scarcity, its energies were focused on an impressive waste-reduction and log-improvement campaign, two objectives that complemented each other. The Service was determined simultaneously to salvage wood previously left to rot in the forest and to utilize more efficiently logs customarily felled for lumber; hence, it continued to pursue its aim of perfecting the tree as tree, the species as species. Enamored of the *form*, foresters tended to lose sight of the *functions* which lumber served.

This failure to evaluate market requirements correctly has indeed been serious in an economy where wood has remained a surplus commodity. Unfortunately, the Forest Service overlooked the need to maintain lumber in a strong competitive position by reducing its costs, perhaps because theory predicated on scarcity assured future certainty of marketing opportunities. Neglecting market instability resulted in indifference to changing consumption patterns and raw materials substitutability, and reinforced a professional identification with "producer's goods." It also hampered efforts to homogenize the wood resource by insisting on the unique virtues of the sawlog for structural support purposes.[66] By excluding uncertainty and unpredictable change from its purview, the sustained-yield concept thereby contributed to a false view of economic reality. In thinking of the environment as one of wood scarcity and market certainty, the Forest Service saw little need to promote product development in some areas. A distorted outlook on change clearly limited its capacity for adaptation.

[65] Paul W. Bedard and Paul N. Ylvisaker, *The Flagstaff Federal Sustained Yield Unit* (Inter-University Case Program No. 37 [University, Alabama: University of Alabama, 1957]).
[66] While Forest Service energies in the direction of wood standardization have been confined chiefly to boards made from sawdust and other waste, a New Hampshire company has recently introduced chip boards made by cutting specially shaped small chips directly from round rather than waste wood. When perfected, this new process will permit molding of structural members and will compete directly for lumber and wood markets.

Internal Administrative Practices

The ideology expressed in conservationists resource policy was also reflected in their attitude toward administrative organization. Foresters saw external and internal efficiency as a seamless web. Their image of the ideal natural and social environment did not allow for uncertain change; their prescription for management reform gave expression to a bureaucratic formalization which minimized internal uncertainty.[67] Indeed, they viewed scientific management as another "technique of conservation." (Frederick W. Taylor gratefully acknowledged his debt to the conservation movement.) [68] In the case of the Conservationists, the organization's *modus operandi* embodied a definition of purpose.[69]

The Forest Service had a pronounced interest in management science. When Gifford Pinchot convened the Keep Committee on Department Methods (1905), it was partly in order to demonstrate the superiority of Forest Service management to that of its competitors in the Department of the Interior. Years later, Pinchot recollected with obvious pleasure the findings of the Keep Committee:

> Incidentally, in this analysis of Department methods the Forest Service came out with flying colors and was pointed out as a model for other Government units to follow. Jim Garfield, then Secretary of the Interior, said, "The Committee was unanimous in the belief that efficiency in the Forest Service was so much greater than that found in other offices that we used many of the methods we found in vogue there as the basis for recommendations for changes in other branches of the Government service." [70]

Pinchot also proudly recalled the recognition won by the Service in 1908 from a distinguished group of management consultants: "The fact is that the Forest Service was good." [71]

This esteem once earned, Pinchot was resolved to protect and enhance it. Owing to his efforts, and to those of his successors, the Service has continued to win plaudits from administrative analysts. As recently

[67] March and Simon, *op. cit.*, pp. 141–142.
[68] Frederick W. Taylor, *Principles of Scientific Management* (New York: Harper, 1957), p. 5.
[69] This instrumental application of conservationist ideology should be distinguished from the phenomenon of goal displacement described by Robert K. Merton in *Social Theory and Social Structure* (2d ed., Glencoe, Ill.: Free Press, 1957), p. 199.
[70] Gifford Pinchot, *op. cit.*, p. 298; Harold T. Pinkett, The Keep Commission, 1905–1909, *Journal of American History*, 52 (1965).
[71] Pinchot, *op. cit.*, p. 298.

as 1951, Luther Gulick took note of its accomplishments: "The performance standards, developed and used in the daily work of foresters
throughout the U.S. Forest Service, are more comprehensive and specific
than any set of administrative standards we have encountered in any
other area of public administration." [72] The Service had introduced vertical filing and a subject-matter filing classification scheme in advance of
most federal bureaus. These innovations anticipated by at least two or
three years recommendations by the Taft Committee on Economy and
Efficiency for government-wide adoption. The agency also pioneered in
devising record disposal and retention plans. Its archival schedule of
1918 preceded by almost two decades the development of systematic
plans for other federal bureaus. [73]

In 1912, F. A. Silcox applied Taylor's approach to the study of
work practices and organization. Silcox, later Chief Forester during the
depression, had examined the operations of the Savenac Forest Nursery
in a test of scientific management techniques. Taylorism gradually established roots elsewhere, notably in California under Roy Headley's influence. [74] Upon his transfer to Washington in the 1920s, work-load analysis
became an object of general attention within the organization. And so,
with painstaking care, the Service developed the first governmental system of executive work-load measurement.

Assistant Chief Earl Loveridge's outline shows the mechanistic
bias of the system. In terms evoking Taylor's assaults on "soldiering,"
Loveridge argued that "morale is not a forced quality, but a natural
human one. If a member of the Service . . . is disturbed by a conscien-
tious administrative attempt to know what he is doing and the effectiveness with which he is doing it, I would not be so much concerned with
the man's morale as with his ability to meet Forest Service requirements." Though he believed that ample time for reflection should be afforded senior executives (unlike district rangers), Loveridge advised analysts to let "tangible job" requirements alone guide their appraisals:

> This procedure may seem to slight the need for that silent contemplation
> which many feel to be invaluable for the birth of new ideas and the de-
> velopment of older ones. Some of the best creative thinking is not done
> as a result of sitting down at a desk with the intent to think, but as the
> result of the stimulus to the intellectual powers resulting from the actual
> doing of tangible jobs and planned experiments, or from contacts with

[72] Luther Gulick, *American Forest Policy* (New York: Institute of Public Administration, 1951), p. 74.
[73] Harold T. Pinkett, The Forest Service, Trail Blazer in Record-Keeping, *American
Archivist*, 22 (1959).
[74] Note his influence on fire control operations; Schiff, *op. cit.*, p. 70.

other minds . . . the hours required to travel from job to job provide time which often has been and will continue to be devoted to meditation.[75]

Job-load analysis was intended for adoption chiefly at the ranger district level, but, as Loveridge envisioned its future status, the plan would be extended to some of the higher grades. He quoted approvingly comments from two regional foresters. One officer found that "scheduling of his own work was necessary if he wished to get certain jobs done"; another asserted that schedules "must become one's 'taskmaster' if the work was to be done." The system breathed a tone of scientific assurance; the work mystique, by accenting techniques, reaffirmed the value of established decisional frameworks. Work plans and sophisticated communication and control procedures, the Service contended, merely constituted rational means for realizing scientifically ascertainable ends. Its assumptions were so little challenged, that not until the 1940s did the system come under vigorous attack. At that time, a highly placed research forester protested to Loveridge that

> The Forest Service is more expert on administration in the narrow sense than on resource management from the technical and fundamental standpoint. I suspect we give too much emphasis, in selecting men for key positions, to demonstrated administrative skill and experience. I think there is danger of placing too little stress on breadth of view, imagination, and deep-seated concern for resource management on its own account and in relation to social objectives and criteria. . . . I realize that much of the recent study of regional office and other organization matters is with the very purpose of improving our resource management, and I don't decry it in the least. I do occasionally, however, get the feeling that there is some danger of carrying it to the point that organization theory becomes the objective rather than the results on the ground in terms of well-managed resources.[76]

Several academicians voiced their objections. One respected professor implored foresters to look beyond professional and bureaucratic horizons for their management cues:

> . . . the Forest Service has a splendid record. It is quite generally recognized as one of the most efficient—if not the most efficient—of the many

[75] Earl Loveridge, "Job Load Analysis and Planning of Executive Work," in *National Forest Administration—A Manual for Forest Officers* (Washington: Government Printing Office, 1932), p. 60.
[76] Memorandum from R. E. Marsh to E. Loveridge, October 19, 1944, National Archives, Record Group 95.

government agencies. But the very independence that has been largely
responsible for their efficiency has isolated them, and their self-sufficiency has cut them off from public contact.[77]

By concentrating on techniques of scientific management, foresters
had neglected to ask fundamental questions about their mission. They
assumed that social needs would be related to forest management without their making any effort to ascertain those needs and develop appropriate policies. They recruited personnel solely from schools of forestry
and therefore could not exploit the insights of other disciplines relevant
to the overall problems of resource management. As a result, the Forest
Service until recently never dealt effectively with the problems of
small-scale private forest owners; with the improvement of grazing, hydrologic, and recreation management; and most generally failed to realize its stated commitment to multiple-use resource administration.

Discussion and Summary

This study has explored the influence of certain value orientations on decision making. Although value orientations toward change in
the resources field revealed profound antipathy to such notions as catastrophe, instability, and uncertainty, there is evidence that ideology correlates differently with organization, function, and discipline. While the
Park Service was most unreceptive to ideas of instability, the Fish and
Wildlife Service proved somewhat more receptive. Similarly, agencies
concerned with maintaining support for ongoing programs displayed
more resistance than their research counterparts. Whereas economists
were once the most conservative subgroup in the Forest Service, they
are at present preoccupied with innovation. It would be a mistake, however, to believe that these differences may easily be exploited. Until recently a remarkable degree of consensus existed among these groups on
the virtues of uniform change, stability, and certainty despite marginal
variations. And, championed by an elite organization as the Forest Service, these values possessed a remarkable capacity for influence and survival. The belief in the necessity of innovation gradually gained ground,
but only against formidable opposition.

Studies of this same normative influence in other contexts may
well enhance the general understanding of administrative behavior. Ac-
quisitions and mergers in the business world indicate sensitivity to the

[77] E. G. Cheney, What is Wrong With the Forest Service, *Journal of Forestry*, 45
(1947), 684–685.

uncertainties associated with rapid environmental change.[78] How attitudes toward change influence internal resource allocations for research and product development warrants additional attention.[79] It would also be of value to determine whether firms faced with the challenge of environmental instability tend to put greater stress on research expenditures or on merger agreements. How would such a decision correlate with various levels of organizational success? Would rival leadership groups hold to different positions on the question?

Among voluntary organizations, the National Foundation for Infantile Paralysis is said to have regarded its goal as "finite." [80] What change perspective did this view embrace? To what extent did this foundation—in contrast with the National Tuberculosis Association—owe its goal flexibility and structural distinctiveness to a more dynamic image of the scientific process and its possibilities for environmental change? Sills's account of the anti-polio campaign is suggestive, but improved comprehension of these relationships awaits a comparative analysis focusing on orientations toward advances in medical science.

Urban planning and renewal efforts have revealed different views of change in city form and function. Indeed, in the early decades of the century, an interlocking directorate served both city planning and conservation. Not surprisingly, their ideological affinity was striking.[81] The garden or new towns concept, emphasizing as it does population and space limitations, and social and economic self-sufficiency, strongly resembles static conservationist assumptions and objectives.[82] Recently, this professional ideology—positing permanence and placing a premium on a high degree of stability—has come under severe attack from Jane Jacobs, who contends that gradual change is more compatible with urban requirements.[83] Charles Abrams has expressed still another attitude toward change after evaluating housing needs in the developing areas.[84] His core-housing, roof-loan, and installment-building schemes reflect a judgment that disposable construction is most suited to present economic capacity and future urban growth. It would appear, therefore,

[78] William Dill, op. cit., p. 1095.
[79] Cyert and March, op. cit., p. 279.
[80] David Sills, op. cit., p. 253.
[81] Dwight Waldo, The Administrative State (New York: Ronald Press, 1948), pp. 4, 66–70; Samuel Hays, Conservation and the Gospel of Efficiency (Cambridge: Harvard University, 1959), pp. 194–195.
[82] Frederic J. Osborn and Arnold Whittick, The New Towns—The Answer to Megalopolis (New York: McGraw-Hill 1963), pp. 2–4.
[83] Jane Jacobs, The Death and Life of Great American Cities (New York: Random House, 1961), pp. 292–294, 435–437.
[84] Charles Abrams, Man's Struggle for Shelter in an Urbanizing World (Cambridge: Massachusetts Institute of Technology, 1964), p. 240.

that an investigation of planning ideology offers a good vehicle for analyzing urban planning and renewal administration.

Finally, the classic view of military innovation as primarily dependent upon the tradition-bound military mind has lately given way to
the thought that the crucial factors are the rate and nature of technological change. Janowitz relates differing perspectives of military managers
in the three services on this factor.[85] He hardly clarifies the problem,
however, by pointing elsewhere to "trend thinking" and other evidences
of "rigidity" on the part of the Air Force.[86] If the impression of the heroic leader comes through quite sharply, the military manager remains
obscured. We still lack a compelling explanation as to why resistance to
innovation was overcome by technological needs in certain cases and
why it succeeded in preventing change in others. This confusion can
only be dissipated by further study into the complex linkages between
the environment, normative commitments on change, and organizational
structure. The present paper has sought to underline the value of taking
this approach.

[85] Morris Janowitz, *The Professional Soldier* (New York: Free Press, 1960), pp.
28–29.
[86] *Ibid.*, pp. 27, 31.

16

Conservation Law I: Seeking a Breakthrough in the Courts

Few terms have greater currency in the United States today than "environmental quality," a cliché that is constantly on the lips of politicians and luncheon speakers. Yet few knowledgeable people believe that, despite successes scored in skirmishes here and there, the battle for environmental quality really is being won. There is growing evidence that pollution problems, noise, urban sprawl, and other environmental ills are generally becoming worse and that an effective overall strategy for coping with these problems is yet to be found. It seems likely, however, that if a workable strategy is found, it will include, among other things, the rapid and imaginative development of what is coming to be called environmental or conservation law.

Environmental problems usually represent conflicts between competing uses of natural resources—for example, a virgin forest may be preserved as wilderness or reduced to pulpwood, and a city park may be kept for recreation or given over as right-of-way for a freeway. It is natural, therefore, that lawyers, who are supposed to have some expertise at resolving conflicts, should be called upon to help resolve problems concerned with the environment. Numerous legal actions over environmental issues are now pending before various courts and administrative agencies around the country.

These include, for instance, suits and petitions to outlaw use of DDT (which no doubt influenced the Nixon Administration's recent decision to institute a partial ban on this pesticide in the United States); to prevent completion of a Corps of Engineers cross-Florida barge canal

° Mr. Carter is a staff member of *Science*. Mr. Carter's article originally appeared in *Science* 166, December 19, 1969.

project that is flooding much of the Oklawaha River basin and causing what some scientists say are disastrous ecological changes; to keep the U.S. Forest Service from allowing Walt Disney Productions to build a commercial resort at Mineral King in the Sierra Nevada; and to bring antitrust charges against major automobile manufacturers for an alleged conspiracy not to compete in the development of exhaust-control devices (damage suits are being brought by the State of New York, two Chicago aldermen, and Los Angeles County). Scientists and other academicians figure importantly in many pending actions, in part because they are strongly represented in the membership of groups such as the Sierra Club which are bringing suits, and in part because they often testify as expert witnesses.

Lawyers and law school professors are becoming aware of conservation law as a potentially important field. This year the American Trial Lawyers Association has established an environmental law committee, which is arranging a series of seminars and is planning to establish an environmental law-reporting service. Significantly, the American Bar Association, a generally conservative organization which tends to resist new trends until they are certified as thoroughly respectable, also is setting up a committee on environmental quality.

And, in September, more than 60 attorneys and law school professors, including some involved in conservation law suits, attended a 2-day conference on law and the environment sponsored by The Conservation Foundation of Washington, D.C., and The Conservation and Research Foundation of New London, Connecticut. They discussed various legal arguments and strategies that might be used in environmental law, a field in which the usable precedents are still few. The conference proceedings, which The Conservation Foundation will have published next year by Walker and Company of New York, may serve as a primer for attorneys venturing for the first time into this unfamiliar legal realm.

Furthermore, law schools, under growing pressure from students to make their programs more responsive to the public interest, have been adding courses on environmental law as well as courses on such topics as consumer and poverty law. And some long established courses on natural resources law are being reoriented to reflect concerns broader than those of the exploitative industries which law schools and many of their law graduates have always served. Some prestigious law firms, such as the Washington firm of Arnold & Porter, which once had their pick of the ablest law graduates, are now finding that to attract such graduates it is helpful to offer opportunities for *pro bono publico* (public service) work in environmental law and other fields.

Arnold & Porter, acting without fee for the Metropolitan Washington Coalition on Clean Air, the Friends of the Earth, the Sierra Club, the Izaak Walton League of America, the Wilderness Society, and other conservation groups, has prepared a brief supporting a suit by some Washington citizens groups that seeks to block construction of the Three Sisters Bridge on the Potomac—a controversial project which many people fear will cause increased traffic congestion and air pollution in Washington and do esthetic damage to the Potomac palisades and the historic Chesapeake and Ohio Canal.

For 2 years now the Environmental Defense Fund (EDF), a Long-Island-based group organized in late 1967, has been asserting in anti-DDT cases and other actions that people have a constitutional right to a clean environment. For example, EDF makes such a claim in the federal suit that it filed last year in Montana to force the Hoerner Waldorf Paper Company to provide an adequate air pollution control process at its Missoula pulp mill. Victor J. Yannacone, Jr., an EDF attorney, speaks of the Missoula suit as the "perfect air-pollution test case." The Hoerner Waldorf mill, he says, is responsible for heavy emissions of active sulfur compounds that are polluting the regional air shed. (The company recently announced plans to try out some new pollution-control equipment.) Such pollution, Yannacone argues, represents a "nonnegotiable hazard" from which citizens should be able to obtain relief under the Constitution's Ninth Amendment, which states that the enumeration of certain rights elsewhere in the Constitution does not deny other rights (such as the right, says Yannacone, to breathe clean air) retained by the people. The Missoula case has not yet been set for trial, and, if and when it is tried, the outcome may turn on legal arguments that are more conventional than Yannacone's Ninth Amendment argument.

Many lawyers doubt that the courts are ready to accept that argument. Most judges are extremely wary about venturing beyond precedent and known law and about deciding questions, such as the general public's interest in clean air (as opposed to a mill's interest in cheaply disposing of its wastes), normally left for legislative determination.

Yet E. F. Roberts, professor of Law at Cornell, said at the September conference on environmental law that the Ninth Amendment allows enough "growth" in the interpretation of the Constitution to extend constitutional protection to the environment. The Ninth Amendment, he noted, was cited by the Supreme Court a few years ago in invalidating a Connecticut law against dissemination of birth-control information. This statute was declared an unconstitutional infringement on personal privacy, even though a right of privacy is not explicitly mentioned in the Constitution.

Enunciation of a right to environmental protection, Roberts said, would "require every agency of government, whether a local zoning board or a federal home mortgage lending agency, to review their plans to make certain that their activities did not actually exacerbate deterioration of the environment." Obviously, however, recognition of a right to environmental protection would have to be reconciled with such necessities as carrying on industrial and commercial activities, providing systems of mass transport, and building homes for an expanding population.

The "trust doctrine" also was discussed at the September conservation law conference. This ancient doctrine holds that all land was once held in trust for the people by the sovereign—or government—and that the government cannot divest itself entirely of responsibility for the uses to which land is put, even though most of it long since has passed into private hands. The government must, according to the trust doctrine, see that no land, public or private, is abused or otherwise used in ways contrary to the public interest. The trust doctrine, though recognized by the courts in certain cases involving submerged lands and publicly owned lands, has not been applied to lands generally.

Joseph Sax, a University of Michigan law professor and specialist in the field of conservation law, views the trust doctrine as a particularly useful and flexible legal concept. A court's finding that a particular proposal or action violates this doctrine, he says, would rarely result in the invalidation of a legislative act. Massachusetts courts, in a series of public trust cases decided in recent years, have set aside administrative decisions in controversial land-use cases when the legislative authority on which those decisions were supposedly based was not clearly spelled out.

In one such case, for example, the state highway department was not allowed to use a public marshland for right-of-way, even though state law seemed to permit such action. The court said that, if it were the legislature's intent to allow such a diversion of parkland to highway use, it should say so explicitly. Sax believes that rulings of this kind have a desirable "squeezing" effect on a legislature, forcing it to face up to the implications of vaguely stated policies which it writes into law.

Sax is the author of a bill now pending in the Michigan legislature which would give Michigan conservationists a potent new weapon. Under this measure, any citizen could bring suit against any person or agency to safeguard the natural resources of the state and to protect the "public trust."

If courts should ever apply the trust doctrine or the Ninth Amendment argument in a wide variety of environmental cases, this would force the executive and legislative branches to move at a faster pace in setting and enforcing standards for environmental protection. Although the environmental problem and the racial problem are not closely parallel, it may be instructive to recall that the Supreme Court's 1954 ruling against racial segregation in public schools triggered the release of dynamic social and political forces that produced the major civil rights legislation of the 1960s.

If courts leap too far ahead of public opinion, they do so at their peril, for, being empowered of neither the "sword nor the purse," they depend on the executive and legislative branches—and ultimately on the electorate—to see that their edicts are obeyed. But today courts are probably behind public opinion with respect to questions of environmental protection. During the 19th century and the early 20th century the courts became, in a real sense, the instruments of laissez-faire economics. In one classic case, decided by a Tennessee court in 1904, two copper smelting companies were allowed to continue their practice of reducing copper ore by cooking it over open-air wood fires, a process that produced billowing clouds of sulfur dioxide smoke which made a wasteland of the surrounding valley.

Farmers who had complained were told by the court that they were not entitled to injunctive relief because "the law must make the best arrangement it can between the contending parties, with a view to preserving to each one the largest measure of liberty possible under the circumstances." Roberts, the Cornell law professor, observes that " 'liberty' here meant that the companies were free to create a wasteland if they paid for it [some damages were awarded], whereas the farmers were free to take jobs with the industry and continue to reside in a valley totally polluted with chemicals."

Judicial attitudes have, of course, been evolving and, in a variety of matters involving the public interest and the social welfare, the private entrepreneur no longer enjoys the freedom of action he once did. Nevertheless, in environmental cases some courts still have not progressed far beyond the kind of "balancing of interests" that characterized the ruling in the Tennessee case just cited. For example, as Roberts has noted, a New York court recently allowed a new cement plant, which had been erected in an Albany neighborhood, to continue polluting the air with cement dust, provided it gave money damages to residents of the area.

With concern about the environment now widespread, it seems likely that the public and most elected officials would support strong court action to curb pollution and other forms of environmental degradation. The "new conservation," calling for the rational use of the environment in the interest of a high quality of life, is as much concerned with the urban environment as it is with wilderness and other natural areas. The conservation movement no longer can be regarded as a "special interest" of concern chiefly to sportsmen, wilderness "preservationists," and the like. On the contrary, conservation has a fast broadening constituency.

Problems such as noise and air pollution bear especially heavily on low-income people who cannot escape from industrial districts and who cannot afford air-conditioned homes or weekends at Aspen or Sea Island. These people, and in many cases their labor unions, are becoming increasingly concerned about environmental issues. Political careers are being built on the environmental protection issue. For example, Representative Bob Eckhardt (D–Texas), before his election to Congress in 1966, had made a record in the state legislature as a crusader on that issue. Many of Eckhardt's constituents are workers who suffer daily the odors and eye-smarting fumes that are emanating from plants along the Houston ship canal.

There is even a strong possibility that the conservation and civil rights movements may form an alliance. Controversies growing out of urban freeway projects, for example, already are bringing together black people threatened with displacement and others who are concerned about worsening air pollution, traffic congestion, and other problems. A leader of the National Association for the Advancement of Colored People in Texas recently joined with several Texas conservation groups, such as the local chapters of the Sierra Club and the National Audubon Society, in a suit to block construction of a golf course in Meridian State Park. The complaint alleges in part that the project would impose a kind of "de facto segregation"—by taking a public park area open to all races and income groups and replacing it with a golf course open only to those with money enough to pay green fees and buy golfing paraphernalia.

Further evidence of the growing interest in environmental protection can be seen in the recent adoption by New York voters of a "conservation bill of rights" as an amendment to the state constitution. If it is true, as Oliver Wendell Holmes once said, that judges must respond to the "felt necessities of the times," it would seem that the time has come when the courts will begin to play an important role in helping to resolve the environmental crisis.

[Ecology is giving conservation its scientific rationale, and scientists are playing a major role in conservation law cases. This is discussed in Article 17, which also reviews gains made thus far in environmental law and considers some potentialities.]

17

Conservation Law II:
Scientists Play a Key Role
in Court Suits

If the genius of a well functioning democratic system is to have reasonable compromises emerge from the clash of countervailing forces, one can say that the forces working for environmental quality have been undermanned and outgunned. At the moment, however, antipollution and other conservation issues have taken hold politically, and prospects for achieving gains for conservation have seldom been better. Conservationists are seeking to commit to the battle all the branches of government, the legislative, the executive, and—the judicial.

In view of the size and complexity of the environmental crisis, the best hope for coping with it surely lies in action by the legislative and executive branches. Citizens' suits and court rulings alone can never do more than a patchy, limited job of environmental protection. But environmental lawsuits, such as those which will be described here, are likely to play a significant role, especially by making the process of decision making followed by government administrative and regulatory agencies more responsive to environmental concerns.

For instance, a suit now pending before a U.S. district court in Colorado is being closely watched by conservationists. If it succeeds, the U.S. Forest Service and other federal agencies will know that, in making plans to dispose of resources under their control, they had better be prepared, through careful assessments of the alternative uses for those resources, to justify their decisions publicly—and perhaps in court. The Colorado case boils down to a charge by the Sierra Club, the Colorado Open Space Coordinating Council, and other parties that the Forest

* Mr. Carter is a staff member of *Science*. Mr. Carter's article originally appeared in *Science* 166, December 26, 1969.

Service has, in deciding on a sale of old-growth timber near the Gore Range–Eagle Nest Primitive Area, neglected its statutory obligations by not properly assessing the wilderness and recreation values affected.

In the first of these articles on conservation law (*Science*, 19 December), two somewhat radical theories aimed at making the lawsuit a major weapon of conservationists were discussed. One of these was the theory that the Constitution's Ninth Amendment, which says that the enumeration of certain rights elsewhere in the Constitution does not deny other rights retained by the people, can be invoked against polluters and others who disturb the environment unnecessarily.

The other [theory] was the public trust doctrine, an ancient theory, given only limited application by courts in the past, holding that the sovereign (the government) has the responsibility of protecting all lands, public and private, from abuse. Wide acceptance by the courts of either of these doctrines would be a breakthrough for conservation. But, in any event, conservationists are beginning to make effective use of the courts, although the usable precedents are still relatively few.

One such precedent may have been set last July when a federal appeals court, responding to the eleventh-hour petition of some Colorado scientists, prevented the destruction of the 34-million-year-old Florissant Fossil Beds by land developers. The court enjoined the development activity long enough for Congress to complete action on legislation establishing a fossil beds national monument. Estella B. Leopold, a paleobotanist at the University of Colorado (and daughter of the late Aldo Leopold, a noted conservationist), had testified that "the Florissant Fossil Beds are to geology, paleontology, and evolution what the Rosetta Stone was to Egyptology and what the Dead Sea Scrolls are to Christianity."

Citizens have often been denied "standing" to bring suit to block government actions or to have a nuisance abated unless they personally faced or were suffering loss or injury, to a degree not shared by the public generally. However, two Wisconsin conservation groups, with the help of the Environmental Defense Fund, the Long Island-based legal action group, were able to petition—in an exhaustive state administrative hearing—for a ban on the use of DDT. And although the Wisconsin statute (enacted in 1943) allowing such proceedings is unusual, citizens in many states may now go to court and challenge government policies and activities which they deem to be harmful to the environment.

In a paper presented in September at the Conservation Foundation's conference on environmental law, Louis L. Jaffe, a Harvard law professor, said that 29 states allow any citizen to file suit to contest official conduct which is alleged to be illegal and that, in at least 27 states, any taxpayer has the privilege. "I would conclude that the constitutional obstacles to [such citizens'] suits . . . are becoming less and less significant," Jaffe added.

Scenic Hudson is a case, which, although the dispute that gave rise to it is still unresolved, has established two important precedents— federal regulatory bodies have been told to give greater weight to esthetic values and to allow conservation organizations to intervene in cases that raise environmental issues. In 1965, the U.S. Second Circuit Court of Appeals set aside an order of the Federal Power Commission (FPC) granting the Consolidated Edison Company a license to build a pumped-storage hydro-power facility at Storm King Mountain on the Hudson River. The court directed the commission to reopen the matter and to consider the preservation of natural beauty as well as such factors as the economics of power generation. The decision was appealed, but the Supreme Court declined to review the ruling.

In later FPC proceedings, the Scenic Hudson Preservation Conference, the Sierra Club, and other conservation organizations sought to show that Storm King Mountain is not merely pretty but uniquely beautiful. Specialists in cartography, landscape architecture, and art history were called to testify. They pointed out, for example, that although a number of rivers cut through the Appalachian Mountains, only the Hudson cuts through at sea level and achieves the effect of a fjord. Thus, these experts argued, even though the appreciation of natural beauty is subjective, certain objective esthetic standards can be applied. An FPC hearing examiner has since recommended that the Storm King project be approved, and the Commission may yet grant the license. But the precedents established in *Scenic Hudson* already have proved useful to conservationists in other suits.

For example, the Sierra Club, citing *Scenic Hudson* and certain other precedents, gained standing to bring suit against federal agencies to block construction of an expressway along the Hudson River, a segment of which was to be built on filled land in the river itself. The Sierra Club's attorneys dredged up an old statute pertaining to navigable waters which says that no dike or causeway may be built in the river without the consent of Congress.

A U.S. district judge, ruling that this statute applies, has decided the case in the Sierra Club's favor. The defendants have appealed.

In another suit, the Sierra Club is trying to keep the U.S. Forest Service from allowing Walt Disney Productions, Inc., to build a ski resort in Mineral King Valley in the Sierra Nevada. As in the expressway case, the club's attorneys have searched the statutes and come up with provisions which they contend make the proposed development illegal.

They also say that public hearings are required by law and have not been held. A federal district court has temporarily enjoined the carrying out of plans for the resort, but the case has not yet been decided.

As in the question of whether a party has standing to sue, burden-of-proof rules can be critical to the outcome of a court case. And, in the past, the burden of proof generally has fallen on the conservationists bringing the suit. However, a 1966 ruling of the New Jersey Supreme Court is viewed by some legal scholars as a sign that judicial attitudes on this point are changing. Texas East Transmission Company was condemning a right-of-way for a gas pipeline across a wooded tract owned by Wildlife Preserves, Inc., a private nonprofit organization, which insisted that the project would be less damaging ecologically if the pipeline were routed across a marsh.

The court held that, since Wildlife Preserves, Inc., was devoting its land to conservation objectives often pursued by government itself, it should not be required to carry as heavy a burden of proof as the ordinary property owner who protests that the condemnation of a particular piece of land is arbitrary. It said, in effect, that if Wildlife Preserves, Inc., made out a *prima facie* case, the burden of proof would shift to the company. The case ultimately was decided in the pipeline company's favor, but not until the trial judge was satisfied that the upland route for the pipeline was as acceptable ecologically as the marshland route and that special protective measures would be taken.

Environmental lawsuits are often supported on a shoestring by the fund-raising efforts of local conservation groups, whereas the defendants are generally well financed industries or government agencies. The struggle is not so unequal as it might seem, however, for the conservationists frequently can call as expert witnesses environmental scientists who are leading men in their fields. These scientists usually receive no more for their services than expense money and the satisfaction of striking a blow in a holy war.

In the hearings on DDT in Wisconsin last winter, for example, the Environmental Defense Fund (EDF) produced witnesses from fields such as fishery and wildlife biology, botany, entomology, chemistry, and pharmacology. These witnesses were all unpaid volunteers, some from the University of Wisconsin, while others were from universities and laboratories in California, New York, and other distant places. The attack in Wisconsin on DDT, which was well publicized nationally and undoubtedly helped to create the present climate of concern about this pesticide, was undertaken on the initiative of the Citizens Natural Resources Association, a small but ecologically sophisticated Wisconsin group in which scientists are prominent.

Clearly, if conservationists should find the courts increasingly willing to help protect the environment, a heavy debt will be owed ecologists and other environmental scientists. In fact, the conservation movement probably would be doomed to deepening frustration and failure if it were not taking on a scientific rationale. In a crowded world, with increasing competition for resources, the most persuasive appeals for conservation are likely to be those supported by hard evidence of impending environmental upsets, large or small.

In hopes of forestalling one such upset, the Florida Defenders of the Environment, a group made up largely of scientists from the University of Florida and other institutions, has had EDF sue the U.S. Army Corps of Engineers to stop construction of the $160-million Cross-Florida Barge Canal, a project which already is far advanced and which will be hard to turn off. The Florida Defenders say that the project is a "crime against nature" that will destroy the Oklawaha River Valley as a wilderness area, turn much of the river into weed-choked or algae-laden impoundments, and alter drastically the flow of nearby Silver Springs (a major tourist attraction). If the case comes to trial, the Florida Defenders will provide a string of expert witnesses from fields such as limnology, plant ecology, and hydrology.

Ecology is not yet a mature science, and ecologists sometimes cannot predict with certainty the consequences of human intervention in an ecosystem. However, as the predictive capabilities of ecology are improved, this rapidly developing glamour science will become increasingly important to the resolution of environmental issues, in the courtroom as well as elsewhere.

David Gates, director of the Missouri Botanical Garden and leader of a new discipline dubbed "biophysical ecology" (wherein the relationship between an organism and its environment is analyzed as a function of energy, gas, and nutrient exchange), believes that eventually predictive models will be developed that will allow scientists to forecast the effect on the environment of various kinds of human activities, such as the clearing of forests from wide areas and the polluting of the atmosphere.

Of course, a court confronted with a lawsuit involving highly complicated environmental questions may doubt its competence to handle the matter. But courts can and sometimes do appoint technically trained special masters to hear cases believed to be beyond the ken of trial judges. The Wisconsin DDT hearings, a quasi-judicial proceeding, were conducted by an experienced examiner who had some background in chemistry and biology; no one doubted his grasp of the scientific issues raised.

Yet it is not uncommon for an ordinary trial judge to sort out and decide the issues successfully in an environmental law case. The judge in the New Jersey wildlife preserves case has confessed that, early in the proceedings, he went to the dictionary to look up "ecology," a word at that time unfamiliar to him. But, according to Joseph Sax of the University of Michigan Law School, who has made a study of the New Jersey case, the judge did a masterful job and rendered an opinion with which it is difficult to quarrel.

As Sax points out, there was never a question of the judge's substituting his judgment for that of the pipeline engineers on any matter in which these engineers were the acknowledged experts. Rather, his task was to hear the environmental experts who testified—some representing the plaintiffs and others representing the defendants—and to decide whether, from the standpoint of protecting the wildlife preserve from needless damage, the utility's administrators and engineers had planned wisely. Neither judges nor the administrators who run utilities and public works agencies are experts on environmental issues. But judges, who ordinarily are not ax grinders, should be better than the administrators at listening impartially to those who are experts on these issues.

As the cases discussed here suggest, conservationists look to the courts for help in making industry, public utilities, and administrative and regulatory agencies give substantial weight to natural values and environmental protection. Such considerations often have been treated as matters of secondary concern by industry and by these agencies, as well as by the stockholders, special "clientele," and political interests which influence their policies. Sax points out the irony of the situation: "To make the democratic system respond properly to the environmental crisis, conservationists are going to the judiciary, the least democratic branch of government."

Legislating for Air Quality Management: Reducing Theory to Practice

Introduction

Air pollution is more or less representative of the nation's increasing environmental problems in that while it has been with us for some time it has only recently grown to a scale where differences in degree have begun to become differences in kind. Up to some level of concentration, disposal of wastes is for the most part a local irritation. But, at a certain threshold, costs to society start to increase significantly. This phenomenon has resulted in a considerable redefinition of air pollution problems. For example, the concern is no longer so much with smoke damage as with harm from photochemical smog and other synergistic effects. Also, a higher aspiration level on the part of the population of metropolitan areas has resulted in a reduced tolerance for anything impairing the quality of the environment. These and other changes in the nature of the air pollution problem suggest a new or at least a broader view of planning for air quality management.

The regulatory machinery for dealing with the air pollution problem is still for the most part of a primitive variety. The Air Quality Act of 1967 assigns primary responsibility for devising the regulatory mechanism to state governments, subject to review by the Department of Health, Education, and Welfare (HEW),[1] and appears to contemplate

* Professor Hagevik is teaching at Rutgers University. This article is reprinted with permission from a symposium, Air Pollution Control, appearing in *Law and Contemporary Problems* 33, 2 (Spring, 1968), pp. 369–398, published by Duke University School of Law, Durham, North Carolina, copyright, 1968, by Duke University.

[1] §101 (a) (3), 81 Stat. 485.

that new legislation or regulatory action will appear at the state and
local level as soon as HEW provides the data and criteria for which it
is responsible under the Act.[2] The resultant need for review of laws and
standards, coupled with changing perceptions of the problem, suggest
that a new generation of legislative responses at the state and local level
is to be both hoped and looked for. In the formulation of this new response, greater sophistication will be needed if the considerable costs involved in air pollution abatement are to be minimized, and it is not
clear that existing air quality management efforts are yielding the experience necessary to guide the legislatures in this direction. Perhaps
greater assistance will come from economists and other experts who can
recognize that the legal attack on air pollution requires a new strategy,
not just further adaptations of old approaches originally designed to
deal with zoning and nuisances.

This paper first attempts to set down some basic social science
theory about the economics of air pollution and about decision making
in general. It then seeks to apply this understanding in the development
of a hypothetical regulatory program for dealing with stationary sources
of pollution. This hypothetical program owes little to existing control efforts and is conceived in the understanding that regulatory officials must
be enabled to operate effectively even in the dim light of partial knowledge defining and relating the social and technological aspects of air
pollution. Since the program is merely sketched, it will not serve as a
blueprint but only as a stimulus to new thinking about air quality management and the organization for carrying it out.

I   The Economist's View—Effluent Fees

Readings in welfare economics published during the last thirty
years are replete with references to smoke damage as a classic instance
of what are called negative externalities.[3] Such discussions, however,
have been of more value to economists interested in the further theoretical development of welfare economics than to the air pollution control
officer concerned with actual abatement and control activities. Unfortunately, in this instance the spillover from theory to practice has been
minimal. Why is this the case? For one thing, the economic theory requires limiting conditions and large assumptions about the data available, neither of which can be fulfilled in practice. The problems of col-
lecting data on such subjects as air pollution damage and the

[2] §§101 (b), 106, 107, 81 Stat. 485.
[3] E.g., A. Pigou, *The Economics of Welfare* 160–161 (1932).

contribution of each emitter to existing concentrations are staggering, to say the least, and economists have not had the fortitude or the means to tackle the measurements necessary to make concrete control proposals. Sheer complexity has discouraged interest, and, until very recently, there was apparently less investment by government and private funding agencies in this field of economic research than the need seems in retrospect to have warranted. In any event, the theory has proved not too difficult to master, but attention is only beginning to focus on the need for data and practical means of developing these data or compensating for the lack thereof. The 1966 volume, *The Economics of Air Pollution*, edited by Professor Harold Wolozin, is probably the best single indicator both of economists' increased interest in the problem and of the gulf remaining between theory and practice.

The practitioner looking for practical answers in the Wolozin volume will be disappointed, for it is little more than a summary—albeit an excellent one—of the state of the art. The primary contribution of the book is that it brings relevant economic theory to bear on the problem, explicitly or implicitly reveals the advantages and weaknesses of the economist's approach, and suggests data deficiencies and research needs. The consensus of the participants in the forum from which the book was drawn seems to be that the problem has been defined and that the task for the next few years is to gather data and do research that might lead to estimates of the necessary answers. If an analogy to water quality management holds, the estimate of a few years seems optimistic. For, even though economists have been concerned with water resource development for some time, Allen Kneese's seminal work on water quality, *The Economics of Regional Water Quality Management*, did not appear until 1964.

The economist's views on air quality management can be usefully reviewed in a brief manner. Most economists would state the problem in this way: The discharge of pollutants into the air imposes on some people costs which are not adequately borne by the sources of the pollution due to the failure of the market mechanism, resulting in more air pollution than would be desirable from the point of view of society as a whole. The "classical" economic theorist's distinctive approach to the problem is manifested in his belief that the objective of pollution abatement programs should be to minimize the total of (a) air pollution damage costs and (b) the costs incurred in any program to alleviate that damage. Any given level of pollution abatement should be reached by the least costly combination of means available, and the costs of any decrement of pollution should not exceed the benefits obtained by the reduction. Thus, the standard theoretical approach would be to calculate the damage to each receptor from polluted air containing various amounts and kinds of effluents. Such a calculation would permit measurement of the benefits to be expected from proposed abatement projects. Next, one would calculate the cost to each pollutant source of abating its emissions in varying degrees. The optimal allocation of the air resource would then require that pollutants be prevented from entering the atmosphere at levels which would inflict more marginal damage on receptors than the marginal cost to the source of preventing the pollution.[4]

The operational procedure which economists would recommend for achieving this optimal condition would include an evaluation of the damage done by the emission of incremental amounts of pollutant into the air at any given location and time and an assessment of a corresponding charge against the emitters. The charge would thus reflect the marginal costs that the sources impose on others. It would be determined by relating ambient air quality to rates of emission, using air monitoring networks and relatively simple atmospheric diffusion models.

The principal advantage from the economist's point of view of "internalizing" the cost by means of a government-levied charge on the source is that the economic units involved can decide on the best adjustment to be made in light of the costs and benefits they perceive. Those firms which can reduce emissions at a cost that would be less than the charge will do so to avoid being assessed the charge. Those firms which *cannot* reduce emissions at a cost that would be less than the charge would elect to pay the fee but would nevertheless have a continuing incentive to reduce emissions. Thus, the optimal level of pollution abatement will be approached by the method that is least costly to society as a whole.

Under this system, management rather than government officials would bear much of the burden of investigation and decision making, and management is said to be better able to evaluate the advantages and disadvantages of the various ways of dealing with the effluent problem and to choose the best mix. This is held to be preferable to being restricted to any one abatement technique. Implicit in the economist's view is recognition that the optimal level of air pollution abatement is closely tied to the technological processes involved, with the least-cost solution being in many cases a complex combination of process changes and treatment of effluent; in some cases, moreover, the least-cost solu-

---

[4] A detailed statement of this approach is found in Crocker, "The Structuring of Atmospheric Pollution Control Systems," *The Economics of Air Pollution* (H. Wolozin, ed., 1966) [hereinafter cited as Wolozin]. For a refinement of the problem of determining which abatement expenditures are justifiable, *see* notes 69–70 *infra* and accompanying text.

tion might involve partial abatement and payment of the lower effluent fees associated with the remaining emissions. The continuing incentive provided by the effluent fee to search for additional or alternative ways of abating discharges involves a much different response than that compelled in a straight enforcement action. Enforcement by criminal proceeding, or by injunction, or cease-and-desist order, for example, would provide no real alternative to incurring the abatement costs, whatever they might be. Moreover, enforcement programs that would compel the adoption of specific technology would altogether destroy the incentive to explore alternative abatement techniques or to combine approaches to achieve the maximum efficiency in pollution reduction.

A system of effluent fees has additional theoretical appeal because of its adaptability to changing or variable circumstances. Fees can be varied up or down in accordance with weather conditions, the time of day, the season of the year, and other factors in order to correlate emitters' costs even more closely with the damage caused. The theoretical advantage of this flexibility may be difficult to realize in practice, however, and indeed may even prove a liability. Given the vast inadequacy of data and the probabilistic character of the factors that might be reflected in variable fees, the schedule would take on an appearance of arbitrariness that might be difficult to dispel. We have here one key to the unlikelihood that effluent fees will soon play a major role in air quality control.

The primary problems with effluent fees are simply the shortage of data and the lack of agreement on many of the theoretical problems that are presented. The major information deficiency is in the measurement of damages attributable to particular pollutants, and myriad conceptual and informational problems inhere in the allocation to individual polluters of the share of the total damages for which they are "responsible." Perhaps most difficult of all is the theoretical problem of allocating damages to specific polluters when synergistic effects occur—that is, where the combination of two or more pollutants, such as sulfur oxides and particulates, causes greater damage than either pollutant could cause alone. Problems of equity are also presented by the need to allocate damage costs between new and existing industries. Finally, there are also doubts that monitoring technology is adequate to permit effective enforcement of an effluent fee system. Especially where there are numerous small polluters to be monitored, such a system would be costly to administer.

Another problem, which must be faced in any regulatory system, with or without effluent fees, has to do with the determination of who should benefit from the use of the air resource. If air is to be treated as a free good for the receptors, including humans, plants, and animals, certain costs are thus imposed on others who may wish to use the air for waste disposal. Theoretical discussions seldom deal with why these costs should not be allocated according to "practical" considerations such as the supposed ability of industry to pass on added costs to consumers and the apparently greater ability of industrial firms to select and apply the least-cost solution (including the possibility of paying adjoining landowners to move or take protective measures). An effluent fee program might be designed to encourage such flexibility, but administrative problems would again seem to be overwhelming in the short run.

While these many problems and data shortages will handicap any program of enforced abatement which purports to compare abatement costs and the benefits derived therefrom, an effluent fee program would also have to survive legal attacks based on arguments of apparent discrimination and abuse of the taxing power. As understanding of the nature of air pollution and pollution damage costs increases, effluent fees may become more feasible and may ultimately fill an important role in air pollution control. But today, while the assignment or sale of emission or receptor rights has theoretical appeal, the pricing of such rights still requires some sort of centralized decision-making system. Such a system, as it might now be constituted in our political and institutional environment, would yield only a few of the advantages that a fully market-oriented system, from which it is conceptually derived, would produce.

Finally, a basic complaint against the theoretical underpinnings of the effluent fee approach has been raised by Wolozin, who states,

> My skepticism is based on the unfortunate fact that we do not know enough in an empirical way about the effects of taxation on business policies and human behavior to be at all certain about the outcome of any scheme of tax like effluent fees. Even the underlying theory can be questioned.[5]

This questioned theory is, of course, the conventional neoclassical microeconomic model, which depends upon the postulate of rationality and the concept of the firm as a profit maximizer. Since these assumptions have often been criticized as unrealistic, Wolozin suggests that a more useful approach might be to view the goals of the firm in relation to its position as an organization in a political and social system.[6] Wolozin's point is not well taken, however, for it seemingly ignores three

[5] Wolozin, "Discussion," in *Proceedings: The Third National Conference on Air Pollution*, 580 (Public Health Service Pub. No. 1649, 1967) [hereinafter cited as *Third Nat'l. Conf. Proceedings*].
[6] *Ibid.*

fundamental considerations. First, many significant polluters will in fact be entrepreneurs in the traditional sense rather than firms in which management has become independent of ownership, the condition usually cited as having undermined the profit-maximization postulate. Second, the proposition that management generally prefers lower costs to higher is a principle which has never been directly criticized, and it holds largely true even in regulated public utilities where "regulatory lag" permits realization of profits wherever unanticipated cost savings can be accomplished.[7] Finally, Wolozin misses the notable fact that management's presumed social responsibilities, which are so strongly emphasized by those who would contest the profit-maximization postulate, are also at work in this field, assisting in the achievement of the social goal of a cleaner environment. One might predict, therefore, that effluent fees, by raising the cost of *not* fulfilling a perceived social responsibility to abate, will yield dividends *greater* than traditional theory would anticipate.

In sum, effluent fees have a solid theoretical foundation, but the practical problems associated with establishing and enforcing a fee schedule appear so great that immediate adoption of this approach seems unlikely. Understanding of the air pollution problem and the regulatory challenge it poses nevertheless requires a grasp of effluent fees' potentiality, since a system of fees may be the ultimate goal toward which regulation should evolve. Vickrey's advocacy of an effluent fee program rests in part on the consideration that it would force the regulator "to bring the problem into perspective, and tends to put something of a restraint on the pure air enthusiast who might at times be inclined to impose standards that would entail too high a cost relative to benefits." [8] One premise of the hypothetical regulatory program developed below is that the cost-benefit principle can also be implemented in a program of direct regulation and that the lesson Vickrey wants taught can be learned without opting for effluent fees as the dominant regulatory approach.

II   Choice of a Control Philosophy

a. *Alternative Approaches to Control*

In addition to the effluent fee approach, payments and direct regulation are other approaches to environmental quality management

[7] *But cf.* comments by Linsky, Mills, and Wolozin, *id.* at 589.
[8] W. Vickrey, Theoretical and Practical Possibilities and Limitations of a Market Mechanism Approach to Air Pollution, a paper presented at the Air Pollution Control Ass'n Conference, Cleveland, Ohio, June 1967.

problems.[9] Direct regulation is somewhat different from the other two in that it is nonfiscal. The payments approach includes not only subsidies but also reductions in taxes that otherwise would be collected. Common examples include the subsidization of particular control equipment, accelerated depreciation, and tax credits for investment in control equipment. Direct regulation includes a mixed bag of licenses, permits, registration, zoning, air quality and effluent standards, and the enforcement of standards through regulatory bodies and the courts.

1. PAYMENTS. One possible payment system might rely on selective payments to waste contributors for the purpose of motivating them to restrict emissions to an optimal degree. These payments would in principle be equivalent to the off-site costs imposed by increments of waste discharge and would vary with atmospheric conditions and effluent location, as well as with the quantity and quality of effluent. Since this sort of payment would be similar in theory but opposite in approach to the effluent fee scheme, the criticisms and difficulties mentioned above would apply here also.

The more typical proposal under the payments heading, however, relates to tax relief or subsidies. Such proposals are a popular topic these days, particularly among industry representatives and members of Congress, but they have only one substantial argument in their favor— there is less resistance to a program of subsidies than to programs of regulation. There are, however, a number of problems with the payments approach. As Mills states,

> [T]here is a strong practical argument against most of the policies under the payments heading. They are simply payments for the wrong thing. The investment credit proposal will illustrate the deficiency that is common to others. An investment credit on air pollution abatement equipment reduces the cost of such equipment. But most such equipment is inherently unprofitable in that it adds nothing to revenues and does not reduce costs. To reduce the cost of such an item cannot possibly induce a firm to install it. The most it can do is to reduce the resistance to public pressure for installation. Common sense and scattered bits of evidence suggest that these payments policies are costly and inefficient ways to achieve abatement.[10]

[9] See generally A. Kneese, The Economics of Regional Water Quality Management 193–95 (1964); Mills, "Economic Incentives to Air Pollution Control," in Wolozin 40.
[10] Mills, "Federal Incentives to Air Pollution Control," in Third Nat'l. Conf. Proceedings 575–576.

More specifically, it would be difficult to decide how much to pay to whom for any level of pollution abatement, since there is no commonly accepted level of air quality from which payments could be computed. The taxpayer's feelings of equity might also be violated, since the industrial firm, in not having to consider pollution abatement as a cost of production in the same sense that labor and capital are, would rely on payments raised at least partially by higher taxes on other taxpayers.[11]

Payment schemes, tax credits, or accelerated depreciation may also bias the technique used for control in an uneconomical direction because they tend to promote construction of treatment facilities when adjustments in production processes, products, or inputs might achieve the same result at lower cost and might even increase productivity. Tax writeoffs of capital cost are also at a disadvantage because they are not capable of reducing all abatement costs. It has been estimated that capital cost accounts for only about one-eighth of the air pollution abatement costs for a typical firm.[12] Indeed, fuel substitution alone is estimated to be the least-cost alternative in over sixty percent of the cases involved in air pollution abatement.[13]

Grants and loans have the same objectives as tax writeoffs in that they lower the cost of capital expenditures. Thus the criticisms suggested above apply. However, it has been suggested that if grants were made for both capital and operating costs and administered through regional air quality management organizations, this particular criticism would lose much of its bite. But it must be remembered that extensive reliance on grants and loans suffers from the uncertainty of fluctuations in legislative appropriations.

2. DIRECT REGULATION. Although the ideal method for dealing with the effects of the unidirectional external diseconomies associated with air pollution would be a system of effluent charges, it is often suggested that the best operational method for dealing with practical problems is direct regulation. Existing federal policies on air pollution abatement mostly fall in the category of regulation and enforcement activities.[14] The advantage of this approach is that it permits the government to take interim steps even though it has almost no idea of rele-

---

[11] See Mills, supra note 9, at 45–46.
[12] Working Comm. on Economic Incentives, Federal Coordinating Comm. on the Economic Impact of Pollution Abatement, Cost Sharing with Industry? 27 (Summary Report 1967) [hereinafter cited as Federal Coordinating Comm.]
[13] Ibid.
[14] For a full discussion of federal powers under the statute, see Martin & Symington, A Guide to the Air Quality Act of 1967, in this symposium, p. 239 [Law and Contemporary Problems, Duke University School of Law, 1968.]

vant measurements. For example, if people's eyes were burning because of obvious emissions from an industrial plant, it would be logical to require filtration of these emissions even if one had no way of measuring the amounts of the emissions. Such regulation can be justified, since, as a report of the staff of the Senate Committee on Public Works states, "Whatever yardsticks are employed, it is clearly evident that the cost of property damages alone from air pollution is great—far greater than the amounts devoted to its abatement by industry and all levels of government." [15] The implication seems to be that there is little chance of the costs of such a program exceeding the benefits.

Not all economists view direct regulation with complete suspicion. Crocker states,

> Given the uncertain quality of available physical, biological, and economic information, and the potentially high costs associated with the gathering of additional information about atmospheric pollution problems, the control authority, in order to impress receptors and emitters with the necessity of regarding the air's two value dimensions as scarce economic resources, appears to be justified in setting minimal standards. [16]

A greater commitment to standards is evident in the writings of Paul Gerhardt, an economist with the National Center for Air Pollution Control. He states:

> A polluter faced with the necessity to comply with a law or suffer punishment will generally find the least cost set of controls or have no one to blame but himself. He will pass cost increases along to customers in the form of price increases or to equity holders in the form of reduced profit shares. Optimum allocation will be preserved as the public makes new choices about their spending and investing patterns. Administrative costs could be less than for some alternatives as there would be no complicated tax revenue emission charge or payment system to operate. [17]

But, as expected, relative simplicity is not achieved without certain costs. One objection to direct regulation is its allegedly extreme inflexibility which results in considerably higher costs than would more selective abatement. To use an example from water pollution, the Fed-

[15] Staff of the Senate Comm. on Public Works, 88th Cong., 1st Sess., A Study of Pollution—Air 20 (Comm. Print 1963).
[16] Crocker, *supra* note 4, at 79.
[17] P. Gerhardt, Some Economic Aspects of Air Pollution, a paper presented at the Mid-Atlantic States Section, Air Pollution Control Ass'n Conference, Oct. 4, 1967.

eral Water Pollution Control Administration found in the Delaware River Basin that simple equal-proportional reduction of all waste loads would cost fifty percent more than achieving the same quality standard by requiring firms to reduce their waste loads in proportion to their harmful effects.[18] In the case of air quality management, the Federal Coordinating Committee on the Economic Impact of Pollution Abatement suggests that the cost of achieving a specific air quality standard could increase by 200 to 400 percent if equal-proportional reduction on a year-round basis were attempted.[19]

The argument over the desirability of direct regulation cannot be resolved on the merits here. It is perhaps more important, however, to note that government already appears to be committed to direct regulation as the preferred means of dealing with the air pollution problem, although subsidies and tax concessions will continue to appear. While Congress did not see fit in the Air Quality Act to enact the President's proposal for a program of national emission standards for all polluting industries, such standards are still under consideration.[20] Moreover, most state and local abatement programs are based on strict prohibitions of the emission of specified concentrations of pollutants. Against this background, the final section of this article, in developing a hypothetical program of direct regulation, is premised on these judgments, among others (1) that government has already opted for a direct regulation approach, (2) that such an approach holds fewer dangers of resource misallocation and inequity than would a payments or subsidy program, (3) that direct regulation would be more likely to operate effectively with necessarily imperfect data than would an effluent fee approach, and (4) that its legal status might be somewhat less open to question than an effluent fee program simply because it is somewhat less of a novelty in the spectrum of public policies. Finally, while it is believed that there is already a commitment to regulation, the shape of the regulatory machinery, the details of the policies to be implemented, and the decision-making methodology to be employed do not seem to be finally determined. The hypothetical program is thus framed to encourage maximum flexibility in pursuit of least-cost solutions, which economic theory tells us are important and can help us to find.

b. A Larger View of Decision Making

To this point the review has been over what should be familiar ground. Unfortunately for many practitioners in the field of air quality

[18] Federal Coordinating Comm. 14.
[19] *Ibid.*
[20] *See* Air Quality Act of 1967, §211 (a), 81 Stat. 485.

management, knowledge relating to benefit-cost ratios, marginal cost pricing, and optimal taxing schemes has been secondary to the necessary concern with temperature inversions, wet scrubbers, filters, and the like. This is the case even though air pollution is in a fundamental sense a social and economic problem the solutions to which have to be worked out within a complex political and institutional framework. Technological means are currently available to purify the air to any desired degree, but costs increase significantly as more control is desired.[21] The economist's view of air quality management is important because we are finally perceiving a condition of scarcity so central to his thinking. Air is now viewed as a congested facility, and without the attempt at evaluation he provides, the desirable objective of reducing the level of pollution in the atmosphere by the least costly means possible would be difficult to achieve.

Since pollution abatement is primarily a matter of avoiding costs, programs need to be initially evaluated from an economic point of view, for as Turvey has noted, "even though an economic calculation of gains or losses is often not sufficient to reach a well based decision, it is nearly always an essential preliminary." [22] This determination of sound economic policy in air quality management requires an accurate and continuing evaluation of the costs of abatement relative to air pollution damages. Viewing costs avoided as benefits, decisions need to be sought that maximize the present value of net benefits.[23] Ideally, this analysis would be directed toward finding abatement efforts that equate incremental abatement costs and the value of incremental damage costs reduced.[24] But even a less sophisticated approach could measure abatement costs so that they include both administrative costs of control and capital and process change costs associated with abatement. Tools of

[21] The main technological problem that remains to be solved is the development of a method of monitoring levels of emission accurately and at low cost.

[22] Turvey, "Side Effects of Resource Use," in *Environmental Quality in a Growing Economy* 52 (R. Jarrett, ed. 1966).

[23] This is essentialy a benefit-cost view of air quality management, since one may alternatively refer to (1) damages (costs) avoided as benefits and (2) costs incurred for abatement as costs, and say that waste reduction up to but not beyond a certain point will maximize benefits minus costs. Cost minimization (including damages as a cost) and net benefit maximization are in this case identical.

[24] It is significant, as Gerhardt points out, that there has been far more interest in assessing the value of the damage by air pollution than in the costs of control. The costs of recent attempts at control have generally been accepted as a fraction of total damages. The interest in incremental costs of control will increase as the point of equality between incremental control costs and incremental damages is approached. *See* Gerhardt, *supra* note 17. For an argument suggesting that abatement costs should be a matter of immediate concern, *see* notes 69–70 *infra* and accompanying text.

evaluation, whether in sophisticated or crude form, need to be applied not only to the theoretical ideal of effluent fees and charges but also to the actual or potential use of payments and continuous and noncontinuous emission standards under a program of direct regulation.

While direct regulation seems to be emerging as the dominant control philosophy, the regulation to be undertaken may nevertheless comprise subsidies, licenses, permits, effluent charges, emission standards and variances therefrom, emergency powers, and some reliance on market forces. Experimentation with regulatory approaches to determine the best mix of such control techniques is desirable, and this need should be recognized by HEW in its review of state enforcement plans under the Air Quality Act. Such experimentation can be accomplished most readily by a control agency that is given broad powers with discretion to choose the tools needed for particular purposes. The hypothetical regulatory program described below contemplates such experimentation.

The overriding decision-making issue in this field is simply the difficulty of regulating an activity requiring prompt and decisive regulatory attention under conditions of imperfect knowledge, information, and understanding. The need for experimentation stems from these uncertainties. Ridker, commenting favorably on the need to get on with the job of regulating and the desirability of regulatory experimentation, quotes a British air pollution control official as follows:

> You Americans behave as if you have sufficient time and money to investigate a problem to death before you decide to act. In Britain we take note of a problem we do not like, take some action to correct the problem, and then do research after the fact to determine whether we were right.[25]

Such a purely seat-of-the-pants approach might not be politically feasible in this country and might be open to legal attack. Nevertheless, regulation must proceed with only partial knowledge, and if sensible and progressive regulation is to be achieved, substantial decision-making powers must be delegated to control agencies along with the discretion to experiment and innovate control approaches. The challenge becomes one of devising an effective decision-making process, with the decision maker's discretion structured and guided by legal principles, growing technical understanding, and clearly defined legislative goals, and with opportunities for participation by affected parties in the decision-making process. Social science theory can again be turned to, this time for guidance in the shaping of such a regulatory program.

[25] Ridker, "Strategies for Measuring the Cost of Air Pollution," in Wolozin 87, 100.

III   The Role of Bargaining

Social scientists have developed a plethora of overlapping and competing theories and models of the decision process. The literature on the subject is vast, and any attempt at synthesis here would only result in confusion for the reader.[26] What is needed at this stage is a theoretical framework that relates social, political, and economic behavior to the institutional structures under consideration in a program of air quality management. Such a framework, concerned with the actors in the decision process, the strategies they pursue, the nature of the information available to all parties, and the environment in which decisions are made, would be of great assistance to legislators attempting to develop more rational regulatory institutions for securing pollution abatement. The following discussion may help to provide a conceptual approach to the formulation of an effectively functioning control program.

a. Theory of Conflict Resolution

Significant public policies originate in the conflict of group interests.[27] The peaceful resolution of these conflicts is generally achieved through reconciliation, compromise, or an award process in which both parties agree to accept the verdict of an outside person or agency.[28] Reconciliation relies on discussion to lessen the differences of opinion between the participants. Compromise uses the mediation and conciliation aspects of bargaining, while an award is achieved through arbitration or legal trial. In air quality management or in any other environmental management program none of the three types of resolution can be considered as an independent technique for pollution abatement, although one form might predominate. Indeed, Boulding asserts that reconciliation and compromise might occur simultaneously, that some reconciliation may be necessary before compromise is possible, that there are likely to be elements of discussion and propaganda in bargaining situations, that in arbitration cases or in court proceedings there are often elements of bargaining and reconciliation before the award is announced, and that an award might not be accepted unless it has been preceded by informal reconciliation and bargaining.[29]

[26] For a useful review of the major contributions in the area of decision theory, *see* Robinson and Majak, "The Theory of Decision-Making," in *Contemporary Political Analysis* 175 (J. Charlesworth, ed., 1967).
[27] *See, e.g.,* J. Anderson, *Politics and the Economy* (1966).
[28] *See* T. Schelling, *The Strategy of Conflict* 3–20 (1966).
[29] K. Boulding, *Conflict and Defense: A General Theory* 310–313 (1962).

Game theory has become one principal avenue for research on conflict resolution, and it is usually defined as the formal study of rational decisions in situations where "two or more individuals have choices to make, preferences regarding the outcomes, and some knowledge of the choices available to each other and of each other's preferences."[30] It is concerned with situations—games of strategy—in which the best course of action for each participant depends on what he expects the other participants to do, with the outcome a function of what choices are made by the other actors. The individual decision units have only partial control over the strategic factors affecting their environment, since the essence of the game is that it involves adversaries whose fates are intertwined. In a sense, each group or individual faces a cross-optimization problem in which plans must be adjusted not only to one's own desires and abilities but also to those of others.

Bargaining, which is defined as the process by which a tolerable settlement for all participants is reached,[31] falls within the theory of games but is a species of game in which relatively little progress has been made, partly because it includes situations involving common interest as well as conflict between opponents.[32] Cooperation is useful in this type of game because within some range of possibilities both parties will be better off with a solution, i.e., bargain, than without one. Conflict is involved because within this range of solutions the participants compete for the most favorable distribution of benefits. Thus, while both parties are interested in the adoption of some solution, they have divergent interests with regard to the particular solution that is adopted.[33]

Although bargaining has been widely studied and discussed, it is not always clear, as McKean has pointed out,[34] just how bargaining works. Because of this lack of knowledge, bargaining is often viewed as a constraint in decision making rather than as a variable that could be

[30] Schelling, "What is Game Theory?" in *Contemporary Political Analysis* 213 (J. Charlesworth, ed., 1967).
[31] *See* Banfield, "Notes on a Conceptual Scheme," in *Politics, Planning and the Public Interest* 307 (M. Meyerson & E. Banfield, ed., 1953).
[32] In the terminology of game theory, bargaining is a positive-sum (as opposed to zero-sum), frequently nonsymmetrical game between participants with a mixture of conflict and cooperation. Zero-sum games are those in which one player's loss is the other's gain. The sum of gain plus loss is zero—hence "zero-sum." A positive-sum game is one in which the gain of one party is not equal to the loss of the other. For example, a gain for A of one unit of value may only cause a loss to B of one-half unit. A nonsymmetrical game results when B's loss varies from move to move even though A's gain with each move is constant. These variations from the zero-sum prototype make the mathematics of a game extremely complex.
[33] This dichotomy gives the bargaining game its unusual character and raises issues quite different from pure conflict or pure cooperation games.
[34] McKean, *The Unseen Hand in Government*, 55 Am. Econ. Rev. 494 (1965).

manipulated to achieve a least-cost solution.[35] The usual explanation for this situation is that there are no generally accepted operational criteria for determining economic efficiency, that there are many competing groups with diverse interests and values seeking to influence policy making, and that a variety of political, social, and ethical as well as economic considerations are involved in the making of public economic policy. The policy process involves the striking of balances and the making of compromises more often than the finding of "correct" policies or the choice between "right" and "wrong" in any absolute sense. Given the suggested importance of bargaining in the decision-making process, bargaining should no longer be viewed as a constraint within which one attempts to optimize. There are obvious costs and benefits associated with shifts in bargaining behavior that can be identified. Current and anticipated research on decision making in air quality management needs to take cognizance of the role of bargaining, and the researcher should seek to identify the costs and benefits attached to any bargaining solution.

While economists and mathematicians have developed highly sophisticated approaches to game theoretic decision making, such methodology might be only tangentially relevant to decision making in air quality management. For the social scientist that which is conceptual and rudimentary in game theory is the most valuable.[36] Rather than being thought of as a formal "theory," it is now viewed as a framework for analysis which can be adapted and modified according to specific needs. In essence, it provides a point of reference for examining a problem and gaining needed insights without accepting the often unrealistic rules of the game. With this in mind, the following section reviews some of the insights gained in the study of the bargaining aspects of game theory that might have potential application in devising a regulatory framework for air quality management. Because it is within the legislative power to change the rules and context within a particular "game" situation, understanding of the forces at work would assist in making institutional and substantive adjustments that will contribute to more nearly optimal outcomes.

b. Some Insights from Bargaining Theory

1. CONTINUOUS GAMES. Research on conflict situations clearly shows that negotiation and bargaining operate best in situations where

---

[35] See R. Cyert & J. March, A Behavioral Theory of the Firm 31 (1967).
[36] See, e.g., Schelling, supra note 30, at 219; Shubik, "The Uses of Game Theory," in Contemporary Political Analysis 260 (J. Charlesworth, ed., 1967).

the subject in contention can be divided into parts that can be dealt with sequentially. This incrementalism, whether achieved by changes in moves or in value systems, is of considerable importance.[37] To draw the analogy of chess, players move in turn, each moving a piece at a time; the game proceeds at a slow tempo by small increments and is of an indeterminate length. The game changes character in the course of play by a succession of small changes that can be observed and appreciated, with plenty of time for mistakes of individual players or mutual mistakes which can be noticed and adapted to in later play. In an uncertain situation, a person is often saved from making a strategic error if he hesitates, so the capacity to make future decisions is not relinquished.[38]

The decomposition tactic in bargaining can be applied to either threats or to promises, and can be viewed as a necessary prerequisite for making a bargain enforceable. This is so since there is a perception on the part of the participants that future possibilities for agreement will not develop unless mutual trust is created and maintained. The participants need to be confident that each of them will not jeopardize opportunities for future agreement by destroying trust near the start of the game.[39] Such confidence is naturally not always in evidence, so decomposition serves to encourage the same expectations on the part of all participants. An aspect of building mutual expectations is that if a threat can be decomposed into a series of consecutive threats, there is an opportunity to demonstrate to an opponent during his initial reaction to a threat that you "mean business," thereby making the continuous game a learning experience.[40] Although it is possible that future opportunities for bargaining are not anticipated, a semblance of a continuing game can be created by separating the issue at stake into consecutive components. The principle is also apparent that it is poor strategy to require compliance in terms of some critical amount or degree that would be deemed mandatory, for action geared to increments has a greater chance of success than one that has to be carried out either all at once or not at all once some particular point has been reached.

This is a concern of some importance in environmental management situations, since they are structurally "lumpier" than chess games. There is no continuous range of choices open to the polluter and the abatement officer. Due to the initial administrative and psychic costs and the initial and marginal capital costs, moves have a considerable impact, and it is usually difficult to project a control situation more than

[37] See T. Schelling, supra note 28, at 170.
[38] See K. Boulding, The Impact of the Social Sciences 43 (1966).
[39] See T. Schelling, supra note 28, at 45.
[40] This learning process is detailed in A. Rappaport & A. Ghammah, Prisoner's Dilemma (1965).

a move or two ahead. The pace of the game can bring things to a head before much experience has been gained or much of an understanding reached unless ways are found to increase the number of possible moves. The use of incrementalism in structuring pollution abatement progress eases the impact of each move and allows the participants to acquire both knowledge of each other and experience with the particular problem at hand. Costs are spread over a longer period of time, and the slower pace of the process and the indeterminate length of the "game" reduce the possibility of crisis. Because of these advantages gained through the use of incrementalism, one would expect that conscious attempts would be made to increase the number of "moves" and extend the life of the game. It is of interest that the Air Quality Act specifies that multiple actions must take place before final regulatory action occurs.[41] These steps make the process more incremental in nature, thus gaining for the participants the advantages described above.

Another aspect of the continuous game which must be considered is that negotiating processes develop certain rituals, and attempts to bypass or reduce these rituals may destroy the negotiating process itself.[42] For example, the parties begin the proceedings with somewhat bombastic statements that set the initial boundaries to the negotiations. There is a period of withdrawal designed to make it appear that the commitments are genuine. The parties know, however, that the commitments are not absolute; otherwise the negotiations would break down. There may follow a process of trading by which mutual concessions are made, and there may have to be a period during which, even though no visible progress occurs, the incipient settlement is in fact developing. The resolution of conflict through bargaining thus involves the difficult institutional problem of arranging these ritual elements in the proper order and proportion.[43] Because legal procedures may be too inflexible to permit the proper mix of ritual elements required by the bargaining and reconciling processes, a formal legal proceeding may often be a poor way of handling a conflict in air pollution control.

2. FOCAL POINT SOLUTIONS. In bargains that involve quantification of solutions, such as the setting of emission and ambient air standards, there seems to be some appeal in mathematical simplicity. Outcomes tend to be expressed in even numbers, since they provide good

[41] See §108, 81 Stat. 485 (1967). See Martin & Symington, *supra* note 14, at 244–247.
[42] See Douglas, "The Peaceful Settlement of Industrial and Intergroup Disputes," I. *J. Conflict Resolution* 69 (1957).
[43] See K. Boulding, *supra* note 29, at 311.

"resting places." [44] Thus a compromise at forty-seven percent is much less likely than at fifty percent. Just as the mathematical properties of a game can influence its outcome, the perception by the participants of the historical, cultural, legal, and moral properties of the game can serve to focus expectations on certain solutions. A "focal point" [45] solution has characteristics that distinguish it qualitatively from surrounding alternatives. Unlike the numerical scale, which is too continuous to provide good resting places, qualitative principles are more difficult to compromise, and focal points thus generally depend on qualitative principles. But a commitment to a principle that provides the basis for a numerical calculation which comes out at a specific number may provide the support for a stand at that point.

The outcome of any game can best be characterized by the notion of converging expectations.[46] A good example is the remarkable frequency with which long negotiations over complicated quantitative formulas or shares in some benefits and costs are ultimately influenced by a seemingly irrelevant previous negotiation. Precedent seems to exercise an influence that considerably exceeds its logical importance, since both parties recognize it as a focal point. Past bargains become precedents for present situations in that they often remove from conscious consideration many agreements, decisions, and commitments that might well be subject to renegotiation as conditions change.[47]

If the outcome of a game is seemingly already determined by the participants' perception of the configuration of the problem itself and where the focal point lies, it would seem that the scope of bargaining skill would be insignificant. But it can be argued that the obvious outcome depends greatly on how the problem is formulated, on what analogies or precedents the definition of the bargaining issue calls to mind, and on the kinds of data that may be available to bring to bear on the question in dispute. Thus bargaining skill in air pollution control can be seen to be important before bargaining actually begins by being able to give prominence to some particular outcomes that would be favorable.

c. Conclusions on Bargaining Theory

Several aspects of the many facets of bargaining have been reviewed. These aspects—incrementalism, ritualization, continuing negotiation, and focal point solutions—all suggest that rationality in bargain-

[44] T. Schelling, *supra* note 28, at 114.
[45] *Ibid.* at 111.
[46] *See Ibid.* at 114.
[47] *See* R. Cyert & J. March, *supra* note 35, at 33.

ing outcomes is a function of basically psychic phenomena. At first this view may appear to run contrary to the accepted economic notion that "rationality" is evident only in the minimum-cost solution. But a broader view of decision making may suggest that the least-cost solution is most readily approximated through procedures which take full cognizance of the psychic elements in any bargaining situation and which channel these elements in the direction of a mutually sought, economically sound goal.

IV   The On-Site Incineration Example

An example of decision making in air quality management that helps to illustrate the discussion of bargaining is the attempt to reduce particulate emissions in New York City. During the mid 1960s the heightening concern of the public in New York City with air pollution was focused on visible suspended particulates. During this time, more than ninety percent of the 50,000 complaints received per year by the Department of Air Pollution Control were related to visible emissions. Public attention was particularly focused on the approximately 12,000 apartment house and commercial incinerators which emitted an esti-mated 8,400 to 9,000 tons of particulates per year into the atmosphere. These incinerators became the first important issue in air quality man-agement to face the city administration.

In 1966, responding to public pressure, the City Council passed, in some haste, a local law dealing with the reduction of sulfur dioxide emissions from fuel burning, the use of bituminous coal, the upgrading of municipal incinerators, the upgrading of existing private on-site incin-erators, and the banning of incineration in new buildings. Of particular interest is the section of the law prohibiting construction of residential and commercial on-site incinerators after May 1968 and requiring the upgrading of all existing ones.[48] The first deadline under the law was May 20, 1967, a year after its passage. At that time the owners of an un-known number of incinerators in buildings of seven or more stories were to have completed construction of unspecified control equipment to meet criteria for levels of emissions which had at that time not yet been defined. Local Law 14, as it was called, also had a May 20, 1968, dead-line for the upgrading of buildings under seven stories. The law states that the process of upgrading includes the "installation and use of an auxiliary gas burner regulated by automatic firing clocks, an overfire air

[48] Local Law 14, May 20, 1966, N.Y. City Admin. Code §§892–2.0 to 897–2.0 (Supp. 1967–1968).

fan and nozzle system and control apparatus as may be defined by the [Commissioner of Air Pollution Control]." [49] Basically the required procedure involved the installation of a firebox that burns the refuse efficiently and a scrubber system—a motor-driven device to force the smoke through a special water bath that will remove the heavy particulates. Only compactors would be permitted in new multiple dwellings. This fairly direct attempt at controlling particulate emissions, although not an ideal approach, might seem to some people a useful first step in the direction of cleaner air. Unfortunately it was not.

Why was this the case? The initial problem was that the Department of Air Pollution Control had relatively little time to develop specific criteria for upgrading as required under the law. As a result, the criteria were not formally adopted by the Board of Air Pollution Control until five months before the actual upgrading of the first group of apartment houses was to have been completed. A second problem was that the Department of Air Pollution Control had no enforcement powers to require compliance before the May 20, 1967, deadline. The options were to seal every noncomplying incinerator on or after that date or expedite compliance later. The first deadline came and passed with few completed upgradings. At one time about sixty incinerators were under seal by the Department. This state of affairs was partially due to questions that were raised as to who would *not* be required to upgrade their equipment. In an interpretation of Local Law 14 the City Corporation Counsel ruled that the law permitted every incinerator which had been installed before on-site incinerators became mandatory in 1951 to be closed down voluntarily rather than upgraded. Then, in August 1967, the Corporation Counsel interpreted the absence of any incinerator provision in the new city housing maintenance code to mean that almost all existing incinerators were now "voluntary" and could close down rather than upgrade, which meant that the owner might convert to refuse chutes and handle raw or compacted refuse.

An additional complication was a virtual moratorium that was declared on public statements on the issue by the city administration on the ground that the Commissioner of Air Pollution Control was being sued by the New York Real Estate Board and some private real estate interests for imposing a law that was deemed to be "arbitrary and capricious." Another factor was that the Department of Sanitation was not prepared to collect an unknown amount of refuse that formerly was burned. Although there were other reasons why the Sanitation Department could not be counted on to collect the refuse, the Department cannot be blamed for viewing with alarm the prospect of picking up some

[49] N.Y. City Admin. Code §892–4.3 (Supp. 1967–1968).

unspecified amount of refuse that was previously burned in on-site incinerators.

As a result of these developments the city administration finally decided that the law in its original form was unworkable. On the basis of the experience gained, the law was amended in two ways that are more in agreement with the minimum cost approach and bargaining theory. These amendments related to the generation of alternatives to upgrading and the timing of compliance dates.

Before the amendments were introduced, a cost study of the alternative ways of approaching the problem of reducing particulate emissions from on-site incinerators was carried out.[50] The study considered the varying size of buildings, operating expenses, labor costs, capital investment, and the distribution of unit costs among a number of apartments. The results of this research indicated that the larger buildings would find it most economical to upgrade and that middle-sized buildings could be left to decide for themselves whether it would be cheaper to compact or to upgrade. It was predicted that only buildings which had about fifty units or less per incinerator would find it more economical to shut down. Using these data, the Department of Air Pollution Control estimated the refuse output from the projected shutdowns and determined that the Department of Sanitation could handle the additional volume over a three-year period. Although the actual amendment to the law as passed by the City Council did not include giving the option to every landlord to choose the method which he considered to be the cheapest, the option to shut down for buildings with forty or fewer dwelling units per incinerator was passed as a direct result of the economic analysis.

Another amendment provided a deadline for submission of compliance plans six months prior to the completion deadline. Various strategies of noncompliance that were so successful under the original law have a much lower probability of success now that the Department of Air Pollution Control can use an incremental approach to pollution abatement, which will avoid unexpected reactions and smooth out the "lumpy" features of compliance programs. In keeping with bargaining theory, the "game" is spread out over a longer period of time.

The on-site incinerator example did not, of course, involve bargaining except in a very general sense, since the behavior that was observed involved noncompliance on the one hand and frustrated attempts at enforcing an unrealistic ordinance on the other. The example does, however, clearly convey both the relevance of decision theory to explain

[50] Task Force 2 of the Comm. for Implementing Local Law 14, Economics of Upgrading or Discontinuing Incineration (mimeo., Oct. 3, 1967).

the way decisions are made and the importance of comprehending the least-cost principle in a program of direct regulation. Some further reflection on the role of bargaining as it is apt to evolve in air pollution control programs and other environmental management programs should suggest that the least-cost solution can and should be sought in a regulatory program, both by explicit recognition of the cost-benefit nexus and by giving bargaining a chance to function in conjunction with market forces. Indeed, it is possible to assert that regulation strategically employing cost-benefit analysis and market forces can yield solutions to particular pollution control problems that the regulators themselves are not wise enough to devise.

V Devising a Hypothetical Regulatory Scheme: Bargaining and the Least-Cost Solution

a. The Shape of Regulatory Programs, Present and Future

New York City's amended incinerator rules represent an across-the-board legislative attempt to control gross pollution from a very common type of emitter. While bargaining theory explains in some measure the experience with the original attempt and the evolution of the amendments, no opportunity for individual bargaining was actually observed. However, control of other types of pollution will almost necessarily involve ad hoc regulation of individual industrial polluters who cannot appropriately be dealt with by general legislation or rule-making.[51] In these circumstances face-to-face bargaining will be almost essential as a means of dealing with individual polluters.

As local air pollution control ordinances and statutes are now formulated, bargaining does not have a clear chance to operate, though practice almost inevitably opens some opportunities for give and take between polluters and the control agency in both the standard setting and compliance stages. Most of the legislation, which appears to have been modeled after zoning legislation, either establishes fixed emission standards or delegates the setting of the contemplated standards to the control agency. Because fixed standards not only conflict with the least-cost principle but may raise potential constitutional problems, the statutes generally provide for variances to be granted by the agency. A typical variance provision is this one from the Illinois statute:

[51] Holden notes the inadequacies of state water pollution control legislation for this purpose. M. Holden, *Pollution Control as a Bargaining Process: An Essay on Regulatory Decision-Making* (1966).

The Board may grant individual variances beyond the limitations prescribed in this Act, whenever it is found, upon presentation of adequate proof, that compliance with any provision of this Act, or any rule or regulation, requirement or order of the Board, will result in an arbitrary and unreasonable taking of property or in the practical closing and elimination of any lawful business, occupation or activity, in either case without sufficient corresponding benefit or advantage to the people.[52]

The hardship required to be shown is a considerable one, though much is left to agency and court interpretation. One would have to conclude that, while the typical statutory language appears to permit variances only in extreme cases—perhaps only in those having constitutional dimensions[53]—an agency might, by seizing on the requirement that there be a "corresponding benefit or advantage," indulge in as much comparison of benefits and costs as it might wish. On balance, however, existing legislation appears to give less than sufficient sanction to methods of finding least-cost solutions.

The Air Quality Act of 1967 provides that states shall give effect to federally determined air quality criteria and control techniques once they are promulgated by HEW, which is also granted power to review the standards established and the proposed plan of enforcement.[54] It was apparently contemplated by Congress that new state and local legislation would be forthcoming, and this expectation, coupled with a fairly clear congressional mandate that pollution control be undertaken selectively in light of technological and economic feasibility,[55] suggests that new thought should be given to devising machinery that will be ca-

---

[52] Ill. Rev. Stat. ch. 111½, §240.11 (1967).
[53] The reference to the constitutional problem simply refers to the general principle that the state cannot curtail one's use of his property without paying "just compensation." The concept of "taking," which appears in the statute, is a constitutional concept which defines whether or not compensation must be paid, and it is applied rather inconsistently. Still, it is possible that curtailment of the property owner's rights to pollute may be classified as a "taking" unless a strong case can be made based on regulation for public health and use of the police power. When aesthetic and generalized environmental quality goals are emphasized, constitutional doubts are increased. See Pollack, Legal Boundaries of Air Pollution Control—State and Local Legislative Purpose and Techniques, in this symposium, p. 331 [Law and Contemporary Problems]; see also Michelman, Property, Utility, and Fairness: Comments on the Ethical Foundations of "Just Compensation" Law, 80 Harv. L. Rev. 1165 (1967).
[54] §§107(c), 108(c)(1), 81 Stat. 485. See Martin & Symington, supra note 14, at 259.
[55] The Air Quality Act of 1967, §107(c), 81 Stat. 485, provides, "Such recommendations shall include such data as are available on the latest available technology and economic feasibility of alternative methods of prevention and control of air contamination including cost-effectiveness analyses."

pable of doing this job most effectively. Indeed, if the concepts of "technological and economic feasibility" are equated with cost-benefit analysis, the question arises whether many existing regulatory schemes might fail to meet the approval of HEW. The issue that is raised is whether the federal act would justify HEW disapproval of state and local legislation on the ground of heavy-handedness, or lack of willingness to discriminate among polluters on the basis of the many economic and administrative factors that are comprised in an optimal, least-cost solution. The act suggests that review is limited to assuring only that maximum effectiveness is achieved,[56] and HEW may be motivated to review only for weakness and not for potential economic hardship on polluters.

The remainder of this article, drawing on these speculations, sets forth some ideas about the shape and function of air quality management programs that can best approximate least-cost solutions. As noted earlier, the outlook is for programs of direct regulation rather than for the sort of effluent fee approach advocated by the welfare economist. While the data shortages that prevent implementation of effluent fees will also plague programs of direct regulation, the latter approach is more familiar and, as noted earlier, can probably sustain a greater amount of regulation in relative ignorance than could a more novel system. But in keeping with the "new federalism," which is often praised as lending itself to experimentation and innovation in ways of attacking particular problems, HEW should not, in exercising its supervisory powers, restrict states to traditional patterns of regulation. Indeed, the regional approach to regulation specified by the Air Quality Act would seem to anticipate and encourage new departures. Such innovation and experimentation at the regional level might produce significantly improved regulatory procedures.[57]

[56] The state control plan will be approved if the Secretary finds, among other things, "that such State *standards* are consistent with the air quality criteria and recommended control techniques issued pursuant to section 107." §108(c)(1), 81 Stat. 485. (Emphasis added.) Section 107(c) provides that control techniques should be based on technological and economic feasibility. *See* note 55 *supra.* But the state enforcement *plan* need only be "consistent with the purposes of the Act insofar as it assures achieving such standards of air quality within a reasonable time," and must provide "a means of enforcement by State action, including authority comparable to" certain emergency powers provided in the Act. §108(c)(1), 81 Stat. 485. Thus the emphasis arguably is on achieving prompt compliance and not on cost effectiveness.

[57] One possible, perhaps even a likely, evolution from the present system would require polluters to *pay* for the variances they seek, the fee to be set in accordance with damage estimates. If variances were purchased rather than granted, the system would change profoundly, with variances becoming more palatable to the public and the control agency. Bargaining over the fees would yield some of the benefits sought in the program hypothesized below.

b. Structuring a Regulatory Program to Facilitate Bargaining

The regulatory setup we conceive of in the following discussion is the one most common in other systems of direct economic regulation. It features an independent regulatory body (the "commission") supported by a staff of legal and technical experts. Membership on the commission is for a relatively long fixed term, and, because of the nature of the issues to be encountered, the members might be required to have expertise of specified types. Thus, a three-member commission might comprise a lawyer, an economist, and a pollution control engineer. The commission would operate as an independent decision maker, and its final rulings would be subject to judicial review. The agency staff bears the major enforcement burden and provides the evidence and expertise which guides the commission's efforts.

Any attempt to hypothesize about the outlines of an enforcement program that attempts to approach a least-cost solution through administrative means must recognize the desirability of avoiding the use of litigation before either judicial or administrative tribunals as the primary means of achieving abatement in individual cases. The limitations of both legal and technical staff resources, the importance of achieving prompt relief, the difficulty of resolving difficult and highly uncertain technical issues in an adversary proceeding, and the considerable administrative costs involved, all point to the need for minimizing the use of litigation whenever possible.[58] The approach that would be most helpful in achieving this objective would be to structure regulation to encourage the use of bargaining and settlements as the primary means of accomplishing regulatory objectives. Such a structuring would most likely include the following conditions:

(1) The control agency's regulations should provide for establishment of formal communication with both actual and potential polluters. Thus it might be required that all polluters within the agency's jurisdiction file reports with the agency on their present emission levels and perhaps a ten-year estimate of anticipated increases or decreases in these emissions. Other continuing contact would also be desirable, and informal conferences could be called that would bring the agency staff, trade associations, and other interest groups together to discuss the local problems. The author's interviews with Los Angeles Air Pollution Control District personnel confirm that informal conferences have been a

[58] The inadequacies of a litigation-oriented approach are detailed in Nat'l. Research Council, Nat'l. Academy of Sciences, *Waste Management and Control* 203–221 (Pub. No. 1400, 1966).

key element in successfully controlling stationary sources of pollution.

(2) The agency's potential sanctions must be substantial but flexible enough so that they could be adjusted to the nature and magnitude of each particular problem confronted. Massive fines for emitting a small amount of pollution, for example, would be a poor agency strategy, since it would distort the credibility of the agency's image as an arbiter of the public interest.

(3) The sanctions must put no premium on delay. Thus, a retroactive effluent charge, perhaps accumulating from the date of the agency's complaint, might be provided as a means of compelling a polluter to engage in bargaining in good faith. Filing of a complaint would thus constitute in itself a significant sanction and would most likely lead to bargaining before a formal proceeding was initiated, much as the Federal Power Commission and the Federal Communications Commission have tended to bargain for rate reductions without starting a formal rate case.[59] With this strategy, bargaining would also be encouraged after a complaint was filed.

(4) Paradoxically, although the agency's sanctions must be strong enough to encourage polluters to bargain in good faith, they should probably not be so strong as to allow the agency to enforce its will without some recourse to bargaining. This surprising condition—that weaker sanctions may be desirable—is dictated by the conclusion of studies of mixed conflict and cooperation situations that the "game" will not be constituted in good faith unless each side has something to win and something to lose, and that both must be in a position to lose if an outcome is not achieved. The final sanction of formal proceedings can and should be costly to both the agency and the polluter. Both this and the previous condition reflect the fact that inequality or imbalance in the strength of each party's sanctions will bias the outcomes of bargaining. The proper balance may be difficult to achieve but must be sought if something approximating the optimal, least-cost solution is to be arrived at.

(5) If informed bargaining is to operate to the public's advantage, the agency must be adequately staffed so that it is known that its sanctions will not go uninvoked if agreement is not reached or if bargaining is not conducted in good faith. The abatement of ninety percent of the emissions from stationary sources of air pollution in Los Angeles County, for example, was achieved in part through the efforts of several hundred Air Pollution Control District employees. The New York experience recited above also illustrates the importance of credibility of sanctions.

[59] See generally Welch, "Constant Surveillance: A Modern Regulatory Tool," 8 Vill. L. Rev. 340 (1963). See also note 65 infra.

(6) Public utility regulation points to the fact that the public's representatives at the bargaining table must be neither altogether free of nor unduly subject to political influence, in order, first, that excessive zeal or laxness can be checked and, second, that polluters may not accomplish through influence what they are unable to achieve by negotiation. Judging with respect to this one point, one might argue that the regulatory framework has been more effective in Los Angeles County than in New York City. California legislation authorizes any county to set up its Air Pollution Control District by resolution of the County Board of Supervisors declaring the need for the District to function. The districts are granted the power to "make and enforce all needful orders, rules, and regulations," [60] and Los Angeles County was given considerable latitude in attacking its local problems. New York City, like Los Angeles County, has the power to adopt and enforce rules and regulations and authority to require permits and control devices on pollution-generating equipment,[61] but experience to date, as was revealed by the on-site incinerator study, has been that the City Council has actively intervened in the Department's regulatory program. A comparative study of the two agencies shows that Los Angeles Air Pollution Control District has had much more freedom in the development of rules and regulations.[62]

(7) Experience with other types of regulation also suggests the desirability of maintaining public control of administrative discretion through openness in decision making. Thus the data submitted by both the polluter and the agency staff, the terms of the settlement itself, the staff's reasons for accepting it, and the commission's approval should be on public file.[63] Also useful might be annual or more frequent reports of settlements, together with underlying data, which could be used by the legislative body to which the agency is responsible.[64]

(8) A final precondition for effective bargaining is a clearly defined legal framework within which bargaining can operate. This is essential so that the bargainers—the agency staff and the individual

[60] Cal. Health & Safety Code §§24260 (West 1967).
[61] N.Y. City Admin. Code §§894–2.0, 892–3.0, 892–5.0 (1966); Cal. Health & Safety Code §§24261–63 (West 1967).
[62] Hagevik, Decision Processes in Air Quality Management (unpublished dissertation, forthcoming).
[63] The Air Quality Act of 1967, §108(c)(5), 81 Stat. 485, states that in connection with hearings conducted under the Act, "no witness or any other person shall be required to divulge trade secrets or secret processes." Some confidentiality must be provided by any regulatory scheme.
[64] Evaluation of agency performance by the legislature is one of the more important aspects of a rational decision process. See A. Maass & M. Hufschmidt, Design of Water Resource Systems, ch. 15 (1962).

polluter—can largely avoid differences on questions of legal principle while concentrating on the development of the technical and economic data needed to reach a judgment about potential least-cost solutions.[65] Included among the many issues that ideally need to be resolved and eliminated from dealings with individual polluters are as many of the overriding facts as possible about the air pollution problem in the particular airshed. Such questions as estimates of pollution damage in general and attribution of this damage to particular pollutants would be best resolved authoritatively after public hearings open to all interested parties. Bargaining with individual polluters could then proceed without calling these matters back into question. Further discussion below considers how certain specific issues are better resolved in general agency rule-making proceedings than in case-by-case bargaining or adversary proceedings.

If conditions such as the foregoing could be created, face-to-face bargaining could be made to serve an important function in the administration of an effective air pollution control program. It is argued that the advantages would be many, including the establishment of cooperative attitudes between regulators and industry, which would encourage a joint search for solutions to problems; a de-emphasis of fact finding through quasi-judicial process and the avoidance of "swearing contests," which are characteristic of adversary proceedings requiring expert testimony; speed, flexibility, and efficiency in the sense that appellate proceedings and time-consuming judicial review would be avoided; and a more efficient use of technical, administrative, and legal staffs.

c. Toward a Least-Cost Solution

There is an axiom among engineers that one can "go slow by running too fast." Although this statement can be interpreted by control officials with some justification as a polluter's excuse for doing nothing, the establishment of the preconditions for an effective control program is a case where the axiom applies. The structuring of the process that will produce efficient resource allocation depends in large part, as we have noted, on the decisions of the legislators who create the sanctions and provide the enforcement staff and on the establishment of a clear

[65] Testimony to the importance of establishing such a framework appears in an opinion of the FCC defending the decision to commence the first full-scale rate case against AT&T. In response to Bell's stated preference for bargaining as a rate-making method, the Commission stated, "Indeed, we believe that the standards and criteria developed on the record here will enable us to employ continuing surveillance [*i.e.*, bargaining] even more effectively in the future." *Re* American Tel. & Tel. Co., 61 P.U.R.3d 554, 559–60 (1965). The words "even more" are self-serving.

legal and factual framework within which to operate. Since a prime
objective is to keep as many issues as possible out of litigation, the
agency needs the authority to negotiate concerning factual uncertainty.
Given the state of the art in environmental management, the legislators
need to realize that the "best guess" approach requires that some substantial degree of discretion be given to the agency and its technical
staff.

The commission will begin developing the necessary legal and
factual framework by holding public hearings as a prelude to authoritative findings on these factual issues:

(1) the total damages attributable to air pollution in the airshed.
(2) the allocation of these damages to each pollutant or each major group of
    sources. The findings on these first two points need not be sufficiently
    detailed to satisfy a welfare economist, and it is obvious that the goal is
    simply the best estimates possible.
(3) an inventory of emissions, including the total amount of each pollutant
    emitted at particular times and in particular areas.
(4) the relationship of emission levels to the assimilative capacity of the am-
    bient air. This would be determined by using a relatively simple atmos-
    pheric diffusion model and air quality monitoring devices. Thus, New
    York City is now putting into operation an aerometric system of monitor-
    ing stations which record and transmit data on levels of sulfur dioxide,
    dustfall, suspended particulates, and smoke shade on a continuous basis
    to the Department of Air Pollution Control; New York has also devel-
    oped a simple model which fairly accurately describes the complex diffu-
    sion of pollutants in the city.
(5) the objectives of the abatement program, stated in terms of air quality and
    the level of damages anticipated as optimal for the airshed as a
    whole.[65a]

Some of the foregoing factual judgments would be based in part
on the air quality criteria to be issued by HEW under the Air Quality
Act.[66] Additional evidence would be required, and the agency's conclusions should be buttressed by subsidiary findings and a reasoned opinion. All such findings would be subject to periodic review and revision,
each time following the procedures employed in the initial formulation.
Taken all together, these findings should give a sufficiently clear picture
to allow our decision-making and bargaining framework to begin functioning.

[65a] See note 70 infra on the derivation of such objectives.
[66] §107, 81 Stat. 485 (1967). But see note 70 infra on the theoretical deficiencies of
the HEW criteria.

An additional matter that the agency would probably find it appropriate to resolve in a rule-making proceeding is the development of a generalized technique for determining a polluter's contribution to the region's over-all concentration of pollutants. Once this issue was settled in principle, the questions at issue with each polluter would be (1) his respective contribution of pollutants to concentrations in the ambient air, which would probably be fairly close to the proportion of total emissions for which he was responsible, adjusted for such factors as wind, timing of emissions, and stack height; and (2) the polluter's costs associated with varying levels of abatement.

Ideally the agency staff would be able to negotiate effectively within this framework of settled legal and economic principles and authoritative general findings of fact concerning the extent and danger of pollution. The issues at stake in the bargaining with individual polluters would be almost exclusively factual and would be susceptible to quantified solutions, thus facilitating some compromise in areas of valid doubt. Focal point bottlenecks could be largely avoided, since matters of legal and economic principle would have been eliminated for the most part by rule making; where legal questions did arise they could be set aside for separate authoritative decision by the commission. Such procedures would allow time for incrementalism to operate to narrow gradually the range of possible results, and the continuing negotiating machinery, which would be focused primarily on technical issues, would provide a hospitable climate for the resolution of these issues.[67]

The strategy of a least-cost solution within a bargaining framework suggests that the legislative body to which the control agency is responsible must clean its own house first by upgrading or abandoning any municipal incinerators it operates and reducing the emission levels from governmental heating and generating plants. This is necessary to avoid the embarrassing—and legitimate—charge that a governmental jurisdiction is forcing the private sector to clean up its pollution while continuing to pollute the air itself. This has been a continuing accusation in New York City where the municipal incinerators had not been upgraded by the time private on-site incinerators were to be upgraded.

The agency's next move would be to tackle the sources of air pollution which can have their levels of pollutant emissions reduced in fairly straightforward ways that clearly yield greater benefits than costs. This might mean that the agency should proceed against those polluters who are perceived by both the control agency and the public at large as

[67] One of the reasons given for the success of the Los Angeles Air Pollution Control District is that there has been a great deal of cooperation between the technical staff of the District and the technical staffs of the regulated industries.

the most significant polluters of the atmosphere in the jurisdiction, but not always. For example, it is now recognized in New York City that the formulators of Local Law 14 made a strategic error in the structuring of the legislation by requiring that initial action be taken against on-site incinerators even though they were a source of easily visible localized particulate concentrations.

Initial agency action, in addition to avoiding potential charges of being "arbitrary and capricious," must consider the impact of highly localized costs in relation to diffuse benefits and whether the technological and administrative solutions to problems are at hand. In the New York case, it can clearly be argued that a much greater reduction of air pollution could have been achieved at a lower cost to individual polluters by proceeding initially against the emissions of sulfur oxides and particulates resulting from the burning of fuel oil. A technical solution —switching to low-sulfur fuel oil—was available which could be implemented without too much difficulty.[68] In fact, due to difficulties involved in getting thousands of on-site incinerators upgraded or shut down, the program to change to a low-sulfur fuel, which was initiated after the incinerator upgrading, yielded tangible benefits much sooner.

Selecting the initial target in this manner has considerable implications in terms of later control efforts. A demonstrated success gives the agency a good image, reflects positively on the elected officials who give the agency support, and lessens the opposition of businessmen to control efforts aimed at them. The stage is also set for conflict resolution procedures such as negotiation and bargaining rather than for the polarization of attitudes that results in litigation.

One of the more important matters that should concern a control agency operating under our system is the establishment of a method of determining the maximum abatement expenditure—or level of abatement—that could be required of an individual polluter. This complex question has practical importance because all polluters cannot be attacked at once, and the marginal unit abatement costs apparently justified when pollution levels are high will seem inappropriate when more nearly tolerable concentrations have been achieved.[69] All polluters

[68] Although making the use of low-sulfur fuel mandatory is in conflict with the economists' rational model, it can still be viewed as a sound decision in keeping with our strategy, which would allow mixing of necessary approaches. At a later stage another approach should probably be substituted.

[69] Since the aggregate cost curve for damage abatement within an airshed is almost certainly nonlinear—costs increase as the more obvious sources of pollution are controlled and as the more serious damage is eliminated—an estimate of the amount of damage reduction obtainable from a unit of abatement by the first polluter proceeded against might be high if this polluter was considered as an isolated source. This would apparently justify imposition of equally high abatement costs. Such a

should be subject to the same maximum, however, and the derivation of this maximum is extraordinarily difficult. A very rough figure can be derived, however, if air quality standards or goals—indicators of the level of air quality desired within a given jurisdiction—have been developed from objectives and constraints specified in the legislative process and in HEW's air quality criteria. Beginning with these goals, which will necessarily include estimates of the abatement outlays required to achieve them,[70] the agency can arrive at a general estimate of the theoretical emission level at which all marginal expenditures would equal marginal benefits. No polluter should be required to abate below that emission level which he would be permitted to maintain under such optimal conditions, or, in other words, to pay more for a unit of abatement than would yield a net gain if optimal conditions prevailed.

Conclusion

Optimizing methods are a guide to decisions, not a philosopher's stone that substitutes for decision. With a view to achieving practical results, it has been pointed out how bargaining might contribute to finding a least-cost solution. Although bargaining is often viewed as a distributional device rather than one that promotes efficiency, it has been shown that the latter view can also be taken. Having been directed, or having found it expedient, to adopt a cost-benefit approach, the control agency would be responsive within our framework to polluters' arguments based on a comparison of marginal benefits and costs associated with alternative emission reduction techniques. The polluter would most likely be inclined to hold out for the lowest-cost remedy and to develop and advance in the negotiations alternative ways of accomplishing the objectives being sought—an advantage, it will be recalled, usually associated exclusively with effluent fees as a control mechanism. Market

view of marginal control expenditures and benefits is deceptive, however, in that if other firms or groups of firms were forced to abate sequentially, their positions on the curve would be lower and their expenditures would yield a lower return, thereby decreasing the amount of required investment. Thus, a simplistic comparison of marginal costs and benefits is not enough, since this would result in applying a different standard to each polluter depending on the sequence in which they are attacked.

[70] See Thomas, "The Animal Farm, A Mathematical Model for the Discussion of Social Standards for Control of the Environment," 77 Q. J. Econ. 143 (1963). Thomas points out that to set a quality criterion is to impute a cost-benefit ratio. Id. at 147. Thus the starting point for pollution abatement programs should be cost-benefit analysis and not arbitrarily determined quality criteria or emission standards. But see H.R. Rep. No. 728, 90th Cong., 1st Sess. 16 (1967), which states that economic considerations are to have no place in the development of HEW's criteria.

forces will thus aid the controllers in seeking the most efficient approach to pollution damage reduction. For these reasons the outcome of a properly structured bargaining process should not deviate too far from economic rationality.

The hypothetical regulatory program we have outlined probably represents an ideal difficult to achieve in our society today. Why it may be so is a matter for conjecture and concern, and the most pessimistic conclusions one might draw is that the law and the legal system are in many respects incompatible with the scientific pursuit of optimal conditions under constraints of uncertainty.[71] We have proposed a scientific approach to pollution control requiring gross estimates of pollution damage and abatement costs. A problem of concern in this framework is the difficulty of making damage and cost estimates having enough objective validity to withstand legal attack when viewed as the product of a hearing record which must contain "substantial evidence" to support the result reached. In many respects informed guesses will be all that the control commission can show, and honesty should compel the commission to admit the depth of human ignorance on the questions in issue and to acknowledge frankly that its findings are made for the purpose of getting on with the abatement job. Courts would then be faced clearly with the problem of allowing regulation to proceed in the dim light of partial knowledge or to cease until science can provide light enough to satisfy the judicial sense of what due process requires.

Experience with the regulatory process in general suggests, however, that agencies do not as a rule confess ignorance but rather pretend to omniscience. While often not disclosing the true basis for their decisions and allowing their opinions to be written in "judge proof" boilerplate by their legal staffs, the agencies assume an air of knowledgeability that belies more than it reveals. This attitude might work in air pollution control as well, and the temptation to adopt it will be great. Control commissions may prefer to fill their opinions with statistics and data and to conclude by solemnly declaring, "Having considered all of the evidence and the relevant legal principles. . . . " The results may be unimpeachable for the simple reason that the underlying principles relating such items as costs to benefits are not stated and thus not subject to review. The alternative may be unattractive in administrative circles because the necessary estimates are of such precariousness that they can be defended only by candor about the depth of the problem and by apparent conscientiousness in approaching it. Nevertheless, the courts should learn to insist on full disclosure in lieu of obfuscation.

[71] For a more optimistic view, see National Research Council, supra note 58, at 204, 207–209, 214–217.

Once this is obtained, judicial review should then require only the exercise of the agency's expert judgment on the best information and data available, incomplete and unsatisfying as it may seem. In no event should the courts prevent effective regulatory action solely because science has not yet yielded the secrets needed to realize the regulatory ideal.

Pollution Control Laws:
The Politics of Radical Change

Pollution represents a threat to the environment supporting human life. It is not a new threat, nor is it a newly perceived threat. As long as man has been a social animal, he has contended with pollution and has devised ways of putting his wastes out of the way. But the problem today is not simply the same problem man has faced in the past. Now the quantities of waste produced are so large that they threaten to make basic, universal ecological changes. In the past, when man so ruined an area that it would no longer support his life, he could simply pick up and move on. In modern society, for many reasons, that solution is not a viable one. There is no longer an inexhaustible number of places to move to. Shortly, it appears, there will be no place on earth free from dangerous contamination.

In the past, when man shocked nature with his wastes, nature rolled and recovered. But today the quantity and quality of wastes are such that it is increasingly doubtful that nature will recover. A sense of the magnitude of the problem can be gained from the fact that over one percent of the gross national product is spent annually on the collection and disposal of municipal, agricultural, and industrial wastes. In 1968 almost one ton of solid waste was produced *per capita* in the United States, an average of 5 pounds per person per day. The average is greater in our highly urbanized areas. In sections of New York City, the average waste produced is 7–8 pounds per person per day.[1] These figures represent the totals for solid waste only, and solid wastes are only

---

* Thomas Vitullo-Martin is assistant professor of political science and education at University of California, Riverside. His article was prepared for this volume.
[1] James H. McCall, "Financial," in *The Affluent and the Effluent* (a symposium), Railway Systems and Management Association (Chicago: 1968), pp. 3–4.

one form of waste. Wastes also are put into the air and into water. The Metropolitan Sanitary District of Greater Chicago (MSD) treats the waste water from 5.5 million people and the industrial equivalent to another 3.5 million people daily.[2] It treats 1.5 billion gallons of sewage a day, from which it extracts 1,000 dry weight tons of solids every 24 hours. An additional 203 tons of particulate matter is lost to the air each day in the drying process.[3] If all water-borne wastes in the nation were treated as efficiently as Chicago's, over 40,000 dry weight tons of solids would be retrieved a day. Furthermore, even with Chicago's high rate of treatment, it is estimated that the treated effluent passed on into the Mississippi River from Chicago is equivalent to the raw sewage from a city of 2 million people.

The sheer quantity of all this waste threatens to overload nature and force her to make a permanent readjustment. It is an increasingly prevalent concern among scientists that the eventual balance reached by nature will either destroy, or seriously reduce, the quality of human life. To avoid these consequences, much greater care must be taken in the production and placement of wastes. Since the problems caused by wastes are general ones affecting all of society, their management has properly been public management. The control of wastes is a public concern and therefore a political problem.

Three political problems are characteristic of pollution control. This paper will argue that the problems are interrelated and that a common solution to them can be found. Most of the examples used in the paper will be drawn from experience with the control of water pollution, but this is not to imply that water pollution is a unique political problem. The political problems for control of pollution are similar for all forms, even though the technological problems and their solutions are quite distinct.

The first political problem for control is that there appears to be a lack of sufficient will to control pollution on the part of a number of political leaders. This is frequently attributable to the fact that many local political leaders are so tied to their local industrial economies that they fear and resist what they believe would be costly steps in pollution control. They fear the costs would damage the local economy. A leading federal air pollution official testified before a House subcommittee in 1966 that "one of the impediments to more rapid progress in pollution abatement relates to the existence and scope of state and local government regulatory and control activities. . . . Not more than half of the

[2] *Ibid.*
[3] Frank E. Dalton, "Metropolitan Sanitary District of Greater Chicago," in *The Affluent and the Effluent*, pp. 19–21.

urban areas which are in need of regulatory and control programs for air pollution control now have them and of these . . . the majority are operated at an inadequate level." The administrator believed the inertia was the result of political and social obstacles, not technological difficulties.[4] Crenson, through detailed case studies and broad survey research covering 50 American cities, convincingly establishes that not infrequently air pollution is deliberately repressed as an issue, deliberately made a nonissue by local political leaders. Crenson cites the case of Gary, Indiana, which had the highest mean particulate count (a measure of air pollution) of any city in the country—a count more than 25 times higher than the national urban mean. Political leaders of Gary identified smoking stacks with full employment and refused to consider the question of reducing air pollution.[5] The will of the Gary legislators to act was so weak that they refused legislation which exempted "for a period of about ten years the following existing metallurgical processes . . . from the suggested provisions: open hearth furnaces, blast furnaces, Bessemer furnaces, ferrous foundries, driers, kilns and roasters." [6] An estimated 50 to 80 percent of Gary's air pollution was caused by these processes.

A second characteristic political problem for pollution control stems from the fact that, while legal controls over pollution are politically balkanized, pollution respects no political jurisdiction.

Political institutions with primary responsibility for pollution control have delegated their responsibilities, decentralizing controls. Pollution characteristically affects large areas, overrunning municipal, county, state, and even national boundaries. The result is that, despite the best efforts of many localities, the environment remains polluted.

The Comptroller General of the United States reported to the Congress on November 3, 1969, the result of a comprehensive study of the federal water pollution abatement program.[7] The federal program began

[4] U. S. Congress House of Representatives, *The Adequacy of Technology for Pollution Abatement, Hearings before the Subcommittee on Science, Research and Development of the Committee on Science and Astronautics* (89 Cong., 2 Sess., 1966), p. 57, as quoted in Matthew A. Crenson, *Non-Issues in City Politics: The Case of Air Pollution*, unpublished Ph.D. dissertation, Department of Political Science, University of Chicago (Chicago, 1969), p. 9.

[5] The counts for 1958, the year in which the Gary City Council refused to act on the recommendation for controls proposed by a dissident councilman, were: Gary 262, National Urban Mean 108, micrograms of particulate per cubic meter of air. Crenson, *Op cit.*, p. 72.

[6] Armour Research Institute, "Air Pollution Survey of Gary, Indiana," typescript 1958, as quoted in Crenson, *op. cit.*, pp. 115–116.

[7] Comptroller General of the United States, *Report to the Congress, Examination into the Effectiveness of the Construction Grant Program for Abating, Controlling, and Preventing Water Pollution (B–166506)*, General Accounting Office (Washington, D.C.: November 3, 1969).

in earnest in fiscal year 1957 and continued through 1969. The Federal Water Pollution Control Administration (FWPCA) allocated grants to the states to enable them to upgrade waste water treatment systems. In the 13 years of the program, the FWPCA gave grants totaling $1.2 billion dollars for constructions of 9,400 projects having a total estimated cost of $5.4 *billion*. The Federal act establishing the program in 1956 required "federal and state planning for water pollution control . . . as a prerequisite to the approval of federal grants to municipalities and other political subdivisions (hereinafter referred to as municipalities) for the construction of waste treatment facilities. Also the act requires each state to certify that the individual projects which are to receive grants are entitled to priority over other eligible projects on the basis of financial and water pollution needs." [8]

However, the GAO (General Accounting Office) found in its review that the comprehensive planning envisioned by the act for the control of pollution became in practice, prior to 1968, "essentially an alphabetical listing, prepared by the states, of all municipalities in each state that were in need of, or might be in need of, waste treatment facilities in the foreseeable future. The listings were published in the *Federal Register* in November, 1956, and were revised periodically to add municipalities not included initially." [9] In effect, the federal program aided the construction of treatment projects on a first-come-first-serve basis. All initiative was in the hands of the local community desiring the facility. The Federal Water Quality Act of 1965 changed these procedures. The states were required to establish quality standards for their waterways. Waterways could be designated as any one of four rankings, from a quality suitable for swimming to one suitable for transmitting sewage without nuisance. It was expected that nuisances would not exist under any quality standard. [10] Plans would have to be drawn to attain these goals and projects would have to be given priority by the state, based in part on their contribution to the general pollution abatement plan. In practice however, the GAO found this to be another instance of the "shotgun approach" to pollution abatement. Only those communities that had drawn up plans for new construction and applied for a grant were ranked. Thus, by leaving the initiative up to the local community, an effective priority system was made impossible.

The consequences of the inability of the FWPCA to enforce coor-

[8] *Ibid.*, p. 22.
[9] *Ibid.*, p. 23.
[10] Class B water is suitable for bathing, recreation and agricultural uses and is acceptable, with filtration and disinfection, as a public water supply. Class C water is suitable for boating and irrigation of certain crops and as a habitat for fish and wildlife. Class D water is suitable for the transportation of sewage and wastes, and for power, navigation, and other industrial uses. *Ibid.*, p. 87 ff.

dinated pollution control on a stream is illustrated by the history of a community of 900 people on a river flowing between the United States and Canada. The river was used for swimming and recreation. The community emptied its sewage into the stream. In 1960, the state ordered the community to construct a plan to treat its sewage. In 1962, the federal government awarded grants to the community totaling $105,000 for construction. The community matched those grants, so that treatment was gained at a cost of over $210,000. This treatment reduced the Population Equivalent of Biochemical Oxygen Demand [11] (PE of BOD) from the 900 population to 600.

However, at least a year before the federal grant was made, a food processing plant, financed by the Area Redevelopment Administration (ARA), was put into operation upstream from the community. In 1964, a second plant was built with ARA funds, also without adequate pollution controls. Fish kills resulted in 1962 and 1963. In 1965, the state, after unsuccessful efforts to make the company reduce its pollution, lowered the classification of the stream, designating it as "suitable primarily for the transportation of sewage and industrial wastes without creating a nuisance." [12] But even that minimal classification was not low enough. Tests in 1965 and 1966 showed that the stream had nuisance conditions. The total PE of BOD from food plants was between 164,000 and 234,-000.

The plant, constructed at great local and federal expense for the community of 900, had an infinitesimal effect on the water quality of the river. The food companies upstream had already lowered the water quality. Residents of the community received no benefit for their expenditure. Effective control of the river required the control of the upstream companies.[13]

The GAO recommended that, at the very least, major polluters of a stream be ordered to correct their problems before minor polluters. The Department of the Interior disagreed with this proposal. Its disagreements reflected the two political problems of pollution mentioned earlier: first, the lack of political will; and second, the difficulty with decentralized controls. Interior wrote:

[11] The BOD is a measure of the amount of oxygen taken from the water by decomposing wastes. One unit of BOD is equal to the amount of waste produced by the average person in one day. A town of 900 would have a PE of BOD equal to about 900. The treated effluent of these 900 persons was equivalent to the BOD of 600 persons without treatment.
[12] It should be noted that only the first two of the four quality goals would protect fish from oxygen starvation.
[13] Comptroller General, op. cit., p. 87.

Since as a general rule state political leverage on a community may be presumed to be inversely related to cost effectiveness of investment, it is not difficult to see why the small community often builds its plant first. Then because of inadequate improvement in stream quality, its weight is added to pressures for action by the larger community or industry. However obvious the situation, the way to implementation of the most cost effective investments first has not been so obvious.[14]

The GAO concluded:

The Department seemed to imply that it was easier to pressure small communities, which contribute relatively little pollution, to construct waste treatment facilities, than it was to pressure larger communities or industries that might be major polluters.[15]

The third political problem for the control of pollution becomes apparent on analysis of the GAO study: the traditional treatment technology is based on a concept of *de minimus*. Traditional sewage treatment technology is, in essence, a series of filters, each of which removes certain contaminants. The first filter is a settling pond and screen that removes heavy solid and floating pieces. In a primary treatment plant, the effluent from this pond is chlorinated to kill bacteria and released into the stream. The second filter, a secondary treatment plant, digests BOD particles through bacterial action. Tertiary treatment, which few systems have, removes specific contaminants through a chemical precipitation method. Often tertiary treatment introduces new contaminants in the course of removing the old. Phosphates or nitrogen would be removed in a tertiary treatment process. Thus, the concept behind the technology is little different from that of a traditional industrial plant. The sewage plant has its raw materials (sewage), its manufacturing process, its waste by-product (sludge in one form or another), its product (sewage effluent) and its distribution channels (the body of water into which the effluent is dumped). The product has to meet certain limited quality standards. The standards themselves are a compromise between what is technologically possible and what is economically possible. In capitalist ideology, quality standards are imposed by the play of the free market. The customer will seek the best for the least. The industry will supply the least for the best price. Similarly, the traditional sewage technology attempts to supply the least treatment necessary. The technology operates on a *de minimus* philosophy. Consistent with the

[14] Letter dated Oct. 17, 1969: Department of Interior to Comptroller General, quoted in *ibid.*, p. 99.
[15] *Ibid.*, p. 99.

free market ideology, the sewage treatment plant does not consider the ramifications of its product for the waterway, since the waterway is not its product. Finally, since the standards for product quality (or effluent quality) are derived from what is technically possible at reasonable cost, rather than from what is the optimum for a particular body of water, pollutions other than the oldest recognized ones are ignored.

The *de minimus* concept is in fundamental error in that it proceeds from an inadequate understanding of the nature of pollution. This error is illustrated in another GAO-cited example.

The GAO intensively studied the utility of federal grants made to the communities along one 14-mile tributary.[16] Grants totalling $451,000 were made in 1964, 1965, and 1967, to ten projects discharging into the tributary.[17] The tributary was dry in the summer and therefore deemed incapable of receiving the effluent. The treated effluent "grossly polluted" the waters. For improvements costing over a million dollars, no benefits were received.

Additional investment in plant improvements would not have been expected to improve the quality of the stream, for the stream had no ability to assimilate wastes. Even the best examples of the traditional technology consign that stream to death. Traditional technology could not have adequately treated the water at any reasonable cost. The *de minimus* concept said low levels of contamination waste are acceptable, high levels are not; therefore, we will lower the quantities and qualitatively change some of the remaining wastes through treatment. In concept, then, it is deemed acceptable for a city to flush its wastes down a stream. In the GAO instances, the heavy technological investment did not benefit the water quality. The previously cited statistic of the quality of the effluent from the Chicago MSD gives further evidence that the concept served by traditional treatment technology is bankrupt. Despite the most sophisticated treatment facilities in the nation and a high cash expenditure for treatment ($14 million annual operating costs), the treated effluent from the MSD is equivalent to the raw sewage of a city of almost 2 million people. The scale of the waste problem makes 80 percent removal, 90 percent removal, even 95 percent removal of wastes from the water inadequate.

The GAO's general conclusion of its report gives emphasis to the inadequacy of the present technology. After evaluating 9,400 water treatment projects constructed from 1957 to 1969, costing *$5.4 billion,* it could not note any significant improvements in water quality due to

[16] *Ibid.,* pp. 45–52.
[17] Federal grants range from 10 to 55 percent of total costs. These were probably about 30 percent.

these expenditures.[18] In a more detailed section of the study, GAO gave evidence of the uselessness of at least substantial portions of the present technology. GAO commissioned a detailed analysis of the treatment facilities on the Merrimac River. One phase of the analysis correlated the investments on treatment facilities along the waterway with improvements in water quality. Table A presents these correlations. The table demonstrates that large amounts of money could be invested in conventional technological improvements with *no resulting improvements in water quality.*

Table A. Merrimac River Study: Improvements in Water Quality Compared to Dollar Investments [19]

Stages of Improvement in Sewage Treatment					
Original ($ in Millions)	I	II & III	IV	V & VI	VII
$0	$8	$20	$125.7	$48	$21.9
Water Quality					
25 Mile Nuisance	25 miles	25 miles	0 miles	0 miles	0 miles
120 Miles Below Designated Quality	70 miles	70 miles	40 miles	40 miles	17 miles

At stages II and III, $20 million worth of investments were contemplated that would show no improvement. At stages V and VI, $48 million more worth of improvements were planned with no gain. For approximately $224 million, the pollution controllers could have raised the dissolved oxygen levels of the river to the desired standards on all but 10 percent of its length. However, important qualifications must be made. Since the conventional treatment plants cannot handle the overloads caused by storm runoff, the plants are bypassed in these crisis periods. In times of storms, waste water is not treated, or is only minimally treated. The quality standards for the waterways are not applied. It was estimated that the correction of this problem would cost another $140 million.[20]

    Even when that would be accomplished, the state standards called for 25 percent (42.4/170 miles) of the river to be designated "D" quality (for industrial uses and sewage transmission) and another 10 percent of the river would be below its quality designation. The treated wastes poured into the river would seriously damage its original quality.

[18] Or, as the GAO diplomatically phrased it, "These projects have contributed to abating water pollution because the problem would have been worse if the projects had not been constructed." Comptroller General, *op. cit.*, p. 1.

[19] *Ibid.*, pp. 85–88.

[20] *Ibid.*

Finally, it should be noted that GAO's conclusions were based on quality parameters established by the traditional technology. These parameters ignored several of the most dangerous constituents of water pollution. First, they ignored phosphate and nitrogen contamination. These chemicals are nutrients that encourage algae blooms on the water and hasten the eutrophication of the waterway. Second, they ignored contamination by heavy metals, such as lead or mercury, a contamination found to be present in potentially dangerous quantities in fish taken from a wide variety of the nation's waterways. Third, they ignored virus contamination, perhaps the most dangerous kind of pollution to humans. While both nutrient and heavy metal pollution can be substantially removed by a series of expensive tertiary treatment processes,[21] virus cannot be removed by the traditional technology. Viral organisms are too small to be trapped by filters and are extremely resistant to disinfectants.

Studies dating back to 1952 have shown the effluent from sewage plants to be highly contaminated with viruses. In fact, public health doctors have been able to determine the viral disease present in an area by testing the effluent from conventional treatment plants.[22]

Viruses are a particular threat because of the way in which they reproduce. Viruses reproduce only within a host cell to which they are uniquely attracted. Viruses, in general, appear to be species specific, and to invade particular cells within that species. When they are expelled into the water, they enter a dormant state until they again enter another human, there to multiply again. Viruses can exist for long periods of time in their dormant state. Thus, in a system that returns viruses to the waterways, there exists a potential for a cyclical, escalating build-up of viral contamination wherever that same water is used for human consumption.

To recapitulate, the traditional technology follows a practically oriented concept: pollution control involves the reduction of the quantity of wastes in water to the extent technically and economically feasible; it ignores the question of whether the technology can remove all of the range of significant pollutants, or whether, in absolute measures, enough pollutants are removed to prevent damage to the waterway.

[21] Processes such as chemical precipitation which, ironically, add other pollutants to the water.

[22] A Houston, Texas, stream receiving treated waste water was found to be contaminated with poliovirus types 1–3 and echovirus type 7. Two paralytic polio cases were discovered in the river basin during the period of study. One was fatal. Joseph L. Melnick, et al., "Virus Isolations from Sewage and from Streams Receiving Effluents of Sewage Treatment Plants," to be published, Bulletin of the World Health Organization. See also McCormick, "Virus Pathogens and their Relation to Waste Treatment," American Journal of Public Health, ff:459, 1965.

The absurdity of this reasoning is shown in the GAO example presented above. Efficient, advanced-design treatment facilities caused a gross pollution problem. Why were the plants built? The engineers seem not to have understood that the wastes would not be passed on. Or, if they understood this problem, they could not solve it. A solution was not possible within their technical competence. What is true for this small tributary in which the water does not flow year round is equally true for even the great rivers which receive large quantities of wastes. The wastes put in the water do not help the water. They do not belong in it. Although they may be passed on, eventually they will be deposited, probably many miles from their origin. The current technology, by ignoring the question of where finally to put the wastes, cannot solve this problem. It is inadequate in concept, no matter how refined a filtration system is developed, to a final solution to the pollution problem. A new conceptual understanding of pollution, and a new technology based on this concept is called for.

Understanding Pollution: Sheaffer's Principles

Traditionally, pollution control has been considered a kind of good housekeeping chore. The housecleaning tasks were carried out by engineers whose goal was to devise an efficient cleaning system. They did not seek a conceptual solution to the problem of pollution. Like the Supreme Court Justice viewing pornography, they didn't know what pollution was, but they knew it when they saw it.[23]

However, environmental planners have begun understanding pollution in a systematic way. The logic of their position leads them to state a fundamentally changed attitude toward nature as the essence of pollution control. John Sheaffer, a noted environmental manager, has formulated this emerging systematic understanding: [24]

1. The environment is a total entity.
2. Any pollution control system must be designed as a closed system.
3. Pollutants are resources out of place.

[23] See the opinion by Justice Potter Stewart in *Roth* (354 US 476, 1957).
[24] For a discussion of this framework, see John R. Sheaffer, *Statement before the Subcommittee of the Committee on Government Operations, Hearings*, U.S. House of Representatives, 91st Congress, 1st Session, December 15–17, 1969, pp. 211–215 ff. See also George W. Davis, "Fundamental Concepts of Environmental Planning," Working Paper WAAOC-WP-i, Center for Urban Studies, University of Chicago, May 22, 1970.

The most important principle is the first: The environment is a total entity. This principle is a restatement and application to environmental studies of the law of the conservation of matter: Matter can be moved, its form changed, but it cannot be destroyed. Waste matter in one form or another will always have its place somewhere in the environment. We do not, for instance, destroy garbage by burning it. We merely move the garbage—in a changed form—into the air (some ash remaining behind). Eventually, the air will cleanse itself of the garbage, returning it to the land or water. The case is similar with water. We dump waste down the drain in our home; it does not disappear. Some of the solids are removed from the water at the treatment plant, and still must be disposed of; dissolved matter, particularly nutrients that cause eutrophication of water, eventually are deposited in the waterway. The treatment plant may incinerate the solids, passing part of them into the air; eventually solids in the air return to the land and water.

Because nothing can be disposed of, it is necessary to plan and control the location of the waste. It is not sufficient to engineer a system that passes waste along. Thus the second principle is: The system must be closed. We must refuse to pass on the waste problem. The system can be closed in two ways: (1) the waste can be stored in a place which contains it and from which it can be efficiently retrieved; (2) or the waste can be recycled and used again. These lead to a third principle, to a new definition of a pollutant: A pollutant is a resource out of place.

The theory provides a groundwork for a solution to the control of pollution. A pollutant can be eliminated by making it a resource. Human activities will be pollution-free when all man's wastes are collected and used as immediate resources for some activity, or are stored in an efficient way so that they can be used in the future as a resource for another activity. Pollution control involves the management of these previously wasted resources, and thus to a certain degree, the alteration of our accustomed actions.

Controlling Pollution: A System Change

There is a difference in kind between the changes proposed by those who would control pollution by the old technology and those who would propose a new technology following a closed-system concept. The old technologists hold to a narrow, compartmentalized view of the environment. They do not see their efforts as part of a whole. The changes they propose are narrow-visioned and short range. Such changes can be called incremental changes.

Incremental change is essentially a tinkering approach, an addition to the powers of some agency or a restriction on some practice or some particular type of pollutant. Or it can take the form of a massive commitment to do more of what has been done in the past with little effect.

The attack on water pollution problems by the construction of new treatment plants was typically incrementalist. The decisions of whether to build, what to build, and where to build were all made locally. The decisions were not made pursuant to some policy providing for the environment's overall needs. Even if there had been a coordinated approach to the construction of the plants, the policy still would have been incrementalist and it still would have failed to provide a solution. Working at optimum, the plants would leave too great a quantity of some wastes in the waters, and would not remove other contaminants at all. The FWQA has proposed a $10 billion program to increase the construction of the same kind of sewage treatment plants already shown to be ineffective in the GAO report.

It is the common practice in our political and legal system to move incrementally, to solve each problem as it arises, to proceed by gradual steps, and to change directions in a slow curve. However, control of pollution cannot proceed piecemeal. It is not sufficient, for instance, to eliminate one pollutant from the air if one is merely going to replace it with another (whose effects may not be known), or if one is merely going to put it into the water or on the land, thus polluting another part of the environment. But facing problems as they appear leads precisely to this sort of *ad hoc* solution. Pollution control requires a different kind of law, which proceeds from some vision of a whole.

Environmentalists hold such a vision. These men believe that pollution is a problem within our environment, and that the environment is a total entity. Therefore a law is needed having responsibility for the whole of the problem, a law that works from the point of view of the whole (the environmental system) back to the parts (the individual pollutant/resource). Environmentalists will ignore or replace all previous efforts to treat pollution if those efforts were narrow-visioned. They will plan total systems changes, that is, they will attempt to transform a large body of socially interdependent behavior in one fell swoop.

The changes sought by the environmentalists must be highly disruptive. All public pollution control efforts are being pursued by bureaucracies with fragmented, compartmentalized responsibilities.[25]

[25] See Theodore White's popular discussion of the multiplicity of jurisdictions and responsibilities in Theodore H. White, "The Environmental Jungle," *Life*, June 26, 1970, pp. 36–44.

These organizations are the flower of incrementalism. No one of them is responsible for treating the waste management system as a whole. But the problem with incrementalism is precisely its neglect of the whole. The environmentalist principles will result in the elimination of this compartmentalization. Furthermore, these bureaucracies are heavily committed to a technology manifestly inadequate to the problem. Since pollution control involves environmental management and global planning strategies, it is apparent that the technical engineering or public health skills of the leaders of the traditional pollution treatment bureaucracies are inadequate. Simply put, the control of water pollution will involve the substitution of the guidance of planners for the past guidance of civil engineers and public health doctors.

The preponderant political activities of our government (and, consequently, the organizations to support this activity politically) must change because they interfere with, or are inappropriate to, pollution control. The changes which must be made are so great that it is questionable whether they can be made by those now in positions of political authority. It would appear that the political support for such changes would have to be greater than any possessed by the legislators responsible for the polluting system. Furthermore, just as the kind of law or policy must change, and the legislator responsible must change, the political support for both law and legislator must change.

The political support must change because both the policy and the legislators being supported are completely changed. But if the support is changed—if different people suddenly become active in the issue or if supporters of the old policy make an about face and turn to the new—then it would be reasonable to assume that the organization of that support, and the expression of that support is also different for the radically changed policy, different from what it had been for the incrementalist policies. If the character of this changed support, and its relation to the kind of law being proposed could be understood, it would be possible, perhaps, to know what characteristics of the proposed law would aid its victory or insure its defeat.

Theodore Lowi has outlined a theory relating different types of policies (laws), modes of government (regimes), and characteristics of political support by the citizenry.[26] Lowi, working with studies of Congressional politics, has described three sets of "arenas of power." Each set is identified by its characteristic policy: distributive, regulative, or

[26] Theodore J. Lowi, "American Business, Public Policy, Case Studies and Political Theory," *World Politics*, Vol. XVI (July, 1964), 677–715.

redistributive. The distributive and redistributive policies correspond respectively to incrementalist and radical pollution control policies.[27]

Lowi describes the distributive arena as having the following characteristics:

1. Individuals or small groups are the most influential in determining the legislation.
2. Coercive force is avoided.
3. Compliance is "bought" (if one does this, he will receive that).
4. Overall (global) policy is not taken into account. Policies are *ad hoc.*
5. Laws are written and amended in the narrowly representative Congressional committee.
6. Differences are settled by compromise. Conflict is avoided. The politics is a politics of consensus.

Lowi describes the redistributive arena as having the following characteristics:

1. Mass-based political organizations are most influential in the conflict.
2. Force is applied discriminately to obtain compliance.
3. Rewards are given discriminately to encourage compliance.
4. Legislation attacks the whole category of the problem. It deals in systems.
5. Laws are written in the Executive or on the floor of Congress, that is, by the most nationally representative body in the government.
6. Short periods of intense political conflict are experienced. Clear lines of opposition are drawn. The choosing of sides is encouraged.

This schema relates the politics to the law and, no matter the subject of the legislation, suggests that there is a characteristic politics appropriate to a law of a certain type.

Incrementalist policies correspond to the distributive category. In a pollution control jurisdiction that pursues incrementalist policies, a kind of incrementalist regime is established. As indicated by Lowi's typology, the regime would be harmonious with a very low level of political conflict, a consensual political style, and an elemental mode of organized political support. Effective pollution control laws must not be

[27] The regulative category describes special laws dealing with functional sectors of the economy. Examples of the laws are the Federal Power Commission and the Interstate Commerce Commission. In reality, federal regulative acts delegate Congressional power to functional legislatures Congress establishes. These legislatures, such as the Interstate Commerce Commission, make laws to regulate their sector. They are concerned with the welfare of the sector. The category is not useful to the present discussion.

compromised to suit such a regime. This regime would not have the political support, if it had the inclination, to enact the radical pollution control legislation needed.

Political and technical experts desiring to implement pollution controls have assumed that the governmental context which exists will continue to exist in the same way. They assume that the organization of government (which is in part reflected in who supports public decisions and who is systematically indifferent to them) and the manner of its operation in the waste management field cannot or will not be altered. The result has been that political circumstances, without challenge, have defined the world of the possible. Experts have concerned themselves with the implementation of technical solutions available within the narrow, politically defined limits of possibility. Their efforts have been abysmally and needlessly insufficient.

Recall, for an example, the case history of Gary, Indiana, previously cited. The single company most responsible for Gary's pollution was the giant Gary Works of the U.S. Steel Company, the second largest steel mill in the world. Gary's pollution control proponents asked the Armour Institute (a research corporation of the Illinois Institute of Technology) to make a study of air pollution in Gary and to recommend effective legislation to bring it under control. The Armour Institute wrote a report which recommended that U.S. Steel be virtually immune from regulations for a decade, by specifically exempting the bulk of the company's equipment. Why? Crenson suggests one answer may be that "the Institute's investigators may have perceived that no pollution control program could be enacted in Gary without the acquiescence of local manufacturers, particularly U.S. Steel, and they may have drawn up their recommendations with an eye to securing their acquiescence."[28]

Why was the Armour draft law, *in its draft*, ineffective? Why is the cumulative experience with pollution control one of frustration in the face of ineffectiveness? It might be that the laws were written in line with what the then dominant political order desired, because it was believed that the support of those powers-that-be was absolutely essential to the law's passage.

Closed-systems policies correspond roughly to Lowi's redistributive category. They are redistributive first of all because they embody a view of the whole. They are universalistic, and are coercive at the same time as they bestow benefits. Because their view is towards the whole, they will be authorized only by political leaders who are oriented towards the larger society. They will also seek the support of political organizations acting for the broadest common good, as opposed to the

[28] Crenson, *op. cit.*, p. 118.

narrow, interest group support for the distributive-incrementalist policies.

Such a policy has recently been enacted in Muskegon County, Michigan. Muskegon County adopted a county-wide sewage system that followed Sheaffer's principles. The county will build a central sewage treatment plant that will replace several traditional treatment plants serving local municipalities. The county plant will collect all local sewage and industrial waste, stabilize the waste in treatment lagoons, and spray the material on what is now barren land. The waste water will provide nutrients to the land sufficient to maintain a large-scale farming operation. Water will be pumped from several deep-wells on the farm and returned to the streams. The water will be pure enough to drink. The nutrients that once contaminated it will have been given up to the soil to fertilize the crops. Virus will be contained by soil particles. The system will put no wastes into the local streams and lakes.

Radical Policies Need Radical Politics

Just as incremental law is incapable of bringing about effective pollution control, so is incremental politics. A radical law needs radical politics if it is to have the authority necessary to its success. Because this has not been understood, it has often happened that would-be pollution controllers have attempted to "reform the pollution problem from inside the system." Efforts have been made to win support for effective pollution control laws from the old incrementalist politicians and political supporters. These efforts were made for one of two reasons: (1) it was assumed that the incrementalist structure would accept and implement the law; and (2) it was assumed that no other political support for the law could be developed, and that success could be obtained working with the incrementalists. The pollution controllers did not understand the political requirements of the changes they were proposing. Crenson presents a case history that illustrates the consequences of such tactics. In 1948, the city attorney for East Chicago, Indiana, announced that he had prepared an air pollution ordinance designed to eliminate the pollution from local industry. He had worked in secret for three years on the ordinance. The ordinance covered all equipment "the use of which may cause the issuance of air contaminants within the city." [29] The law would establish fines and jail sentences for violators, and would permit the Air Pollution Control Officer to license new equipment that would have the potential to pollute and to seal offending equipment until

[29] Ibid.

corrections were made. The lawyer then went into secret session with the East Chicago Chamber of Commerce, an organization composed of virtually all the local industries. He met with them for over a year to gain their support for the law. At the end of a year's time, and before the city council had seen the proposed bill, he had conceded a series of exemptions and changes to the Chamber, and gained some highly-qualified support from the organization. In 1949, the law was passed, but the industries in the town refused to license equipment designated as sources of pollution by the newly appointed control officer. One year later a new control officer was appointed, a man agreeable to local industry. Thirty-two additional pieces of equipment were exempted from the law at industry's request, and the first-year license fees that industry disputed paying were forgiven.

The success of the law could not be measured until 1957, when regular sampling of the air began. From 1957 to 1961, the East Chicago air quality improved. But in 1962 it began to worsen once again, reflecting the introduction of a new and highly-polluting steel production process into the local industries. However, even the pre-1962 "success" of the East Chicago ordinances must be highly qualified. In 1958, East Chicago's air contained over twice the number of suspended particles than the mean for the nation's cities.

The law in East Chicago was not sufficient to the pollution problem. Significant polluters were exempted, standards were ill-defined, and the pollution control officer was without real sanctions. As the city attorney anticipated, a law that would have actually controlled pollution would not have been supported by the local influential industrialists. The lawyer attempted to work a moderate change in existing ordinances. His ordinance officially replaced a smoke-abatement ordinance favored by local industrial leaders which put the burden of pollution on individual households in the town and exempted the industries. Although he did win a moderate change, he did not establish real controls over pollution, which had been his goal. The law's failure was clear. A 1966 study estimated that over 90 percent of the local air pollution came from industries regulated by the law.[30]

Incremental solutions are proposed because of an insufficient understanding of the politically possible. If the technical experts possessed a clear understanding of the political context in which they were operating—and in particular an understanding of the nexus between pollution and political order—they would see that what they considered an incremental solution was in reality a system change, the full ramifications of which they had denied.

[30] G. Ozolins and C. Rehmann, "Air Pollutant Emission Inventory of Northwest Indiana," mimeo, Northwest Indiana Air Resources Management Program, 1966.

A law that would induce a system change has different political characteristics from one that would only incrementally affect events. An incremental law, to be enacted, must have the support of those who support what has gone on in the past in the area of its concern. The incremental law assumes a continuation of past actions and directions and attempts only to modify them slightly for the future. Politically, the fights establishing the old directions and old order have already been settled, perhaps settled long ago. Some segments of the polity have won, others lost; but the fights have been settled. The incremental proposal cannot afford to renew these old fights because it could not win. On the one hand, the old victors who support the established operation would sharply oppose the proposal's challenge. And on the other hand, those who had opposed the victors in the past would not support the incremental law because the law would clearly intend to continue the old order, only slightly modified. Having lost the fight once, the old losers would not be likely to fight again to continue the existence of what they had opposed. Thus an incrementalist law must avoid conflict, because conflict will engender the opposition of those in power and will win no support. An incrementalist law must be supported by those who support the current order of things. It, therefore, must be adopted by compromise so as not to antagonize its supporters.

That the predominant support for the incrementalist law comes from the supporters of the status quo has important consequences for the kinds of change that such law can effect. The inequities of the old order, the abusive privileges which over time often accrue to those long in dominance, could rarely be changed by incrementalist laws and politics. For the law would, in effect, seek support from the old victors for a change that would remove their prerogatives. It is incapable of bringing about any of the hard changes which must, from time to time, be made in government and in the social life of a people.

A law that would bring about a radical change needs political support sufficient to overcome the support of the incumbent policies. Only a strong, effective law that envisages a revolution-by-law could deserve such support. The support needed will be manifest in political conflict during the time in which the new policy (law) is seeking its adoption. The law must be strong enough to affect, in the case of pollution, the way of life of most of the members of society.

The creation of this support is crucial. It is this support—this widespread, dominating agreement about what should be done or what should be proscribed—that effects the changes. In other words, it is not the law itself that forces revolutionary changes, but the will of the people that the law formally expresses.

How does the necessary support for the change develop? The conditions that encourage this support are at least partially known. The support for radical change must be widespread and intense. But widespread and intense political participation is the practical definition of political conflict. Thus political conflict is necessary to the development of support for radical change, though conflict situations will not always mean victory for the challengers. Conflict develops over *concrete* proposals for change—either over specific laws proposed, or over a combination of the laws and the political offices responsible for their enactment. The laws at issue must have a vision or a principle worth fighting for. That is, they must be effective laws for bringing about the change they intend. And those who propose these laws must be willing to engage in political conflict.

The law proposed is important because of its own efficacy, but is just as important for the support it develops among the people. This latter function is crucial since, as has been said, the radical change that does occur is more a product of the widespread belief that the change should take place than it is a product of the law itself. Thus, if the law proposes an effective and total control of pollution, and is uncompromising in its position, there exists a much higher chance of its causing political conflict, gaining support and winning.[31]

In sum, radical change is needed to control pollution. Laws that seek their support through compromise and the avoidance of conflict do not have the political base to effect the radical change.

Only laws (or proposals) sharply at issue with current polluting practices, laws which embody a principle that has the promise of successful control, can be expected to attract the broad support needed. Such laws, because of their challenge to the entrenched methods, will of necessity attract opposition. The more serious the challenge, the more serious the conflict which will result. If the conflict is sustained, a strongly supported victory for the law and those who support it is possible. Only a strongly supported and sharply principled law is capable of bringing us to abandon our exploitation of nature, an exploitation that is deadening us and the world.

Thus a radical solution ought to be sought for reasons of political prudence (that is, prudence sometimes dictates extreme measures). Only a radical proposal that would directly affect a large portion of the public could develop the interest necessary to effect change. Inasmuch as a great proportion of the problem of pollution control is attributable to its

[31] It could be argued that the efficacy of the law comes from the intensity of its support in two important ways. First, there is the moral force of a law that a great number of men strongly affirm. Second, there is the threat of mass violence if the law is disregarded.

possessing a politics of low conflict, low level of public interest, which invites corruption and other special considerations, a radical politics alone would supply the needed corrective independently of whatever the specific policy at issue would propose. That is, if a proposal which would create public conflict were advanced, the conditions encouraging the corruption would be removed.

Radical Politics from Radical Law

By applying an analytic approach similar to Lowi's to the study of pollution control policies, it is possible to remove some of the mental fetters that have restrained appropriate policy formation. For instance, when characterized by Lowi's typology, the East Chicago air pollution ordinance would be a distributive policy, since the law contained many exemptions and was therefore particularistic in its impact, since support for it was sought through consensus with the status quo, since its standards were vague and were eventually defined in consultation with local industry. What would be the effect of adopting a redistributive policy? [32] Suppose clean air standards were announced which said that no contamination could be put into the air and a program devised whereby airborne wastes could be transported to a central treating plant that would process them into usable products. Charges for processing would be apportioned equitably and air polluters would be subject to immediate and severe sanctions. Let us suppose the proposal is a technically coherent system, is economically feasible (because of the resources it reclaims and conserves), and reduces to a minimum the pollution from waste disposal. The policy could be expected to produce great opposition from those who benefit from the present manner of disposing of wastes into the air. The arenas theory would suggest that the politics of such a policy would be totally different from the previous distributive type, and that independent of its technical merit, it would have a much greater chance of solving the pollution problems. The redistributive policy would have the advantage of creating a high level of public conflict, which would legitimate the policy (if successful) and fill the political void that had been the source of much of the exploitation of the pollution controls.

---

[32] Lowi uses the redistributive category to correspond to policies that rationally determine to relocate resources of the country. But the category also includes policies that are "system conscious," such as policies concerned with the equity or functioning of the whole system. The important word here is "whole." Hence, the redistributive category is appropriate to the radical pollution control policy discussed herein.

An adequate history of the Muskegon plan is now being developed, but preliminarily, it is possible to conclude that the plan for sewage treatment and the policies supporting its adoption conform to the redistributive model. As has been discussed, the plan embraced a concept of the whole. It eliminated pollution by turning the waste into a valuable resource. Lowi's model would predict that such a plan would be characterized by sharply-drawn political lines, broad-spectrum political organizations embracing citizens rarely on the same side of political issues on prior occasions, and political leaders different from those supporting previous incremental policies. The Muskegon plan did take a clear and uncompromising stand against the old technology. Its proponents refused a compromise with the city of Muskegon, offered at a time when it appeared the county plan was doomed to defeat in the office of the Michigan Department of Public Health which had to approve all sewage treatment plans. Muskegon desired to modernize and expand its traditional sewage treatment plant. A heated political battle was fought with the state Water Resource Commission and the state Department of Public Health, and was won because of the broad coalition that formed behind the issue. Republican leaders of a neighboring county, joining with Muskegon County for the first time on any issue, worked with the Democratic leaders of Muskegon in fighting the traditional treatment forces in the state administration. The fight was led by newly-elected leaders of the county board, men who had been the first in the county to run for election in support of county-wide issues. The pollution control forces were joined in their fight by both conservation clubs and the major industrial polluters in the area. The unusual coalition was forged by a combination of factors: the vision of the plan, the sharpness of its stand against pollution (the Muskegon policy went so far as to criticize the Michigan Water Commission's water quality standards), and the danger that its opposition would overwhelm it. The Muskegon fight has not ended. The new technology is not yet in operation. But it is still possible to see the ultimate effectiveness and practicality of redistributive laws for bringing about social changes of great magnitude from an example taken from experience in another field of social policy.

In the field of education, school boards were advised to integrate their school systems through incremental changes affecting only a few schools at a time. However, investigation showed that the incremental changes were a form of distributive politics and inappropriate to the fundamentally redistributive goal of integration. The result of the inappropriate policy was political catastrophe. Extreme local hostility resulted even from within the most liberal groups in the community. Only impotent support developed for the narrowly applied and half-hearted policy. Most potential supporters were alienated from the policy because it discriminated against them, or they were not touched by it. When, however, universal and coercive rules were established for integration, and all members of the community were affected, then extreme opposition but also extreme support for the move developed. The violence (figurative) of the conflict was sufficient to break the remnants of the distributive organization of the politics of the community. Integration won. Only highly authoritative political actions (those actively involving a significant segment of the population) can cause the change in political organization from one type of politics (distributive) to another (redistributive).[33]

The political advice given to the sanitation board (or its equivalent) today is similar to what was originally given to the school boards. It is equally misinformed. The crux of the matter is the understanding of the place of political conflict in policy formation. Conflict politically expressed is by definition the involvement of a large number of citizens in an issue, and only broad political involvement is capable of supporting policies that seriously change the established order. Thus conflict-producing policies are essential to effective pollution control.[34]

[33] For a detailed discussion of the experience with redistributive integration policies in Berkeley, California, and Teaneck, New Jersey, see Thomas W. Vitullo, "Integration Through Conflict," unpublished M.A. thesis, University of Chicago.

[34] Difficulties with classification of type of conflict, type of law, and regime character clearly remain. Further work along these lines is continuing.

APPENDIXES

Although the focus in this volume has been upon current environmental problems in the United States, clearly the Spaceship Earth conception is a valuable one. As D'Amato mentioned in his paper, the "alternative futures" idea also aids us in escaping both complacency and an exclusive focus on the here-and-now. An imaginative paper by Pelowski looks at some of these futures from a perspective of providing incentives for the international business community. Pelowski argues that it is in the enlightened self-interest of business to encourage (and help finance) population control.

From a methodological perspective, this paper is valuable in illustrating the use of regression-based models for the projection of various futures. There are a number of assumptions in such models. Perhaps the most important assumption is that the causal patterns are mirrored in the regression equations. This assumption is both controversial and central to the models generated here.[1] But the modeling done by Pelowski presents an approach to data analysis which complements the other techniques discussed in this volume. The student should be cognizant of the tools at his disposal for the study of both politics and the environment.

[1] For a discussion of such assumptions, see Hayward R. Alker, Jr., "Statistics and Politics: The Need for Causal Data Analysis," in Seymour M. Lipset, (ed.), *Politics and the Social Sciences* (New York: Oxford University Press, 1969), pp. 244–313.

ALLAN L. PELOWSKI *

A Global Eco-tactic:
Population Control as a
Multinational Business Proposition[1]

The primary focus of this paper is on alternative ecological-societal futures involving population control and the role of multinational corporate enterprises. Regression-based models of multinational business are employed to project four futures, each with somewhat different empirical and normative assumptions.

Variables used include European (West German, British, and French) and United States affiliates located in 28 nations, diplomatic exchange, population levels and growth rates, GNP and GNP per capita, and GNP growth rates.

Computer experiments were performed to generate futures data. The principal result is that both the United States and European multinational business systems stand to gain considerably from population control programs—especially if population control proceeds quickly—and under conditions where businesses help to finance such programs.

A plan for the 1970s is outlined in terms of these findings.

° Mr. Pelowski is a doctoral candidate at Northwestern University. This paper was presented at the September, 1970 meetings of the American Psychological Association at Miami Beach, Florida.
[1] The author wishes to thank members of Northwestern University's Global Society Seminar (Department of Political Science) for stimulating comment and criticism of ideas expressed in this paper. Special gratitude is due the staff (Professors Harold Guetzkow, Michael R. Leavitt) of Simulated International Processes Project, Northwestern University, ARPA SD-260, for the provision of time-sharing computer facilities with which this experimental work was carried out.

Proposals for intra- and extracorporate revamping and coordination (including pollution control) are put forth.

A Conservationist's Lament:

> The World is finite, resources are scarce,
> Things are bad and will get worse;
> Fire will rage with Man to fan it,
> Soon we'll have a plundered planet.
> People breed like fertile rabbits,
> People have such disgusting habits.

The Technologist's Reply:

> Man's potential is quite terrific,
> You can't go back to the neolithic.
> The cream is there for us to skim it,
> Knowledge is power and the sky's the limit. . . .
> Men will grow to pastures greener,
> Til all the Earth is Pasadena.

ANONYMOUS

The fictional dialogue of the conservationist and the technologist characterizes in some respects today's public discussion about whether our species can survive its accelerating "environmental" crisis. In this discussion, which is becoming increasingly ground in simplistic dichotomies between dreadful fatalism and naive optimism, one can do no worse than to submit blindly to the position that either no solution exists (other than catastrophic die-off) *or* that the solution must be more (perhaps doomed) Pasadenas.

The research reported in this paper is based upon the belief that innovative methods are needed for sensitizing human decision makers to *possibilities as well as probabilities*, to longer-range desired states as well as immediately feasible ones. While both conservationist and technologist can point out trends that support their respective world-views, the point here is that trends *can be—often are* in the first place, and in my opinion *ought to be*—infused with explicit normative considerations (values, goals, attitudes, sentiments), such that *change* rather than (or in addition to) *stability* becomes our primary focus. In the models developed below we use the term "pathway" to refer to trends (for example, corporate investments, population levels) that are *explicitly* linked to values (for example, maximize earning potential, decrease population growth rates). Developing a pathway requires explicit normative as well as empirical parameter estimation; a pathway is less a "given with which we must live" than an "heuristic to be employed" in the determination of societal plans and contingencies. We must be willing to assume that a given pathway may at first be judged "unadaptive" for apparently legitimate reasons (for example, hyperconsumption), but that as the system changes over time the same pathway may reveal subtle connections with other components and relationships in the system (for example, population control as a result of increased societal wealth [2]) that could substantially alter our initial assessments of the future.

This article is concerned with the experimental development of alternative pathways for global decision makers who desire the means to bring the population explosion under control, but who are unwilling to "go back to the neolithic" in order to do so. Specifically, we will consider the *possibility* and *probability* that European and United States multinational corporations, acting in concert with United Nations agencies and nation-states, might increase substantially their earning potential through the *financing* of large-scale, global, population control programs. Four pathways are developed, each with somewhat different normative assumptions. Probability estimates of how much earning potential for how much population control spending are developed through correlation and regression analyses. Futures of these pathways are "projected" out to the year 2000 by means of computer experimentation. These futures are then discussed in terms of a plan for population (and pollution) control in the 1970s.

Delineation of the System

Experiments will be performed on a system composed of distributions of 9 variables over a selected sample of 28 nations. The nation sample includes 10 European, 7 African, 4 South American, 5 Asian nations, and the United States and Canada. Taken together these nations contain 1.48 billion people, or 42 percent of the world's 1969 population,[3] and generate approximately 70 percent of its Gross National Product (as measured in U. S. dollars). The selection criteria included data availability and whether a nation is an important part of the multinational business structure.[4]

---

[2] This relation has been argued by Richard A. Easterlin, "Effects of Population Growth on the Economic Development of Developing Countries," *The Annals* (Jan. 1967), pp. 98–109.

[3] These estimates are based upon data developed by the UN and presented by the Information Service, Population Reference Bureau, Washington, D.C., (April, 1969), a report.

[4] A nation was included if it contained at least ten affiliates from each of the United States and European business firms. Some nations otherwise in this category were

Two dependent and seven independent variables were selected on the basis of previous research on the correlates of international business and population.[5] The first dependent variable is called European Business (EURBIS) and is composed of the sum of French, West German, and United Kingdom multinational corporate affiliates located in the 28 nations.[6] The second dependent variable is called United States Business (USABIS), and refers to the number of United States affiliates in the sample of nations. Data for these variables were drawn from work by A. J. N. Judge,[7] for the period 1966–68.

Independent variables include numbers of diplomats representing France, West Germany, and England who reside in the 28 nations (EURDIP), numbers of United States diplomats (USADIP),[8] population levels in the sample of nations (POP), rate of population growth (POPINC), Gross National Product (GNP), rate of change of GNP (GNPINC), and GNP per capita (GNPCAP), all drawn from sources in the period 1967–1969.[9]

Relative to the Judge data on 15 distributions of multinational firms, the two dependent variables used here represent 81 percent of the total number of "parent corporations" located in Europe and the United States (7,046 as against 5,738 corporations in this study), and 82 percent of the total number of affiliates as reported by Judge for 88 nations (26,409 as against 21,632). Thus, while we have restricted our analysis to 28 nations and 2 business distributions, we have nonetheless included a very large proportion of multinational corporate activity. These figures are roughly consistent with data collected independently and reported by Vaupel and Curhan.[10]

---

excluded because of missing or unreliable data on other variables (especially GNP growth rates, diplomats exchanged).

[5] Allan L. Pelowski, "International Business and Diplomacy: A Regression Analysis," Northwestern University, mimeo, June 1970 (forthcoming in *Peace Research*); "National Attributes and Cross-National Business: A Combined Regression-Simulation Study," Northwestern University, mimeo, May 1970.

[6] Aggregating these firms by simple addition has practically no effect upon the resultant correlations (*see* Pelowski, June 1970, p. 1).

[7] A. J. N. Judge, "Multinational Business Enterprise," *Yearbook of International Organization*, 12th ed. (1968–1969), pp. 1189–1214.

[8] Both diplomacy distributions are drawn from magnetic tapes of data originally collected by Brams and Alger, Vogelback Computing Center, Northwestern University, and for which an analysis has been published by Chadwick F. Alger and Steven Brams, "Patterns of Representation in National Capitols and International Governmental Organizations," *World Politics*, 19 (July 1967), pp. 646–63.

[9] UN *Statistical Yearbooks* (Washington: Population Reference Bureau, April 1969).

[10] James W. Vaupel and Jean P. Curhan, *The Making of Multinational Enterprise* (Boston: Graduate School of Business Administration, Harvard Unversity, 1969), p. 122.

Correlation and Regression

Previous correlational and regression analyses of up to 37 variables and 82 nations [11] revealed that multinational business distributions have strong positive relationships with distributions of diplomats (coefficients ranging from 0.46 to 0.82), moderately positive correlations with GNP per capita (−0.05 to 0.63), and moderately negative relationships with population growth rates (0.07 to −0.44). A series of regressions of business distributions on politics, wealth, and size variables yielded positive coefficients for numbers of diplomats and for GNP per capita, and negative coefficients for population levels and population growth rates. For the 15 business distributions reported by Judge, the multiple correlation coefficients ranged from 0.61 to 0.84. The principal finding from these analyses was that "international business and diplomatic relations are highly interdependent, especially for nations in which international business is relatively small or restricted to few sectors of the economy; but, as international business increases in scope and depth, it becomes less dependent upon historical political ties (that is, diplomacy), and more dependent upon a complex of wealth, growth, and size variables (that is, GNP per capita, population)." [12] This finding is reflected in the 28-nation, 9-variable data with which this analysis is concerned. See Table 1.

For European business (variable 1) we note that diplomacy and GNP per capita (variables 3 and 8) have positive coefficients of 0.90 and

Table 1   Correlations (× 100) °

		(1)	(2)	(3)	(4)	(5)	(6)	(7)	(8)	(9)
EURBIS	(1)	100								
USABIS	(2)	50	100							
EURDIP	(3)	90	47	100						
USADIP	(4)	16	87	24	100					
POP	(5)	06	25	18	36	100				
POPINC	(6)	− 54	− 38	− 44	− 19	04	100			
GNP	(7)	30	92	36	98	34	− 29	100		
GNPCAP	(8)	47	66	32	46	− 10	− 75	54	100	
GNPINC	(9)	07	11	− 11	− 01	− 32	− 52	07	42	100

° Although significance tests are not strictly appropriate here, coefficients above 47 would be significant at 0.01 if random sampling from a universe of nations had been employed. (These are Pearson Product-Moment correlations.) $N = 28$.

[11] See Pelowski, May 1970, pp. 9–10, 23–25.
[12] Pelowski, June 1970, p. 2.

0.47, respectively, while population increase has a negative coefficient (−0.54). For United States business in the 28 nations we note that the same variables now have coefficients of 0.87, 0.66, and −0.38, respectively, and that GNP totals correlate at 0.92 with business. The relative strength and direction of these relationships are consistent with findings in the 82-nation study. These correlations also highlight other relationships found in the 28-nation data set. For example, nations high or low in GNP per capita are very likely to be low or high in population growth ($r = -0.75$). The two diplomatic distributions are less similar ($r = 0.24$) than are the two business distributions ($r = 0.50$); and national size indicators (GNP, POPulation) share more variance in common with the diplomatic variables than with the business variables.

In terms of the strength and consistency of correlations with multinational business, these results suggest, as in the previous analyses, that diplomacy (EURDIP, USADIP), population growth rates (POPINC), and GNP per capita (GNPCAP) may be important determinants of business activity levels in the 28 nations. A principal components factor analysis of these independent variables supported this claim; a three-factor solution more adequately reflected the correlations than any two-factor or single-factor solutions.[13] The relative importance of each variable was then estimated by least-squares, multiple-regression analysis, the results of which are given in Table 2.

The beta coefficients for European multinational business levels tell us that diplomacy is by far the most important independent variable, with GNP per capita a distant second, and with population growth rate relatively insignificant. For United States business we see that diplomacy is still most important, but that GNP per capita has increased in importance while population growth has diminished to virtual unimportance. Both prediction equations reach a fairly high level of reliability as measured by variance explained ($R^2 = 0.85$ and 0.83) and/or by the F values. In the European case the major deviations from predicted business levels occur in former colonies (Union of South Africa, Australia) and in the Scandinavian countries. For United States business levels, the largest residuals are found in geographically proximate nations (Canada, Mexico) and in European allies (West Germany, France, United Kingdom). With these exceptions, the overall "fit" between ac-

[13] A varimax rotated single factor accounted for only 22 percent of the variance common to the variables; the two-factor solution accounted for 49 percent, but neither factor was interpretable in terms of the correlation matrix. The three-factor result was interpretable (United States factor, Europe factor, and a population growth-wealth factor) and it accounted for 51 percent of the variance. The three-factor solution was closely similar to other factor analyses of the 37 variable study. Pelowski, May 1970, p. 7.

Table 2 Regressions °

Dependent Variable	Independent Variable	Coef-ficient	Std. Error	T-value	F-value	Beta	R	Intercept
EURBIS	EURDIP	3.54	0.38	9.39	45.75†	0.82	0.92	63.3
	POPINC	−29.44	51.06	−0.58	—	−0.07		
	GNPCAP	6.18	4.82	1.28	—	0.15		
USABIS	USADIP	2.74	0.36	7.60	43.52†	0.72	0.91	0.45
	POPINC	1.21	66.33	0.02	—	0.01		
	GNPCAP	17.59	7.32	2.41	—	0.33		

° $N = 28$; D.F. = 3.24.
† Significant at 0.001.

tual data and model-implied data is quite good for both multinational business distributions.

Because of the high correlation between United States business and GNP levels ($r = 0.92$), it would have been possible to construct an equally reliable model with this variable rather than, for example, diplomacy. While we have left the United States model "as is" in Table 2 for the sake of consistency, we shall nevertheless attempt to take account of the alternative model when interpreting the results of the experiments with decision-making pathways. For our purposes, then, the two prediction equations can be expressed as follows:

$$EURBIS_j = 3.54 \times EURDIP_j + 6.18 \times GNPCAP_j - 29.44 \times POPINC_j + e_1 \tag{1}$$

$$USABIS_j = 2.74 \times USADIP_j + 17.59 \times GNPCAP_j + 1.21 \times POPINC_j + e_2 \tag{2}$$

where "j" refers to one of the 28 nations, and "e" to an error associated with each estimate.

Experimental Design and Apparatus

In developing alternative decision-making pathways we will be focusing upon comparisons between two future states of the global system. The first state, which we are told is quite probable, consists of little more than the simple extrapolation of today's population and GNP trends. This will result in the rich getting richer, the poor getting poorer, and in approximately 7.52 billion people (mostly poor) by the year 2000.[14] The second state, which many policy makers, scientists, and other people see as highly desirable, involves the gradual approach to zero-population growth and to a more equitable distribution of wealth in the system.[15] These will be quite different worlds, depending, of course, on *how soon* zero-population growth is reached, if at all, and upon whether or not and how soon wealth redistribution occurs. In our experiments we will compare simple extrapolations to *three* different zero-population future worlds. We will attempt to demonstrate—within the limits of the models and data—that the international businessman stands to gain considerably in the latter worlds, especially if he should help finance a *rapid* approach to zero-population growth.

[14] These are "constant fertility" UN projections as reported by the Population Reference Bureau, April 1969.
[15] For personal reports of these values, see Joseph M. Jones, *Does Over-Population Mean Poverty?* (Washington: Center for International Economic Growth, 1962).

Our strategy of experimentation requires three sets of mutually interdependent assumptions. First, we assume that a viable, global population control program would necessitate very heavy financing, at least for the first few years of such a program, and that corporate expenditures on this scale would have direct negative effects on GNP totals in Europe (United Kingdom, France, West Germany) and in the United States. In effect, this is to assume that population control on a large scale would lead to an outflow of GNP from these nations to areas with high population growth rates and (for the most part) lower GNP per capita.

Second, we assume that a multinational corporation's earning *potential* (not "actual profit") is directly proportional to the *number* of affiliates (branches and subsidiaries) it has operating in the system. Data with which this assumption could be tested are not available for any large number of multinational corporations; however, the growth curves of United States and United Kingdom dollar investments in foreign countries is roughly equivalent to growth curves for numbers of affiliates.[16] This assumption will enable us to interpret the effects of different zero-population growth policies in terms of earning potential.

Third, and perhaps most fundamental, we assume that growth in the numbers of affiliates is directly related to product and management *diversification*. Again, data upon which to base this assumption are fragmentary, but the limited evidence available suggests that the greater the number of affiliates in the system, the more likely that more of the various categories of firms will be represented,[17] and the greater the likelihood that different cultures will be represented in top management roles.[18] As we interpret the experimental outcomes, this assumption will be related to possibilities and probabilities of pollution control and waste recycling in multinational corporations.

Experiment 1

The first experiment to be performed is the simple extrapolation of the existing parameters to the year 2000. This means that GNP is multiplied by GNP growth rates for each country, that population is multiplied by its growth rates, and that the dependent variables as estimated in the two regression models are "updated" each year to produce new

[16] See data comparisons reported in Sidney E. Rolfe, *The International Corporation* (monograph of the International Chamber of Commerce, 22nd Congress, Istanbul, 1969), pp. 146–147.
[17] *Ibid.*
[18] This is revealed in analysis of the Judge data for some 500 specific United States and European corporations; see Judge, 1968–1969.

estimates of numbers of affiliates. We have assumed diplomatic levels to remain constant—in effect assuming that some political relationships in the system will remain at the 1960s levels.

Experiment 2

The second experiment involves the manipulation of two of the variables in the models. First, multinational corporate investment in population control is simulated by GNP "transfers" from Europe and the United States to the rest of the system. Second, a zero-population growth policy is instituted such that all nations in the system reach stable population levels by 1980 (that is, in 10 years). GNP transfer is set at 0.001 (one-tenth of 1 percent of GNP) per year for each of the years of the 10-year program. In dollar value this is equivalent to a GNP transfer of 1.29 billion per year (0.001 × 1291 billion). The other nations of the system do *not* gain this amount; rather, we assume that all this money is absorbed in the population control program.

Each nation is able to reach zero-population growth at its own rate, depending upon its existing rate. For example, the Philippines, with a growth rate of 3.5 in mid-1969 must decrease its rate more each year than Belgium, which has a growth rate of 0.1. This calculation is equivalent to the amortization of a debt that is being compounded annually.[19] As in Experiment 1, we assume constant diplomatic levels.

Experiment 3

The third experiment is exactly the same as Experiment 2 except that nations are given 20 years to reach zero-population growth. This does not increase the yearly cost of population control (which is left at 0.001) or the total cost of the program (payments are stopped after the first 10 years of the program).

Experiment 4

The last experiment is the same as Experiment 2 except that the rate of GNP transfer is reset to 0.002 (two-tenths of 1 percent per year).

[19] This is represented as an inverse compound interest formula:

$$R = A \frac{1}{a_{\,n|i}},$$

where R is the yearly decrement in population, A is the initial population level, and $a_{\,n|i}$ is an annuity of one year (n = no. of years, i = rate of population growth). For the computer program (subroutine POP), we have translated this formula to an algorithm provided by Samuel Goldberg, *Introduction to Difference Equations* (New York: Wiley, 1958).

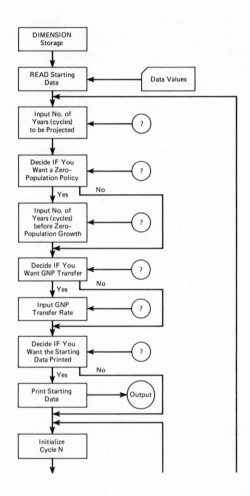

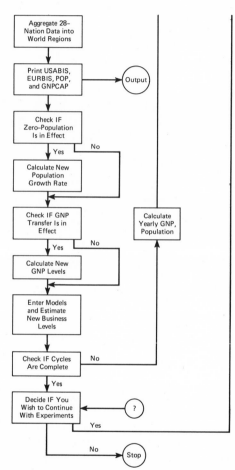

Figure 1. *Experimental design and inputs and outputs (question marks refer to an experimenter's decision)*

This means, in dollar terms, a loss in GNP of 2.58 billion in Europe and the United States. Nations reach zero-population growth by 1980 and diplomacy is left constant.

These experiments were performed in an interactive, time-sharing

Table 3   Experimental Results °

Region	N†	Time	Exp. 1	Exp. 2	Exp. 3	Exp. 4
Europe	10	1970	4879	4877	4876	4873
		1985	6777	7163	6932	7116
		2000	9733	11330	10862	11250
Change overall			+ 99.5%	+ 132.3%	+ 122.8%	+ 130.9%
N. Amer.	2	1970	3412	3412	3411	3411
		1985	3803	4019	3905	4005
		2000	4336	5121	4904	5098
Change overall			+ 27.1%	+ 50.1%	+ 43.8%	+ 49.4%
Africa	7	1970	752	751	752	751
		1985	809	889	847	889
		2000	903	1236	1144	1236
Change overall			+ 20.1%	+ 64.6%	+ 52.1%	+ 64.6%
S. Amer.	4	1970	892	892	892	892
		1985	843	928	885	928
		2000	808	1049	979	1049
Change overall			− 9.4%	+ 17.6%	+ 9.8%	+ 17.6%
Asia	5	1970	1536	1537	1537	1537
		1985	1994	2258	2135	2258
		2000	2738	3799	3540	3799
Change overall			+ 78.3%	+ 147.2%	+ 130.3%	+ 147.2%
World	28	1970	11471	11469	11468	11464
		1985	14226	15257	14704	15196
		2000	18518	22535	21429	22432
Change overall			+ 61.4%	+ 96.5%	+ 86.9%	+ 95.7%

° Numbers of U.S.A. affiliates in 28 nations for simulated time 1970–2000:
Exp. 1 = simple extrapolation of 1960s parameters.
Exp. 2 = zero-population growth in 10 years with GNP decrement set at 0.001.
Exp. 3 = zero-population growth in 20 years with GNP decrement set at 0.001.
Exp. 4 = zero-population growth in 10 years with GNP decrement set at 0.002.
† N refers to the number of nations in a given region.

computer environment. Figure 1 illustrates the flow of experimenter decisions, the use of the regression models and the data base, and the experimental design.

Experimental Results

A summary of the results of the four experiments is given in Table 3 (U.S.A. business) and in Table 4 (European business). By comparing Experiment 1 with Experiment 2, we see that the 10-year population control program with 0.001 GNP transfer results in dramatic increases in the numbers of affiliates over and above the simple trend projection. For United States business the largest increases occur in Asia (India, Japan, Philippines, New Zealand, and Australia), while the smallest but still significant increases occur in North America (U.S.A., Canada). The South American regional increases are particularly interesting, since the simple trend projection results in *negative* growth (−9.4 percent), while population control boosts affiliate formation to increases of 17.6 percent over the 30-year period. A similar though less spectacular growth picture is obtained in the case of European business. Here we note the largest increase in South America (−5.7 to 72.6 percent), and the smallest (but still impressive in view of the large number of firms involved) in Europe (27.6 to 39.8 percent). The difference between affiliate growth in the two experiments for the entire system (28 nations) can be seen in Figure 2.

The plot (Figure 2) illustrates that while United States multinational affiliates increase by 61.4 percent under the 1960s growth rates, this becomes 96.5 percent if zero-population growth is reached by 1980; *this is a difference of over 35 percent* (which translates into an increase of over 4,000 new affiliates). In the European case, the simple trend projection yields increases of 24.6 percent, while Experiment 2 boosts affiliate formation to 51.8 percent. *The difference here is 27.2 percent* (which is equivalent to nearly 3,000 new affiliates). It is important to remember that these increases were obtained under conditions of GNP transfer; that is, where the United States, France, West Germany, and the United Kingdom lose at least 1.29 billion per year in real GNP.

Looking further at Tables 3 and 4, we see that doubling the GNP transfer rate to 0.002 per year still results in affiliate increases nearly on a par with Experiment 2. The conditions of Experiment 4 thus have little effect on affiliate formation—*so long as zero-population growth is reached by 1980!* Comparing Experiment 3 with Experiment 4 shows the effects of delay on affiliate growth. For United States corporations we

Table 4   Experimental Results °

Region	N†	Time	Exp. 1	Exp. 2	Exp. 3	Exp. 4
Europe	10	1970	6179	6200	6189	6198
		1985	6848	7201	7065	7184
		2000	7889	8669	8505	8641
Change overall			+27.6%	+39.8%	+37.4%	+39.4%
N. Amer.	2	1970	1267	1267	1261	1266
		1985	1395	1561	1498	1556
		2000	1583	1949	1873	1941
Change overall			+25.9%	+53.8%	+48.5%	+53.3%
Africa	7	1970	961	1016	989	1016
		1985	981	1564	1410	1564
		2000	1014	1686	1654	1686
Change overall			+5.5%	+65.9%	+67.2%	+65.9%
S. Amer.	4	1970	506	543	525	533
		1985	489	855	755	895
		2000	477	937	913	937
Change overall			−5.7%	+72.6%	+73.9%	+72.6%
Asia	5	1970	1180	1212	1195	1212
		1985	1340	1755	1632	1755
		2000	1603	2299	2207	2299
Change overall			+35.8%	+89.7%	+84.7%	+89.7%
World	28	1970	10083	10238	10159	10226
		1985	11053	12976	12390	12954
		2000	12566	15540	15152	15504
Change overall			+24.6%	+51.8%	+49.1%	+51.6%

° Numbers of *European* affiliates in 28 nations for simulated time 1970–2000:
Exp. 1 = simple extrapolation of 1960s parameters.
Exp. 2 = zero-population growth in 10 years with GNP decrement set at 0.001.
Exp. 3 = zero-population growth in 20 years with GNP decrement set at 0.001.
Exp. 4 = zero-population growth in 10 years with GNP decrement set at 0.002.
† N refers to the number of nations in a given region.

note that delaying zero-population until 1990 results in the loss of over 1,000 new affiliates. For the Europeans this loss is somewhat less—382 new affiliates will fail to form under Experiment 3 as compared to Ex-

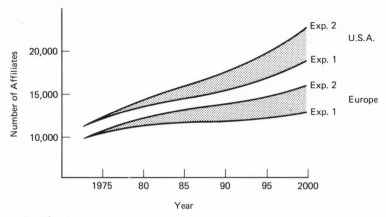

Figure 2. *Plot 1*

periment 4; all this, despite the doubling of payment in Experiment 4! Thus we conclude that *delaying population control, under the assumptions of the models used here, is less than optimal business practice. A better alternative is to pay more, over a shorter period, to achieve population control as quickly as possible.*

Comparing population with affiliate outputs under different delay functions results in the relationship expressed in Figure 3 (plot 2). This plot reinforces the conclusion that excessive delay is bad business practice; under the conditions of Experiment 2, as delay increases, total world population is left at higher levels while the total number of affiliates (U.S.A. + Europe) is left at lower levels. The drop in affiliate formation is particularly sharp after a delay of 15 years. We see also that speeding up population control results in a world (28 nations) "population saving" of up to 300 million people—a figure equivalent to 20 percent of the mid-1969 population of these nations.

Discussion

In terms of our empirico-normative decision pathways, these results emphasize the importance of speedy population control programs in global decision making. If our assumptions are correct, the multinational business system can increase its earning potential by around 30 percent under conditions of zero-population growth policies. In the concrete terms of dollars and people, this increase represents one new business affiliate for every 43,000 people who do *not* reach birth! Thus, if we were to speculate that each deleted birth would cost around $5 (contra-

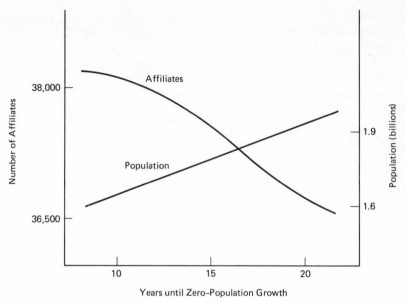

Figure 3. *Plot 2*

ceptives would be cheaper, but the education that must go with them would raise costs), then each new affiliate would need to generate only $215,000 profit *over its life span* in order to pay for the entire program.

Similarly for the national political decision maker; with multinational corporate financing of population control on this scale, he would have (on an average) 20 percent fewer mouths for which food would otherwise have to be found. Also from his perspective as well as the multinational businessman's, such a program of population control would make raising GNP per capita much easier; that is, the consumption part of the investment-consumption ratio would decrease, permitting increased societal savings and more diversified national development programs. But, from the particular perspective taken in this analysis, more important than all of this is the idea that "population savings" are necessary for the very survival of societies on this planet. A serious attack on pollution is not possible in many parts of the globe unless population growth curves drop sharply within the next few years. Turning deserts and oceans into gardens is not feasible unless the capital necessary for this can be freed by limiting population growth. Costly educational programs, communication and transportation channels, national arts development, and such things all depend upon getting population under control rapidly. In short, by changing the *probabilities*

associated with today's trends we can begin to approach some of the desirable *possibilities* that politicians, businessmen, scientists, and citizens
all claim to be working for.

The projections we have developed and the models on which they
are based are not *exact* in the sense that X dollars will flow from limiting population by Y people. These are rough, linear, and clearly limited
pathways whose validity with respect to the "real world" of the next 30
years cannot be directly assessed. The parameter estimates come from a
cross section of time in the 1960s, and there is no guarantee that they
will continue to operate in the near or distant future. However, even if
we were to assume considerable error, let us say in the neighborhood of
25 percent, the international business system still could make considerable gains in many parts of the world; it would still seem "profitable" to
invest in population control.

It is also true that other models can be found that will "fit" the
1960s data equally or better than the ones used here. We alluded to the
high correlation between GNP totals and United States multinational
business earlier in this paper; however, such a model does not destroy
the direct and positive relationship between business and GNP per capita. In fact, this model shows even more spectacular business affiliate increases than the one used here. Somewhat more confounding is the possibility that business distributions may depend upon population
magnitude as well as upon growth rates and GNP/population. This
would have the effect of reducing the growth rates of affiliates relative
to projections based upon models without this variable. In actual analyses, however, the influence of population size on business growth has
been found to be either weakly negative or insignificantly positive.[20]
This occurs because correlations between population magnitude and
business distributions fall in the range between 0.00 and 0.26—much
weaker relationships than between GNP per capita or growth rates and
business variables.

The chief weakness of the models and pathways developed in this
article is that most findings and prescriptions depend upon the maintenance of stable political relationships (as reflected imperfectly in diplomatic exchange). Should such relations be severed, the international
business system would be seriously set back, at least in areas of the
world where business relations are young or where only a few sectors of
economy are involved. Because of the strength of the diplomatic variable in our prediction equations, there appears to be little in the way of
statistics or data transformation that would compensate for this. Never-

[20] Pelowski, May 1970, p. 25.

theless, there may be several means by which the global businessman can protect and nurture existing political relations and at the same time utilize the increased earning potential associated with the financing of population control programs. These means will flow out of sound (ecologically and socially) resource, personnel, and interorganizational coordination and utilization practices—a subject we will at least touch upon in the concluding section of this article.

A Tentative Plan for the 1970s

Let us assume that global businessmen have opted for further investigation of the possibilities of a population control investment pathway (as in Experiment 2 or 4). How then shall they conduct their intra- and extracorporate activities so that a substantial deflection of existing trends can be accomplished? Or, to put it another way, how can possibilities for the future be translated into desirable probabilities? What amounts to a skeletal plan for this is outlined below.

Intracorporate Relations

In my view, the socially and ecologically viable corporation of the 1970s will be based, at least in part, upon the principle of "requisite variety." In general systems theory this is the simple idea that, in order to survive, an organization should contain sufficient variety of men, ideas, skills, and relationships among them to ensure the early recognition of varieties in the organization's internal and external environments.[21] This idea has many practical applications in the fields of organizational design and management. Consider for example the issues associated with environmental pollution and waste products recycling. It is a reasonable assumption that industrial pollution will become fully capable of causing political conflicts between host nations and headquarters nations. Multinational firms may well become "targets" in such conflicts; they may be blamed for pollution they have caused as well as for pollution caused by others (including the host country itself). The nation-states will often resort to ordinary international relations like scapegoating and face saving along with low-intensity, tacit bargaining moves like the removal of diplomats. Can "requisite variety" help the corporation prepare for such entanglements? In answering this question

[21] For a philosophical and theoretical discussion of requisite variety, see Ludwig Von Bertalanffy, *General System Theory* (New York: George Braziller, 1968).

let us consider a hypothetical corporation that is in many ways "typical" of today's multinational business enterprise.

Corporation "X" is engaged in aluminum extraction and sheet metal production in five nations. The nations differ substantially across a wide range of economic, political, and social characteristics. The parent company operates ten affiliates in these countries, each under at least 51 percent control, with the remainder held by the host nations' central governments. It has decentralized production through the affiliates, but top management is centralized in the headquarter nation—a large, rich, "Western-oriented" nation. Hiring criteria and skill development procedures are based on Western models (highly motivated, company-oriented, technically educated individuals are preferred to others), but wages paid reflect the host nations' living standards and GNP per capita. The age profile of top management is "bottom-heavy"; that is, the proportion of executive roles filled by older people is much greater than would be expected solely on the basis of host nations' age profiles. Two affiliates, one extracting aluminum, the other making sheets of it, have developed and partially implemented antipollution procedures. Both affiliates are located in the most economically developed nation. Other affiliates have minimal antipollution plans, but so far these are not ready to implement. Rivers and the atmosphere continue to absorb effluents from these subsidiary installations. It is corporation-wide policy not to engage in controversial political issues (such as multinational population control or East-West power struggles).

In short, Corporation "X" depends upon diversity in its environments (that is, aluminum deposits occur in quite different cultural, political, and economic settings), but fails to "map" this diversity in its internal structural and human components. Management seems quite aware of global political issues like pollution and is, of course, keenly aware of cost-benefit ratios in the various extraction and production processes, but in some significant ecological sense it fails to design and plan futures around this awareness.

Requisite variety in Corporation "X" can be said to be very low. First, top-management age profiles and cultural-political-social background should reflect more closely the age profiles and demographic characteristics of its production and marketing areas. Hiring criteria should be made "culture-specific" in the sense of other than strictly Western models. This would permit the intake of greater variety. Such variety is the "prophylactic medicine" of organization. It includes not only the intelligence and creativity of managers but also the much more fundamental value and attitudinal predispositions associated with cultural and social background. The intracorporate transactions will then better mirror those in its external environments.

Second, requisite variety demands social anticipation and creation; anticipating political problems and designing hypothetical solutions to them early in the game will lead to effective organizational responses to environmental changes. Anticipation means utilizing internal varieties to develop working solutions to problems *before they become crucial to survival*. Anticipation and creation cost money. Even hypothetical working solutions to big problems like pollution require high initial investment with perhaps only long-term "promises" of returns (political or monetary). *The immediate problem thus becomes one of financing the increase in the protective requisite variety. And this is where the plan for the 1970s should include massive investments in global population control.*

Population control information and free contraceptives should become part of each plant's fringe benefits. This will affect company employees and, indirectly, other people associated with employees; but this "token" population control effort, although admirable and sorely needed, will not be enough to ensure the increased earning potential associated with global population control. Developing requisite varieties will require intercorporate, corporate-nation, and corporate-nonbusiness organization intermeshing of plans and investment tactics.

Interorganizational Relations

Will not the change of Corporation "X" from a low-variety organization to one with higher variety create more political problems than it solves? Will population control efforts be tabbed as "meddling" in the internal affairs of others? Will this become another "capitalistic plot" in the world press? There does indeed seem to be a dilemma between increasing corporate anticipatory viability and dominant ideological images of international relations. There is probably no easy solution to dilemmas of this sort. However, we must also entertain the possibility that ideological parameters on world politics are as unadaptive as are the polluting parameters of industrial plants. Both are trend-maintaining, ecologically harmful, and socially undesirable constraints on social anticipation and creation. Any plan for the 1970s must therefore include tactics for surmounting the provincial dominant images of how international systems work to solve (or fail to solve) important problems that face it.

The United Nations General Assembly has proposed that a conference on "Problems of the Human Environment" be held in 1972.[22] The purpose of this conference is to provide a "world-wide focus for action to avoid a possible crisis which could endanger the well-being of mankind." [23] Multinational business should have a strong voice in this conference, not only because its future is as tenuous as everybody else's, but also because it has a direct role to play in the financing of the number 1 environmental problem—population control. This conference (which is tentatively scheduled for Sweden) will provide a forum for businessmen, scholars, politicians, and secretariat personnel to interact, to explore, and to initiate alternative pathways for human survival. In my opinion, the global businessman should be ready with population control and pollution control pathways already worked out in some detail. He should propose to the conference that 1972 be declared "International Demographic Year," a year for macro and micro research, for communication, and for the working out of detailed nation-business (with UN mediation if necessary or desired) cooperation on problems of the environments that they all share and with which they all must live or die.

Let us take hypothetical Corporation "X" again and assume that one of its representatives has a proposal for the conference's attention. Our "typical" corporation has realized (after detailed study of its particular production and marketing schedules and operations) that its internal variety must be increased, that this will cost money, and that investments in population control in its broadly defined operations areas is one important way to finance it. The representative's proposal contains ten central points:

1. Ministries of Interior (or Health) of each nation should immediately begin work on the internal subdivision of the country into "demographic sectors," each sector rated on its population control needs relative to its human well-being (that is, health, food, richness of social and artistic relations, and so on).
2. This demographic information should be made available to all nations and multinational corporations at UN expense and with UN supervision (for example, as part of normal UN demographic data collection and dissemination activities).
3. Corporations will then be asked by the individual nations to submit "bids" on how much population control in the demographic sector it is willing

[22] U Thant, "Report to the General Assembly on Problems of the Human Environment," ECOSOC, E/4667, May 26, 1969, pp. 4–6. Reported in *Bulletin of Peace Proposals*, 2(1970), pp. 102–103.
[23] *Ibid.*

to finance, and how much money it proposes to spend over what period of time in each sector.

4. Contracts will be awarded to corporations on the basis of criteria set up by each nation's government. These criteria should be based upon ratios between population saving and time spent as well as upon the nature of population control (that is, the mix between education, contraceptives, economic incentives, and such).

5. The winning corporation in each sector will be given a franchise to work out relations with public health and UN agencies (World Health Organization, the World Bank, and so on) for the actual carrying out of population control programs. Corporations will in effect "subcontract" the parts of the program that it is not capable of handling directly. All these relations will be worked out on paper beforehand; that is, before the bid is received.

6. Corporations will finance these agencies according to the criteria set out in each bid.

7. For every birth saved in each sector the corporation will be given preferences and/or a certain percentage rake-off of capital generated by the population control.

8. Corporations will in turn guarantee that a certain percentage of its rake-off will be spent in pollution control and in culturally diversifying its organization.

9. Some of the sectors will have the benefit of direct UN supervision (that is, where business-national relations have been strained or where ideological problems are particularly acute).

10. The UN will keep records of population control programs up to date and readily available to all concerned; this will decrease the probability that errors committed in one sector will be repeated in others.

The Corporation "X" representative will argue that his proposal, despite some technical or political loopholes, has the capacity to generate a great deal of population and pollution control on a global scale, and that a major reversal of existing trends can be accomplished through these or similar steps. His argument will rest on explicit empirico-normative models and theory-based projections of alternative futures. He will present the more than 12,000 multinational corporations as a force for change rather than narrow, unadaptive, trend maintenance.

II

Politics and the Environment— A Suggested Course Outline

Since several writers have suggested that college curricula should be made more relevant to environmental problems,[1] it is the goal of this essay to suggest how this may be done particularly within the discipline of political science. Political scientists should help students evaluate the many attempts at improving environmental quality that originate in and are directed through the political system.

A course dealing with politics and the environment should have at least two broad objectives:

1. To educate students to the nature of contemporary environmental problems, and
2. To demonstrate the importance of political science to the resolution of such problems through a study of both governmental structures and their evaluative, planning, and decision-making processes.

Introductory lectures should survey the origins and magnitude of contemporary ecological problems. Discussion of the following topics is appropriate to this end:

1. The historical-philosophical bases of contemporary attitudes toward the environment [2]
2. The finite nature of the Earth and its resources [3]

---

* Mr. Liroff is a doctoral candidate at Northwestern University. His article was prepared for this volume.
[1] An extensive though not exhaustive Bibliography has been appended to this article. The numbers in brackets in the text and footnotes refer to numbered items in this Bibliography. For material on education and environmental concerns, see [1–6].
[2] See [50].
[3] The best general introductory text to all items in this section is Ehrlich and Ehrlich [17]. See also [10, 26].

3. The existence and complexities of ecosystems [4]
4. The consequences, known but often unknown, of technological change [5]
5. The esthetic and economic value of pollution abatement, resource and wilderness conservation, and regional planning [6]
6. The nature of particular problems:
    (a) air, water, noise, thermal, and radioactive pollution [7]
    (b) waste disposal
    (c) urban blight [8]
    (d) conservation of resources and recreation areas [9]
    (e) population control [10]
    (f) pesticides and CBW [11]

The impact of environmental pollution and the concomitant need for wilderness conservation can be made quite vivid through the use of field trips. For midwestern students, for example, Gary's cracking towers belching forth clouds of thick reddish-black smoke present a brilliant panorama of environmental violence, while the Indiana dunes provide a gentle picture of unspoiled natural beauty; the contrast of the two scenes underscores the importance of the congressional struggle over establishment of an Indiana Dunes National Lakeshore.[12]

Should field trips be difficult to arrange, motion pictures may be profitably substituted; while the visual media, with other institutions, have overlooked for too long the threats to our environment, several documentaries have recently been produced which not only vividly portray the problem but also present the viewpoints of various business and political leaders.[13]

More generally, it is appropriate to examine the attitudes of businessmen, economists, and the general public toward the reorientation of priorities, reallocation of resources, and innovative governmental policies that may be necessary to improve environmental quality.[14] What are often involved are opportunity costs—who will pay how much, and what

[4] See particularly [9, 49] and issues of *Environment* [104].
[5] See [8, 34, 44].
[6] See [18–20, 22, 41, 109–113].
[7] Air pollution, see [23, 36, 41, 45]; water pollution, see [36, 37, 41]; noise pollution, see [41, 45]; thermal pollution, see [14]; radioactive pollution, see [11, 23, 30, 31, 38, 39, 41].
[8] See [32, 41].
[9] See [41, 47].
[10] See [12, 15].
[11] Pesticides, see [7, 22, 24, 39, 42, 43, 51]; CBW, see [28].
[12] See [115].
[13] For a humorous view of technological advance, one might screen Charlie Chaplin's classic, *Modern Times*.
[14] A sampling of business attitudes can be found in [55].

are they willing to sacrifice in order to do so? Perceived from this economic perspective, the following questions are automatically suggested:

1. In low-income areas, or in areas dependent upon marginal industries, how can the problem of economic well-being and/or economic development be reconciled with the requirements of pollution abatement?
2. What role do government economic incentives and regulations play in stimulating a market for technological innovations that combat environmental problems? What are the attitudes of business toward these various modes of governmental actions?
3. What is the role of economic analysis as a guideline for governmental policy? What are the strengths and weaknesses of benefit-cost analysis and what have been the problems in translating pollution problems into economic terms? How much are esthetic valuations considered in planning activities? [15]
4. How viable are the recommendations and demands of environmentalists in light of the foregoing considerations?

Having attempted a synthesis of the "environmental" and "economic" approaches, the groundwork is laid for an examination of the evaluative, planning, and decision-making processes of government. Here again some relevant questions for discussion are

1. What are the innovative and evaluative capacities of various government bodies? What is it in their procedures that mitigates for or against rapid innovation, as opposed to incrementalism? [16]
2. If the range of alternative actions for government includes creation and enforcement of standards of behavior and granting of incentives or use of negative sanctions to encourage particular modes of behavior, research, and production, a number of questions arise. What are the particular means available for implementing these alternatives? What are the relative advantages and disadvantages of each, how successful has each been in the past, and which agencies and branches of government appear to be best suited to each task? [17]
3. What are the consequences for long-term planning and short-term coordination of the existence of 90 separate federal environmental programs? What are the implications of the division of labor between federal, state, and municipal governments? What suggestions can be made for restructuring institutions and reordering relationships so as to improve policy output? [18]

[15] See [54, 56–59, 61–63, 67, 69, 70].
[16] See [68, 71, 80].
[17] There is a large and growing volume of literature on the subject of policy analysis, but none of the general works in the field has been listed in the Bibliography. For more specific work, see [72–78, 87–91, 93, 95].
[18] See [72–78, 87–91, 93, 95].

4. How does one quantitatively measure congressional "environmental" output —by the number of bills introduced into or passed by Congress, number of hearings and investigations by committees, absolute amount of environmental verbiage in the *Congressional Record,* or amount of money authorized and/or appropriated by Congress for environmental purposes?
5. How can government activity be evaluated both in terms of improvement of environmental quality and in terms of influencing public opinion? Can "symbolic" gestures be readily separated from "concrete" actions? [19] What is the relationship of public opinion to representatives' behavior? [20]
6. With regard to the appellate process, do the length of litigation, the nature of enforcement, and the size of maximum fines make it economically feasible to pollute? Have injunctions been widely used, and are they functional in obtaining compliance with federal laws? [21]

While much of the existing literature on the politics of environmental problems has dealt with the "process" questions listed above, so too has much of it been institution-specific. For example, the Atomic Energy Commission's role as both advocate and regulator of peaceful uses of atomic energy has been the subject of an excellent case study.[22] More generally, the nature of agency-clientele relationships (by which agencies tend to become "regulated by the regulated") and of agency-congressional relationships have been widely analyzed.[23]

The congressional committee system, sanctum of powerful economic and geographic interests, has often been the target of those seeking innovative policy change. The Senate Interior Committee, dominated by western senators beholden to extractive industries, and the Senate Agriculture Committee, controlled by senators representing powerful farm interests, have been the scourge of environmentalists seeking approval of conservation and pesticide control bills in the Senate.[24]

One might also focus upon other characteristics of Congress. The particular nature of Senate and House constituencies affects environmental legislation and certain congressional rules (such as those pertaining to non-roll-call voting) serve to screen legislators' actions from their constituents and from interested partisans.

Although the syllabus has to this point encompassed at least one semester's work, many other aspects of the structure and processes of

[19] See [119].
[20] See [118, 120, 122, 123].
[21] See [22, 96–100].
[22] See [11].
[23] See [79–86].
[24] See [115].

American government merit exploration. Thus, it is worthwhile to ask the following questions:

1. What are the consequences for the environment of jurisdictional disputes between the federal and state governments, and between state and municipal governments? [25]
2. What are the benefits of and obstacles to the establishment of regional jurisdictions that cut across preexisting municipal and state jurisdictions?
3. What are the particular obstacles to the passage of state and municipal environmental protection acts? What are the economic problems that governments must cope with in regard to such legislation?
4. Can mass public environmental action be more effective at the local and state levels because of the particular constituency configurations of such governments? [26]

This last set of questions is an obvious attempt to add some state and community dimensions to a syllabus that is primarily federal in focus. The abbreviated treatment of these former dimensions as well as the total absence of international considerations should serve as a challenge to other students of political life to make learning in the classroom more relevant to contemporary events through the development of equivalent syllabi devoted to these areas.[27]

Bibliography

Education and the Environment

1.   Hafner, Everett, "Toward a New Discipline for the 70's: Ecography," in Mitchell, John G., and Stallings, Constance, *Ecotactics* (New York: Simon & Schuster, Pocket Books, 1970), pp. 211–219.
2.   Jeffrey, David, and Kageyama, Glenn, "Innovating Relevant Curricula,"

[25] See [25].
[26] See [121].
[27] In support of the belief that formal education need not be confined to the classroom or the library, for a class of "eco-activists," participation in or organization of on- or off-campus environmental groups may be required, with a written record of such participation submitted in lieu of a research paper. Where grades may be required, they may not depend solely on the quality of written work or classroom participation, but perhaps on such things as success in gaining favorable coverage in local media, success in introducing controversial environmental issues into local politics, or success in achieving changes in pollution practices by local residents or businessmen. As for classes comprising less active students, research papers on local environmental problems may be in order.

in Mitchell, John G., and Stallings, Constance, *Ecotactics* (New York: Simon & Schuster, Pocket Books, 1970), pp. 220–239.

3. Maslach, George J., "The Reorganization of Educational Resources," *Daedalus* 96:4 (Fall 1967), pp. 1200–1209.
4. Morison, Robert S., "Education for Environmental Concerns," *Daedalus* 96:4 (Fall 1967), pp. 1210–1223.
5. Office of Science and Technology, Executive Office of the President, *The Universities and Environmental Quality—Commitment to Problem-Focused Education.* A Report to the President's Environmental Quality Council by John S. Steinhart and Stacie Cherniack (Washington, D.C.: G.P.O., September 1969).
6. Ripley, J. Dillon, and Buechner, Helmut K., "Ecosystem Science as a Point of Synthesis," *Daedalus* 96:4 (Fall 1967), pp. 1192–1199.

Introductory

7. Carson, Rachel, *Silent Spring* (Boston: Houghton Mifflin, 1962).
8. Commoner, Barry, *Science and Survival* (New York: Viking Press, 1966); on the role of technology.
9. ——, "Soil and Freshwater: Damaged Global Fabric," *Environment* 12:3 (April 1970), pp. 4ff.; on ecosystems.
10. Crowe, Beryl, "The Tragedy of the Commons Revisited," *Science* 166 (Nov. 28, 1969), pp. 1103–1107. [Reprinted as Article 2 in this symposium.]
11. Curtis, Richard, and Hogan, Elizabeth, *The Perils of the Peaceful Atom* (New York: Ballantine Books, 1969).
12. Davis, Kingsley, "Population Policy: Will Current Programs Succeed?" *Science* 158:730–739. Reprinted in Hardin, Garrett (ed.) *Population, Evolution and Birth Control* (San Francisco: W. H. Freeman, 1970).
13. Dubos, Rene, *So Human an Animal* (New York: Scribner's, 1968).
14. *Environment* Staff Report, "A New River," *Environment* 12:1 (January–February, 1970), pp. 36ff.; on thermal pollution.
15. Ehrlich, Paul, *The Population Bomb* (New York: Ballantine Books, 1969).
16. ——, "Paying the Piper," *New Scientist* 36:652–655. Reprinted in Hardin, Garrett, *Population, Evolution and Birth Control* (San Francisco: W. H. Freeman, 1970).
17. Ehrlich, Paul and Anne, *Population, Resources, Environment: Issues in Human Ecology* (San Francisco: W. H. Freeman, 1970).
18. Ewald, William R., Jr. (ed.), *Environment and Change: The Next Fifty Years* (Bloomington: Indiana University Press, 1968).
19. ——, *Environment and Policy: The Next Fifty Years* (Bloomington: Indiana University Press, 1968).
20. ——, *Environment for Man: The Next Fifty Years* (Bloomington: Indiana University Press, 1968).

21. Fremlin, J. H., "How Many People Can the World Support?", *New Scientist* No. 415, pp. 285–287. Reprinted in Hardin, Garrett, *Population, Evolution and Birth Control* (San Francisco: W. H. Freeman, 1970).

22. Gesteland, Robert, and Putnum, John (eds.), *Project Survival* (Evanston, Ill.: Project Survival Press, 1970).

23. Gofman, John W., and Tamplin, Arthur, "Radiation: The Invisible Casualties," *Environment* 12:3 (April 1970); on radiation levels.

24. Graham, Frank, *Since Silent Spring* (New York: Houghton Mifflin, 1969).

25. ———, *Disaster by Default: Politics and Water Pollution* (New York: M. Evans, 1966).

26. Hardin, Garret, "The Tragedy of the Commons," *Science* 162 (Dec. 13, 1968), pp. 1243–1248.

27. Health, Education, and Welfare, Department of, Public Health Service, *The Effects of Air Pollution* (Washington, D.C.: G.P.O., 1967).

28. Hersh, Seymour, *Chemical and Biological Warfare: America's Hidden Arsenal* (Indianapolis: Bobbs-Merrill, 1968).

29. Iltis, Hugh, "Corn and Cows Are Not Enough!—The Uses of Diversity" (mimeo, based on *Field and Stream* editorial, June 1970).

30. Inglis, David, "The Hazardous Industrial Atom," *Bulletin of the Atomic Scientists* 26:2 (February 1970), pp. 50–54; a review of books by Novick and Curtis and Hogan.

31. ———, "Nuclear Pollution and the Arms Race," *The Progressive* 34:4 (April 1970), pp. 55–60.

32. Jacobs, Jane, *The Death and Life of Great American Cities* (New York: Random House, 1961).

33. Kardos, Louis T., "A New Prospect," *Environment* 12:2 (March 1970), pp. 10 ff; on recycling.

34. Krutilla, John V., "Some Environmental Effects of Economic Development," *Daedalus* 94:4 (Fall 1967), pp. 1058–1070.

35. McCarthy, Representative Richard D., *The Ultimate Folly* (New York: Alfred A. Knopf, 1969); on CBW.

36. Marine, Gene, *America the Raped* (New York: Simon & Schuster, 1969); on the pollution of nearly everything.

37. Moss, Senator Frank, *The Water Crisis* (New York: Praeger, 1967).

38. Novick, Sheldon, *The Careless Atom* (New York: Houghton Mifflin, 1969).

39. ———, "Earthquake at Giza," *Environment* 12:1 (January–February 1970), pp. 2ff; on atomic wastes and natural disasters.

40. Patterson, Robert, "The Art of the Impossible," *Daedalus* 96:4 (Fall 1967), pp. 1020–1033.

41. Rienow, Robert and Leona, *Moment in the Sun* (New York: Ballantine Books, 1969); also on the pollution of nearly everything.

42. Risebrough, Robert, and Brodine, Virginia, "More Letters in the Wind," *Environment* 12:1 (January–February 1970), pp. 16ff; on pesticides.

43. Rudd, Robert, *Pesticides and the Living Landscape* (Madison: University of Wisconsin Press, 1964).

44. Shepard, Paul, and Mckinley, Daniel (eds.), *The Subversive Science* (Boston: Houghton Mifflin, 1969).

45. Shurcliff, William, *The SST and Sonic Boom Handbook* (New York: Ballantine Books, 1970).

46. "The 'New Citizenship' for Survival"—An interview with Senator Gaylord Nelson, *The Progressive* 34:4 (April 1970), pp. 32–37.

47. Udall, Stewart L., *The Quiet Crisis* (New York: Holt, Rinehart and Winston, 1963).

48. ———, *1976: Agenda for Tomorrow* (New York: Holt, Rinehart and Winston, 1969).

49. Von Den Bosch, Robert, "Pesticides: Prescribing for the Ecosystem," *Environment* 12:3 (March 1970), pp. 20 ff.

50. White, Lynn, Jr., "The Historical Roots of Our Ecological Crisis," *Science* 155 (March 10, 1967), pp. 1203–1207.

51. Whitten, Representative Jamie, *That We May Live* (Toronto: D. Van Nostrand, 1966); pro-pesticides—if you're not part of the solution, you're part of the problem.

Some Economic Perspectives

52. Boulding, Kenneth, "Economics and Ecology," in Darling, F. Frazer, and Milton, John P., *Future Environments of North America* (Garden City, N.Y.: Natural History Press, 1966), pp. 225–235.

53. Breslau, Jon, "Economics and Ecosystems," in DeBell, Garrett (ed.), *The Environmental Handbook* (New York: Ballantine Books, 1970).

54. Clawson, Marion and Knetsch, Jack, *The Economics of Outdoor Recreation* (Baltimore: Published for Resources for the Future by Johns Hopkins Press, 1966).

55. Editorial, "The Environment: A National Mission for the '70's," *Fortune* (February 1970).

56. Jarrett, H. (ed.), *Environmental Quality in a Growing Economy* (Baltimore: Johns Hopkins Press, 1966).

57. Kneese, Allen, *Water Pollution: Economic Aspects and Research Needs* (Washington, D.C.: Resources for the Future, 1962).

58. ———, *Managing Water Quality: Economics, Technology, Institutions* (Baltimore: Johns Hopkins Press, 1968); for RFF.

59. Kneese, Allen, and Herfindahl, Orris, *Quality of the Environment: An Economic Approach to Some Problems in Using Land, Water, and Air* (Baltimore: Johns Hopkins Press, 1965); for RFF.

60. Lewis, Jack N., and Headley, Joseph, *The Pesticide Problem: An Economic Approach to Public Policy* (Baltimore: Johns Hopkins Press, 1967); for RFF.

61. Ridker, Ronald, *The Economic Costs of Air Pollution: Studies in Measurement* (New York: Praeger, 1967).

62. Teller, Azriel, "Air-Pollution Abatement: Economic Rationality and Reality," *Daedalus* 96:4 (Fall 1967); pp. 1082–1098.
63. "Waste Water Treatment and Costs for Organics 1969–1973," *Environmental Science and Technology* (April 1969); FWPCA estimates.
64. Wollman, Nathaniel, "The New Economics of Resources," *Daedalus* 96:4 (Fall 1967), pp. 1099–1114.
65. Wolozin, Harold (ed.), *The Economics of Air Pollution* (New York: W. W. Norton, 1966).

Decision Making, Budgeting, and the Bureaucracy

65. Brinser, Ayers, "Standards and Techniques of Evaluating Economic Choices," in Darling, F. Frazer, and Milton, John P., *Future Environments of North America* (Garden City, N.Y.: Natural History Press, 1966).
67. Gilliam, Harold, "The Fallacy of Single-Purpose Planning," *Daedalus* 96:4 (Fall 1967), pp. 1142–1157.
68. Lindblom, Charles, "The Science of 'Muddling Through'," in *Public Administration Review* 19 (Spring 1959), pp. 79–88.
69. Maass, Arthur, "Public Investment Planning in the United States: Analysis and Critique," *Public Policy* 2:1 (Winter 1970), pp. 211–244.
70. Schick, Allen, "Systems Politics and Systems Budgeting," *Public Administration Review* 29 (March–April, 1969), pp. 135–171. [Reprinted as Article 10 in this symposium.]
71. Wildavsky, Aaron, *The Politics of the Budgetary Process* (Boston: Little, Brown, 1964).

The Federal Role: Independent Agencies, Structural Change, Congressional Responsiveness, and Clarity of Goals

72. Caldwell, Lynton, "Environment: A New Focus for Public Policy?" *Public Administration Review* 23 (September 1963), pp. 132–139.
73. ———, "Administrative Possibilities for Environmental Control," in Darling, F. Frazer, and Milton, John P., *Future Environments of North America* (Garden City, N.Y.: Natural History Press, 1966), pp. 648–671.
74. ———, *Environmental Studies*, 2 vols. (Bloomington: Indiana University, 1967).
75. ———, "Authority and Responsibility for Environmental Administration," *The Annals* 389 (May 1970), pp. 107–115.
76. Citizens' Advisory Committee on Environmental Quality. *Report to the*

President and to the President's Council on Environmental Quality
(Washington, D.C.: August 26, 1969).

77. Cooley, Richard A. and Wandesford-Smith, Geoffrey (eds.), *Congress
and the Environment* (Seattle: University of Washington Press, 1970).

78. Grant, Daniel R., "Carrots, Sticks, and Political Consensus," in Caldwell,
Lynton, *Environmental Studies* (Bloomington: Indiana University, 1967),
pp. 19–41. [Reprinted as Article 8 in this symposium.]

79. Maass, Arthur, *Muddy Waters: The Army Engineers and the Nation's
Rivers* (Cambridge: Harvard University Press, 1951).

80. National Academy of Sciences, Ad Hoc Panel on Technology Assess-
ment, *Technology: Processes of Assessment and Choice*, prepared for the
House Committee on Science and Astronautics (Washington, D.C.:
G.P.O., 1967).

81. President's Science Advisory Committee, *Restoring the Quality of Our
Environment* (Washington, D.C.: G.P.O., 1965).

82. ———, *Use of Pesticides* (Washington, D.C.: G.P.O., May 15, 1963).

83. Ross, Charles R., "The Federal Government as Inadvertent Advocate of
Environmental Degradation," in Helfrich, Harold (ed.), *The Environmental Crisis* (New Haven: Yale University Press, 1970).

84. Schiff, Ashley. *Fire and Water: Scientific Heresy in the Fire Service*
(Cambridge: Harvard University Press, 1962).

85. ———, "Innovation and Administrative Decision-Making: A Study of
the Conservation of Land Resources," *Administrative Science Quarterly*
2:1 (June 1966), pp. 1–32. [Reprinted as Article 15 in this symposium.]

86. Selznick, Phillip, *TVA and the Grass Roots* (Berkeley, Calif.: University
of California Press, 1949).

87. U.S. Congress, Senate Committee on Interior and Insular Affairs and
House Committee on Science and Astronautics, *Hearing, Joint House-
Senate Colloquium to Discuss a National Policy for the Environment*,
90th Congress, 2nd Session (July 1968).

88. U.S. Congress, House of Representatives, Subcommittee on Science and
Research and Development of the Committee on Science and Astronautics, *Hearings on Environmental Quality*, 90th Congress, 2nd Session
(1968).

89. U.S. Congress, House of Representatives, Subcommittee on Science and
Research and Development, *Managing the Environment. Report to the
Committee on Science and Astronautics* (1968).

90. U.S. Congress, Senate Committee on Interior and Insular Affairs, *A National Policy for the Environment*, a special report to the Committee
(July 11, 1968).

91. U.S. Congress, Senate Committee on Governmental Operations, Subcommittee on Intergovernmental Relations, *Hearings, Establish a Select
Senate Committee on Technology and the Human Environment* (1967).

92. U.S. Congress, Senate Subcommittee on Reorganization and International Organizations of the Committee on Government Operations, *In-*

teragency Coordination in Environmental Hazards (pesticides), 88th
Congress, 1st Session (1964).

93. U.S. Congress, Senate Committee on Interior and Insular Affairs, *Hearings, National Environmental Policy*, 91st Congress, 1st Session (April 1969).

94. Wengert, Norman, "Perennial Problems of Federal Coordination," in Caldwell, Lynton, *Environmental Studies I* (Bloomington: Indiana University, 1967). [Reprinted as Article 9 in this symposium.]

95. Curtis, Richard, and Hogan, Elizabeth, *Perils of the Peaceful Atom* (New York: Ballantine Books, 1969), pp. 203–229. *Also see* Democratic and Republican party platforms for 1960, 1964, and 1968, and Presidential messages to Congress dealing with environmental matters (all are in *Congressional Quarterly Weekly* and *Congressional Quarterly Almanac*).

The Courts

96. Carter, Luther J., "Conservation Law I: Seeking a Breakthrough in the Courts," *Science* 166 (Dec. 19, 1969), pp. 1480ff. [Reprinted as Article 16 in this symposium.]

97. Cohen, Bernard S., "Legal Defense of Environmental Rights," *Trial* 5 (August–September, 1969), p. 27.

98. Hagevik, George, "Legislating for Air Quality Management: Reducing Theory to Practice," *Law and Contemporary Problems* 33, 2 (Spring 1968). [Reprinted as Article 18 in this symposium.]

99. Sax, Joseph L., "The Search for Environmental Quality: The Role of The Courts," in Helfrich, Harold, Jr. (ed.), *The Environmental Crisis* (New Haven: Yale University Press, 1970).

100. ——, "Emerging Legal Strategies: Judicial Intervention," *The Annals* 389 (May 1970), pp. 71–76.

Journals

101. *Air/Water Pollution Report.*
102. *Congressional Quarterly Weekly.*
103. *Congressional Quarterly Almanac.*
104. *Environment.*
105. *Environmental Education.*
106. *Environmental Health Letter.*
107. *Environmental Science and Technology.*
108. *The Environmental Monthly.*

and the following publications by environmental groups:

109. *Conservation Report* (National Wildlife Federation).
110. *CF Newsletter* (Conservation Foundation).

111.   *Outdoor America* (Izaak Walton League).
112.   *Sierra Club Bulletin* (Sierra Club).

Bibliographies

113.   Caldwell, Lynton, and DeVille, William B., *Science, Technology, and Public Policy, A Syllabus for Advanced Study,* 2 vols. (Bloomington: Department of Government, Indiana University, 1968).
114.   *Choice,* a magazine (January 1970).
115.   Cooley, Richard A. and Wandesford-Smith, Geoffrey (eds.), *Congress and the Environment* (Seattle: University of Washington Press, 1970).
116.   Mitchell, John G., and Stallings, Constance, *Ecotactics* (New York: Simon & Schuster, Pocket Books, 1970).
117.   Rudd, Robert, *Pesticides and the Living Landscape* (Madison: University of Wisconsin Press, 1964).

Addenda

118.   Chudde, Charles, and McCrone, Donald, "The Linkage Between Constituency Attitudes and Congressional Voting Behavior," *American Political Science Review* 60 (March 1966), pp. 66–72.
119.   Edelman, Murray, *The Symbolic Uses of Politics* (Urbana: University of Illinois Press, 1964).
120.   Forbes, Hugh D., and Tufte, Edward R., "A Note of Caution in Causal Modelling," *American Political Science Review* 62 (December 1968), pp. 1258–1264.
121.   League of Women Voters, *The Big Water Fight* (Brattleboro, Vt.: The Stephen Greene Press, 1966).
122.   Miller, Warren, and Stokes, Donald, "Constituency Influence in Congress," *American Political Science Review* 57 (March 1963), pp. 45–46.
123.   Truman, David, *The Governmental Process* (New York: Alfred A. Knopf, 1951).